Osho ⌐ ⎯ ⎯ ⌐ ⌐

21 well known therapists describe how
their work has been inspired by an
enlightened mystic

Compiled by Svagito

Perfect
ublishers Ltd

ISBN 978-1-905399-99-4

Consultant Editor: Anand Subhuti

Proof Editor: Anand Chetna

Cover Design by Hamido Kardell

Cover Painting by Meera Hashimoto (www.meera.de)

Dedicated to Osho

Contents

Introduction

Svagito

This book is about therapy that is connected to meditation, inspired by the enlightened mystic Osho and his vision of life. For this reason, it is referred to as 'Osho Therapy'. In this context, therapy is not just a method to solve personal problems, but also prepares and leads a person towards meditation.

Therapy can be defined as a way to create a state of well-being within the body and mind, while meditation leads to a state that is beyond the mind. Peace, harmony and personal fulfilment are never fully possible within the dimension of mind, because mind by its nature is a problem-creating mechanism. If you solve one problem, it will inevitably create another. If you find the answer to one question, many more questions arise.

This is why some mystics have likened the mind to a tree that is being pruned or trimmed: you cut off one branch and in response the tree grows many branches in its place.

The real solution is to step outside the dimension of mind and enter the dimension of No Mind in which silence, peace and bliss are experienced naturally. Meditation techniques are ways to arrive at such a state.

This book presents a way of working in the field of self-development, healing and therapy that has this understanding as its base. So, while different therapeutic methods and styles are being introduced, the core aspect is the same: the fundamental importance of meditation.

The art of living consciously, connected to the present moment, is considered as the best way to live a real, authentic and fulfilled life.

Birth of a New Vision

Therapists and group leaders who present their work in this book have all been profoundly influenced and guided by the enlightened mystic Osho and his vision of bringing eastern methods of meditation together with Western therapy techniques. They use Osho's meditation techniques in their work and regard therapy as a stepping stone towards higher states of consciousness.

In Osho's own words:

My therapists are not only therapists, they are meditators, too. And therapy is a superficial thing. It can help to clean the ground, but just to have a clean ground is not to have a garden. You will need something more.[1]

East and West Shake Hands

In the late 1970s, therapists trained in Western methods of psychotherapy gathered around this controversial mystic and explored eastern methods of meditation. This gave birth to a unique experiment.

Maybe for the first time in history, Western psychotherapy and eastern mysticism shook hands. With Osho's guidance, therapists using a wide spectrum of growth methods developed new ways of working with people, looking at the human psyche from a broader viewpoint.

Deeper insights became possible for everyone involved, including the therapists themselves, as well as for those participating in their workshops, seminars and trainings.

Therapists with different skills learned from each other and experimented with new forms of working with people, without needing to stay within the restrictive guidelines of each specific therapeutic discipline.

Of primary importance in this process was the eastern understanding of putting aside the personal ego and allowing a higher energy to manifest – beyond a therapist's own personal knowledge and skills.

There is a profound difference here that needs to be emphasized: Western culture cultivates the individual ego, so that skilled and gifted people in all professions – politics, business, medicine, therapy – have a tendency to acquire a sense of self-importance that accompanies success.

Eastern culture, on the other hand, regards the absence of ego as an achievement far superior to self-aggrandisement. As a result, in the community created around Osho in Pune, India, there was less identification with professional status, not least because roles and jobs were flexible and tended to change quickly – an individual working as a therapist in one moment might be a cook or a cleaner in the next.

When Osho added Western therapies to his work he personally monitored what was happening in these workshops. After each course, he met with the group's participants and its facilitator, inviting everyone to share their experiences and ask questions.

Therapists learned to ply their craft in a totally different way. In a specific workshop – say, for example, Primal Therapy – a therapist would act as the guide and be in a position of authority; but, in the wider context of the community, both therapist and participant would be learning and experiencing meditation together. There was a sense of oneness, with little distinction. This has continued to be the case, long after Osho's death.

Fundamental to this understanding is that meditation is a mysterious process that cannot be quantified, measured, or even understood by the rational mind – since it is, after all, a state of No Mind. So, even though a therapist has a valuable skill that can be of help to others, he has no greater status or maturity in a spiritual sense.

This revolutionary approach was supported by the fact that no therapist was paid for the work he did. Their work was given out of love and a wish to contribute to the community, supporting the greater priority of meditation.

The reader may wonder about the strange Indian names of the therapists who have contributed to this book. Some background will help: in the 70s, when people started gathering around Osho, he began to initiate them into *sannyas*. Traditionally, in India, a sannyasin is one who renounces the world and dedicates his life to meditation, changing his name and style of dress.

Osho's revolutionary approach to *sannyas* was to remain 'in the world' – exploring relationships, business, careers and on so – while learning through meditation to be free from attachments. He taught his new *sannyasins* to live life fully and joyfully, while at the same time seeking their own innermost 'Buddha Nature'. He called his approach 'Neo-Sannyas' and asked his *sannyasins* to dress in the traditional orange colour and wear a necklace of wooden beads – called a *mala* – with a locket containing his portrait.

A person, who took *sannyas* in this way made a commitment with himself to meditate, declaring to the world that he was now ready to enter a new stream of consciousness, where the art of living life joyously and exploring meditation went hand-in-hand. It was not about withdrawing from the world, or being part of any religious group, or becoming a follower of any kind, but about learning to stand alone and unburdening oneself of past knowledge, traditions, religions …

In the late 80s, Osho declared it was no more important to have any outer symbol of this inner spiritual commitment, so the distinctive clothing, colour and *mala* were dropped. Now it is everyone's choice to take a new name or keep the old one, but the commitment to meditation and self-inquiry is the same as ever.

Osho's work went through many phases and so did the communes that evolved around him. Maybe never in history was there an experiment of such magnitude, where people from all walks of life and backgrounds, from any nation, race or culture, gathered around an enlightened mystic, creating the most diverse and unparalleled melting pot.

Osho's Multiversity, which acted as the umbrella organization for his therapy work, started in India in 1974, then moved in 1982 with Osho and his *sannyasins* to Oregon, USA. In 1987 it came back to Pune, where it greatly expanded, offering over fifty different kinds of therapy, courses and sessions for body, mind and spirit. Therapists, health professionals and artists shared their skills, knowledge and insights with each other.

Enriching Experience

Nowadays, therapists who once trained together in Pune work more on their own, without being connected to a specific Osho community. Still, there remains a common link between them, as the reader will discover in this book.

Through years of sharing, co-operation and communion, while at the same time respecting uniqueness, these therapists have learned to appreciate the richness that can be brought to a comprehensive, multi-dimensional understanding of the human psyche.

For example, during a bodywork training in Pune in the 90s, in a course that lasted several months, various teachers were introduced, covering a wide range of body-oriented therapies from strongly physical, deep-tissue massage to the most subtle energy work.

The teachers sharing their skills worked differently and sometimes plainly contradicted each other. Yet the programme's facilitators had no problem with this paradoxical situation. They knew it would be an enriching experience and a challenge to help people find their own style of working.

Outside of the training, these therapists would send clients to each other and there was an overall feeling of working together for a common purpose.

This was reflected in the Osho Therapist Training, a therapy process lasting two to three months, where various therapists contributed to a single long-term course, teaching people how to work with clients.

The idea to create this compilation came from those times, when many Osho therapists worked closely together. This book presents their approaches, which are different and yet complementary. Each covers a different aspect of human experience and offers a different model of man's reality.

Those therapists selected have been with Osho for a long time and have developed their own personal styles. Theoretically, they could all contribute to a single Osho Therapist Training that would, indeed, be a kaleidoscope of psychotherapy.

In order to keep the book to a reasonable length and also to avoid repetition, the number of contributing therapists has been restricted. This does not constitute an evaluation of those who have not been invited. There are many more who could have made equally valuable contributions.

Given the uniqueness of every human being, the reader is bound to feel more rapport with some therapeutic styles than others. Yet, rather than taking a comparative standpoint, the reader is invited to embrace different approaches that are all part of a bigger movement towards the growth of consciousness. Osho's approach to life is multi-dimensional, hence the name 'Multiversity'.

This book can be read in a straight sequence, but does not need to be. Each chapter stands on its own. Each chapter serves as an introduction to a way of working that may inspire you to explore deeper, perhaps even joining one of the courses that these therapists offer.

Beyond the Therapist–Client Relationship

Osho therapy gives dignity to human beings by understanding that answers to life's existential problems come from inside, not outside. They arise from the deepest core of one's own being, not from anyone else. At its best, therapy helps to remove obstacles in order to allow us to find our own answers.

In other words, consciousness is not a commodity that can be given. So the work of an Osho therapist is to create the right atmosphere in which the inherent wisdom and understanding of the client emerges into the open. The therapist functions more like a midwife. It is not a progress from *here* to *there*, but to a deeper and deeper *here*.

Ultimately, a therapist is not a guide who knows more than the client, but a friend who is aware that, even though he possesses a particular skill, he is essentially in the same boat. In Osho's words:

When the therapist and the patient are not two, when the therapist is not a therapist only and when the patient is not a patient anymore, but a deep 'I–thou' relationship arises, where the therapist is not trying to treat the person, when the patient is not looking at the therapist as separate from himself, in those rare moments therapy happens.

When the therapist has forgotten his knowledge and the patient has forgotten his illness and there is a dialog, a dialog of two beings. In that moment between the two, healing happens. And if it happens the therapist will know always that he functioned only as a vehicle of a divine force, of a divine healing. He will be as much grateful for the experience as the patient, in fact he will gain as much out of it as the patient.[2]

CHAPTER ONE

Self Love

Anando

The old adage that therapists specialize in what are in fact their own issues, is certainly the case with me. I had not even realized that I did not love myself until I met Osho. When I first experienced his unconditional love, which never wavered no matter how stupidly I acted, I resisted. I didn't trust it.

It took me a long time to learn trust, kicking and fighting all the way. Fortunately he was patient beyond words with me. Finally, I gave up fighting and allowed myself to feel loved – something that brought tears and tears and tears, which somehow melted years of old wounds and helped me to be more real.

Before that I had been very busy avoiding myself by becoming first a lawyer and then a wife and then a successful businesswoman. I was so focused on the outside and 'achieving', that I thought that was all there was to life. I managed to achieve success and even a certain amount of fame. I was also earning a lot of money, had a good husband, a nice house and good friends – in short, everything that is supposed to make you happy. And yet I wasn't.

Only years later, after I started becoming aware of the inner dynamics running my life, did I realize that underneath my veneer of 'a successful person', there had always been an unconscious voice saying 'You are not as good as people think', 'You are a fraud', 'If people really knew you they wouldn't like you.'

Of course, because it was unconscious, I had no idea that it was there. It was only after I started the journey of discovering myself that I realized the stress and tension that was making me unhappy was a direct result of those powerful inner voices. At the time, however, I was totally blind to all that.

At first, I thought it was only me who felt somehow wrong,

14

who felt that I was an outsider, a misfit, and I thought it was because I came from a highly dysfunctional family. Everyone else, I imagined, had their act together and were as confident and happy as they seemed.

But slowly I began to see that most people feel at least a little out of place, a little insecure behind whatever image they have erected to impress the world. And this insecurity, or lack of self-love, is the basis of the walls we erect around ourselves to protect ourselves from showing, or even feeling, this vulnerability.

Unfortunately, those walls also prevent other people coming too close to us. We all long for intimacy, but at the same time we are afraid that if we let people come too close, they will see our vulnerability and reject us. So we let people come close only up to a certain point, and no closer, which is not a great basis for an intimately nourishing relationship!

Searching for a New Way of Life

The tension from the inner conflict caused by my unconscious doubting voices and the outer image of dynamic businesswoman and wife that I strove to keep, became so unbearable that I decided to quit my job – and soon after, my husband and home – and look for a different way of life. I felt there had to be more to life than material success, which was not giving me the contentment I wanted.

My journey took me overland to India and I arrived at the Pune ashram of Osho in 1976. I had already started practicing his famous Dynamic Meditation in London, without realizing quite how powerful it was – it was in fact the catalyst that sparked my rebellion against the whole lifestyle I had been living.

I had intended to stay in Pune for only two weeks; I just wanted to 'look around'. And I certainly had no intention of becoming a disciple of Osho and changing my name and wearing orange clothes. People who did that, I thought arrogantly, were just social drop-outs who couldn't make it in the real world.

One week later I had joined them.

15

Meeting Osho was an energy event that my cynical pragmatic lawyer-businesswoman's mind couldn't understand. In fact, I don't think it ever caught up. But it was the beginning of a whole new way of life for me – exactly what I had been looking for. And I ended up staying for thirty years.

The Pune Ashram in the seventies was an amazing cauldron of eastern mysticism and meditation plus the new psychological and energetic therapies that were beginning to arise in the west. I jumped in with no idea of how much my life was about to change.

In the beginning, I must confess, it was rather depressing to discover that my entire life up until then had been lived unconsciously – that inner voices, such as I mentioned earlier, were in fact running my life, without my having the least idea. For example, I came to realize I had lived my whole life in fear: fear of other peoples' opinions and judgments, fear of being criticized, punished, etc.

When I first faced my fears they seemed overwhelming, as if I was at the bottom of a huge pit. The image of success that I had used to cover up those fears didn't last long in the ashram – the first job I was given was scrubbing the kitchen floor!

Meditation: the Essential Ingredient

I jumped into course after course and soon realized that the daily meditations were what helped me to keep going through the pain and fear I was uncovering. No matter how discouraged I felt, after looking at my unconscious in some course, Osho's Kundalini and Dynamic meditations always gave me some distance, and listening to Osho's daily talks transported me to a space from where I could have a different perspective from my unconscious mind.

When I started creating my own courses later, I always incorporated these meditations. I realized that if we just stay in the mind, trying to figure things out, then nothing can change, because the mind controls everything unconsciously, automatically. It just incorporates new information into the same old ruts it has always run on. Its 'job' is to keep us in the familiar, in the old 'comfort zone'.

But meditation is outside the area of the mind's control, so it gives us the possibility to have some distance from the old patterns and to see things differently. It is that different perspective that gives us the choice to also respond and behave differently. So for me, meditation is *the* essential ingredient.

One of the groups that particularly resonated with me was the Self Love Group, based on insights by Osho, plus Western therapy. Through it, I discovered how to recognize and not be influenced by those old voices that had made it so difficult for me to relax and enjoy my life previously. I learned the process and then adapted it to fit with my own ongoing understanding and experience.

I also became interested in new scientific discoveries that were being made about how the brain functions. And I realized they fitted very well with what Osho had been saying since the 60s about the workings of the conscious and unconscious minds. I read up on the 'neural plasticity' of the brain – the discovery that we can reprogram the brain – and started to incorporate it into my work.

Understanding How our Minds Work

Here is how I teach this today:

Our thoughts run our life – we basically live in our minds.

Our thoughts are mostly unconscious. Any cognitive scientist will tell you that between ninety-five to ninety-nine percent of our thoughts are automatic, pre-programmed. Even when we think we are having a 'conscious' thought, sophisticated brain scans show that seconds before, a part in our unconscious mind was activated, which then triggered that thought. This means that we are conscious only one to five percent of the time – pretty depressing, when you realize it ... but it also means there is great scope for improvement.

As an example, do you remember a time when you were driving from A to B and you arrived at B without remembering how you got there? It's rather scary, isn't it? But that's how we are most of the time: on automatic pilot. Or, remember how many times you have made a 'conscious' decision to go on a diet or to exercise regularly, or be more loving or less irritated … and it doesn't happen?

Why? Because as well as the conscious desire to do that, there is an unconscious voice inside that says 'Not today, maybe tomorrow', or something like that. And which voice is going to win? The one percent of your thinking that is conscious, or the ninety-nine percent that is unconscious?

So, it is important to become aware of our unconscious thoughts if we want to change, if we want to move out of the automatic comfort zones we live in.

In the Self Love work, we start to become aware of the unconscious thoughts that make us doubt ourselves, or hesitate to go for what we want. Most people have some hidden theme along the lines of 'I am not good enough as I am, I need to be different to be loveable or acceptable or respected'. I think Osho is the only person I have ever met who doesn't have some version of that.

We were not born with these ideas. We would not have survived birth if we felt inadequate. So that means we learned these ideas – we picked them up from someone, usually a parent, although we often don't remember this. We pick up these ideas mostly in our early years, almost from the moment we are born.

How we Learned our Identity

Those first years are the time when we learn that we are separate individuals, when we learn who we are, who other people are, and what is expected of us – how we should be. And unfortunately we pick up not only information that is helpful, but also information that is not helpful, such as 'you are stupid … you are not as good as your brother … you have to be serious and responsible … you don't deserve … ' etc.

These ideas are sometimes picked up directly from our parents, but often indirectly. Maybe daddy comes home tired from work and the child runs to him, 'Daddy, daddy, come and look at this,' and daddy naturally says, 'Not now'. The message the child picks up is 'I am not good enough for daddy as I am right now', 'I have to be different for daddy to listen to me', or something similar.

These ideas go straight into the unconscious mind as 'truths'. And a child has no ability to question whether that is really true or not. A child's mind mostly just absorbs – look at the face of a young child, it is like a sponge, innocently absorbing everything.

Once something is lodged in the unconscious as a 'truth', we never question it again. The job of the unconscious is to prove it is true. So it will interpret every bit of information we pick up from other people or situations *through the eyes* of that 'truth'.

For example, if nine people tell you that you are a wonderful, lovely person, and one person says you are not, which one affects you more? When I ask this in my courses, almost everyone recognizes that they are more affected by the one negative assessment than the nine positive comments. You can take a moment to check if this is true for you as well.

It is as if we have lenses over our senses that interpret everything that happens to us according to our inner, unconscious image of ourselves, which is for the major part negative.

Feeling Unworthy of Love

The most important first step is to start to become aware of these negative messages which are always in the background, and which naturally affect our energy and our emotions, not to mention how we react to situations.

An example from my own life: as a teenager and even into my early 20s, I jumped from one boyfriend to another because I never trusted that they really loved me. My unconscious told me that I was not loveable, something I'd learned from my mother, who'd learned the same thing from her mother. And that's another problem with all the garbage that's dumped in the unconscious part of the mind – unless we become aware of it and how it is influencing our lives, we will unconsciously pass it onto our children.

So whenever a boy told me he loved me, I wondered what was wrong with him and immediately lost interest and started looking for another. Or, I would constantly test them by interpreting any small thing as a rejection and provoking them until they left me, at which point my unconscious could say, 'See, you are not worth loving'. And because I had no idea of my unconscious at that stage of my life, I always thought it was the boy's fault, not mine.

Once we learn to recognize that we are reacting from an old unconscious idea, either by becoming aware of the message inside or by recognizing the emotional *funk* it provokes, at that point we have a choice. We can do something different than our usual unconscious response.

And that awareness also gives us an opportunity to heal the 'wounded' space inside. Our strong emotional reactions are almost always the reaction of the small child we once were, the child who learned that he or she is not okay as they are – who learned that they need to earn love, or try harder, or be different, in order to be respected and accepted.

That space is still there inside us, in our unconscious, and our emotional reactions still come from that space even though we have grown up. Watch any couple fighting and you will hear and see the children they once were. Their voices, words and behaviour are clearly that of a child – the child they once were.

The Unconscious Need to be Loved

I was working recently with a client, let's call her Elizabeth, who was blaming her ex-partner for all her problems. She sounded logical – the mind is very good at rationalizing. But her voice, when she was talking about her ex, was the voice of a hurt little girl. And she was making herself a victim – of course, when we blame other people or situations for our problems, then we are victims, because we have no control over other people or situations.

First, I helped Elizabeth to see that she was angry at her ex because he wasn't being the way she wanted him to be. How did she want him to be different, I asked her. Her lengthy list could be boiled down to the fact that she wanted him to hear her, understand and respect her, and to love her.

"Do you love yourself?" I asked.

This elicited a long silence. Then a wry smile. This is something we all do – we expect other people to treat us better than we treat ourselves. But if we don't love ourselves, how can we expect someone else to love us? How can we trust someone else's love for us?

So part of Elizabeth's work was to take responsibility that it was her job to fulfill her need to feel loved and accepted, not the job of her ex. And the way for her to start that process, was to become aware of the negative messages she was carrying in her unconscious which were making her feel not loved.

Once she became aware of those messages and recognized that these were ideas and beliefs about herself that she had picked up as a child, then she could begin to change them inside by reconnecting to the little girl she had once been. Later chapters in this book go into this work in more detail.

It sounds easy. It is not. We are our own worst enemies, and for many people it is difficult to even want to help the child we once were, let alone start to love them unconditionally. When Elizabeth could finally see that little girl with compassionate understanding eyes, rather than seeing her through the judging eyes of her parents, she could begin to understand that it was not the fault of that little girl that she learned she was not loveable. That little girl was innocent and beautiful, just the unfortunate victim of her parents' unconscious message that she was not good enough.

So Elizabeth's ongoing work is to make that loving connection to the child space inside stronger and stronger, so that she can start to correct those wrong messages in the unconscious. As the small Elizabeth begins to trust those new messages, she relaxes and starts to trust herself. And then she can grow up into the present without being so needy. And then, of course, everything changes.

What is our Business and What is Not

If we can learn to love and respect ourselves, as we are, without trying to become perfect, then we automatically become relaxed

21

and natural, and this makes us very attractive. It is strange: we don't expect our friends to be perfect, but we expect ourselves to be perfect. This puts tremendous pressure on us, and has the opposite effect – it makes us behave in a very tense and unnatural way, which is unattractive.

As we begin to realize how much our unconscious has been affecting us, we realize that other people in our lives are also affected by *their* unconscious. They also have their limits that come from the hidden messages they carry inside.

Part of the work is to understand that their unconscious ways are not your business. Your business is to acknowledge that the other provokes a reaction in you, and that is *your* reaction – coming from your unconscious needs and fears. And it is not the other's job to take care of that. It is your work, and in fact you are the only one who can take care of those needs, because you are the only one that can understand your unconscious.

In Elizabeth's case, the work involved understanding that her expectations of how she wanted her ex to be were totally unrealistic. He was not like that. And he would never be like that. And there were very good unconscious reasons why he was the way he was – and those reasons were not her business. It was not her business to change him. Her business was to recognize that his unconscious behaviour was triggering old child wounds inside her.

He was triggering old fears from her childhood about being abandoned, or rejected if she didn't get her parents' approval. Elizabeth was able to recognize that she was experiencing exactly the same feelings she had had as a child when she felt rejected. So then the work becomes clear: when the small Elizabeth inside understands that she will not be abandoned, and that she is okay as she is, then she can start to relax. And eventually her dependence on the 'other' to make her feel okay will lessen.

The work is very healing, and liberating. Because when we learn to love and accept ourselves just as we are, without becoming perfect, then, and only then, can we start to love others as they are, without judging them or wanting them to be different.

Changing the Unconscious Programmes Inside

So, the work involves healing and changing the old programmed messages in the unconscious about not being good enough. And it *is* possible to change those old messages. Modern neuroscience research shows that it doesn't matter how old you are, you can change the connections between the synapses in the brain – that's why the brain is now referred to as 'plastic'.

What that means is that you can change the old fixed pathways that your thoughts unconsciously circulate on. It's not easy, and as far as I know it is only possible by using meditation as a way to slip out of the grip of the unconscious mind. But it is certainly possible. I have seen thousands of people, including myself, change their inner attitude about themselves in this way.

So the Self Love work uses self-awareness to understand the unconscious nature of our minds, plus hypnosis to re-programme the old mind, plus meditation to allow the change to be permanent.

Love is perhaps the most powerful element in that mix. And by love I mean unconditional love – the kind that I witnessed and experienced over and over again from Osho. The kind of love that understands that we are all unconscious, and it is not our fault, or indeed anyone's fault. The kind of love that understands we are not our minds. We are much, much more. And that we can change the way our minds work.

I remember one incident, when I was working as Osho's caretaker: I was feeling quite neurotic, as I often did when I was premenstrual. I was also running late, so I didn't have time to calm down before entering his room. I just kind of burst in … Osho looked up and said, 'How are you, Anando?' The reply jumped straight out of my mouth, 'I am feeling neurotic and psychotic and totally fucked-up.'

A huge smile came over Osho's face and he said, 'That's great!' *Immediately* the neurotic feeling disappeared and I also laughed. That was a wonderful lesson of the instant healing power of acceptance, and I have used it many times since with people in courses and sessions. If someone accepts you totally, as you are, then it breaks the automatic association in the mind that there is something wrong in you that needs fixing. You immediately jump out of that mind-set into the present. Of course, it only works when it comes from a genuine space of lovingness, not when you're just using it as a technique.

That kind of lovingness, in my experience, can only be born out of meditation, because it comes from a different part of the brain. It can't come from the mind, the part which thinks and judges. It comes from a part of us that we can discover only by going beyond the mind, through meditation.

This is what I think makes therapy based in Osho's vision different from therapy that works only with the mind.

Exercise: Examining Old Beliefs

Here is an exercise you can practice for yourself:

Choose your favourite judgment or criticism about yourself and formulate it into a succinct belief about yourself. For example, 'I feel unworthy', or 'I don't deserve to be happy', or 'I am a failure', or 'I am not loveable', or 'I am inadequate', or 'Other people are more important than me', etc.

If you look back, you will see that this is an old idea that has been lurking inside you for most of your life. You may have covered it up well, by constantly proving that you are good enough, but you know that whenever things get out of your control, whenever you feel the rug slipping from under you, then this old fear creeps back again.

Now, I want you to ask yourself: were you born with that belief? I can assure you, you were not, otherwise you would not have survived birth. Why would you leave your nice cosy womb to go out into a world where you feel inadequate?

So you were not born with it. You picked it up from the unconscious mind of someone bigger than you – probably an unsuspecting parent. And because at that time you had no capacity to doubt its truth, it went straight into that trusting innocent young

24

mind of yours as a truth. And you have never questioned it since.

Now I want you to remember a situation where you strongly felt this belief. It will probably be a situation where you were feeling a bit vulnerable, or even shaky, or maybe you were having a strong emotional reaction like anger or jealousy.

Close your eyes and remember where you were, what was happening, who else was involved, etc. And as you remember, feel yourself back in that situation. And notice something you may not have been aware of at the time – notice how you feel in your body when you believe this thought. Notice how it affects your energy and body posture. Your attitude. Really feel what it does to you.

Then, still remembering yourself back in that situation, notice how you project that thought – how it makes you behave, what kind of things you say, or don't say. And how you say them. Notice how it affects your attitude to others.

Remember other situations when you believed that thought. Do you see how you prove that belief is true, just by your behaviour? That you actually perpetuate that belief? Take your time with this, and really look hard.

This will give you some understanding about how much this belief is affecting your feelings and your behaviour, and how it has been running your life up to now and limiting what you want to do.

If you feel you don't want to live the rest of your life like that, then use your imagination to see yourself without that belief. In your imagination, see yourself in that same situation, with the same people, but without having that belief about yourself. And notice how that would feel in your body. Notice how your attitude would be, how you would behave and communicate, even how your posture would be different, if you didn't believe that about yourself.

Notice the feeling that actually comes in your body as you visualize yourself being without that belief: this is your natural feeling. And if you practice this visualization, you will find yourself feeling this more and more in your life.

Really use your imagination – it is a very powerful tool. Energy follows imagination. For example, in an experiment at Harvard Medical School, scientists discovered that students who imagined they were playing a certain tune on a piano, had the same changes in the area of their brain related to musicology and the movement of their fingers, as students who actually played the tune on a real piano. So imagining something realistic – as distinct from a Hollywood movie – can actually influence our brain wiring.

After all, you have spent most of your life living out that old belief, which was just an idea which had been planted in your unconscious mind by someone else's unconscious mind. You were not born with it, so it is not part of your nature.

Now you are using your imagination to visualize yourself without it, to visualize yourself as you really are – natural and easy, the way you were before you picked up that belief.

If you find yourself unable to visualize yourself in that situation – without that negative belief about yourself – then acknowledge to yourself, 'I am not ready to drop this belief yet. I want to keep this idea, because it is part of my identity and I am afraid to think of myself without it'.

Taking responsibility for this will allow something to relax inside you; the fight about how you 'should' be, will stop. And this will leave the door open to your changing the belief in the future.

Yes, it is scary to drop these old beliefs about ourselves; they are our identity, our comfort zone. But is it really an identity that is worth all this suffering and misery?

Ask yourself: 'How does it feel to live the rest of my life with this belief getting in the way of everything I want to do'?

In everyday life, when you notice these old beliefs – or the feelings they generate – coming up, give yourself time to pause, to come into the present. And then question: is this really true? Or just an old idea I picked up when young and have never questioned?

Remind yourself that you are unique, so you don't need to be any different. This is a scientific fact, not some New Age fantasy.

There has never been anyone else exactly like you, in the whole history of the world. And there never will be again. If you are good enough for existence to invite into this world, you don't need anyone else's permission, or approval, in order to enjoy being the unique person that you actually are.

CHAPTER TWO

Arun Conscious Touch
Anubuddha

Anubuddha, a totally new kind of education is needed in the world... ~ Osho [1]

These words, spoken by Osho in Buddha Hall in 1988, in response to a question of mine, address the fact that humanity's natural sense of touch has been crippled and distorted. Our education systems, both religious and secular, contribute to almost everyone being uneasy, inhibited, and fearful about touching and being touched. Even growing up in 'liberal' California in the 50s and 60s we were all subliminally programmed to be full of doubts, guilt and longings around the subject of touch, and definitely *not* loose and natural.

To me, this is a crime. Touch is one of our most basic needs... it is food for our hearts and a healing balm for all of our physical and emotional pains. Touch gives us life and energy. I don't think total relaxation is possible while we carry this fear, because our whole inner and outer life is revolving around touching and being touched.

Osho, with his enlightened vision, altered forever the way I perceive and share touch. Many times I've heard Osho say, "I am here to remove all guilt"... and that is what transpired in his presence.

In 1976, Osho told one of his sannyasins, who was giving massage in the ashram in India:

Massage is needed in the world because love has disappeared. Once, the very touch of lovers was enough. A mother touched the child, played with his body, and it was massage. The husband played with the body of his woman and it was massage; it was enough, more than enough. It was deep relaxation and part of

28

*love. But that has disappeared from the world. By and by we have
forgotten where to touch, how to touch, how deep to touch. In fact,
touch is one of the most forgotten languages ...* [2]

Until that time, no one was talking about touch and the human
body as an organic whole. For me and other 'touch-based' healing
artists to apply what he was indicating in our daily work opened
up many new mysteries that we never learned in our Western
trainings. I realized that everyone is born to touch and we all come
to this Earth with unique talents to share, and all of us are touching
every day in all of our activities.

For me, touch has become synonymous with life itself. Human
touch is a big subject, rich and complex beyond measure, multi-
dimensional and amazing in its potency. Touch always and only
happens in *this moment* – never in the past, nor in the future.
Conscious touch can never be a technique; it is always here-now
and no two touches are ever the same.

Touch flows in and out of all our senses: looking, we touch
through our eyes, smelling we touch through our nose, hearing we
touch through our ears... we touch with much more than just our
hands and feet. The English expression 'being touched' is used
very significantly. We may use it without understanding what it
means, when we say we are 'touched' by a person or experience.
Seen from this perspective, our whole daily life consists of
touching and being touched.

I can think of no better way to share meditation, love and
compassion with another person than through ARUN Conscious
Touch, which is the name of the teaching Anasha and I have
developed under Osho's guidance, distilling the essence of healing
touch from almost all the methods arising in Eastern and Western
cultures.

In my life-time, an incredible worldwide phenomenon has
occurred. Never before have so many touch-based healing
modalities been created, practiced and taught. Right now, more
people are touching as a profession and as a form of creative
expression than ever. In the last twenty-five years, thousands of

spas, wellness centres and healing resorts have opened, all of them offering massage and a multitude of touch-based sessions. We are witnessing a global evolution in the field of touch, in which Osho and his sannyasins are playing a big role.

In Western cultures, the most important innovations in touch-based healing have occurred during the last hundred years, while in Eastern cultures touch as a healing art has been firmly established and practiced for millennia. In India, China, Thailand, Japan and other oriental countries the medical and healing professions relied on various methods of touch, conscious movements, breath awareness, cleansing, nutrition, herbs and meditation for maintaining physical, mental and spiritual well-being. These traditional methods include Ayurveda, Shiatsu, Thai Massage, Chinese Medicine and Acupuncture, Qi Gong, Tai Chi, Yoga, Vipassana, Pranayama and many more.

Many of these healing arts were practiced in Osho's ashrams and communes spanning the years from 1974 until the mystic's death in 1990 and, indeed, into the years beyond. The Healing Arts department offered a full spectrum of treatments in such diverse fields as Massage, Psychic Healing, Shiatsu, Acupuncture, Rolfing, Postural Integration, Kirlian Photography, Colorpuncture, Feldenkrais, Alexander Technique and Osteopathy.

Osho helped us to create our own style. For example, in 1980, we began to offer Rebalancing, which was perhaps the first method of deep bodywork that actively spoke of awakening love and meditation in its recipients, as well as relaxation, healing and realignment of the body's physical structure.

What transpires, or comes to light, through conscious touching is one of the greatest mysteries in existence. Did you ever observe that the way you touch people, animals, plants and objects around you, demonstrates how you feel about them? It does. Our human hand is the place where our inner love and awareness meets and interacts with whatever is outside us. Our whole personal history and present psychology is in our hands.

The average person has never taken time to intimately feel

30

and become aware of the life force in their hands, experiencing this phenomenon subjectively, from the inside. If you do, it may change your life, because love and awareness flowing through your hands, in any activity, always brings joy.

I feel blessed for the part I have played in the evolution of touch as a meditation and I feel the best is yet to come. If humanity as a whole can learn to touch with love and awareness, so much violence and suffering would disappear immediately.

As a part of the first wave of sannyasin touch-based healing artists, I was immersed in a living spiritual laboratory orchestrated by Osho to erase the negative imprint of humanity's past, and to bring moment-to-moment love and awareness to all facets of our daily activities.

In the period 1976-1992, living and working in Osho communities, I gave over ten thousand individual sessions, but my main focus during these seventeen years was helping to create and teach trainings in Osho Rebalancing, CranioSacral, Massage and Hara Awareness, all of which amounted to working with thousands of students.

To appreciate the multi-dimensional potential of Osho's gift to the art of conscious touch some awareness is needed of the spiritual vision of an enlightened mystic. For example, Guatama the Buddha and Osho were both born in India, two thousand five hundred years apart, and both Osho and Buddha created large spiritual communes in which people could experience their enlightened message for harmonious living and self-realization. Osho has said:

The Master simply means a certain Noosphere. The word "Noosphere" is coined by Pierre Teilhard de Chardin... we are acquainted with the word "atmosphere". Atmosphere means the air that surrounds you, the climate that surrounds you. "Noosphere" means the world of subtle vibes, thoughts, feelings that surround you... the Master carries a noosphere around himself... I call it the Buddhafield. [3]

Living with Osho and his sannyasins is difficult to describe. We were exploring, creating and on the cutting edge in so many different activities. Osho encouraged us to 'squeeze the juice of life' and that's what we learned to do. His Buddhafield was an alchemical laboratory of creativity, where every activity was infused with the qualities of totality, laughter, love and meditatively watching inside.

Many polarities merged in our experiment: work and play, material and spiritual, male and female, yin and yang, left brain and right brain. Bridging all of these elements was the influence of Osho's daily discourses and *darshans* – individual meetings with the master.

The three main areas where Osho's sannyasins brought ground-breaking innovation to the world at large were meditative music, spiritually-based therapy and the healing arts. Perhaps there was another area, too: the community itself, in which meditators were gardening, cooking, cleaning, singing, dancing, shopping, building, doing maintenance, accounting, hugging, organizing, playing music, plumbing, driving, sewing, typing, painting, leading therapy and meditation groups, massaging, doctoring, teaching, exploring Tantra and unconditional love, welcoming newcomers and countless other tasks.

My clients were not just ordinary clients; they were spiritual seekers coming to learn meditation. It was in this atmosphere that the various therapies and healing arts were refined, created, and developed.

ARUN Conscious Touch is a new kind of education in the sense that its focus and method for learning are different than those found in our traditional schools. What I would like to share is something of the magic of Osho's loving way of being present in the body, and how this understanding can be applied to a person's relationship with his own body and sense and appreciation of visible and invisible touching.

Our Human Energy-Field

Have you ever been overwhelmed by the mystery and the beauty and the miracle of your own body? Have you ever noticed the minute, moment-to-moment interaction between your physical body, your mind, your emotions and your spirit? Have you realized that your body is much, much more than simply 'a body'?

To say it accurately, each one of us is a vibrating, electro-magnetic, human energy field, infused with consciousness. These are not just fancy words. What is happening under our skin is more psychedelic and inter-connected than we can conceive. Every cell, muscle and nerve of our body, which I prefer to call our human energy field, is vibrating and pulsating with life and consciousness … right now – in this moment.

With every breath we take, with every heartbeat that resonates through our whole body, with each fluctuating wave of the cerebrospinal fluid surrounding our brain and spinal cord, life flows through us and rejuvenates us. If this is true, then why are the overwhelming majority of people so tense? Why is everyone full of mental and physical pain, so out of touch with their own bodies?

We don't usually talk about it, or reflect on it, but I think everyone has experienced what mystics refer to as our 'energy body'. It is a sensation or awareness that is not limited to an obvious material, physical reality. For example, you know how a particular thought can make you depressed, or full of joy. The sight of something you find beautiful can cause your muscles to relax, your mood to lift, while the sight of something cruel or painful may cause you to contract with fear or sadness. The sound of music, or a particular voice, can make you feel happy, or on the contrary put you in a negative mood.

A particular smell can help the pores of your skin to open, your body tissues to expand and make your lungs want to breathe deeply, or can have the opposite effect. One person touching you, or coming close to you, will generate a feeling of 'yes', while another will cause your energy to contract and say 'no'. Walking on pavement or tarmac in a big city affects you differently than walking on the earth, in nature. A strongly held negative mental attitude can limit and control the movement of your breath, which will affect the muscle coordination and range of motion in your skeleton, as well as your mental outlook.

Watching Inside

Buddha, Osho, the founders of Yoga and other mystics have taken these simple observations deeper and deeper inside. Finally, the only way they could explain the subtle, intricate interactions of the mind-body mechanism was to use a new vocabulary, and a new anatomy, based on 'watching inside'.

It can be said that our energy, thoughts and consciousness are 'immaterial', whereas our muscles, nerves, blood and bones are 'material', but for the enlightened Seer both are equally real. You can dissect the body and see the pathways of muscles, blood vessels, nerves, the arrangements of the bones, organs and so on. But you will not be able to see the wireless life-force – *prana* in Yoga terms – that flows through the living body, nor the mind that moves our muscles and bones, nor the 'heart energy' that either loves or hates.

For a Buddha, thoughts, sensations, feelings, moods, attitudes and judgements are all real energies. What is even more valuable and important for a meditative person is the experience that an essential part of each human being is capable of observing all of these internal energy phenomena. This is what is termed the 'witnessing consciousness', which is beyond the body, the mind and the emotions.

Osho's insight is that love and compassion are absolutely needed for your body and its nourishment. The better body you have, the more is the possibility for growing consciousness. It is an organic unity. Your body is the home of your essential nature, your inner witnessing consciousness.

Life Moves through Touch

Whether you are aware of it or not, you are being touched right now; it's happening on the inside and from the outside. When you understand touch the way that a meditator does, you realize that touch is life. This 'touching' is happening on so many levels of our Being simultaneously that it is a moment-to-moment miracle. At the same time, it presents a great challenge for us all. The challenge is how to make our body, mind and consciousness fully alert in each moment, so that we can allow life to touch us deeply and to trust in our ability to touch life.

In my experience, Osho can be described as a Master of Conscious Touching. Around Osho, my own sense of touch expanded in ways that I would have never dreamed of. One important 'click' or 'Aha!' moment happened for me in 1984. While living in Osho's commune in Oregon I heard him say, while talking about the long-term effects of watching inside:

Slowly, you will also become able to feel the touch through the rays. That is what is called the ‚vibe‘. It is not a non-existential thing. The other person feels it, you will also feel that you have touched the other person. And then those rays go on spreading to people, to animals, to trees, to rocks ... and one day you will see, you are touching the whole universe from within ... [4]

We are an energy-field and a consciousness as an organic unity. As I mentioned earlier, our energy field is made up equally of material and immaterial energies: physical, mental, fluid, emotional and electro-magnetic energy components, with every part intimately interconnected with every other part.

We have *voluntary* energy and potential as well as *involuntary* energy and potential. All of these aspects can be observed by watching inside. Again, the body is the home of our inner consciousness. The body is always in the present moment and it is the door to inner consciousness.

A New Paradigm for Human Touch

For a meditator, in all forms of touch, value is placed equally on the art of giving and the art of receiving. Giving and receiving need to flow equally. All forms of touch are inter-active, requiring an innocent loving heart and a deep understanding of electro-magnetic energy: we are made of vibrations and light. And all forms of touch are miraculous when we open ourselves up to the mystery. But sincerity is also needed: if we don't allow ourselves to receive the touch then even the spiritual touch of a mystic cannot penetrate us. We have first to become aware of, and then let go of, resistance and fear in order to be touched profoundly.

When we see something, it is light touching us from outside our energy field. Light is being perceived and felt. The amount of light we allow – in other words, what we allow ourselves to really see – depends upon our utilizing consciousness without fear, guilt or expectations. When I look at whatever is around me, then through my eyes I am touching whatever I look at. There is a palpable difference between the touch of a loving look, an approving look, a critical look and a judgmental look – everyone has felt this.

Anyone can verify this by trying a small experiment: when looking at an object, or at someone, first feel that from inside you, through your eyes, you are touching what you are seeing. Then reverse the sensing and feel that you are being touched by what comes through your vision.

When we hear, or talk, it is a similar process. The vibrations and frequencies of outer sounds touch us and resonate within our energy field and we translate these vibrations into thoughts, feelings, responses and movements. By paying attention and listening consciously, in each moment, our hearing becomes richer, our understanding deepens and we experience that sounds are touching us all the time.

Similarly, the vibrations of our words and our breath are touching those around us. Everyone has felt the difference between the energy of an encouraging word and a critical word and the affect it has on the one who is being touched by this energy. In fact, when we change the tone of our voice, the meaning of what we say also changes. Everyone should learn to sense the vibration of the words they are sharing... and also learn to consciously sense how the vibrations and meaning of their words are touching others.

Our involuntary body rhythms: heartbeat, breath, craniosacral pulse, can be minutely felt with practice and consciously utilized as an ‚inner touch‘ that nourishes and heals body and mind of tensions, fear and pain. If we are not aware of this, we miss contact with our own inner healer.

Although our breathing is involuntary and works without our awareness or will power, it can be voluntarily used by everyone as a door to the inner consciousness and psycho-physical healing. This was one of the most valuable contributions of Guatama the Buddha, twenty-five centuries ago: his understanding of the subtle secrets of conscious witnessing of the incoming and outgoing breath, which came to be known as Vipassana Meditation.

Vipassana has helped millions of people on the path of meditation and self-realisation. Think about this truth: each breath is unique, only happens once and can never be repeated. Realizing this, we can learn to come into this very moment without comparison, fear, or expectation. For me, this awareness has helped me on so many levels and in so many situations.

Everyone knows that music touches and transforms our reality. Nature – the countryside, rivers, mountains, ocean, valleys – certainly touches us and renews our energy.

Food touches us through our mouth from outside, then continues touching inside and renews our energy by miraculously transforming into blood. Water touches us and every one of our trillions of cells. The sun and all forms of heat touch us. Cold touches us and also serves as an important inner balancing ... I could go on and on. The written word touches and influences us. Even thoughts and ideas touch us. Your thoughts affect your mood, your muscles, your nerves, your heart and these thoughts immediately affect and touch the people and things outside of us. Love touches. Anger touches. Fear touches. Compassion touches.

So, in an elusive yet obvious way, we are constantly touching and being touched through our eyes, our ears, our mouth and voice, our nose, our hands and skin, our mind and its thoughts, our feelings, the atmosphere around us... Touch, the way I am defining it, is a vast moment-to-moment happening.

Five Possibilities of Touch

All touching experienced through the medium of our own personal electro-magnetic energy field has several subconscious, though voluntary possibilities in it. It is helpful to understand and appreciate the subtle nuances of each of these five possibilities and how each one can alter one's experience of touch:

1   Our eyes (or ears, hands, mind, etc) can be clouded with fear, suspicion, mistrust, anger, desire, or other alienating emotions. This will prevent accurate, direct seeing, hearing, or sensing. By letting go of fear and conditioned attitudes, a new possibility opens. Our pitiful education systems have programmed almost everyone to be afraid and suspicious of touch... even to feel guilty about touching, which is one of the most precious gifts we are born with.

2   Mechanical touching, out of habit... with no sense of wonder, presence, or innocence. Our thinking and comparing mind, which dominates our awareness, keeps us from feeling what is actually happening in this moment. It is mind-boggling how many things we can do every day without any awareness of what we are doing.

3   Our consciousness, which is living in the body, can be alert, sensitive, loving and can actively send energy and acceptance to what is both outside and inside our personal energy field. Touching without fear, judgements, or expectations, with a deep sense of acceptance and gratitude – this way of seeing, listening and connecting allows a deeper experience of touch and sharing between the inner and outer phenomena.

4   Eyes, ears, and hands can learn to be more consciously feminine: receptive, involuntary and trusting, yet alert and ready

to respond and share. It is possible to allow the energy of people, animals, nature, sounds and light come into us with less and less filtering or expectation. The feminine energy, which is part of every conscious touch, functions like the energy of the Divine Mother and is available to us all. Consciousness can be given more space and permission to touch through the eyes, voice, energy and hands. In this way, something of the principles of ARUN Conscious Touch, or meditation, can be brought into looking, listening, talking, eating, moving and touching.

5   Here and now: with an element of what Osho and other mystics call 'No Mind' or 'meditation', the art of touching consciously – whether looking, listening, or sensing through our hands – is always in the present moment. There is no past to duplicate, or any future goal to achieve. For the look or touch to be conscious, we need to experience it by feeling it more than by thinking about it, commenting for or against, comparing this touch to other touches, analyzing, etc. The touch is an experiencing of life in this moment. Nothing needs to be added, or changed and everything moves through touch. Again, thanks to our all-prevailing education systems, we have been heavily trained to judge, compare and criticize... and this makes it very challenging to be in the moment with touch. Remember, no two touches can ever be the same.

Inner Touch

An essential thread in the rich tapestry of ARUN Conscious Touch is contained in Osho's understanding of Yoga and the subtle ,wireless' inner anatomy of man. As one of his representatives and teachers of Yoga in his communes in both India and USA, I came to an elusively obvious realization: whenever I change the angle between any two bones of my skeleton, an inner touch is generated that I am able to perceive and this can be a healing force for the part that feels the touch. This awareness makes meditative movement – a key component of Gautama the Buddha's teaching – easy to experience.

Yoga, as taught in ARUN Conscious Touch, is entirely non-comparative and non-competitive. We use whatever sensations, thoughts, feelings, tensions, fears, or energies that are generated by doing the various *asanas* as a focus for our awareness in the present moment; and as a way of becoming more familiar with our body and consciousness as an organic unity.

Think about this: your body moves through a miraculous, intricate system of pulleys (muscles, tendons and ligaments), levers (individual bones of the skeleton) and shifting fulcrums (round articulations of the joints) powered by the *prana* (or consciousness) within your breath. An *asana* is a body position that is maintained for an extended period of time, so each asana gently and safely encourages the bones of your skeleton – and the muscles and fascia that holds the skeleton together – to temporarily change their angles relative to each other.

When you stretch, one side of the articulation shortens, while the other side lengthens. Every movement or stretch is felt because the bones of that part are changing their angles relative to one another. The nerves and blood vessels flow along and between the bones, carrying messages back and forth to your brain, and you have over two hundred and twenty bones in your body.

This stretching can be felt as an inner touch and can be gradually and minutely directed to the deepest tissues of your body. It is in the deeper tissues and the spaces between the bones where tension and fear accumulates, as well as most physical and emotional pain. This tension, fear and pain naturally pollutes the mind, the brain and the emotions – making it even more difficult to enjoy this moment.

Touching, whether through your own conscious movement, or received from the hands of someone else, has immense healing and meditative potentials. Touch simultaneously activates sensory nerve pathways, hormones, endorphins, feelings and motor nerve passages. It also activates our awareness. Within us, there are ingenious feedback loops, or circuits, that enable this inner-activity to take place. These pathways are made stronger and healthier through conscious movements and by meditatively watching inside. Improved co-ordination, flexibility, gracefulness, health, freedom from pain, and relaxation are just a few of the many benefits.

Your body movements, including both voluntary and involuntary motion, can also be perceived and felt as all-the-time touching inter-action. It just depends upon your sensitivity and ability to watch inside. Inner movements that occur as you move position in space while standing, sitting, lying down, walking, or dancing – the rearrangement of bones, rotations, contractions, stretches – mixed with all the intricate interactions of our muscles, nerves, blood flow, breath, brainwaves, together with motions of the cerebrospinal fluid, hormones and lymph systems is a never-ending inner touch that is always available to our witnessing consciousness. That was a very long sentence! But I am trying to emphasize the delicate inter-connectedness of everything that goes on inside us. With awareness and appreciation of the in-built wisdom of the body-mind, our consciousness is able to expand and utilize its richest potential.

Touch Implies Two

All of us living with Osho had many different roles in the commune. My main work was guiding Dynamic Meditation, teaching Yoga, Rebalancing and CranioSacral Balancing. Another important turning-point in my comprehension and awareness of how meditation and touch can be joined together happened for me when Osho asked me to tune in to his own energy field and function as his personal touch-based 'doctor' to see what could be done for the overall health of his body. In 1988, I gave him about one hundred and fifty individual sessions, each one unique, over a nine-month period. I also used a variety of electro-magnetic acupuncture devices with him such as the 'Mora Machine', 'Indu-Med' and 'Bi-Com' high frequency inventions.

While touching Osho, something became obvious to me that I feel is very significant, something I had never valued so deeply before. That is: while I was touching Osho, he was touching me! I not only refer to energetic and spiritual dimensions when I say this, although he was definitely touching my heart and my soul. It was something else. I began deeply pondering the hidden implications of this and a whole new window into the phenomenon of touch opened for me. Immediately, I started utilizing this awareness in my trainings and individual sessions.

Ask yourself: is it possible for you to touch anything without it simultaneously touching you? I don't think so. The very word 'touch' implies two. Anything that I touch is in that same moment touching me. We cannot accurately say that one is 'giving the touch' while the other is 'receiving the touch'. It's a two-way process.

So I began experimenting with this new awareness and trying to fathom the hidden implications. This is the practical reason that Anasha and I are always emphasizing that human beings are electro-magnetic energy-fields: the ‚electro‘ part is expanding out of our body, while simultaneously the ‚magnetic‘ part is drawing into our body. Our consciousness is the medium that allows this to happen... just like the earth is the ground for the positive and negative poles of electricity.

Giving and receiving need to flow equally. It needs an innocent loving heart and a very deep understanding of electro-magnetic energetics: we are made of vibrations and light.

When you touch something knowing that it is also touching you, a new and transformational possibility opens. You start listening, allowing and responding moment-to-moment. The touch travels from your hands into the body, radiates towards the centre and rebounds back into your own energy field. For instance, you can probably create a graph showing how much energy ‚rebounds‘ when your touch carries ten kilograms of pressure as compared to a touch carrying ten grams of pressure; the body touches you back differently and in this way you can learn to interact minutely with what you perceive.

All of the primary involuntary body rhythms can be touched,

which means you can become sensitive to the rebound touch of the heartbeat, the breath and the movement of cerebro-spinal fluid inside the human energy field. You simply need to allow your hands ‚to be‘, without moving and you will be able to sense the pulse of the heart, the breath, the fluids surrounding the brain...

I encourage you to trust your hands, take your time and allow the life energy to come to you. You will start feeling things inside the body of which you were unaware and the person you are touching will also benefit greatly by tuning into their natural body rhythms. When you are simultaneously giving and receiving, a new alchemy of healing and meditation becomes available that is impossible to predict and an effortless pleasure to share.

Love and awareness simultaneously flowing through your hands, in whatever activity, always brings joy.

It was a total joy to be with Osho and touch his body for ninety minutes. Sessions happened daily for over two months and sometimes he would ask for two sessions in one day. I used to get totally ‚in the zone‘ when being with him this way... his body was so free of fear, so full of presence and let-go, and his movements were extremely graceful – especially his hands.

The Man of Awareness

One day, after our session, as Osho was walking back to his room, he turned to me and said something that fundamentally altered my relationship with touch, and set me on a quest that continues to this day. This is how I remember it:

Anubuddha, people have a misunderstanding about the man of awareness... they think that when you are aware, you won't feel pain any more. This is not true – the man of awareness feels the pain more clearly, more intensely. But if you are truly aware, you also become dis-identified with the sensations... you observe them, but you know the pain is not you. You are an unattached witness to the body and mind. What you are doing with touch can make a meaningful contribution to the world of medical science and the

43

world of meditation. Many physical problems that medical doctors cannot help with drugs can be helped by conscious touch. And many people who want to learn and experience meditation have great difficulty because there is so much pain in their body and mind... so this way of touching is ideal for them. Help them to feel and go into the pain without fear, and stay alert.

Needless to say, this was another turning-point in my comprehension and awareness of touch, but there is one more key insight from Osho that really opened up the gift of ARUN Conscious Touch. I asked him if there was anything he would like me to share with sannyasins giving different healing sessions and trainings. I'm not sure what I expected him to say, but Osho's answer took me by surprise:

Every form of treatment has equal value and potentials. What is important is that whatever they are sharing that they put their total energy and love into it.

So Osho was saying that the technique or the method was actually secondary – the essential ingredient was the presence of the practitioners. This became a quest for Anasha and myself: a totally new vision of touch and meditation.

Visible and Invisible Touch

I would like to communicate another essential thread in the beautiful tapestry of conscious touch that is very subtle and important to understand. Just as every touch implies two, every touch has visible and invisible aspects. With each touch, whether it moves through our hands, our eyes, or our voice, there is a material and visible part that can be observed, but there is an equally important immaterial and invisible part which has to do with the ‚intention' of the one who is touching. Sometimes, the intention can be obvious, while at other times it can be sensed only by a meditator, or by someone who has awareness of the human energy body.

You can see the outer actions of a doctor, healer, or therapist: their movements, words, gestures, etc. But for me, what is less visible is even more important: do they touch with respect, with presence? Can they touch without judging, comparing, or criticizing? Are they in the present moment, or acting mechanically, daydreaming, or comparing this touch to other touches? Are there hidden expectations or desires in the treatment, masking a deep sense of insecurity? Or, are they touching with love, a sense of wonder, searching for the essence inside the one whom they are with?

Meditative Touch

ARUN Conscious Touch is not a technique, it is an inter-active meditation. A technique requires memory and a preconceived progression. For the touch to be meditative, it requires presence, trust and the ability to respond moment to moment.

Conscious Touch is the meeting of awareness and love. Love is expressed through touch – the loving caress of the hands on the body, the loving gaze, or love in the tone of the voice. Awareness is presence, totality, spontaneity. Conscious touch is fearless, without expectations, without wanting anything that is not present. It is a silent mirror that reflects what is, without judging or trying to change anything. Conscious Touch is a blessing.

Each touch is like your breath – it happens only once and can never be repeated. Try not to compare this touch with any other touch. When you compare, you lose presence. There is giving and receiving in each touch. For the touch to be truly meditative, it needs to be non-judgmental and have the quality of *tathata*, which is Buddha's word for 'unconditional acceptance of what is'. By the way, this is almost impossible for the average body worker! Most systems train you to depend on judging and analysing, in one form or another.

If you learn to use the touch to watch inside, without trying to change anything, moment-to-moment, without fear and without expectations, you will be amazed. Feel each touch with all your senses and centres of perception open and alert. Trust your intuition, trust human touch, relax and enjoy. No need to be serious. Love, awareness, radical acceptance and the natural wisdom inside the body is what transforms tension and pain. As I heard Osho say:

Your body is the greatest mystery in the whole of existence.

There are few problems, whether of the body or the spirit that ARUN Conscious Touch cannot treat in a healing, meditative way. Those parts of our being, or energy field, that never receive a conscious touch become dormant or asleep, and every part of us is equally vital to our overall life-experience – we are one organic unity.

Many secret, or essential parts of us exist in seed form – for instance, our glands and chakras – and without being touched by our love and awareness they will never grow spiritually – or physically, for that matter. Pain and injuries, both physical and emotional, also cause various parts of us to become fearful, tight and disconnected from other parts of us. We become unaware of it, and suppress the pain. This unawareness, over time, becomes tension. Tension, over time, becomes pain and dis-ease.

This is why I am against almost all allopathic pain-killers and drugs used for physical and emotional problems – they add to our unawareness of the roots of the pain.

Love beautifies, heals and cleanses both the observer and the observed – it is like an inner sun, emanating from us. Awareness does something similar to the body tissues and organs: they begin to vibrate and function at their optimum level. We use conscious touch to promote health, flexibility, sensitivity and more importantly, as a door to expanded consciousness. ARUN is a loving touch that is relaxed, alert and non-judgmental.

The body is the door, the body is the stepping stone to the inner consciousness.

CHAPTER THREE

Osho's Meditation Methods

Shunyo

Meditation has been mainstream for a long time now. There are hundreds of specific styles and different types of activity commonly referred to as meditative practices. Chanting mantras, the use of prayer beads, contemplation and concentration are all understood to be part of meditation.

The word 'mindfulness' is often used for meditation these days. It actually means awareness and has been used for thousands of years by Eastern mystics, also referred to as self-remembrance, witnessing, watching and right- mindfulness.

There are many websites promoting mindfulness, many good teachers and organizations whose concern is to bring positive social change and more happiness through mindfulness. This is great news, an indication that on a certain level many people are becoming more aware and interested in improving the quality of their lives.

'Mindfulness' has helped to bring meditation into the market place. It is understood that meditation doesn't need to be practiced at a certain time of day, as something separate from daily life, although if you can manage to take some time each day to relax into yourself and simply be, then mindfulness, or awareness, becomes easier. What is needed, as a solid base, is to learn the knack of relaxing into the present moment.

In my understanding, mindfulness, or awareness, is not so much a 'practice' like, for example, yoga, or working out in the gym; nor is it any kind of work, but more an understanding of how it feels, or what it means, to be present in the moment, aware of what you are doing whilst doing it.

There are a few common pitfalls to be avoided. For example,

when mindfulness is presented as a technique that has a certain goal – even if that goal is relaxation – then the very fact that you are 'doing' mindfulness as a practice to achieve something means you are still somehow controlling the method and therefore not completely relaxed. There is still a subtle form of effort, ambition, tension or manipulation in what you are doing.

Meditation is sometimes promoted as easing health issues, such as depression and anxiety, managing stress, building positive emotions and happiness. Positive benefits are said to include improved performance in the workplace, including decision-making and greater productivity.

In this way, relaxation and peace of mind are sometimes offered as desirable goals in meditation, because a relaxed person can become more successful. However, when meditation is used as a means to achieve such benefits, you may find yourself adjusting to daily life in a more easy way, but it will not necessarily help you to become more conscious.

Methods to Wake Up

Osho's methods wake you up and this can be risky, because you might just wake up to the fact that you want to live your life in a different way, in a different job, or with a different partner.

I began meditation – Osho Dynamic Meditation to be exact – about forty years ago. I was not stressed, or unhappy, but somehow had the feeling that there was more to life than a likeable job, a steady boyfriend and a comfortable house.

Some part of me was stirring, as if turning in its sleep. I had the feeling that I was not yet seeing things as they really are. I discovered a book by Osho and saw, written in the back, the address of a meditation centre in London, so I decided to investigate.

I did this meditation technique every day for about six months, but was caught the first time I did it. Each time I left the meditation centre I felt inexplicably happy and this happiness continued throughout the day.

The centre was located in one of the worst parts of London,

near Paddington train station where the red brick buildings are old and ugly. The streets and the flyover were crowded with trucks and cars, yet I would look around, thinking to myself "How beautiful everything is!"

There would be moments in the day when I would suddenly become aware of a breeze touching my face that would feel exquisite, or the evening sky would seem luminous. I was becoming more sensitive, both to myself and everything around me. Doing the meditation not only gave me great joy, but increasingly gave me the feeling that everything I had known until now was losing meaning.

During those first few months as a meditator it was as though I began looking at things for the first time. Veils were falling from my eyes. Dynamic Meditation awakens a vital energy that brings freshness and clarity to the seeker's vision.

The effect meditation had on my life was not unusual. Many friends whom I would later meet had the same kind of experiences. A radical change happened in the way they saw their lives and a feeling, or longing, for something deeper and more meaningful urged them to explore further.

Grasp the Fundamentals

To be on the path of meditation is a great adventure. I travel to many countries sharing meditation methods and, of course, everything is so different today. It's almost as if we have outgrown the old, wild phase and people are more sensible; yet the new generation is also more intelligent and they grasp the fundamentals of meditation much quicker than I did.

Osho's techniques transform you and they are revolutionary. The techniques are simple and powerful, yet they require a commitment to change and the courage to let go of old ideas and habits. His methods are not a quick fix – more like long-term transformation. They differ from traditional methods because they are non-serious and include movement, dance and catharsis as well as silent sitting.

There is an important distinction to be made between meditation techniques and the state of meditation itself. The techniques are not the state, but they prepare the ground for meditation to happen. I like to emphasize that it helps to enjoy the technique for its own sake and then if meditation happens ... great. If it doesn't ... well, anyway you have enjoyed the dance, the method, and a few moments of relaxation.

A relaxed and alert state of consciousness brings us to simply witnessing, or watching: watching the body and its movements, and even watching the mind, which is more difficult because thoughts are more subtle and continuously coming and going. Finally, we develop the capacity to watch how emotions come and go. And, as I said earlier, this can become a part of daily life and not something separate to be practiced at certain times.

Information Overload

It is not easy to simply sit and be silent when we lead such busy lives and this is why Osho created his active meditations. They are specially designed to cope with our hectic, stressful lifestyles. During one of Osho's talks, someone asked him "What is neurosis and what is the cure for it?" Osho answered:

Neurosis has never been so epidemic in the past as it is now. It is almost becoming a normal state of human mind ... The modern mind is overloaded, and that which remains unassimilated creates neurosis. It is as if you go on eating and stuffing your body. That which is not digested by the body will prove to be poisonous. And what you eat is less important than what you hear and see.

From your eyes, from your ears, from all your senses, you go on receiving a thousand and one things each moment. And there is no extra assimilation time. It is as if one were constantly sitting at the dining table, eating, eating, twenty-four hours a day.

This is the situation of the modern mind: it is overloaded; so many things are burdening it. It is not any surprise that it breaks down. There is a limit to every mechanism. And mind is one of the most subtle and delicate of mechanisms.

A really healthy person is one who takes fifty percent of his time to assimilate his experiences. Fifty percent action, fifty percent inaction – that is the right balance. Fifty percent thinking, fifty percent meditation – that is the cure.

Meditation is nothing but a time when you can relax utterly into yourself, when you close all your doors, all your senses. You disappear from the world. You forget the world as if it exists no more – no newspapers, no radio, no television, no people. You are alone in your innermost being, relaxed, at home.

In these moments, all that has become accumulated is assimilated. That which is worthless is thrown out. Meditation functions like a double-edged sword: on the one hand it assimilates all that is nourishing, and it rejects and throws out all that is junk.[1]

Osho Dynamic Meditation

This meditation changed my life, and I have seen it change the lives of many, many people. The first three stages are active and this prepares us for the silence in stage four. Dynamic was created over a period of many years, with Osho observing its effects on thousands of people.

The meditation is done with closed eyes and is an hour long, in five stages with music for four of the stages. The best time of the day to do it is early in the morning.

First Stage. Stand with feet shoulder-width apart and breathe chaotically through the nose; let the breathing be intense, deep, fast, without rhythm, with no pattern – and emphasize the exhalation. The body will take care of the inhalation. The breath should move deeply into the lungs. Do this as fast and as hard as you can until you literally become the breathing. Use your natural body movements to help build up your energy. Feel it building up, but don't let go during the first stage.

This chaotic breathing brings more oxygen in your blood, more energy in your cells. Your body cells become more alive and this oxygenation helps to create body electricity or you can call it bioenergy ... When there is electricity in the body you can move deep within, beyond yourself, because this electricity will work within you ...

The body has its own electrical sources. If you hammer them with more breathing and more oxygen, they begin to flow. And if you become really alive then you are no more a body. When you are fully alive you feel yourself as energy, not matter. ~ *Osho*[2]

Second Stage: Catharsis. Explode. Let go of everything that needs to be thrown out. Follow your body. Give your body freedom to express whatever is there. Go totally mad. Scream, shout, cry, jump, kick, shake, dance, sing, laugh, throw yourself around. Hold nothing back; keep your whole body moving. A little acting often helps to get you started. Never allow your mind to interfere with what is happening. Consciously go mad. Be total.

I tell you to be consciously insane, and whatever comes to your mind – whatever – allow it expression and cooperate with it. No resistance, just a flow of emotions ... ~ *Osho*[2]

Third Stage: With arms raised high above your head, jump up and down shouting the mantra, "Hoo! Hoo! Hoo!" as deeply as possible. Land on the flat of your feet, making sure your heels hit the ground. Let the sound hammer deep into the sex centre. Give all you have; exhaust yourself completely.

In the third step I use the mantra "Hoo" as a vehicle to bring your energy upward ... Whilst shouting the mantra 'hoo' we jump with both arms raised straight up into the air. ~ *Osho*[2]

Fourth Stage: Stop!

On hearing "Stop!" you freeze exactly as you are. No movement. You just be a witness – a conscious alertness; not doing anything, no movement, no desire, no becoming, but silently witnessing whatsoever is happening ... ~ *Osho*[2]

Fifth Stage: Soft music begins to play and we dance in celebration.

Osho Kundalini Meditation

Kundalini is another of Osho's well-known methods that is practiced world-wide. It is to be done preferably in the late afternoon.

We do Kundalini Meditation here, but the purpose is not to awaken the kundalini; the purpose is something different. The purpose is to give a dance to the kundalini energy that is within you.

The purpose is very different. The energy that is inside you is, as yet, asleep, and to awaken it you will have to impact it, shake it. My own experience is that there is no need to awaken it; it should just be given a dance, it should just be made musical; it should just be transformed into a blissful celebration. So there is no need to push it or jolt it ...

The purpose of my Kundalini Meditation is not that which has been there for centuries. As far as I am concerned, I am changing the purpose of everything. Here, Kundalini Meditation means, dance – be soaked in bliss, become immersed. Become so immersed that your ego does not remain separate.

This is not the old traditional process of awakening kundalini. This is the process of imparting a dance to the Kundalini. ~ Osho[3]

The meditation is one hour long in four stages, each stage lasting fifteen minutes. Three stages have music. Eyes can be open or closed for the first two stages, and then closed for the second two stages.

First Stage: Shake your body. The purpose of shaking is that whatever energy is lying suppressed or dormant anywhere in your body melts and begins to move; wherever it is lying stuck or blocked, it starts flowing from there.

You stand silently and feel the shaking coming from up your legs. When the body starts a little trembling, help it until the whole body is shaking.

Second Stage: Dancing. The purpose of dancing is that the energy that has been released and spread all over your body can be transformed into bliss. Dance as if you are celebrating.

So dance blissfully, because the more blissful you are the more your energy rises up. A lukewarm effort will not help. Your dance needs intensity. One is dancing, as if one has gone mad. ~ Osho 3)

Third Stage: Stand still or sit down so that the energy can have full opportunity to flow. You simply observe and listen to the music.

Fourth Stage: Lie down, silent and still.

Osho has created many more meditations and they can be obtained via the internet at www.osho.com. When you have found an active meditation that suits you, it is important to practice for twenty-one days continuously. This gives the meditation a chance to work.

When experiencing Dynamic the first few times, your muscles may be sore and stiff, but this will ease as your body adapts to the new movements. By the second week, most people can easily express the chaos of the mind in the cathartic stage. By the third week you settle deeper into the silent stage.

Listening as a Meditation

In 1975 I went to live in Osho's ashram in Pune, which later became his commune. It was during this time that meditation became a way of life for me and not something separate from life.

Osho gave public talks every day for nearly forty years. His talks are spontaneous, filled with timeless wisdom and great humour, but he would often remind us that his real message is not in the words, but in the silent gaps between the words.

Listening to Osho was – and still is – a meditation experience. Remembering those days when we would sit on the meditation hall's marble floor, in stillness and in silence, as the seasons passed from the heat of summer, to stormy monsoon, to the cold mornings of winter, I thought I was just listening to a discourse, but I was also being seduced into the silent gaps between Osho's words. He speaks in such a way that meditation happens by simply listening to him.

I have heard Osho say that listening can be used as a meditation method if you not only focus your awareness on him, but also be aware of the one who is listening. Don't get lost in the speaker, or the music or whatever you are listening to. Do not forget who is listening, because the listener is more important. With this remembrance, the arrow of consciousness is double pointed: one point goes towards the speaker and one point goes towards the listener.

If the listener can be remembered then understanding will go deep, but if the one listening is not aware or is asleep, then the speaker cannot really communicate. If the listener is awake, then even if the one speaking remains silent then you will be able to understand the silence.

It is mysterious how the same silent transmission still happens today while listening to Osho or watching a video of him. I should also add that the content of his talks is relevant for people today and covers all aspects of life, both mundane and spiritual.

For fourteen years my work was doing Osho's laundry. Even then, in that atmosphere of devotion and meditation, friends would ask me in wonder if I didn't get bored or fed up with my work. I never did. Still today, when I need to relax I go for the ironing board.

Osho says he does not *do* meditation, he is living *in* meditation. Watching him, I could sense this, and it has been a teaching for me – to see that meditation is deep relaxation and total awareness at the same time.

Where Have You Been?

When my work in Osho's house included being his caretaker, I would walk with him to the morning and evening discourse, which at that time was being held in a small auditorium attached to his house. One morning, after discourse, we arrived back at the door of his room. As I opened the door and he walked past me, Osho looked at me and with a chuckle asked me "Where have you been, Shunyo?"

I answered that I'd been to the morning discourse with him, but in that instant I realized it was not what he meant. He knew

I had indeed been somewhere, somewhere wordless – to say it was an experience of meditation is enough. And yet this precious experience may have passed unnoticed by me, if Osho had not provoked my recollection, because it was not part of my known mind. It was a reminder for me that we do not always know, or remember, what happens in meditation because it is not part of our mind.

When I began meditating and first heard Osho speaking about 'the mind' I believed I was my mind. I could not – and would not – consider that 'I' was separate. As time passed, I began to understand that I was separate from my mind. I could manipulate my mind, I could think about this … or that … and I could even force my mind to stop for a few moments. So, I considered that I must be separate, I must be more than my mind. I must be the awareness, or watcher.

I came to this understanding in an unusual way. When we shifted the commune from Pune to Oregon, in the United States, Osho liked very much to go for a drive each day. When I was in my 'caretaker' role I was given the incredible gift of going with him. He would drive for a few hours into the remote and desolate countryside. Most of the time, there was nothing around to see or hear and Osho was silent.

In contrast, I found that my own thoughts were on maximum volume, so that they seemed to fill the car. It was shocking to me just how loud and insistent (and embarrassing) my thoughts were and I was sure Osho could hear them.

Somehow, I wanted to do something about it, so I would say to myself "I will think of nothing until we reached the next crossing … " or whatever landmark presented itself. I would fail, but then find another spot in the distance and start again, and in this way my thoughts would slow down. As a method it seemed a bit crude, a bit forceful, but it did help me understand the thinking process.

The years that I spent in a commune of people, whose intention was to grow in love and awareness, was a gift for which I can never be grateful enough. We learned a certain secret to the art of living: the work you do is not as important as how you do the work.

This is a simple understanding that is available to everyone, providing we can stop focusing so much on climbing ladders to success. Work itself can become a meditation when we are present, here and now, in what we are doing, whilst doing it.

In other words, to grow and mature as a spiritual being, Osho's meditation methods should not stop at a one-hour sitting, but can, and must, become part of our daily lives.

Evening Meeting Meditation

This is the last meditation created by Osho. It happens at Osho centres throughout the world at 7:00 pm each day and is in four stages. We begin with about ten to fifteen minutes of music, celebration and dance. Then we sit silently, listening to music that is interspersed with sudden gaps of silence. After three drumbeats, this part of the meditation ends and is followed by an Osho talk. The final stage is a special Gibberish and Let-go meditation guided by Osho himself.

In the last two years of his life, at the completion of each discourse, Osho included a guided meditation where he would guide us to our *hara* centre, about two inches below the navel.

Osho's talks and the Evening Meeting Meditation are available in multiple media formats via the internet at www.osho.com.

Osho's Vipassana Meditation

I think Vipassana is totally under-rated as a method that can help us in our daily lives, in the market place. We may begin by getting the 'knack' of it in a retreat but afterwards the opportunity arises to take it into daily life as a wonderful support for living in a relaxed and calm way.

Osho's version of Vipassana differs from the traditional method. The traditional method can be very strict and Osho's way is more friendly and relaxed, less serious. So, while sitting in silent meditation, watching the breath coming in and going out – the basic Vipassana technique – we can make ourselves very comfortable and also change our sitting position at any time. Moreover, including early morning Dynamic Meditation as part of the process gives us a great chance to release any stiffness and pent-up feelings.

This is one of my contributions, which will be condemned by all the religions – the religions of the cold. I teach you a religion of warmth, love, singing, dancing, music. These are all tremendously helpful to make you alert, wakeful. ~ Osho[4]

During an Osho-style Vipassana retreat, active meditations are included as an essential part of the process. Without Dynamic, the meditator is likely to be suppressing emotions throughout the daily sittings. The energy used for suppression can be much better used for watching.

Loving Ourselves While Meditating

A Buddhist sutra says:

Love yourself and watch
Today, tomorrow and always ~ Osho[5]

Osho tells us that this Buddhist sutra can become the foundation of a radical transformation, and it is one of the most profound sutras of Gautama the Buddha. But it seems that many Buddhists have forgotten about the 'love yourself' part and this makes meditation very dry.

To have a loving attitude is important in Vipassana and, indeed, in our exploration of all meditation techniques. If we are not loving towards ourselves then we leave the door open for our 'mind' – that habitual nagging voice that continually finds problems to think about.

The meditators' worst enemy is himself – 'himself' being the judgmental mind, the critic, the doubter. And you must have noticed how this 'mind' tends to complain and find fault as though it is stuck in a groove called the Complaints Department.

When we condemn ourselves for not being good enough, for

not doing something in the right way, or when we are comparing ourselves negatively with someone else, then we are giving nourishment to a mental image of ourselves that has been with us since childhood.

This image is formed from a collection of ideas about who we are and how we should behave. It has been given to us by society. We have accepted these false ideas about ourselves from our parents and teachers, and when we give attention to these negative patterns we are helping them to grow because attention is food.

When we move into meditation we are susceptible to self-criticism, because meditation is not something that can be proved logically. It is easy to criticize ourselves, or our progress, or lack of it, because our thinking process does not understand meditation. It cannot. Our minds know only what we have already experienced – the known – whereas meditation belongs not only to the unknown (that which one day will become known) but to the unknowable. We can be it, but we can't think about it.

Sometimes in meditation workshops people share their disappointment that although they have been meditating for some time, anger is still there, jealousy still happens ... There is a collective idea that to be a meditator means we will immediately be full of peace and love, becoming almost like saints.

So it is a bit of a shock when so-called negative characteristics are still being experienced. This is where 'love yourself' becomes very important. To be able to acknowledge that anger or jealousy is there, inside you, and not make judgments is itself a kind of meditation. Not an easy one at first, but with love and a sense of humour, you will notice a distance arising between you as a 'watcher' and your emotions and thoughts. You are becoming dis-identified from whatever you are watching and this needs an attitude of loving acceptance.

To understand that there is no goal in meditation can be a relief. Goals create stress and it is a natural tendency, born out of old habit, to bring the same conditioned attitudes to meditation that we have acquired in our daily lives, such as competition, comparison, the drive to succeed, to be the best ... and so on.

Without a goal, nowhere to go, just enjoying the technique, enjoying being in this moment and watching whatever is arising in the mind without condemnation, or thinking it should be different, will bring relaxed awareness. It will give you a sense that you are doing what you can towards creating a state of meditation and simply watching in a loving way.

Whether you are watching a busy mind or a quiet mind it does not matter. What matters is that you are watching, observing without judgment, whatever is there.

Meditation Counselling

Vipassana is an encounter with yourself. In a retreat, all our normal distractions – friends, mobiles, Internet, gossip, television, shopping, work projects – have been put on hold and we are left alone with ourselves.

When counselling clients during a retreat, the focus is to help them to keep watching whatever is happening, without trying to change anything or solve any problems.

Participants in the retreat can choose to speak to the facilitator in private whenever they feel overwhelmed by the unfamiliar situation: emotions may be coming up, old memories may be surfacing that are painful, sitting for so many hours may be causing physical discomfort ... and so on.

The facilitator's main role is to support and encourage people to keep going. Sometimes it is enough just to give a reminder of the simple instructions of the meditation. It is important not to get caught up in any stories that may be arising and yet not reject or cut short whatever the person is saying. Even if someone is sharing an experience that sounds outrageous to you, this is an opportunity to watch your own judgmental mind.

As a facilitator, it's helpful to remember that our thinking minds know nothing of meditation and never will, although it is natural for people – especially beginners – to want to 'know' what is happening, to understand exactly 'what is meditation' and how to 'do' it.

We cannot 'do' it. We can practice a technique, but meditation is something that happens and we cannot *make* it happen. If we understand this and enjoy the technique for its own sake – whether we are sitting silently, dancing, or shaking – then to know that 'it' (a silent moment, or no-mind experience) is not in our hands, can free us of our goal-orientated habits.

As a counsellor, it is a support for people to help them understand that whatsoever is happening is neither right nor wrong, it is just something to watch, or be aware of, and with a little patience thoughts do slow down.

Many people think meditation is something serious, or spiritual, which can make a retreat feel more like a burden, or duty, so in my experience it is good to have a sense of humour when counselling people, to help lighten their load.

Vipassana retreats are a different experience from my other meditation workshops because everyone is in silence for the duration of the retreat – except for the counselling sessions – and this in itself creates a more serious atmosphere. Each person is really on their own, looking within, enjoying moments of inner silence, feeling and sensing in a new way, and sometimes having fresh insights.

These moments are beautiful and it is tempting to try to hold onto them, but this inevitably creates expectations, hopes and desires that can destroy your state of relaxed watching and then everything changes. You may suffer disappointment, or feel bored or angry.

It is a great merry-go-round and this is what I love about Vipassana: one sees the peaks and the valleys and through this see-saw it becomes possible to experience that something deeper and more inner never changes. Something like awareness remains constant.

This is what we can take into our daily lives: this understanding that no matter what happens, we have the opportunity to watch it all.

The Book of Secrets

The Book of Secrets consists of one hundred and twelve meditation techniques from the ancient Indian text of the *Vigyan Bhairav Tantra,* with Osho's commentaries on each method. According to Osho, these one hundred and twelve methods are essentially one technique in different formats, and the basic technique is witnessing. By applying the art of witnessing in different situations, a new technique is created.

There are meditations on listening, seeing, feeling, breathing and making love; there are methods for centring and methods for feeling expanded without a centre. In fact, there is a technique that will suit every possible type of person. These are not just techniques but can become a style of life, a way of living.

The workshops that I create based on these methods are attended by people of all ages and all backgrounds; some may be new to meditation, some may have been traveling the path for many years. I am always impressed by how intensely people want to be more in touch with themselves and how difficult this can be at first.

In this situation, a light and joyful approach to meditation is very helpful and with this in mind it is beautiful to travel and work with Marco, a musician who creates music especially for these meditations.

We practice five or six meditations in one day. Sometimes we may go outside in nature, if the venue is suitable. Some methods we explore with a partner. Some we practice alone.

Heart Meditation

Energy follows imagination and visualization, which are both powerful forces that move through the mind and can affect the body. Just try it for a moment: close your eyes, place both hands on your heart, and as you inhale imagine you are breathing into your heart. You will soon find that your heart and its associated feelings are being energized. Hence, the stories of Tibetan Monks and Hindu Sadhus who can stand in the snow naked and imagine their bodies are hot and not feel the cold.

Absorb the Senses in Your Heart is a meditation from Osho's *The Book of Secrets* that works in a similar way. In this meditation, we practice feeling that every sense goes to the heart and dissolves into it. We use the senses of listening, looking and touch as ways to bring awareness to the heart centre.

When we focus on feelings, our thinking process slows down. In those moments when thoughts do enter and distract us – slipping back into the habit of thinking – I encourage people to just notice the mind has come in, then gently bring the focus of attention back to the heart centre.

Osho tells us that once we are centred in the heart energetically, we have the possibility to go deeper, falling down into a centre just below the navel. Osho has put much emphasis on the importance of this centre, known as the *hara*. He has given us many meditations for this centre, including the guided meditations that follow his evening talks.

Who Is Sensing?

Another meditation is *Be Aware Who is Sensing* and this technique uses looking as a technique to be aware who is behind the sense of looking. Or, you could say, you become aware of yourself looking, rather than focusing on whatever your eyes are looking at. Our senses are doors, receiving stations, mediums, receptors and you are the consciousness, looking through the eyes.

You see through your eyes. Eyes cannot see; you see through them. The seer is hidden behind, the eyes are just the opening, just the windows.
~ Osho[6]

In the second part of the meditation, we use listening as a way to become aware. Our ears are receiving stations, receiving information for us, but who is inside receiving the sounds? Who is aware of listening? It is a process where the act of enquiry, of looking in, is the meditation itself – not that any verbal answer is there.

Darkness Meditation

In *The Book of Secrets* there are meditations on light and on darkness. In the Darkness Meditation, Osho tells us that if we can love darkness we will become unafraid of death, and if we can enter into darkness without fear, we will achieve total relaxation.

Light is born and dies; darkness simply is. It is deathless. ~ Osho[7]

When I decide to introduce the Darkness Meditation in a meditation programme, the first challenge is to find a room where no light enters. This is surprisingly difficult, even at night. At home, I have done the meditation in my clothes cupboard, but that becomes a bit claustrophobic.

In this method, we sit for forty-five minutes. Keeping our eyes open, we look into darkness, allowing the darkness to enter our eyes. In complete darkness, we lose all boundaries, we cannot say where we end and the room begins.

I recall one occasion, sitting with a group of people in a rather small space, when I realized that in complete darkness I wouldn't be able to see the time. So I asked a friend if he would whistle outside the window when one hour had elapsed. I was not to know that the sound of his stumbling footsteps through the undergrowth surrounding the building would be heard with thunderous clarity inside our little room.

I also didn't know that the sound of rapid, laboured breathing and frightened groans belonged to one of the meditators who hadn't told me that all his life he had a phobia of the dark. Fortunately, it was a very sincere group and nobody reacted, commented, or got the giggles. In fact, when the meditation ended, the person who had been so afraid talked about his life-long fear of darkness and how in that one hour he felt he had gone beyond it.

A more advanced stage of meditating on darkness is to carry a patch of darkness within you, just as in meditating on light, the method is to carry a flame inside.

It is recommended that we experiment with a meditation continuously for between three weeks and three months. When

I introduce these methods in groups, it is so that people can get a feeling of which meditation resonates with them. I then encourage them to 'play' with the method for a few days, and then, if it still feels good, to practice it for a longer period. It is surprising how easy it is for people to move deeply into one of the techniques.

Include Everything

I remember a wonderful scene in an old farmhouse in England, where fifty people were participating in a meditation called *Include Everything in Your Being*.

The technique is a little difficult, but if you can do it, then it is very beautiful.

The basic point is to remember inclusiveness. Don't exclude. This is the key given in the original sutra in *Vigyan Bhairav Tantra*: inclusiveness. Include and grow. Include and expand. Try it with your body and your thoughts, and then try it with the outside world also.

You can make it not only a meditation but a style of life, a way of living.

Stage One: sitting, don't divide. Sitting still and silent, be inclusive of all: your body, your mind, your breath, your thinking, your knowing ... everything. Be inclusive of all.

Just say, 'I am all' and be all. Don't create any fragmentation within you. This is a feeling. With closed eyes include everything that exists in you. Don't be centred anywhere. Be without a centre for this technique and include everything in your being – don't discard anything. Don't say, 'This is not I', say, 'I am' and include everything in it.

If you can do this, then wonderful, absolutely new experiences will happen to you. You will feel there is no centre in you. And with the centre gone, there is no self, there is no ego, only consciousness remains – consciousness like a sky covering everything. When this feeling grows, not only your own breath will be included, not only your own form will be included, ultimately the whole universe becomes inclusive to you.

Stage Two:

After sitting in a room with this feeling of 'I am all', the participants move outside. They might look at a tree, then close their eyes and feel the tree is inside them; or look at the sky, close the eyes and feel the sky is inside.

And this is not imagination, because the tree and you both belong to the earth. You are both rooted in the same earth and ultimately rooted in the same existence.

So when you feel that the tree is within you – the tree is within you. You feel the tree's aliveness, the greenery, the freshness, the breeze passing through it.

This technique expands your consciousness. Looking at the sky one can start feeling that the sky is also part of you. You close your eyes for a moment and allow that feeling of being one with the sky. It is beautiful.

And indeed it is. Everything we see, feel, touch is a part of us. A feeling of 'I am all'. And finally, as you look at the other participants around you, this understanding is there that this person in front of you is also part of you. ~ Osho[8]

Watching the whole group going through this experience of inclusiveness was an amazing experience for me. They were outside the farmhouse, moving in slow motion, their eyes filled with wonder, their faces luminous and I was thinking "My goodness, if people could see this they would think everyone is taking LSD." Such a scene in the gentle rolling hills of the English countryside is really quite surreal.

Equally surreal was our *Full Moon Meditation* that did not end, but went on and on. I found myself looking at a moonlit field where fifty people were standing like statues, not moving, even after I clinked the Tibetan bells several times, to indicate the end of the meditation.

I love to share Osho's meditation methods because to teach is the best way to learn and I am still learning. I began this journey knowing there was more to life than I was experiencing, and after

66

a lifetime of experiencing and practicing meditation I still have this feeling that there is more.

The difference is that life has become so much bigger. Life itself has expanded in all directions and yet I still know there is more. Strangely, this feeling is a source of joy, of excitement and peace at the same time. I go on living in a simple way, knowing that everything is actually extraordinary.

CHAPTER FOUR

Osho's Meditative Therapies

Leela

In May 1988 I was working as coordinator of the therapy department in Osho Commune International in Pune when I got a phone call from Anando, who at that time was Osho's private secretary. "I've got something for you," she told me. She arrived with a couple of pieces of paper in her hand; she gave them to me without saying anything other than "Here, read this."

The first page was Osho's explanation of the Mystic Rose, a new kind of course in which participants would laugh for three hours a day, for seven days, and then cry for three hours a day, for seven days – a two week process. There was to be no laughing during crying, no crying during laughing.

Osho was talking about how this new meditation would function as a deep cleansing, a physiological change and a medical transformation, and bring out the inner child with its freshness and wonder. Turning over to the next page, it said "Person to run it: Leela."

I was flabbergasted. I looked at Anando and asked, "What is this?" In her matter-of-fact way, she simply shrugged and said, "It is what it is."

Much later, I was curious and asked Anando "How did I come to get the Mystic Rose?" Because it seemed obvious to me that if Osho was personally creating a new kind of therapeutic process then the right person to lead it would be one of the commune's leading facilitators.

This is what she told me: she was going through the list of commune therapists with Osho and they hadn't hit upon anyone who was free, available and somehow suitable, so she said to Osho "Maybe I should ask Leela, because she is the coordinator of the

Group Department; she may have a suggestion."

Osho said, "Leela? The one who gave me the massage?"

Anando said, "Yes."

Osho said, "She can do it."

And that's how I got to lead the Mystic Rose. Just a note to clarify: I'd given Osho a series of massage sessions a couple of months earlier, because the two body workers who usually massaged him – Satyarthi and Anubuddha – were away from Pune. I'd also been teaching massage to people who were training as body workers.

So, having the Mystic Rose landing in my lap was a surprise, to say the least, because I was still quite a timid person in those days with no idea of myself as someone who could take on such a prominent role. What I did know, however, was that I could laugh easily and naturally, and what I found out quite early in the development of the Mystic Rose was that I could cry easily, too.

Facilitating the Process: First Steps

As a first step, I invited a group of people, mainly commune residents, to join me for a pilot session, a kind of rehearsal to see how things went. Osho had given me no detailed instructions – no "do this, do that" – so I needed to figure it out as we went along.

Anyway, about forty people showed up for the evening experiment and for a couple of hours it was like a madhouse. If I'd had a video camera it would have been a sight to see. There was a lot of laughing, fooling around, theatre and acting-out, a lot of interaction, with people entertaining each other in all kinds of ways.

I was astonished, because people who normally looked very holy when going about their daily business in the commune were suddenly transformed into wild, crazy people ... I couldn't believe what they were getting up to.

After two nights of these experimental sessions, I wrote to Osho and asked him, "Is it okay to have interaction in this process?" Because I could see difficulties in trying to control a group with so much acting-out. I also noticed people's tendency was more towards catharsis and letting go of personal inhibitions, in a humorous way, than focusing on the energy of laughter itself.

Osho's response was clear: "No interaction." So that was his answer to my first question about how to run this new kind of therapeutic process. It was the beginning of a period of trial and error, in which we gradually found the way to move deeper and deeper into an experience of the Mystic Rose's transforming power.

It was a paradoxical situation, because when we normally laugh, in a social way, it can easily be regarded as a superficial and momentary experience – indeed, laughter is often dismissed as superficial, in contrast to negative emotions. But the message coming from Osho was just the contrary: laughter can, in itself, be a very deep and meaningful act. So I was determined to create a process in which participants would be able to taste what Osho was offering to them.

A few days after receiving the note to create the Mystic Rose, Osho introduced it to the public in his daily discourse. He was talking about the significance of ‚Yaa-Hoo!' a playful expression which had entered his vocabulary in the form of a joke – he always told jokes at the end of his discourses. Then he said:

I have chosen Leela, one of my therapists, to create a new meditative therapy. The first part will be Yaa-Hoo! – For three hours, people simply laugh for no reason at all. Digging for three hours you will be surprised how many layers of dust has gathered upon your being. It will cut them like a sword, in one blow.

And then the second part is 'Yaa-Boo!' The first part removes everything that hinders your laughter – all the inhibitions of past humanity, all the repressions. But still you have to go a few steps more to reach the temple of your being, because you have suppressed so much sadness, so much despair, so much insanity, so many tears – they are all there, covering you and destroying your beauty, your grace, your joy.[1]

He went on to point out that nobody in the past had used laughter and tears as a form of meditation, but these qualities were extremely helpful to clean the heart of all inhibitions. He also said that laughing and crying were beneficial for the body as well as the mind.

"This is absolutely my meditation," he declared, then stated once more "Leela will be in charge of it."

The Healing Power of Laughter

In both his note to me and in his discourse, Osho referred to the health benefits of laughter and this is in line with a great deal of recent medical research that points to the healing power of laughter.

In the early 80s, Norman Cousins, a well-known American journalist and academic, was one of the first people to draw the public's attention to laughter as a form of healing, when he wrote a popular book – *Anatomy of an Illness* – about his struggle with a severe form of arthritis. In it, he described how he could create pain-free episodes by watching old Marx Brothers' movies and laughing. Cousins firmly believed that human emotions and illness were deeply connected.

A couple of decades later, another author, Sandra Kornblatt, explored how laughter can make you feel better. On the basis of evidence gathered from a large number of research projects, Kornblatt made the following list of what laughter does: lowers blood pressure, increases the flow and oxygenation of the blood, reduces certain stress hormones, increases the response of disease-killing cells, defends against respiratory infections …

The list is long and impressive. It also includes a study at Johns Hopkins University Medical School, which showed that humour during instruction led to increased test scores.

Humour works quickly. Less than a half-second after exposure to something funny and an electrical wave moves through the higher brain functions of the cerebral cortex. The left hemisphere analyses the words and structures of the joke; the right hemisphere 'gets' the joke; the visual sensory area of the occipital lobe creates

71

images; the limbic (emotional) system makes you happier; and the motor sections make you smile or laugh.

Medicine aside, having the capacity to laugh at ourselves is one of the greatest and most intelligent factors in being human. Unfortunately many of us have lost or forgotten the value of this dimension of life. Those of us who take ourselves and life seriously can have a hard time laughing about anything.

In learning to dissolve seriousness, it helps to have an environment in which we can feel relaxed and open to experiencing others who are laughing *with* us not *at* us. This is a very important distinction that needs to be understood, otherwise laughter can have a derisive, judgemental and cynical attitude which is hurtful and aggressive.

Each participant comes to the group with his or her own unique history of repression. It is impossible – and in fact undesirable – to expect everyone to respond in the same way to laughter. For some it is easy to laugh and for others it takes a bit more time. However, releasing seriousness and developing the capacity to laugh at oneself becomes much easier in the playful, supportive environment of a group such as the Mystic Rose.

Many thousands of people who have gone through this process have been astounded at how it has benefited them and brought so much more joy into their lives. Many people return again and again to the process as they appreciate the healing and freedom it creates in them.

Laughing at Oneself

Learning to laugh at oneself requires that we see how identified we are with our social roles, with many of our actions, beliefs and judgements that we carry about ourselves. There are wonderful moments where, in deep laughter, it is suddenly possible to see a past image of ourselves in one situation or another, serious and lost to the moment, completely identified with some trivial personal drama of our own making, but now we are able to have a good laugh at our absurdities.

When we can laugh at ourselves and are able to see the humour in the world around us, it gives us a distance, a clarity, from our identification with negative beliefs and patterns of behaviour in which we habitually function. Many participants have shared that after the experience of the first week, they often burst out laughing in the middle of apparently serious situations, such as in an argument with their partners. Suddenly the whole scenario takes on a different meaning and they simply cannot remain in the seriousness of it all. This change in perspective can affect all areas of our lives: work, relationships, with our families ... in fact, life in general.

Modern society has developed in such a way that most people's lives revolve around work, with little time for play. How sad is that! All of nature is at play, but we, supposedly the most intelligent creatures on this beautiful earth, are all too often sad and serious.

Immediate action needs to be taken. Laugh more! Your health and well-being may depend on it. And the benefits of that will spread to all those around you. This doesn't mean that we should become entertainers and performers but simply happier within ourselves.

As our ability to laugh at ourselves grows, humility and a more loving understanding can also begin to grow within us. It is vital that we lose the serious view of life and become more accepting of ourselves and our fellow humans.

Slowly, it becomes easier to connect with a light-hearted attitude throughout the day, so it is important to encourage ourselves to become aware of the humour in life and integrate this lightness on a daily basis. We can learn to be less concerned about what others may think of us and this is very liberating, because if we are continuously looking at ourselves through the eyes of others – judging ourselves, always trying to please, keeping up appearances – then, of course, we cannot function naturally. Having a good sense of humour keeps us healthy, balanced and relaxed.

My own experience says to me that if you can laugh rightly, in the right moment, it will bring you out of unconsciousness into the open sky, from the darkness to the light. I am introducing laughter as a meditation because nothing makes you so total as laughter; nothing makes you stop your thinking as laughter does. Just for a moment you are no more a mind. Just for a moment you are no more in time. Just for a moment you have entered into another space where you are total and whole and healed. ~ Osho[2]

Helping the Tears to Flow

People who are drawn to join the Mystic Rose process already seem to have an innate understanding that this is what they need, and even if there is some initial hesitation, a deeper intuition helps them overcome any uncertainty. Generally, people who join the process are simply sick and tired of living in pain and sadness, so they commit to throwing themselves wholeheartedly into it.

When participants arrive for the start of the crying week, many are ready to just let go into their tears, while others are more nervous and anxious. Allowing feelings that have been buried for so long can be quite confronting. During the introduction of the second week, the facilitator explains to everyone that fear and pain is something we all carry within us, and that by allowing ourselves to cry deeply, it is possible to move through the pain and fear to experience an enormous release and healing.

It is made clear that participants know they have permission to let go totally and cry as loudly as they like. If the crying becomes a disturbance to others, we recommend they cry into soft cushions but it is important not to hold back.

A large selection of carefully-chosen, sad and evocative music is played from time to time, which helps to generate the tears. The collective group energy supports the entire process. Just like laughter, tears too can be infectious, so the sound of others crying is of enormous help for every participant.

An important understanding to convey to participants is that whatever fear or pain they may be going through is merely an echo of a past event, and that they need not fear the same punishment, trauma or violence that happened when they were children. We need to allow the repressed memories to surface so that the intensity of these feelings can rise again.

The deeper we go into the process, the greater is our understanding that we will be encountering layers of repression and deeply buried emotions – feelings that in the past we tried to avoid by stuffing them down inside us. As we begin to pass through blocks and holding patterns, we gather courage to encounter more pain. It becomes clear that the more we cry out these emotions, the more unburdened and light-hearted we feel.

For those who were unable to cry, help was at hand. Osho had said that "nobody should be left for dead" and it was okay for other people to come and hold each other providing they themselves were already crying.

This was an important distinction: the other participants had to be crying, not comforting each other. In normal life, that's what we do in order to avoid feeling our own pain: when somebody cries, we show our sympathy and tell them "Never mind … It'll be okay … don't cry … "

The only problem with sadness, desperateness, anger, hopelessness, anxiety, anguish, misery, is that you want to get rid of them. That's the only barrier. You will have to live with them. You cannot just escape. They are the very situation in which life has to integrate and grow. They are the challenges of life. Accept them. They are blessings in disguise.

… Sadness goes to the very bones, to the marrow. Nothing goes as deep as sadness. Remain with it and sadness will take you to your inner-most core. You can ride on it and you will be able to know a few new things about your being that you had never known before. ~ Osho[3]

The Watcher on the Hills

I noticed that, when the crying week was over, many people were feeling raw and this was my own experience, too – by the end of the crying we were all feeling very emotional and vulnerable.

So I wrote to Osho, asking "Can we perhaps do a couple of days of meditation afterwards? Because people need time to integrate what they've been through." By way of reply, I was given a note from Osho in which he talked about the 'Watcher on the Hills' – his term for a meditator who has the ability to watch his own thoughts and feelings – with an instruction to add a third week of meditation to the two-week process.

So that's how the Mystic Rose became a twenty-one-day process for three hours every day. It might seem that I was being very intuitive, asking the right questions to co-create the process, but I wondered, with hindsight, if these were questions that Osho himself felt I should be asking him. These things kind of came to me in a way that was obvious, as a natural development of what we were all experiencing.

As we were about to do the 'Watcher' stage of the Mystic Rose for the first time, I realised we didn't have enough space to do any walking – we were doing it on Krishna House roof – because there were so many people in the group.

Maybe I should back up here, for a moment, and explain that in Osho's version of Vipassana, which is essentially the same as the Watcher on the Hills, people would meditate for about forty minutes, then stand up and walk very slowly around the meditation hall, putting their awareness in the soles of their feet and feeling the sensation as each foot touched the ground.

But walking around wasn't practical for so many participants, so I had the idea of people standing up, just in front of where they'd been sitting, and doing some very gentle dancing movements, on the spot, to relax their muscles and get any stiffness out of the body.

I asked Osho if it was okay and his response was "Yes that is fine but remind people to hold the Watcher and not to get lost in the dance."

So, I divided the three-hour session into three periods of sitting, with two fifteen-minute periods of dancing in between, and that worked beautifully. In accordance with Osho's guidance, I explained to everyone "Don't come out of your meditation when you stand up to dance, hold the space..." and they managed it very well.

Refining the Process

Slowly, more people started to lead the process, because it was hugely popular and happening frequently, and I couldn't coordinate the Group Department and run every Mystic Rose as well. Soon, we formed a Mystic Rose facilitators' group in the commune and met regularly to share our experiences. I needed to hear how it was for others and they needed to hear from me, so we were sharing information to raise our standards as facilitators and get a deeper understanding of how to do it.

One thing we all agreed was that the Mystic Rose is a pure energy process. In this context, we needed to be aware of our attitudes – any judgements we might be having about people in the group, the way they were doing it – because these kinds of negative vibes would prevent a facilitator's energy from flowing towards certain people.

It used to happen, in the beginning, that I'd start thinking "This person is stuck ... that person isn't laughing enough ... this one isn't crying enough ... " and I'd become irritated with them. Then I would be subtly cutting my energy towards those people, because when you have a charge it blocks your energy and sends out a negative vibe instead.

So this was one of the benefits of having assistants. If a facilitator was unable to feel open towards somebody who was having a hard time, then he or she could allow the assistant to take over for a while. This kind of thing happened until we reached a point of such depth of understanding of the human condition that whatever state anybody was in did not affect us personally – that's what we were all striving towards. It didn't take long. In this kind of intense process, facilitators naturally develop empathy and compassion for the participants.

During the first two weeks of the process, participants are not involved in any of their usual mental activity. When you're in a state of full, abandoned laughter, you're not sitting there with the mind chattering away as it normally does in daily life. It's a No Mind experience and when you're in your tears it's the same.

But then, at the beginning of the third week, when you sit down to meditate, the mind can sometimes come back with full force and wants to take control again. To me, when I experienced the 'Watcher' stage for the first time, it felt like my mind was having a kind of survival panic and desperately trying to reassert itself, and several participants felt the same.

I wrote to Osho, saying "The mind has come back with a vengeance and what I've said to people so far is 'don't worry it will settle down'. Is this okay?"

He said "Yes, you're right, not to worry, it will settle." And this was true. After two or three days of sitting silently, mental activity gradually slowed down and became less frantic. Many people expressed to me that after the first two weeks of Mystic Rose their meditation was deeper than they'd ever experienced it before.

Breaking the Dam

Over time, I gained deeper insights into how the Mystic Rose works with blocked energy, which is similar to what happens in Dynamic Meditation. In Dynamic, the first stage of fast, chaotic breathing opens the energy blocks, which are then discharged through catharsis. Three hours of laughing or crying creates such a dynamic flow of energy throughout the body that an enormous amount of stagnant energy is replaced with fresh, vital aliveness.

It is a massive energetic detox, a deep cleaning process, working on many levels, encountering different qualities at each level.

For example, when you go beyond the superficial layers of laughter there comes a moment when the process shifts from being *your* laughter to you *being laughed*. When the energy is flowing through you that strongly, you're not even precipitating the laughter, you're not bringing it on, it's as if you *become* the laughter.

And that's what Osho meant when he said, "It breaks the dam." All you have to do is break the dam and then the flow of energy overtakes you and the process happens by itself.

Dynamic Meditation itself became an issue of controversy for a while, because Osho told us it was okay for people not to do Dynamic during the first two weeks of the Mystic Rose, adding "save your energy for the group." Some people just couldn't believe it, because Dynamic had always been regarded as a foundation to start each day and all the group leaders were urged to tell their participants to begin the day with Dynamic, which started at 6:00 am and lasted an hour.

So this instruction from Osho surprised some people, but when I checked with my own experience, it felt right. If you do Dynamic and then a couple of hours later come to the Mystic Rose you are kind of chilled, relaxed and somehow pleasantly tired. You've already done a big workout and expended a lot of energy. But in the Mystic Rose you need all your energy if you're going to explode into the laughing and crying process and continue nonstop for three hours. Only in the third week, during the Watcher on the Hills, did we bring Dynamic back into the program.

When I ran the Mystic Rose in centres around the world it was a different situation. Many people did Dynamic in the morning because the group was held from 6:00–9:00 pm at night, so that did not interfere with the process at all.

From the very beginning, after being given this process, I was eager to find out what Osho had been saying, over the years, about laughter, tears and meditation. So, together with my assistants, we went into the commune's research library and spent a long time gathering short excerpts from his discourses that could be played during the first, second and third weeks.

This was a great support for the process and helpful to people doing it. But even so, I had to be careful. For example, in the beginning, I played Osho quotes about laughter before we started the process, but then I realised it chilled out the energy too much. Listening to Osho, people quieted down and became a little spaced out, which made it more difficult to get going, so we switched to playing quotes at the end.

This worked much better and also gave participants time to come down off the high of laughing and get a bit more grounded – the energy was so expanded, typically they felt blissed out from all the endorphins flowing through their system – before leaving the room and facing the so-called 'real world' again. So that worked perfectly.

I did realise, from the very beginning, that you can't have absolutely no interaction in the laughing stage. But I'm careful to explain it through guidance, because it's okay for two people to enjoy laughing together, making eye contact, holding hands, or lying down side by side and sometimes gently tickling each other, but it should not develop into a pillow fight, or wrestling match, or entertaining and putting on a show.

"That's a way to distract yourself," I explain, "Rather than getting lost in performance, stay real with what's going on inside you."

This was all part of the facilitator's job: to encourage people and give them freedom to explore the process, while at the same time keeping the energy pointing in a single direction: to release negative, blocked energy through the power of laughter.

As Mystic Rose spread to sannyasin communities all over the world, problems developed with people trying to run the process without having any experience of working with people or having much understanding of Osho's meditations.

Osho was notified of the situation and a short time later I was asked to create a training. This became a regular feature in Pune. As more and more people completed the training, I made the effort to keep in touch with them and help them maintain the standard. I'm happy to say that many of the people I have trained as facilitators are now offering Mystic Rose around the world.

Born Again and No Mind

Two more meditative therapies were created by Osho in the last year of his life:

Born Again: a week-long, two hours per day process that encourages people to move back into the energy of being children before shifting to silent sitting. One hour is provided for each stage.

No Mind: a week-long, two hours per day process that invites people to express themselves verbally through speaking nonsense, or gibberish, for one hour, before entering into an hour of silent sitting.

When Born Again was announced, Osho again said "Let Leela do it," so I was coordinating the group department, running the Mystic Rose and then Born Again as well!

Sometime later, I was given the Osho Institute for Meditative Therapies, which included all three – Osho's Mystic Rose, Born Again and No Mind Meditations – and I also created trainings for people wishing to run them.

I felt that, energetically, these processes were all very similar, so I had the knowledge of how to work with them because of my experience with the Mystic Rose.

Osho's instruction for Born Again was that people should enter into their childhood and do what they always wanted to do, and he mentioned a few things … Laughing, crying, jumping, screaming … All the things that parents had typically prevented us from doing when we were growing up.

Again, there was to be no interaction. I learned by my mistakes and noticed that if you do allow a degree of interaction, some kids will play gently with each other, but if some 'kid' got into a nasty mood he could really create havoc and interfere with everybody, acting out rather than exploring what he wanted to do alone, by himself.

As a facilitator in the Mystic Rose, I was able to enter into the process totally – but with Born Again I realized I had to 'sit out' and remain in the role of group leader, with the focus of protecting and supporting 'the kids'. If you go into a collective energy of regression, you don't feel any separation between yourself and the group, you become one of 'the kids', just like everybody else, so then it's difficult to remain in control, guiding the process.

Born Again is very liberating for the inner child, very immediate and direct, simply going with the dynamic and playful energy. Again, it's not about talking, therapy, or concepts. You just dive into the experience of being a child again, go straight into the energy and come out of it feeling fantastic.

When he gave us No Mind, Osho talked about a Sufi mystic called Jabbar, who never spoke in ordinary language. He travelled around with his disciples and none of them ever spoke anything but gibberish and many of them became enlightened.

Osho had included a few minutes of gibberish in the 'let go' meditation at the end of his daily discourse and once joked "Speak Chinese if you don't know Chinese, speak Japanese if you don't know Japanese; don't speak German if you know German!" So the idea is to dive into a flow of pure verbal expression.

With both No Mind and Born Again, a facilitator needs to be aware that these processes can be taken in any direction. For example, one facilitator was encouraging his No Mind participants to be angry and bang pillows on the floor, or hit against the padded walls of the room, because for him gibberish meant expressing anger. Another was a Primal therapist, so this became the emphasis and he was booking his participants for Primal sessions in the afternoon.

Both these approaches are too narrow. The invitation has to be kept very wide and a facilitator has to be aware of what he or she is saying. For example, one day I came into Born Again and said "if tears happen you should just allow it." I didn't say anything more, but that day the whole group cried! So then I realised "I have to be careful what I say" and next day kept it more general, saying "laugh, jump, cry..." Just as Osho did in his introduction, so that the mind is not focused on any one thing.

The quality of meditation is different in all three meditative therapies. Many people have said to me that the state of meditation they entered in the 'Watcher' phase of the Mystic Rose was the deepest they ever experienced up to that time, and I had that same feeling. After such a major cleanout, the sitting went very deep.

The quality after Born Again has more the flavour of deep relaxation. It's as if every bit of tension has been sucked out of your body through expressing what you always wanted to do with your long-suppressed childlike energy, which has finally been given the freedom to express itself.

I remember looking at people after the first hour was over and noticing how still and completely relaxed they were. I allowed them to sit or lie down in any posture. I didn't expect them to come out of the child space and immediately sit up straight and be good meditators. I said "just relax" and played an excerpt from an Osho discourse.

With No Mind, it's a different quality again. The gibberish, if done in a total way, empties the mind of all content which creates a deep space of 'no mind', or non-thinking, during the second hour of meditation.

A Different Kind of Therapy

There is a big difference between Osho's meditative therapies and other kinds of therapy. It's not that either approach is better, yet the distinction is worth noting.

The meditative therapies allow you to access that which is natural in you, that which we were born with. The child is born with laughter and tears and the art of self-expression. These are natural elements, so it is therapy in the sense that has a beneficial effect on the person doing it, but it has no concept or structure, no specific theme or issue on which to focus.

This is why I decided we should be called 'facilitators' rather than 'group leaders' – that was my idea – because our role is to explain how to work with the process and support people through it, but the work they do is all their own. In a way, they become their own therapist, going at their own pace, doing it themselves.

To me, Mystic Rose is all-encompassing, covering elements of primal, breath work, trauma work and so on – you cannot believe how much trauma is released in the crying phase. Arthur Janov, the American therapist who first introduced the idea of Primal Scream, has written in his book *The New Primal Scream* that unless you cry very deeply you do not heal and I know this to be very true.

Basically, in all three therapies, you're using your own energy and also inviting the energy of existence to flow through you, without doing anything through the mind. So, naturally, people are surprised afterwards at the changes they feel and the healing that has happened, because they haven't been dealing consciously with any particular problem.

People come to me afterwards and say "I can't believe how amazing I feel! I can't believe how much more spontaneous I feel!" It happens in spite of ourselves. Of course, there are specific memories that arise during the laughter and the tears, but there's no particular focus, so it's different experience for everyone, even though they are all in the same structure.

People work individually, in their own way. There is no right or wrong way to do it. Some people have a bit of difficulty laughing and crying, others just flow into it. The process has a kind of spaciousness in which everybody is okay the way they are, and just doing their best.

So it's different from regular therapy and in its own way extremely powerful and effective. Something quite phenomenal and mysterious happens to people and I cannot tell you how many of them come back and do it over and over again, because of how wonderful it makes them feel and how profoundly so many areas of their lives are affected after experiencing Mystic Rose

As I mentioned earlier, one of the most powerful effects of the Mystic Rose is that it expands your perception. When you're lying on the floor, laughing for no reason, it's rather like viewing your life from outer space … it sort of happens automatically. You get insights into yourself, you see your preoccupation with trivia, you see your life passing by in front of you and you laugh at the worries, the mistakes, the victories …

It's no accident that so many mystics burst into laughter at the moment of spiritual awakening, because they see the whole drama of human existence from a totally new perspective.

Laughter has a rebellious quality, too, because you're laughing at everything you thought was so serious and so important … and suddenly none of it matters. So, not only do you go deeper, you also see a bigger picture – you see what's really important in your life.

Let me end by saying this: I learned to run the Mystic Rose and the other two Meditative Therapies by listening carefully to all that Osho had said about each aspect of these processes. For over twenty-five years, I have been sharing my understanding with thousands of participants around the world and as a result my capacity to communicate the benefits of these gifts from Osho has deepened – both as a facilitator and as a human being

I, and many others who offer Osho's Meditative Therapies, pass on our insights to others, so they can derive maximum benefit from participating and sharing in these three extraordinary processes. These Meditative Therapies are a gift from an Enlightened Master, whose depth of understanding of the human condition has lead to the creation of these dynamic techniques through which we can flower.

CHAPTER FIVE

Conditioning and Counselling: Changing the Path of Your Life

Tarika

When I first met Osho I was a fledgling psychotherapist. My head was full of all the right things to say in order to create rapport with my client and all kinds of ideas about how to look competent enough to be helpful. I knew a lot about what was normal and abnormal. I knew that my job was to help people maintain a normal lifestyle.

It all made sense until the day I sat in front of Osho and looked into his eyes. Suddenly, all of what I thought I knew just flew out of my head. I was dumbstruck. There in front of me was a beautiful being, the likes of which I had never seen before. I can still hear my mind saying, "What is this? It looks like a man, but I cannot understand the space that I am experiencing at this moment". It was like falling into an abyss but with a sense of total calm. And so began my journey: to find out how to have this experience in my own life.

I had studied many therapeutic approaches, both for my own personal growth and as a training for working with people. Adding meditation to these experiences was helpful because it gave me the taste of this new, unknown space in small doses. But, at the same time, it left me feeling dissatisfied. I could sense that creating a better personality was not enough. I needed to find a way to go beyond personality in order to find myself. There needed to be a tool that would allow me to come back to this place of 'being' inside, which remained untouched by any of the influences I'd experienced in my early life.

For me, the first step was to find out as much as I could about how my personality got created, how it was made up, and for what

I needed it. This led me to work with early childhood conditioning. It became clear to me that an understanding of how conditioned behaviour runs our lives is essential for any transformation to take place. We cannot pave over the habitual paths created by early conditioning and expect to find a new way to think and be. We must be willing to dig up those old pathways, confront what lies beneath them, then walk on new paths created by conscious awareness and understanding.

Counselling needs to offer the opportunity to go beneath the surface and discover we are much more than our conditioning would ever allow us to be.

What is Conditioning?

Conditioning is a fact of life. As long as we are born into families where ideas and beliefs are handed down, just like family heirlooms, we will be carrying around a closet-full of stuff for which we never asked. But, unlike heirlooms, which can be seen and discarded, or maybe sold at auction, conditioning goes deep into our unconscious and runs our lives from there.

This conditioning is habitual. Like all habits, we do not have to think before we make a move. If we were to stop, even for one second, and ask ourselves why we are doing what we do, we would begin to discover how much our lives are in the hands of unconscious patterns. So, how is it possible that we can be brought up to believe that what we think and feel is true, even if it does not support us in any way to grow?

We arrive on this planet as a complete being. As far as I can tell, we bring the raw material of essential qualities here, but with no user manual. So, we look to those people close to us to give us some idea of what we need to do with these qualities. They must know, because they are big and we are small. It makes perfect sense to us that we need to follow their example in order to grow up and be happy human beings.

What we don't know is that these 'big people' are carrying around an outdated set of ideas and beliefs which were unconsciously handed down to them from other 'big people' a long time ago, when they, in turn, were small. This is a very important point: no one consciously wants to pass on dysfunctional garbage, but as long as we remain unaware of the fact that what we say and do is creating pain and unhappiness, we just pass it on. We think we're doing something valuable, helping the next generation.

So, there we are, freshly arrived on this planet, with this wonderful bundle of qualities wrapped in a small child's body. With the innocence of a child, we present these qualities as gifts to those big people. If they are conscious and aware of their own qualities, then we are accepted and supported in the pursuit of happiness. But if they have been put down, or diminished in some way – which is almost always the case – then we get the message that there is something wrong with us and we should bury those qualities.

Once we are wounded in this way, we spend the rest of our lives defending ourselves against pain, since it is very painful to have a gift rejected. We harbour the feeling that there is something wrong with us and spend the rest of our lives looking outside ourselves to prove that we are okay.

After the child becomes convinced that he or she is *not* okay, we are confronted by old fears every time we want to make a move. Will I be loved? Will I be accepted? Am I good enough? As we get older, we do many things, acting from the rational mind, to overcome these fears, but the wounded little one inside is constantly being triggered. This activation undermines and sabotages our actions.

Although we think we are acting from our free will, we are in fact creating a big inner conflict. If we move forward, how will we manage to survive? The wounded child is clear: he will do anything to ensure survival. This means taking in the conditioning, making a contract with it, and fitting ourselves into the environment in whatever way is needed. This is what we learn to call 'love'.

But, in reality, all we manage to do is stay alive. Our needs and longings are hardly ever met, and we grow up believing that others know better than ourselves who we are and what we need. A great dependency is created and we are not free to even imagine that we can get what we need and want without having to compromise.

Connecting to the Wounded Child

So, the first priority in my work is to bring the person back in touch with his/her wounded child. This creates an understanding that unless we are able to embrace this hurt little one inside we will never be free to actualize and live our amazing qualities in a way that honours us. Bringing the wounded child into our conscious awareness is essential and also scary. This is where our pain is housed, this is where our defences were created – and we have managed for so many years to stay alive through those defences.

In opening a relationship with the child, we must first be willing to acknowledge that we have been hurt. This brings us directly in touch with vulnerability. It is difficult to imagine that a small hurt child is running our lives, but when we make this first step it gives us an amazing release. Trapped behind those wounds is an enormous reservoir of energy. Once we open this understanding, and stop blaming ourselves and others for what is not working in our lives, we can then take a further step.

Next, we need to learn how to embrace this hurt little part of ourselves in a loving way. We have spent most of our adult lives denying it, or even putting it down, because this part is holding so much pain. This means coming in touch with that unconscious programme of conditioning that I call, 'The Radio', which is playing inside our heads 24/7. Recognizing how much negative talk we have circling repeatedly through our heads – and where it comes from – brings us to the next step.

This step asks us to let down our defences and feel the pain: to express what hurts, to acknowledge how we got hurt, to break the contract of protection we have been buying into since we were small. Since the child was wounded by the very people who were supposed to love him, it is difficult for him to allow the pain of how much damage they caused. Instead, the child's mind creates many different ways to protect these people.

The child has limited resources and in fact is being held hostage, so making contracts to stay alive is the brilliance of the child's mind. But, at some point these defences are in the way and we need to be able to break these contracts. This can happen only when the child knows there is a grown up person on his side. It means going from the childish position of dependence to the grown up realization of freedom and responsibility.

Taking Responsibility

Often people are willing to make the first couple of steps in this direction. They want to feel the anger of having been wounded, they like the idea of raging against those who did the wounding, but then they want to stop. They want to feel they are entitled to be treated better and that they are owed something. In other words, they want to remain a child but with better weapons.

For me, it is essential to bring people out of the past and help them to view the present from a grounded and loving position; to be able to embrace responsibility and enjoy the rewards of freedom in a conscious way.

So, breaking the contracts can only happen when we feel grown up, when we truly sense that we do not need to honour the contracts in order to stay alive. Once we can honestly say, 'I am big enough now', then the child can allow the contracts to be broken.

The child can never break the contracts – this is important to understand. From a psychological point of view, those contracts kept us alive when we were small and helpless, and this feeling persists at an unconscious level into adulthood. Unless we feel our capacity in present-time to live beyond our conditioning, the contracts will stay active. If we try to break them before this understanding is clear, we create a big conflict inside and we will get hurt. We would be doing something against ourselves in the name of healing.

When we are aligned with the needs and feelings of the hurt child, then we are able to take the necessary action to break free from what is binding us. Once this action is taken, a crucial part of the work begins. What does it mean to be grown up and live in present-time? This is a learning experience we all need if we really wish to live a more loving and conscious life.

The process of growing up needs to be in our hands. Growing old happens all by itself – for this we can just sit silently and do nothing. But, if we want to experience a life that is full of delight and gives us the opportunity to live our potential, we must do whatever is needed to clear the path on which we are walking.

The focus in my work is to support the person to find his or her own way. As a therapist, I am conscious of staying out of the way as much as possible. I bring the work with the inner child to a place where the person can lovingly put the painful experiences into the past, without disconnecting from the hurt child. Then what begins to appear is a willingness to bring the child to a more healthy and alive present experience.

I invite clients to understand that the defences they created in the early time of their lives was an intelligent and necessary survival strategy. But this is the intelligence of a child who is in a helpless situation. Once the client is able to acknowledge all of what he had to do to stay alive, it becomes easier for him to move on.

Once there is a trusting relationship with the hurt inner child, the 'child' does not feel threatened and the defences can be lowered. It is from this point that it becomes possible to begin cutting ties with conditioning. This cutting can be done in many different ways, but the intention is to break the trance of the past and to start to feel sensations of present-time.

Creating a Tool for Transformation

I am interested in sharing as many tools as I can that support people in living a more vital and happy life. I feel that if the work cannot be done at home, then it is not producing a long term effect. Just feeling good in a session, or a group, is not the goal as far as I am concerned. Being able to recreate that good feeling in daily life is foremost for me.

Keeping in mind that initial meeting with Osho, listening to his discourses, doing his meditations, working more and more from what he says about going beyond personality, I began to feel the need to create a tool that would give me the opportunity to live my deeper experiences on a daily basis. So, with the cooperation of a therapist friend, I started to explore what would happen if I could step out of my old history and feel myself in the so called 'here-and-now'.

I was my own guinea pig. I would take an issue that was distressing me, at that moment in time, and begin to explore the cause of the distress. I understood that the mind works in duality and so, when I was in distress, it was connecting to two parts of my conditioning that were in conflict.

Over time it became clear that my personality was made up of all the conditioned information I had received. I could actually feel, see and hear what each of these parts was holding. The work then became to recognize the personality parts (characters), to be able to see and sense that I was not that personality, and to be able to describe the sensations I had in the present moment.

As soon as I was more connected with the present, I was able to find solutions to the distressing issue – solutions that were creative and very different from what I would 'normally' do. This began to excite me and I started to feel that I had choices I would never have imagined.

Once I had a better idea of what made up my habitual, conditioned way of thinking, I could easily name it as history and this enabled me to step into a more open and free space. Life started to get easier and I was feeling more in touch with a sense of my authentic self.

Then the defining moment for this experiment happened: I worked with a very distressing situation, one that was a causing me a great deal of anxiety. Once I was able to see the parts of my conditioning that were in conflict, once I could experience a distance from them and come in touch with a solution from my present understanding, this distressing situation did not return.

Naturally, as I am a realist, I was sure that it would recur and that I would need to look again at this conflict and find another solution. But, in fact, the conflict did not arise again. This was an 'Aha!' moment. I had actually managed to dis-identify and stop feeding my conditioned mind. In fact, thirty years have passed now and I have not revisited this anxiety-producing conflict.

The Birth of Transessence

This was the birth of the Transessence technique, a tool for essential living. The name Transessence describes what the tool is aiming at: a transit to essence. It is a simple but profound tool for stepping out of old habitual ways and stepping into new possibilities.

The technique helps us see more clearly how we live with our history. It gives us an opportunity to put the history where it belongs, in the past, and to start living from our alive, present being. It works well as a counselling tool and is client-centred, allowing the client to slowly become aware of the difference between personality (conditioned reality) and present-time individuality.

Breaking the ties that bind us is the goal of any helpful therapeutic technique. My greatest moment in the work is when my clients feel they can take life into their own hands. When they are able to recognize they are not their conditioning, they simultaneously experience they are more than conditioning would ever allow them to be. This is a miracle which takes love, understanding, courage, willingness, longing, patience and whatever else can be thrown into the pot. But, for me, it is worth everything. I would not want to miss these moments.

At the start a Transessence session, I explain that when we are having difficulties the conditioned mind is triggered and we get caught in old habits. The personality is made up of different aspects of our early childhood ideas and beliefs with which we identify. It is helpful to be able to see those parts of the personality which are activated and in conflict. Once we are able to do this, we can find new solutions, in the present moment, which did not exist in the conditioned mind's way of thinking.

The work is done with clients facing an open space in front of them – the work space – and with me sitting outside the space as the guide. I inform them that the place where they are sitting is called the neutral place, or present-time place, and that the action of the work will happen there. Once the basic set up is clear, I ask them to tell me what issue they would like to look at.

The Need for Perfection

A young man came to look at his feelings of responsibility for a woman with whom he'd had a relationship, which had ended some time ago. Although he was now in a new relationship, he found it difficult to stop having contact with the old girlfriend. This was causing distress in his new relationship and he felt determined to stop connecting with the old girlfriend, even though he also liked having contact with her. He was experiencing anxious moods and was unable to concentrate on what he needed to do in his life.

After questioning him, it became clear that he did not know for sure if he was finished with the old relationship. But, since he had a new girlfriend, he felt he had to be clear and could not allow himself any doubt.

Me: Can you hear who is talking right now? Who is it who feels he cannot allow himself any doubt?

Client: The perfectionist part of me. There is no space to make mistakes.

Me: Would it be possible for you to bring this part, out here, and take a look at who, or what, this is?

The young man closed his eyes and takes some time to sense what is going on inside.

Client: Yes.

I asked him to place a cushion in the work space that will represent this part, then to gather all the information he could about this part. After some time, he opened his eyes and placed the cushion at a distance from where he was sitting.

Client: I see an uptight young student who is afraid of making mistakes. He is serious and wants to make sure that he is doing everything right.

Me: From where you are sitting right now, what is your feeling about this perfectionist student out there, who is separate from you?

Client: I feel upset and do not want to see him.

Me: Who doesn't want to see him? What part of you is this?

Client (closing his eyes): It feels like my father.

Me: Would it be possible to bring this father part, out here, and take a look at who, or what, this is?

Client: Yes.

He took another cushion, which he placed at a distance from himself and from the student cushion.

Me: Can you describe who, or what, you see?

Client: Yes, I see a man who is hunched over and very disconnected. He is saying he does not want to look.

Me: From where you are sitting now, when you look at the student and father parts out there, how do you feel in yourself?

Client: I feel relaxed, grounded and straight. I can feel my spine and I feel very present.

Me: Take a moment and breathe into this relaxed, grounded and straight feeling; breathe into it from wherever you are feeling it, through your whole body. This lets you anchor the present sensations. Is there anything you need to say, or do, with either one, or both, of these parts?

Client: I'm surprised to see the father part like this and to realize how hard I've been working to get him to see me. I never realized this before.

Me: Is there anything you feel you need to say, or do, with either, or both, of these parts that are out here?

Client: No, there is nothing I need to do or say at this moment. It is good to be able to feel the distance from these parts.

Me: Now take a look at the issue of having to make a clear break from your ex-girlfriend from this more grounded, relaxed and straight place where you are sitting right now. What happens?

Client: Actually, I am not ready to make a final break. I still need to see what there is between us. What I need to do is be straight about it with my new girlfriend. It is okay not to be clear right now, I need more time.

From this understanding the client finished the session in a calm and easy space, saying it was the first time in weeks he had been able to feel okay about himself.

Connecting with present time allowed him to come in contact with the essential qualities of strength, aliveness and intelligence. He was able to see the issue from a dis-identified perspective; he is not the perfectionist student needing to get his father to pay attention to him. He is, in fact, a young man who understands that even if he makes a mistake he will be able to take responsibility for it.

Learning to dis-identify with personality parts that have their origin in the past gives us the possibility to recognize our capacity in the present moment, bringing us directly in touch with all the wonderful qualities we carry inside. We begin to feel that we are whole, not lacking anything, and from this place we can create a loving, beautiful relationship with life.

Individuality is Our Essence

When we are more in contact with our natural qualities, we change the way we talk to ourselves. For example, we are no longer telling ourselves that we have to do better, or that we need to please someone else. We realize that, in this present moment, we are the best person we can be. This gives us freedom to develop our strengths and become more relaxed with who we are. When we feel better about ourselves, we can, in turn, relate in a better way with the world around us.

The Transessence technique helps us to see more clearly how we live with our history, our conditioning. It gives us an opportunity to put the history where it belongs, in the past, and to start living in present-time. It works well as a counselling tool because the client can slowly become aware of the difference between personality and individuality.

Individuality is your essence, you come with it, you are born with it. Personality is borrowed, it is given by the society to you. It is just like clothes, subtle clothes. A child is born naked and we hide his nakedness, we give him clothes. A child is born with essence, individuality, we hide that too because naked individuality is rebellious, nonconformist.

Individuality is exactly what it means: individual. Personality is not individual, it is social. Society wants you to have personality, not individuality, because your individuality will create conflict. The society hides your individuality and gives you personality. Personality is a learned thing. The word personality comes from the Greek root which means mask, persona.....

When the personality disappears do not be afraid. For the first time you become authentic, you become real. You obtain to essence. ~ Osho[1]

CHAPTER SIX

Voicing

Pratibha

In 1973 I had a most striking singing experience which ten years later brought me to create the teaching I called VOICING.[1] I literally heard myself singing. What was coming out of my mouth was a totally spontaneous song with its own unique, individual melody. Every cell of my body was involved in it, while my mind was silent.

As the song had risen, so it would end, leaving me in a state of trembling and yet pervaded by immense gratitude. I 'knew' that something fundamental had shifted inside of me: I was seeing the same world around me but in a different way, with different meanings, with a deep feeling of love and knowing.

From that moment on, I focused my attention on listening and singing, as these were the means through which my spontaneous song had poured out of me. This phenomenon would happen again and again, always when least expected. By observing it deeply, I discovered many precious aspects connected with the power of spontaneous singing.

Merging with Humanistic Psychology

In 1976, when I found myself in Osho's presence, I understood that here was an enlightened mystic who could access all my systems of reference. To me, none of the spiritual teachers I'd met before had the knowledge and capacity to penetrate the human mind and its belief system with such precision.

Joining Osho's international commune in Pune, I allowed singing to temporarily take a back seat while I explored humanistic psychology. With Osho's supervision, we were combining

1   Voicing®

meditation with new therapy techniques that had been developed in the late 60s and early 70s in California, Holland and England.

During this time, I took part in many experimental groups and trainings like Emotional Bodywork, Bio-Energetics, Psychic Massage, Holistic Healing, T'ai Chi, Hypnosis, and Esoteric Science.

Around 1989, all of these experiences merged into one body of teachings for me, whose base was spontaneous singing. From then on, I began running my first voice groups in Pune and later enjoyed taking my new creation all over the world.

In 1994, I called this approach VOICING, intending to give it a name that would include all aspects of singing that can become pathways to self-discovery.

My approach continues to evolve, including new elements of understanding such as those of the Diamond Logos work of Faisal Muqddam, which I have studied for twelve years, plus new experiences and observations in my workshops.

Spiritual Context

In order to place VOICING within the context of spiritual therapies developed around Osho, I need to briefly describe the understanding from which it emerged:

The absolute dimension of Being pervades everything.

We enter into the physical body as part of this Being.

Although it is not separate from the source, this 'part' acquires an individual identity that has been called Soul, Atman, Essence.

The newborn child is a natural expression of Essence, but this is gradually lost as the child develops a social personality and develops strategies to win approval and acceptance from others. In place of Essence, we create ego.

VOICING can be envisioned as a bridge between the dimension of ego and that of the soul, or Essence. It can be a tool that uses the ego structure and then transcends it, opening to a spiritual dimension of meditation.

Spontaneous singing starts from an ego level, but through

celebration melts the ego's defences, passing through barriers such as opposition, blind obedience, adjustment and inauthenticity to connect with the truth of one's being.

To be able to sing not only joy but also feelings like pain, sadness, anger and jealousy, one needs to be able to say 'yes' to these aspects of oneself.

What is essential to spontaneous singing – in order for it to become a tool for transformation – is to engage oneself totally, giving expression to every kind of emotion or psychological issue that is manifesting itself.

VOICING is actually something very simple and innate, accessible to everyone. It is much simpler to do it than explain it. No explanation can replace experience. In fact, it is only through experience that we learn.

For example, I can describe water from a scientific point of view – its chemical composition, our possible psychophysical reactions when we touch it, the various possibilities of inter-acting with it. But only when those listening to my description actually touch water do these words make sense.

Everybody Can Sing

While the main thread of VOICING is singing, it differentiates itself from the common definition of singing, which usually involves knowing how to reproduce a sound track, or melody, that one has heard before and is trying to imitate.

In this traditional way, memory and the skilful reproduction of sounds play the main roles. To me, this form of singing is limited and has unfortunate consequences. For example, if somebody is unable to reproduce one or more sounds and cannot replicate the notes, she/he is considered out of tune, or tone-deaf, which generally equates with 'not being able to sing'.

According to my experience, this assertion is not only false but also abusive and damaging. It would be more appropriate and certainly less destructive to consider this phenomenon for what it is: the inability to repeat and imitate a specific sound.

This inability should spark an investigation to discover why and how this is happening. In my sessions and workshops, when we explore the phenomenon of being 'out of tune', I have seen suppressed emotional traumas emerging. Once these traumas have been faced and expressed, the person will usually be able to reproduce the missing notes correctly.

Unfortunately, our culture's compulsive habit of defining how we should sing, using narrow criteria and specific techniques, is the cause of many peoples' frustrations and deep suffering. Their pain is difficult to integrate, because singing is linked to each soul's unique expression. So, in fact, this condemnation is akin to receive a negation to one's own soul. It is an indescribable, intimate pain.

The truth is just the opposite:

Everybody can sing!

Singing is our birth right because singing is the language of the soul.

Even people who have problems with their vocal cords can sing. Their song will be hoarse, whispered, guttural, broken, but nonetheless a song, full of their personal experience and therefore of great beauty.

The shamanic songs from the various parts of the world cannot be defined as 'bel canto' according to our society's standards, and yet they can deeply touch those who listen to them, activating powerful healing energy and spiritual rebalancing.

Telling someone she/he cannot sing is a form of abuse, and the younger the person is, the deeper her/his pain will be.

It would give me a great sense of fulfilment to know that music teachers around the world have dropped the practice of saying "You cannot sing". We need to abandon the model we know and rediscover the immediacy of singing expression.

Sufficient Unto Itself

Usually, we sing other people's songs. Even when we are creating our own song, in the moment of singing, our brain is at work reproducing something we have heard, or visualized, or written before. It is almost inconceivable for us to sing spontaneously, allowing the immediacy of emotional expression.

When our brain is busy 'remembering' and 'reproducing' a song – accompanied by the anxiety that we might not manage to do it – control is in place and spontaneity is destroyed. Moreover, this kind of singing depends on being appreciated – or not – by a listener. It is as if singing needs an audience.

Singing does not need a listener, as talking does.

Those who enjoy singing in the shower, or in the car, know this very well!

On the other hand, language is a type of communication that implies at least one more person. When we speak, we often describe, speculate, justify and then seek a response from the listener.

Also, in our inner mental dialogues the scenario usually involves two people. Our soliloquy is between 'I' and 'her/him', or between two or more parts of ourselves, or we may even have an imaginary audience. Meditators know this phenomenon very well.

Singing, on the other hand, is sufficient unto itself.

It is the expression of something that goes beyond the limitation of words, even when it uses them. It is the emergence of something unspeakable that finds its way through singing: a deeper authenticity, finding its own means of communication, recovering a newfound sense of fulfilment and Being.

Our drive to communicate remains, but it is now aimed at Existence itself, of which we feel a natural part, offering to Existence our deepest self in celebration.

Seen from this perspective, the fantasy – which many of us have had – of being able to sing in front of a big audience is very narrow. Moreover, the main motive may not even be the singing itself. Often, it is a narcissistic need to fill ourselves with the approval of others, avoiding a profound feeling of inner emptiness. We look for public appreciation in an attempt to reproduce those essential dimensions that have been lost to us.

As I understand it, singing can be more meaningful when no one is listening, when it is simply and solely an intimate communion with Existence. This is an offering and a celebration that should stay out of the realm of judgment, no matter how it sounds.

In this dimension, the notion of singing out of tune has no place at all, because there is no measure of comparison – and the idea of being out of tune is always the result of comparison.

When the singing voice gushes out with uncontrolled spontaneity, without a preconceived sound track, with no references, the notion of singing out of tune is simply inconceivable. The tonalities, timbres and quality of sounds that spring out can be very unusual, far from what we consider 'singing' in our culture. Yet still, it is a true song.

It is astonishing to see the profound impact this experience has on the singer. It is as if suppressed or forgotten 'strings' of our essential 'instrument' are rediscovered and vibrate again, providing a new sense of fulfilment as they come to life and are accepted and celebrated.

Singing as Celebration

Some people ask me: what is the difference, in a therapeutic situation, between singing and other vocal forms of emotional release like screaming? If normal musical standards and social criteria are set aside, how does singing differ? To me, the difference is celebration.

The scream has its place in therapy, bringing a sense of liberation, or freedom, but its relief is temporary. It also presupposes our intention to eliminate something we do not want that is buried inside of us. It is like unloading a weight, offloading baggage we do not wish to carry any more.

In VOICING, energy is transformed, not eliminated.

Every aspect of the personality is accepted and understood for what it is, for the function it has had – and maybe still has. It is seen and used as a springboard for a dive that plunges us inwards, into the deepest spaces of our interiority, until we reach our Essence.

All we need to do is keep singing, without stopping, without letting the mind interfere. In this way, singing without pausing, it's easier to erase the censorship of the mind, which otherwise is committed to preserving our personality structure.

When we allow our pain, anger, joy, to be expressed through singing, this means that we have accepted them. It is an act of surrender. Removing judgment, singing raises our sense of acceptance to the level of celebration. This dimension causes a deep psychological resolution that can become a spiritual experience.

During the experience of spontaneous singing, the singer 'becomes' his singing and there is no longer a separation between the one who sings and his song. His identity disappears in his singing and only his ability to listen stands witness to the phenomenon. We hear ourselves singing or, better said, the singing and the listener merge and only witnessing is left.

Gibberish

In order to learn, or re-learn, the ability to sing spontaneously, without mental interference, we use an invented language to bypass conceptual meaning.

The value of verbal expression is, in fact, very important. Language is composed of groups of phonemes and articulations – combinations of vowels and consonants – separated by intervals. How to maintain this type of verbal structure without connecting it with conceptual meanings?

In Italy, Nobel Prize winner Dario Fò used this type of language in his theatre – he called it *grammelot* – as an effective and outspoken communication tool.

In English, we use the term gibberish, which derives from an eighth century Sufi mystic called Jabir Ibh Hayyan who expressed himself through an unintelligible language. Gibberish sounds like a language, but it is not a real, existing language.

The use of gibberish gives our inner world a tool of direct, unique and un-repeatable communication. We can stay in the immediacy of the intent to express ourselves through a 'language' that develops its own momentum and, by and by, reveals itself.

In this way, even without the usual conceptual references, we feel the fulfilment of real verbal communication accompanied by a sense of freedom. With gibberish, the anxiety of having to express a conceptually and grammatically correct language vanishes. Its immediacy and flexibility makes it easier to express emotions and release energy.

In VOICING, gibberish is not used as a continuous sequence of inarticulate sounds, but is articulated through sound-groups, separated by short pauses, as in the texture of any language. The intent is to 'speak' because a song that uses only vowels does not reach certain inner layers and therefore misses engaging emotions and dimensions of Essence.

Consonants give colour, quality, drive, and meaning to vowels. Different consonants connect to different inner experiences.

How to Proceed

Spontaneous singing should be an innate, easy-to-express phenomenon. Some people find it accessible and simple, but the majority need to practice it. Luckily, it is not something new but rather a natural expression that already belongs to us. It only requires us to rediscover it, dust it off and polish it up.

Here are a few simple instructions on how we proceed:

● First, it is important to learn to 'listen' to ourselves both literally and metaphorically, that is to say, to be in touch with what is happening inside.

● Then we need to recognize and understand that every inner experience is vibrational and can therefore be sung. It is not necessary to determine precisely how each kind of vibration corresponds to experience. It is enough to direct our inner attention to what is happening in this moment – whatever is being felt or sensed – and translate this into an auditory modality by lending it our voice.

● We dive into singing without asking ourselves what we want to achieve, what we have to do, or even how we should sing. Instead, we agree to become a vehicle, a medium, offering our voice to our inner reality. Even when we think nothing is happening, or do not feel anything, in reality it is not so. In such cases, it is best to jump into any sound, sustain it, hold on to it and invite the sound to develop into a melody. It is important to keep a connection with our inner contents, even if they are unknown, and not allow the mind to anticipate or direct the development of the song.

• At all times, we need to be in contact with our belly and heart.

• We keep singing and ignore the mind when it tries to creep in with judgemental comments: "This is not okay"... "It is not what I want"... "I cannot do this"... "This is stupid" and so on. If we do stop, however, it is important to start again exactly from the note we were singing when we left off.

• We engage all our energy in the song: totality prevents the mind from interfering.

• We allow the body to move freely and breathe deeply, synchronizing our breathing with the singing.

Dis-Identification with Self-Image

The process of reconnecting with our spiritual dimension implies a process of learning how to dis-identify from our self-image, which, with rare exceptions, doesn't correspond to our true, unique Essence.

This self-image is false. It was fabricated when we were young in response to our parental conditioning, which in turn was derived from collective social and religious beliefs, and also through hereditary traits we carry through our DNA and other forms of memories. Once formed, this image conceals our direct perception of reality and produces habitual attitudes, predictable emotions and repetitive behaviour.

Our image feeds on explanations and justifications, which are aimed at relieving the pain and distress we experience from having been disconnected from our healthy pulsations. We seek to numb ourselves in an effort to forget the traumatic events that created the disconnection.

For example, if the child is not surrounded by an atmosphere of love and support, a simple mistake or inability to accomplish something – quite a normal occurrence in the growing process of a small child – might be transformed into a terrible sense of failure, especially if it is accompanied by criticism, threats, or condemnation from adults.

Out of this, a belief may be created that 'not being able to' is synonymous with something bad, something to be avoided and feared. This reaction can manifest later in life in contexts that may be quite different from the original one. Just a vague similarity, a faint echo, of the original trauma may be enough to provoke a reaction, like an automatic pilot.

In this way, reality is not experienced as a constantly renewing, unrepeatable flux, but is perceived through a set of beliefs, based on past experiences, that create predefined reactions.

The capacity of the brain to store past associations is useful, especially for survival, but stored memories of trauma often have the negative effect of eclipsing the possibility to make new associations based on the present moment.

Instead of embracing a new situation, we may seek to negate it, or develop antagonism towards it, or attempt to deal with it through the dictates of past conditioning. Mental explanations, justifying a certain type of behaviour, also belong in this category.

Slowly, we stop trusting our original, unique perception of reality and instead live our lives through a fixed personality. Rather than springing from spontaneity of Being, our life experience becomes a mental phenomenon, which might explain why Renee Descartes declared the ultimate expression of self to be "cogito ergo sum" – "I think therefore I am." He was wrong. Thinking is a very superficial layer, when compared with Being.

The true task of therapy and spiritual practice is to de-construct the personality and reconnect with Essence. As you can imagine, this is not an easy task. Each time we are about to step beyond the identity created by our childhood experiences and defence mechanisms, we are faced with the panic of no longer knowing who we are – it's a kind of death.

Modern therapies use several different approaches to re-frame, actualize or erase the limitations of self-image. Verbal and cognitive methods include Hypnosis, Gestalt, Cognitive Therapy, Internalize Object Relation and Somatic Experiencing. Work with energy and breathing techniques includes Bio-Energetics, Rebirthing, Breath, Emotional release and Primal.

VOICING makes use of both avenues. It enquires into the deepest structures derived from infancy using cognitive understanding, and uses bio-energetic and emotional- release methods to unblock obstructions connected to energy and feelings.

The Core of the Process

Spontaneous singing, though, remains at the core of the process, both to remove blockages as well as integrate new opening into Essence.

Our belief systems are imprinted in our brains through sentences that have repercussions in other parts of the body. These sentences have the tonal, rhythmical and qualitative structure of the language through which we first absorbed them. Almost always, these sentences have assertive, mandatory, justifying, manipulative, complaining inflections that contain feelings of guilt, anxiety, inadequacy and so on.

VOICING uses the modality of singing to de-structure these beliefs and to dis-identify from them. Since a belief is not stored in the brain as a song, singing it loosens its grip and in some cases erases it. Another fundamental aspect is that the song doesn't antagonize an identification, but uses it. As I already explained, to be able to sing spontaneously one needs to accept what one is singing.

In this simple and effective way, those aspects of our personality that would be on guard, trying to defend the personality and opposing its de-structuration, are neutralized. Singing is therefore a dis-structuring process in itself, since it certainly wasn't the way the building blocks of our belief structures were assembled in the first place.

While working specifically on one's belief system, we choose a sentence that exemplifies the belief we want to address and then sing it, following the emotional contents as they unwind, without trying to modify any of it.

Once the song subsides and the sentence representing the belief is repeated in a normal talking voice, most of the time it ceases to have a hold, or meaning. Sometimes it even sounds absurd or ridiculous. A distance has been created that allows us to see the belief like a sentence floating in space, outside ourselves, and we are able to realize "I am not my belief".

In this way nothing has been negated, on the contrary the belief has been 'celebrated' while the mere act of singing has stripped it of its original purpose, loosening its grip on the brain. The dimension of celebration, implicit in singing, allows detachment from the limiting belief, and can even create a benevolent space of compassion and understanding that will prevent the belief from having future power over us and our behaviour.

Naturally, this result doesn't always last, because the habit of a particular behaviour or thought is arduous to erase. The fresh input, however, lays a new circuit in the brain that can be sustained through an ongoing attitude of self-enquiry.

This process of singing the sentence of a belief is a technique aimed to obtain a specific result, so it is not the same as singing with complete spontaneity. However, it represents one of the many modalities used in VOICING to guide singing to specific psychological applications and it is a component of the general VOICING approach.

The Dimension of Being

Dis-identifying from beliefs is a delicate inner work that should never be imposed, but rather suggested. Otherwise, a client could try to reinforce an attachment to a particular belief in order to avoid falling into a kind of panic – unable to cope with the space of emptiness that has been created and which may be perceived negatively. This negative perception may, in turn, stimulate the compulsory mechanism of the mind to fill the space with explanations, which can only belong to the past.

In order for transformation to happen, it is imperative to have a deep desire and intention to modify one's self-image, beginning with the understanding that "I am not my belief". The work begins by challenging a specific belief and its related behavioural symptoms without associating the ensuing gap, or void, with panic or a sense of helplessness. This space is, in fact, the door to Being.

The experience of Being and our ability to sustain it are necessary for a deeper and more permanent change. Generally, classical psychology doesn't acknowledge the dimension of Being and is satisfied with the achievement of updating or replacing an old belief. In spiritual practice, no substitution is offered. Instead, one is invited to abandon the mechanism of 'giving oneself an explanation' for what is happening inside and outside oneself.

The process of dis-identification and de-structuring also passes through a phase of replacing beliefs, including the concept that 'we are not what we think we are', since this will remain an idea until it becomes actual experience. Rerouting the mind is almost always an essential passage to be able to embark on the spiritual search.

Totality: a Mystical Experience

When spontaneous singing becomes an act of totality it has the power of dis-identification. Only then, the running mental dialogue stops and all layers of our system fuse in a single act.

When we are total, even our voice is not recognizable as ours. Something more vast, expansive, rich and free is expressing than any aspect of our self-image. We enter in what can be called a mystical experience.

When this happens for the first times, a certain panic can be felt, but the flow of singing functions as an anchor that supports and 'leads' us, almost as if it were an independent life force.

When the singer cannot surrender completely to the singing and the mind manages to interfere, stopping the flow, I suggest to begin again, immediately, exactly where the process was stopped, to avoid giving time and space for mental interference.

Once we gain the experience of stepping beyond personality, we will never be the same again. It's like jumping into the sea for the first time. Afterwards, we will always know what the ocean is like and carry the experience with us – even if it does not repeat itself.

When we experience our divine dimension we have the confirmation of a deep longing we have always felt within us. Then we know that we are so much more than the roles we have carved out for ourselves, so much more than our cultural, religious and social backgrounds have led us to believe.

Obviously, we want to be able to repeat such an experience. Here, as with all types of spiritual occurrences, the danger is that our desire to reproduce the experience becomes a hindrance in itself. Every meditator knows this dilemma, because it is our expectation for a result that drives us to explore meditation techniques and yet the expectations themselves may make it impossible to enjoy a quantum leap into Being.

Spontaneous singing functions in the same way: if we exploit the singing, aiming at a result, we cannot be total, here and now, because part of us will be in the future and therefore not totally in the present.

Totality is the key. As Osho once commented:

When you surrender your actions to the divine you start flowing with the river – and when the river flows there is no ego.[1]

Physical Pain

It would be fortunate if we were trained to enquire into our physical pain and develop a capacity to feel it without immediately creating antagonism towards it.

In VOICING, we are invited to stay with pain, to recognize its vibrational aspect and give it a voice with an attitude, such as "Pain, I give you my voice, express yourself through singing".

Physical pain can be viewed as the language of a body that

wants to communicate a somatic or energetic dysfunction. In this regard, it's worth noting that many indigenous tribal cultures recognize and understand a great variety of bodily sensations that we call pains and can address them accordingly.

I am not advocating the elimination of modern medical pain killers. Everyone has a threshold where pain becomes unbearable, where it would be counter-productive to endure it.

Singing one's physical pain means directing voice-sound-song to and through the place where pain is felt without wanting to modify or get rid of it. Here, the intention is to provide pain with a medium of expression. In so doing, the sense of separation between 'me' and 'the pain' – something we generally want to get rid of – can be dissolved and union can happen when the spontaneous song reaches a dimension of totality. Pain is then transcended through singing.

When the song is complete, often the pain, or its perception, has disappeared and the client's attitude towards it has been modified. Above all, the client feels more connected and serene within himself.

However, it's important to understand that if one uses singing like medicine it probably won't work, since the intention and goal – to get rid of the pain – maintains the separation between 'me' and 'the pain'. It is important not to have an agenda, to maintain an attitude of sincerity and innocence.

Singing as a Resource

With every therapeutic approach, especially those that use strong energy activation, it is imperative to evaluate the capacity of the client to deal with any repressed emotions that may surface, without being overwhelmed by them.

Remember, the nature of our defence system is to maintain a state of repression, which it learned to do many years ago, aimed at preserving our psycho-physical survival. This mechanism had a valuable and necessary purpose during the formative years of our childhood and adolescence, when we were incapable of handling stressful, restrictive and traumatic situations.

Our defences have created neurological reactions that nourish a constant alertness, generating inhibiting and destructive behaviours. Even when, as adults, our defences are obsolete, we cannot easily let go of them, since they are strongly rooted in our personality.

It is advisable to proceed with care when evaluating the ability of a client to open up. This is best done by first targeting areas that can be described as resourceful and by avoiding traumatic areas.

Regardless of the intensity of the traumas we experienced and the pathological behaviours we adopted, we all have access to valid inner resources: the main resource being the capacity of preservation of life – otherwise we wouldn't be here.

The first step is to identify a resource that has a valuable symbolic representation, such as a person, object, place, practice, or situation that is connected to feelings of love, protection, security, peace, encouragement. A resource can also manifest in the form of skills and talents.

Once a person has connected with a resource, the next step is to activate it, sensing it in all its dimensions, finding a space where it can dwell in the body. This becomes a place where the nervous system can relax and recharge; a place where it can always return for support.

In VOICING, the first step is to locate a resource and then focus on it, creating a clear picture of it, a felt-sense, a location in the body, an association with peace, love and support. Then we elicit the vibrational side and externalize it, first as a sound, then as a song. Singing the resource as a starting point is reassuring and creates an anchor that we know we can always go back to, if needed.

However, the power of spontaneous singing relies on the fact that it is a resource unto itself. The song acts as a vehicle. It allows us to connect with repressed and frozen material, and also allows us to express these emotions without the fear normally associated with them.

113

This is possible because spontaneous singing absorbs the fear through acceptance and celebration – a very different experience from how the fear was stored in the first place. In this way, a re-enactment of the trauma is prevented and, consequently, we avoid the danger of being engulfed by our emotions, which would not offer any therapeutic benefit but would only serve to strengthen our defence system.

Any negativity is erased by the singing itself. In spite of the intensity of the experience, spontaneous singing embraces and neutralizes any panic and fear, sustaining the delicate process of voyaging through the episode and allowing us to land on a completely different shore.

When this expression comes to its completion, the system doesn't show any symptoms of stress, agitation or distress. Rather, the person feels an impressive sense of relief, peace and expansion. A state of fine trembling in the body that sometimes happens is a beneficial response to an inner readjustment of the system.

Singing the resource offers another advantage: it is common to feel awkward and embarrassed when invited for the first time to sing spontaneously, freely, without a memory, or a sound track. In the beginning, there aren't many people who can do this without feeling a subtle panic, generated by the idea of 'not being okay', imprinted by continuous reproaches received in the past.

One of the main sentences I hear from clients is "What shall I sing?" My response is to invite them to connect with the resource inside, as this gives them a target on which to focus and naturally opens the door towards a sense of validation and strength: "I sing the resource I have".

Another advantage to sing the resource rests on its positive aspect. The song will have a quality of sweetness and reassurance, even when it refers to qualities like strength and courage. This will help to broach spontaneous singing and erase any inhibitions.

The Quantum Dimension

The development of the ego and our identification with the intellect is not just the result of inheriting Greek Aristotelian ways of thinking, but has also been heavily influenced by the Newtonian vision of the universe – more generally, by science and our accelerating scientific progress.

'Seeing' reality as a scientific phenomenon has developed the functioning of our left-brain hemisphere, which is more rational, to the detriment of the right one, which is more intuitive. The linear thinking of the left-brain feeds our representation of reality as a sequence of cause and effect, which is also related to our perception of space and time.

To sustain this logical, materialistic perception of reality, we must necessarily antagonize all those dimensions that don't belong to it, reducing our field of enquiry by denying any explanation that cannot be described as 'scientifically proven'.

This way of seeing reality has developed an attitude of control, dominion and exploitation of our environment, to the point where we are in danger of destroying the very biosphere we need for our own existence. This attitude has also forged a highly sophisticated social system of control over each other, as well as a propensity of devaluing and negating all feminine values. And it has taken us further and further away from Being.

Our experience of the Essential qualities of Being belongs to a perception of reality that can be defined as 'quantum'. Nowadays quantic discoveries are expanding beyond the realms of mathematical and physical speculation. There are signs that quantic comprehension is helping foster a new vision and experience of oneself, of the world, of the interrelations between people, things, events, etc. Such understanding perceives reality as a dynamic fabric of interrelations between everything, in constant movement, and responding to everything else in one cosmic organic harmony as an awakening reciprocity as a form of living.

A quantum vision doesn't negate the mechanical approach but contains it and goes well beyond it.

I like to think of spontaneous singing as a quantum dimension, since it shares some of its aspects:

- You never know beforehand the melody, the tonality, or where you are heading.
- There is no 'how' – you don't control the pace, the quality, the tone, the texture, etc.
- It can never be repeated in the same way.
- It has infinite possibilities of expression.
- It is easily influenced by surrounding events.

Singing has the tendency to harmonize, mirroring the tendency of quantum particles to influence one another.

I have witnessed many times that magical moment when all participants of a singing group are absorbed in their own songs, regardless of others, then suddenly stop singing, all at the same time, without any external input or invitation. The ensuing silence creates a magical suspension of time and mind.

It is equally common to hear a spontaneous harmony, when all the different singing expressions of the group come together in almost the same key, or share a common volume level.

This phenomenon becomes more frequent with the practice and amplification of listening. Spontaneous singing then acquires a beautiful and spontaneous choral dimension, which is a sign that the group has acquired a wider awareness and an intimacy as a living organism.

The Sacred and the Singing

Talking and singing are communication modalities that exist only in the moment, like dance and, in general, like all body gestures. These expressions dissolve in space and time without leaving a perceptible mark. Similarly, sound waves begin to fade beyond human audible range as soon as they manifest.

On the other hand, written and pictorial signs remain in time and space, even if they no longer convey the original experience of their creators. Writing and painting extend well beyond the moment of creation in a vast, spreading fan, even after the writer or the painter is no longer alive.

In singing, there is a difference between the regular and spontaneous types. With the former, expression is tied to meaning, to concepts of what one wants, what one needs to say, and the sounds are easily reproduced. The sound of the voice may disappear once it is expressed, but the meaning contained in the sentence remains and can be remembered and reproduced.

In spontaneous singing this doesn't happen, since the motive for expression is not preceded and sustained by any conceptual reasoning. Rather, it coalesces in an unpredictable expression of the moment. Such expression can neither be memorized, nor reproduced. Even if one tried to do so, the original spontaneous significance would be lost because it would be subject to a different motivation.

Spontaneous singing, like spontaneous dance, is a powerful vehicle to bring us into the flow of the present moment, ultimately bringing about a spiritual experience. The coalescing of various layers of inner events, expressed through spontaneous singing, has more energy at its disposal than we normally access, since nothing is dissipated in inner fragmentation and in mental activity.

This dimension of totality takes us on a different plane, in a quantum leap, where the ego is dissolved and only awareness remains.

Spontaneous singing, which is a bodily instrument, can open us to the light of pure awareness and celebration as an expression of the divine. Everything is accepted and finds its place as a manifestation of the divine through the instrument of song.

The uniqueness of spontaneous singing is that it cannot be programmed, cannot be repeated, and lives totally in the present. It has the taste of divine creation and our sacred connection to the Absolute.

Teaching Modality

When we begin to sing spontaneously, we are bound to move within the area of our personality, reflecting its limits in our voices. To be able to extend one's boundaries and consequently enlarge the voice spectrum, I proceed by working with different voice layers, starting with very low tones.

Different layers of tone address and trigger different sets of inner experiences, including different levels of consciousness. I like to follow a map that is similar to the Indian chakra map, with different tones corresponding to different levels of consciousness related to different chakras.

1st Chakra: Very low tones trigger spaces that, like those of the first chakra, reconnect us with our roots, the mystery of human incarnation, our relationship with the body and its physical strength. Issues concerning our body, our fears of survival, fears of physical weakness or strength, will be activated. As with other layers, specific bodily exercises and breathing techniques are used to facilitate the opening of the voice in these areas. The resonance of the singing voice in these very low tones will bring about resolution of those fears and provide an overall sensation of deep peace and strength.

2nd Chakra: The journey continues by activating the emotional body, discovering how the rich variety of emotional voices is located in the belly, not in the throat or the heart. The belly is the location of the second chakra.

3rd Chakra: The solar plexus and diaphragm, home of the third chakra, hold a special place in Voicing. In order to be able to assert oneself, to sustain loudness in the voice and feel confident to command and involve other people, one needs to be open in this area. Resolution of third chakra issues depends on recognizing and embracing what is held in our 'shadow'.

4th Chakra: Our song is at home in the heart and we naturally experience this 'heartful' quality of love and compassion once the weights that keep it closed are lifted. Delicacy, sweetness and the purity of the open sound will be the outcome.

5th Chakra: Freedom of expression is the theme of the throat area, and work here revolves around the de-structuring of our belief-systems through singing as well as releasing falsity.

6th and 7th Chakras: The very high tones of voice needed for the 6th and 7th Chakras require special care, since they involve more subtle dimensions of the brain and meditation.

This exploration can take anything from a short introductory course to a two-year process. The longer the time, the more accurate becomes the exploration of the intricacies of oneself and the greater the benefit gained from the infinite possibilities of one's own voice.

When it comes to individual sessions I have no definite set approach. Each session is unique in itself and, to some extent, unpredictable and unrepeatable. The first input that can determine the way I proceed is the voice of the client. The client's motivation for requesting a session, as well as his or her psychological history and previous experiences in therapy will influence what my intuition will then dictate.

Since singing is connected to energy, body, emotions, behavior, consciousness, very often a session starts with activating the body energy through shaking, grounding exercises and emission of simple sounds at random.

Also for individual sessions it is advisable to start with the client accessing an inner resource and encourage her to sing it. This creates an anchor for use in possible future situations of confusion or stress, and while at the same time helping the client overcome the hesitancy of exposing oneself through singing.

If the client shows a feeble, rather high-pitched voice, lacking in substance and roundness, I might bring her to focus and work on the low-tones ranges. When I feel the client is not likely to get engulfed emotionally if the emotional body is activated, I might venture to touch disconnected issues related to disregard of the body, sexual or emotional frigidity, fear of one's own powerful drives, etc. as well as emotional vulnerability. This can lead also to more targeted emotional release related to fears, behaviors, beliefs adopted in childhood and related to parental attitudes.

Sometimes this process requires also specific verbal phrases that need to be expressed with specific voice tones and qualities. Even in these cases, though, the final outcome is the singing.

When a client intends to have a series of sessions we can establish a kind of map that begins either at the heart level or, more frequently, with the low tones, focusing on different tones during each session in a similar way to groups.

After some sessions, the magnifying glass on different tone ranges will be dropped in order to experience the increased availability of sounds in one's own voice when engaging in spontaneous singing.

In some cases, when I evaluate that the client is very sensitive and in a rather fragile space, I might use different sound-healing techniques, like deep-relaxation and/or the use of more finer qualities of sound, both vocal or of specific musical instruments.

It can also happen that, from the very beginning, I ask the client to jump directly into spontaneous singing and continue without stopping for quite some time.

Singing, in fact, remains the main track to follow and trust.

The main focus for the VOICING therapist is always the voice, which is the best leader in a session. Whenever the tone of spontaneous singing is resonant it means it is heading towards a dimension of authenticity that generally needs to be supported and encouraged.

The therapist needs to be master of her own voice in such a way that she can pace exactly the client's voice, sustain it, expand it and, if need be, lead it towards a more differentiated harmony. At this point, merging with the client, mastering and displaying one's own voice and exactly synchronizing with the voice of the client, is the main ingredient nourishing the intuition to determine in which direction the client's song is heading.

In this way, facilitating a VOICING session is comparable to being a midwife.

Results

My desire is to transmit the practice of spontaneous singing as a tool for discovering deeper levels in ourselves and opening a channel of expression both for the unconscious and the superconscious. In addition, I dare to say that VOICING can raise the unconscious to the level of the superconscious.

The practical results I have witnessed are connected to a heightened self-awareness that brings about an increase of self-value and courage, as well as a new ability to express oneself in all fields, from personal to social to professional.

I have observed an increase in courage to undergo big changes in life, in areas than stretch from intimate relationships, to family, to jobs, to changing one's living environment. Often, I also see an increase in creativity and a greater capacity and willingness to accept and deal with the unknown.

Continuous practice of VOICING fosters a steadier contact with oneself, the ability to recognize and express emotional issues, the readiness to deal with difficulties in accordance with one's own personal integrity.

I'd like to cite the case of a woman whose experience touched me:

In her youth she had been violently sexually abused. This trauma had left deep marks of low self-esteem, of low trust in herself and in others, and a disconnection from her body. One evening, after an eighteen-day Voicing workshop, she was strolling down a street in Copenhagen when she was confronted by three men who visibly and audibly announced their aggressive intentions towards her.

Instead of falling into a panic and feeling helpless, she stopped and uttered such a fierce, powerful sound that her would-be assailants took fright and ran away. She considered this event as the true mark and threshold of her healing.

Later, she found the courage to leave her teaching job in order to commit herself fully to her love of painting and a couple of years later she had her first personal exhibition.

This is one of several examples I've heard through the years, of incidents of successful self-defence using the voice, transmitting deep sounds intended purely for defence.

Often, people who approach VOICING confide in me that "I don't like my voice". In such cases, the first part of my work focuses on eliciting those aspects of voice my client judges as undesirable, by asking the person to expose them audibly. This step can have unexpected results.

I can quote the example of a Norwegian woman who complained to me that her voice was ugly, aggressive and she felt it was scaring people.

Actually her voice sounded harsh, dry and choked, with fast binary rhythms, revealing a lot of energy, possibly related with a repressed anger that she was trying to contain.

This woman had been a spiritual seeker for many years and had participated in self-awareness groups with Osho's therapists. Her experience made it possible for me to invite her into the middle of the circle of participants and encourage her to give vent to her 'ugly' voice in an uncontrolled way, with the intention of frightening the other participants.

She threw herself into the challenge, riding a release of energy that quickly became very strong. Since her husband was also present, I suggested that she address him as well. As a result of letting go all control, her voice gradually became a song: a powerful, raw, resonating song springing from her belly that impressed and touched everybody, including herself.

When the song came to a natural end, there was an unexpected and surprising result. Her voice had become lower in tone, more round, warm and relaxed, with a slower rhythm and sweet, touching, heartful inflections.

The episode helped her understand the value of listening to her own voice and recognizing the messages it contained, instead wasting time criticizing it.

In my long experience of working with people, the voice doesn't fundamentally change, but it can become more connected with one's Essence and therefore more resonant, with more inflections and tonalities revealing a wider range of moods, emotions and purposes of communication. This is only possible if one continues the practice of listening to oneself and singing spontaneously.

Often I am asked if VOICING is useful in clinical cases, such as chronic sore throats, throat polyps, cancer, thyroid problems, etc.

I'm not a medical doctor, so I can't evaluate VOICING's healing effect, but I prefer not to accept participants who are under medical treatment. However, considering the body's many-fold psychosomatic interrelations, it would be interesting if one day someone would do research on this issue.

Generally speaking, VOICING teaches us how to regain the capacity to sing spontaneously. When this ability is awakened it is always a healing agent. The healing process is not always smooth and quick, since we have been taught the habit of 'doing' and 'controlling' our voices and in this way creating damaging pressure on the throat, which makes spontaneity and healing difficult.

In some cases, when there are no medical limitations in the use of the voice, I agree to work with people who have, or have had, some kind of throat illness. But in these cases I prefer to work individually – not in group formats – to be able to ensure continuous supervision of their vocal expression.

I'd like to mention a woman who'd been operated for throat cancer, sometime before coming to me, and had also been treated with chemotherapy. To me, her manner of presenting herself to others was phoney; very pleasing and forcibly sweet, even though her energy suggested a hidden strength.

Working with her voice created a big shift in her life. Focusing on the repressed, shadow aspects of her personality, she discovered qualities like meanness, envy, aggression and selfish impulses, all in marked contrast to her attempts to be seen as a 'good girl'.

Through VOICING she managed to accept these hidden parts. Singing full blast, she connected with her own witchy side, becoming the Queen of the Night, opening up to her energy and power. After a few VOICING groups, she told me she'd discovered not only one 'dictator' inside herself, but several. She'd also found the courage to change her job, her place of residence and other aspects of her former life. Many years have passed and she continues to be well, with no relapses. She continues singing.

CHAPTER SEVEN

Pulsation

Aneesha

It was the idea of sexual freedom which attracted me to both Osho and Wilhelm Reich. I grew up in the United States in the 60s, a time when many aspects of the 'old social order' were being questioned and challenged, and for me sexual mores were at the top of the list. As a young woman in my early twenties, the issues concerning women's liberation, birth control, abortion and marriage were very important to me.

Early in his life, Reich, as a pioneering psychotherapist and student of Sigmund Freud, understood that sexuality is a basic instinct and human need. He believed that the lack of sexual fulfilment, caused by sexual misinformation and dysfunction, was one of the greatest causes of human misery in modern times.

For many years, Reich operated clinics where ordinary people, including adolescents, could come and receive counselling and sex education. He also pioneered many techniques for releasing suppressed energy, claiming that Freud was wrong in assuming modern man is forced to be neurotic.

My training in Reichian breathing and bodywork techniques at the Radix Institute in California gave me a chance to explore my own emotions and make conscious much of what I had buried inside myself. I remembered all those years of swallowing down my sadness, my anger, and protecting my vulnerability. Now, I had the chance to cry deep tears, scream with rage and let out old feelings that had been suppressed during childhood and adolescence.

Gradually, as my body and my emotional turmoil relaxed, I re-connected with a spontaneity of feeling and expression, and a freedom of movement in my body that I had not felt since childhood.

This brought me tremendous joy. Even in the midst of deep emotional pain in response to some agonizing memory, I always had a solid and connected sense that *this is good, this is healing.*

Such powerful work on the physical body is bound to touch the basic energy of sexuality, and I began to understand how much I had been disowning my sexual feelings. Step by step, during my personal therapy sessions, pain gave way to the full positive force of my physical vitality and I began to unlock the pleasures of free-flowing energy.

In addition, I discovered a natural talent for working with people using neo-Reichian methods – breathing, bodywork and emotional release – and in time learned how to practice this deep, powerful and sensitive energy work with clients. My teacher, Charles Kelley, introduced me to his colleagues in California, the Mid-West and Eastern United States. It wasn't long before I found myself working in many different locations, including the prestigious Esalen Institute in Big Sur, on the West Coast, where I lived and practiced for two years.

During my time at Esalen I heard about Osho, an enlightened Indian mystic, who had created and fine-tuned some revolutionary meditation practices, designed for contemporary seekers, very different from what I'd so far known. Instead of sitting silently in rigid postures, focusing on who-knows-what, these meditations used vigorous body movement, dancing, breathing and emotional catharsis as precursors to silence and stillness.

From the early 70s onwards, Osho offered these contemporary meditations to his disciples and other seekers, who were drawn to India from around the world. His 'body-active meditations' were designed to shake up, dislodge and throw out whatever childhood conditioning these Westerners might have 'swallowed' in the course of growing up.

I first tried Osho's Dynamic Meditation at Kalptaru Meditation Centre in London, when the centre leaders invited me to come and try it. The meditation is described in detail elsewhere in this book, so I'll just state the five stages briefly:

- Ten minutes of deep, fast, chaotic breathing through the nose, emphasizing the exhale.
- Ten minutes of cathartic expression: shouting, screaming, crying, laughing.
- Ten minutes of jumping, with arms raised, shouting the mantra "Hoo! Hoo! Hoo!"
- A sudden stop, followed by fifteen minutes silence and stillness.
- A final section of fifteen minutes free-form dancing.

The effect of Dynamic Meditation – on my body, my energy, my feelings – was profound. Even with my experience in emotional release work it was challenging to do this meditation, especially the first few times. But I could immediately understand its value and, over a period of time, noticed it had the effect of helping life energy flow more freely through my body.

Experiencing Dynamic Meditation made me realize I had found the right spiritual Master to teach me meditation. Through the techniques Osho created, I realized he knew the principles Reich had outlined in his theory of *orgone energy* in his book, *Function of the Orgasm*. Osho understood the laws of energetic *charge* and *discharge* which Reich called *the orgasm formula* and also what Reich referred to as *muscular armouring*. Later, I learned Osho had spoken lovingly about Reich and kept many of the psychotherapist's books in his own extensive library.

I arrived at Osho's ashram in Pune in 1976 and after a year of practicing Osho's active meditations was invited to lead workshops using my skills as a Reichian and Radix therapist. Osho was keen on adding Reich's work to the wide spectrum of groups and workshops being offered at his ashram, explaining that these therapies helped people to come into deeper contact with their bodies, release suppressed energy and discharge emotional tension. This, in turn, allowed them to be more vitally alive and relaxed – an ideal combination for experiencing meditation.

It was during these years that my own particular style of therapy developed, which I call Pulsation. This is what I still teach, some forty-odd years later, travelling around the globe, leading workshops, giving individual sessions and also training people as Pulsation practitioners.

Osho supported and guided my work, answering my questions during evening *darshan* – personal meetings with the Master – as well as in his daily discourses, and occasionally consulting me when participants in my workshops sat in front of him, seeking more understanding about what they'd been experiencing.

For example, one of my participants might sit in front of Osho and describe what was going on in his body, or perhaps in his energy flow, and Osho would turn to me and ask, "What do you say, Aneesha?

I kept my answers practical; pointing out, for instance, a constriction in the person's diaphragm and a related incapacity to breathe deeply – nothing very profound in terms of spirituality but certainly accurate in terms of my work. Osho would nod and say "That's exactly right" and then continue offering guidance to the person.

With Osho's support, I developed an intuitive style of working with people that went far beyond the methodology of the neo-Reichian therapeutic approach. I bridged the gulf between therapy and meditation, guiding people deeper and deeper into their own interior worlds, journeying from mind to heart to being.

So, as I describe my work in the following paragraphs, please remember that these methods are conducted within a wider atmosphere of trust, self-acceptance and wisdom that acts as a kind of spiritual container. Reich didn't know about meditation. That was the missing ingredient in his recipe for human fulfilment. It was Osho who added the missing spice.Meditation in Pune went far beyond techniques like Dynamic and Kundalini. It was present in the silence in Buddha Hall, as we waited for Osho to come and give discourse. It was in the air after *darshan*, as we walked silently along the ashram pathways. It was in those magical moments I experienced, as a participant and as a guest medium in Osho's *energy darshan* phase, when we would all disappear into inner cosmic spaces, vast and empty, yet pulsating with an ecstatic energy that filled us with awe and delight.

Now, coming back down to earth, let's take a look at the therapeutic background of my work.

Early Life Experiences

The idea of 'childhood psychological conditioning' and the fact that we are influenced both positively and negatively by early life experiences, is well known in today's world of psychology, self-help therapy and personal growth. Through the discoveries of Sigmund Freud, the idea of repression and the unconscious mind has become ubiquitous in the Western world.

What is less well known is that our emotional and psychological wounds are stored and recorded, not only psychologically through the brain and nervous system, but in all parts of our bodies: the muscles, the fascia, the cells ... even, according to recent research, in our DNA.

Many muscles are involved in the movements that accompany emotional expression. Those same muscles do the work of controlling and repressing feelings that arise during traumatic or painful experiences. The energetic imprint of these experiences, too painful to feel, too scary or overwhelming to express at the time, are pushed down into the unconscious mind, where they can be more easily forgotten.

Freud, and those who followed in his footsteps, employed verbal and analytical techniques when working with patients: dream analysis, association and other predominantly mental approaches to 'untangle the knots' of the neurotic mind. But one of Freud's young students, Wilhelm Reich, began to understand, through studying his own patients, that the physical body is also deeply involved in the expression and repression of emotions.

As a young medical student in Vienna, Reich began to recognize the significance of sexuality in human life. He was drawn to Freud's work, particularly his theory of *libido* which the professor described as a biological, sexual energy in the body.

Unfortunately, this vibrant concept of *libido* was diluted and toned down by Freud and his closest followers, reduced to little more than a psychological idea. But to Reich this biological energy was much more than a concept. His life's work led him through many fields of scientific research and clinical practice to pursue the secrets of sexual energy and life energy, which he named *orgone energy*.

Pregnancy, Birth and Childhood

In the last few decades, scientific studies of the brain and nervous system have informed us that adult human patterns of behaviour and response have their roots in the experiences of the foetus in the weeks and months before birth. Inside the mother's womb, the child is suffused with the energetic, biochemical and emotional atmosphere of the mother – her thoughts, feelings, emotional reactions – as well as everything she eats, drinks and puts in her body.

If the mother is relaxed, contented, feeling loved and supported by those around her, she will create an energetic and biochemical atmosphere of loving support for her child. If the mother is surrounded by disharmony, violence, hatred, poverty or emotional rejection, how can she create a safe space within which her baby can thrive?

All of the abuses and support the mother supplies to her growing foetus will affect the delicate processes and biochemical settings underway in the nine months of pregnancy. Because the extremely sensitive foetus is affected at the very roots of its formation, its body, as it grows, will be imprinted by those experiences. A developing individual will carry those influences, good and bad, within his or her physical body for their lifetime.

Birth 'lays down' another layer of experience that, for all of us, is a powerful and often traumatic event. Many people undergoing therapy have reported 'reliving' painful birth experiences through Primal techniques that 'take us back' to previously unremembered events.

Our parents' influences mould us consciously and unconsciously into the grown beings we become. Our relationships in the present day often mirror the unfulfilled or distorted relationships from earlier times in our lives. Our life experiences – whether hurtful, frightening, enraging, happy, joyful – are recorded, somehow imprinted, into our energy system, our nervous system and our physical body. Hence, Freud's assertion that experiences too uncomfortable or painful to consciously remember are denied, pushed away and repressed deeper into the unconscious.

The effort of pushing away what we don't want to feel can be experienced through the body as physical tension, pain, numbness, deadness, limited or uncoordinated movement and many other uncomfortable symptoms. These symptoms 'live' in the physical body in our muscles, ligaments and bones as we develop the habit of holding in what wants to burst out.

One of the most powerful ways we employ, as children, to block unwanted feeling and expression is by controlling our breathing. As we hold our breath, muscles in the chest and diaphragm become tense, the throat closes and in this way feelings are swallowed down. If repeated often enough, the tension becomes rigid, chronic, and we are no longer able to relax, even with a conscious intention to do so.

The body is held in a controlled and rigid manner, or perhaps takes on a collapsed posture. The breathing is all but immobile, shallow and tight. Wilhelm Reich called this rigidity, when it manifested in the body, *muscular armour*. And when it manifested through emotions, mind, and behaviour, he called it *character armour*.

Energy and Life Force

To say that Pulsation is body-oriented is only half true. There is another element that comes into the equation and that is the idea of a life force, or life energy. Life energy is an invisible undercurrent that flows and pulsates through the bodies of all living things and is more subtle than the physical world.

131

In the process of becoming a Radix teacher, I studied teachings of Franz Anton Mesmer from the 18th century and Hans Reichenbach from the 20th century, each of whom described theories of some sort of vital energy that flows through the human body. In fact, this energy is said to permeate all space, all matter, perhaps like the *prana* in Yoga, or the *chi* in Chinese medicine, which flows through specific channels or meridians in the body. These ideas, discovered and re-discovered throughout history, at the fringes of science, point to a hidden, invisible, yet tangible force or energy, which animates life.

Freud's *libido* was one of those theories but he shied away from going deeper into sexuality. And surely, this vital, energetic understanding underlies many of the Shamanic healing practices and celebrations of tribal peoples around the world.

Reich named this life force *orgone* and Charles Kelley called it *radix*, meaning 'root', or primary cause.

Life energy pulsates through living organisms by various means; for instance, the heartbeat and the circulatory system, the breathing and the digestive system. Our bodies are alive with hundreds of flows and rhythms, some of which are physical, others more subtle. Our energy systems are continuously engaged in charging and discharging, expressing energy in life's everyday activities.

In fact, the *breathing pulsation* serves as a kind of pump for the life energy, to help it flow through the body. Every time we breathe in, we charge our energy system, taking in not only oxygen-rich air, but also *prana* – life energy that we need and use as a kind of fuel. Every time we breathe out, we discharge not only carbon dioxide, but also work energy that moves outward into the world in the form of practical actions and creative expression. Giving and receiving are parts of a whole wave of energy, just as masculine and feminine energies are two halves of one circle.

As we live our daily lives, life energy flows into and through every part of the physical body, in and out, up and down, transmitted like waves through the liquid contents of the body, supporting us to walk from place to place, to communicate, eat, talk, smell the roses ... responding to whatever the world brings before us. These are mechanical acts: doing something, moving the physical body.

We are also constantly responding to whatever we feel inside, to impulses that have an emotional impact, such as unexpectedly bursting into tears while watching a sad movie, or instinctively running away from danger. Many of the feelings and emotions that arise in us are unwelcome – things that our upbringing and social training has taught us not to show or express, but instead swallow down and keep silent. Children are quieted, or ignored when crying, punished for showing anger, humiliated for showing fear.

Thus, we have learned how to regulate and control our expression of emotional energy, to adapt our behaviour to what is expected by our parents, teachers and others, so that we grow up to be well-behaved citizens, controlling our emotions in order to conform. All of this is reflected in the way we hold our bodies as we stand, sit and move through life.

Seven Segments of Muscular Armouring

As I mentioned earlier, the muscles that we use to express emotions are the same muscles that tighten to prevent expression from happening. These muscles are located inside the body in coordinated groups that form rings around the central core of the body, rather like the segments of a worm or snake.

The sphincter-like opening and closing of these muscular rings creates a wavelike movement in these legless creatures as they slither forward. In the human body, energy flowing up and down the spine is intersected by seven rings. Reich called these muscle groups the seven segments of muscular armouring.

Segment 1: The Ocular Segment (Eyes)

Located at the top and sides of the head, this segment includes the eyes and all the muscles within and around the eye sockets and forehead, as well as muscles at the top, sides and back of the head.

Segment 2: Oral Segment (Mouth and Jaw)

Includes the mouth and jaw area, the lips, teeth, tongue, and a group of muscles linking the jaw to the back of the neck. It is a major doorway for the passage of energies flowing through the throat.

Segment 3: Cervical Segment (Throat and Neck)

Involves the muscles of the neck and throat. Much energy passes through the neck and throat in the form of outward-directed expression and also in receiving breath, energy and nourishment from the environment.

Segment 4: Thoracic Segment (Chest, Back, Shoulders, Arms, Hands)

Refers to the muscles in the chest and back, including the rib cage, pectoral muscles, the shoulders, arms and hands, as well as feelings and expressions that arise from the heart centre.

Segment 5: Diaphragmatic Segment (Diaphragm, front and back)

Here we have the diaphragm, an umbrella-shaped group of muscles located just beneath the ribs and attaching to the ribs, all the way round to the back. Its function is to support our breathing, to swing freely down with the in-breath, filling the lungs, and to swing upwards with the out-breath, emptying the lungs.

Segment 6: Abdominal Segment (Belly, Lower Back)

Comprising the muscles in and around the abdomen and lower back.

Segment 7: Pelvic Segment (Pelvis, Legs, and Feet)

Includes the muscles of the pelvis, anus, genitals, tailbone and muscles connecting the legs to the body. It controls the function of energetic grounding through legs and feet, as well as the function of reproduction, elimination and survival instincts.

These seven segments include not only muscles but also organs, glands, nerve plexes and other anatomical parts affected by the energetic flow – or lack of it – through each segment.

Reich theorized that cancer and other diseases grow in tissue that has been stifled by physical tension and a lowered oxygen level due to shallow breathing. In Pulsation, we mainly address muscular tension and the energy this holds back, but many health professionals recognize that certain medical conditions have their roots in blocked emotions.

Reich's model of the seven muscular segments is an important map that informs us, as practitioners, about what is happening in a client's body in terms of energetic charge, tension, aliveness and relaxation. We closely observe the body as it breathes, as it builds a charge of energy. We touch the body to support and guide the client, while at the same time assessing levels of tension in key areas of the body. Tension gives us information about what feelings are being blocked or protected in those parts of the body.

The Segments and the Chakras

Another important but non-Reichian 'map' that we use in Pulsation is the system of Chakras, discovered thousands of years ago in the East by yogis following the teachings of Patanjali, the founder of Yoga. Even before I heard of Reich, I had become interested in the chakras, or energy centres, which were brought to public awareness in the West by Charles Leadbeater, Annie Besant and the Theosophical Movement.

Reich never knew of the Eastern practice of Yoga, yet his description of muscular segments corresponds almost exactly to the locations of the Chakras. Within each muscular segment there is a vortex of subtler layers of energy, deeper inside the body. Each Chakra not only regulates the functioning of the organs and nerves in its segment, but also indicates psycho-emotional issues that actually 'reside' and are processed through these places in the body. Understanding the Chakra map has helped me to understand human energy even more deeply.

The Breathing Pulsation

The Breathing Pulsation is the connecting link between the physical body and the subtle energy body, which is the medium of emotions. A complex interplay of movement and breathing is the driving force behind the expression of feelings and emotions. Along with the beating of the heart, breathing is the most powerful and life-connected physiological function of the body. Without these two repetitive, pulsatory, cyclical actions, the body will die.

Breathing has two basic movements: in, and out. This repetitive rhythm, breathing in, breathing out, keeps the body supplied with the oxygen it needs to support life, and frees the body of carbon dioxide and other wastes. We can control our breathing up to a certain point, but life depends on breathing and nature intelligently arranged for breathing to continue without our conscious control, or even our attention.

I have already mentioned that life energy – *chi, prana, orgone, radix* – is absorbed into our bodies as we breathe. It also circulates through our bodies by means of the breath. Life energy 'rides' on the pulsating waves of breathing. Our overall energy level affects breathing, just as breathing affects our energy level.

Through deeper, intentional breathing we accumulate more energy than is needed for 'base-line' existence. This is called building a charge of life energy and happens on the in-breath. Similarly, energy is discharged or expended on the out-breath. When we breathe out, energy is released, expressed.

The Orgasm Formula

Breathing is the foundation of neo-Reichian work because through breathing a charge of energy is built – we can call it a bio-electric or bio-energetic *charge*. It is something similar to electricity, but not the electricity we know. In turn, this bio-electric charge creates a potential for energy *discharge* or release.

As I've already indicated, Wilhelm Reich had a name for this process of bio-electric charge and discharge – he called it the *orgasm formula*. This formula has four stages: charge > tension > discharge > relaxation.

The same process, more or less, happens in a therapeutic emotional release session, using Reichian methods:

The *charge* phase: as breathing deepens, waves of life energy start to surge through the body and we begin to build a charge. However, the muscles are already 'charged' and 'armoured' to a certain extent with all the hurts, wounds, betrayals and tensions through a lifetime of holding back feelings. By deepening our breathing, an increasing energy charge activates the muscles to do something, while more tension grows in the muscles to ensure containment.

The *tension* grows as the breathing pulsation builds, the charge gets higher and the muscles have to work harder to hold everything inside. Finally, the tension cannot hold the charge anymore and it bursts forth in emotional expression, loaded with the emotional charge of the old wounds as well.

The *discharge* phase: in an emotional catharsis, memories flood the mind, emotions flood the heart, tears flow of rage or pain, arms and legs pummel the mattress with full force. For a moment, everything is felt, expressed and released. In such a release, it is as if one is taken by a storm, or flooded by a wave. Like a full-bodied sexual orgasm, the wave becomes irresistible – the body convulses involuntarily as it surrenders to expression via waves of feeling.

The *relaxation* phase: gradually all becomes still, relaxed, breathing returns to normal. This is a moment when integration can happen in the body, the nervous system and the psyche. It is a moment to absorb the healing benefits from restored life-energy flow, which is more open and relaxed.

Reich's work led him to discover physical, hands-on techniques as well as verbal ones, as a way of encouraging his patients to feel and express painful emotional memories as they worked together. Asking his patients to breathe deeply, he prodded and massaged tight muscles in their bodies; muscles which were involved in holding back the expression of feeling.

He also encouraged his patients to show their feelings through their eyes, to express the full, energetic force of their feelings by moving the body, beating the couch with fists, shouting, kicking and so on. After one of these sessions, Reich's patients reported experiencing relief in their muscles and joints, in their nervous system and in their hearts and minds ... eventually, in their lives.

Allow me to emphasize once more: the most important key to contacting deeper feelings and emotions is the breathing, so this is a prime focus in Reichian methods. We need to let the whole body move as it breathes, so the energy spreads all over the body. This movement is combined with vocal sounds of all sorts: gibberish and nonsense language, shouting sounds and words. These three things: breathing, body movements and vocal sounds are the keys. When combined skilfully with the sensitive healing presence of the therapist, together with accurate and appropriate touching on tense musculature, much can be released, relaxed and transformed.

These releases often involve the expression of emotions that seem to pour forth from unknown sources, deep inside the body. What remains when the storm has passed is relaxation into an inner well of peace, silence, stillness and acceptance.

It is important to acknowledge the joy, the delight, the love and deep trust that arise from within once we open our windows and doors, allowing fresh breezes to blow through us. What is discordant within us can loosen, shake free and possibly find a new inner harmony.

The Feeling Pairs

I want to introduce a concept that was formulated by my teacher of Neo-Reichian techniques, Charles Kelley. Kelley's Radix 'brand' and his personal working style of applying Reichian methods, was generally high-charge, hands-on and very interactive between therapist and client.

138

This style can generate discharges of explosive anger and rage, convulsing pain and crying, fear and terror. It is important, therefore, to understand the dynamics of emotional expression – how each emotion has its characteristic ways of inhibiting breathing.

The three basic emotions – anger, fear and pain – are energetically related to the breathing pulsation. Understanding the direction of each emotional expression, we can be clearer how to support expression and release in the most helpful way.

The Feeling Pairs are: Anger/Love, Fear/Trust, Pain/Pleasure.

Anger is associated with the outward movement of energy, from core to periphery. Fear is related to the inward movement of energy, from periphery to core. Pain is related to the rapid contraction and expansion of muscles that we experience in expressions like laughing, sobbing, and orgasm.

Each negative emotion, when blocked, has a characteristic way of holding itself in the body in the form of muscular tension. This enables an experienced therapist to 'read' the body of a client and detect the predominant blocked emotion.

Anger/Love: Anger is a hard, explosive, aggressive expression of energy in the form of a sudden rush to the periphery. In a fight, the fist is really nothing but an extension of an energetic impulse, traveling outwards. Love, the other half of this pair, is a soft, tender, compassionate expression of the outward movement of our energy. Although they are very different, love and anger ride the same highway, moving in the same direction, from core to periphery.

If one aspect of outward expression is blocked, it tends also to block the other aspect as well. Love is a much softer, more delicate feeling than anger. It will not be able to pass through a hard layer of chronic armour created by the habit of blocking anger. Even if, at your core, you long to express your love, to reach out towards others in an expansive movement, you cannot. The highway is jammed, the traffic is blocked, nothing can move.

Anger needs to be released and expressed in order for love to flow.

Fear/Trust: Fear makes people shrink. It is a contractive, inward pulling of energy, because our basic survival instinct is saying "Run away!" It is the urge to take ourselves out of a situation that is perceived to be dangerous. Adrenaline is released into the body to promote action and the animal inside us wants to run, to flee.

In some situations, flight is a practical option. However, for the young child, trapped in a scary domestic situation, it is another story. Unable to flee, helpless and dependent on the parents who are making him afraid, there is no other option but to shrink, to retreat to the core; to build a wall, an inner fortress, to protect the scared little one inside.

It is understandable that a fearful type of person has difficulty trusting people or the surrounding environment, because trust requires openness and receptivity. Trust is a decision to allow energy from the outside to penetrate you. Like fear, trust rides on the inward stroke of the pulsation, moving from periphery to core, so it follows that if a person is armoured against fear this will prevent the soft, receiving, inflow of trust.

Fear needs a safe space in which to be felt, allowed, and in which to surrender. Out of the melting of fear, trust naturally arises.

Pain/Pleasure: When a small child is really crying or laughing, its whole body is in a state of natural, healthy pulsation. But when these feelings are suppressed or blocked, the pulsation is diminished, so that both directions of the breath – inhalation and exhalation – are minimized in an effort to deaden unwanted or unacceptable feelings. In the blocking of pain, every effort is made *not* to feel, *not* to recognize what wants to be felt and expressed. It's a kind of holding, or suspension, of the pulsation.

If we can allow pain to be felt, if these hurt feelings can be accepted and embraced, deep crying and convulsive sobbing are likely to follow, tension will be released and the body will become more alive and sensitive again.

Freeing pain opens the capacity for joy and orgasmic pleasure.

Pulsation and Counter-Pulsation

When we work individually with a client, we generally begin with breathing. As the breath moves in and down, the ringed segments of musculature expand to make space for more air. As the breath moves out, these rings contract to push the breath up and out of the body.

As the charge of energy gradually expands, more energy begins to circulate and flow through the body. Breathing deeper and deeper, in and out, the muscular segments are pulsating, opening and closing each muscle group, pulling in and pushing through another wave of energy, feeling and emotion.

In a relatively unarmoured body, or in the body of someone who has done a lot of emotional release work, there is a larger capacity for full, uninhibited pulsation. It is possible for such a body to contain a strong charge of energy without catharsis, tightening up, or spacing out.

But we have learned to control our feelings, deny them, disown them. Almost everyone develops habits and patterns of tension, holding against fuller breathing, deeper feeling and natural expressiveness. So our muscular segments get tighter and start to fight with the breathing pulsation.

There might be expressions of avoidance – general irritation, a 'premature' catharsis, extraneous body movements, or the breathing stops, or there is a 'drifting away' of attention. There are numerous avoidance tactics that we employ to prevent a charge from building up to a discharge.

Each time a wave of feeling arises – we can call it a *pulsation* – it encounters a chronically blocked muscle segment that prevents movement and expression. When this happens, a secondary wave forms – we can call it a *counter-pulsation* – which pushes back in the opposite direction.

It's as if the body is saying "No, I don't want to feel anything! Don't make me cry, or shout!"

As the charge grows and old feelings become activated, these patterns of tension become visible in the muscles and body movements become tighter, more inhibited. As we learn to recognize counter-pulsations we also come to understand how to loosen the muscular blocks so that life energy can flow freely again.

The skilled Pulsation therapist can see, as well as feel, the tensions in a client's body. Through a variety of interventions, both physical and verbal, we can invite, support and facilitate a healing emotional experience.

Practical Application of Pulsation Techniques

Throughout any group or individual session, we are continuously engaged in breathing, employing the process of energetic charge and discharge as a healing tool. We work consciously with Reich's *orgasm formula* to flush out chronic, energetic holding in the muscles, and to free up energy flow in the body.

At the beginning of a group or individual session, the body is more or less in a state of rest and the energetic charge is relatively low. So the first step in the process will be to build a charge in the body.

As previously indicated, we use a variety of physical exercises, combining deep breathing with body movements and vocal sounds, to help loosen muscular tensions, increasing the flow of bio-energy in the body, opening the capacity to feel more deeply. We shake the body, talk gibberish, loosen necks, shoulders, arms, pelvis … moving everything. Dancing is one of my best-loved tools to move energy through the whole body and loosen up whatever might be stuck inside.

One function of these exercises is *grounding*, which refers to our basic and primitive connection to the pelvis, sex, legs and feet, and our sense of rootedness into the earth. These exercises are done standing, sometimes in a circle, sometimes in pairs, often with eye contact with others. Stamping the feet, walking in different ways, moving chaotically, playing with sounds and movements … all serve to loosen the body so breathing can deepen. Grounding brings our awareness deeper into the physical body, which is the 'venue' for our work in Pulsation.

Reich himself worked with individuals but not with groups. Group work seems to have developed out of the experimental 'group therapy culture' that arose in the 60s and 70s at Esalen Institute and other centres in the US and Europe.

Charles Kelley created many structures for work in groups, based on Reichian principles. Usually, participants work in pairs: one lying on a mat as the 'worker', the other partner sitting on a cushion by the side, as a 'supporter'. Many of these partner processes and other exercises are described in my book, *Tantric Pulsation: The journey of human energy from its animal roots to its spiritual flowering.*

Osho, Reich and Tantra

Once the body and the psyche have become looser, less armoured, more free of repressions, so that energy can begin to flow again, there is a new possibility to re-connect with authentic feelings and expressiveness, both emotionally and energetically. We begin to live in the light of a growing awareness of our true nature, of our essential selves. The body expands its capacity to experience deep pleasure, joy and trust in its natural life.

It is important to reiterate that what makes Pulsation so effective in terms of lasting change is meditation, so I include a full range of Osho's meditations in my groups and trainings. Through witnessing, we learn to take distance from the whirlwind of emotions and to dis-identify from their compulsive mental roots. As the grip of mind relaxes, the body becomes more sensitive and we can perceive subtler flows and pleasurable streaming of energy through the body.

In a discourse in 1986, Osho answered a question about Wilhelm Reich. It impressed me very much when I heard him say that although Reich had never been to the East, nor was ever exposed to the practices of Yoga and Tantra, his writings and his work show that he intuitively knew the secrets of Tantra. Osho added that Reichian-inspired work should, in future, be developed in collaboration with Tantra. He added that perhaps some of his

143

sannyasins who work with Reich's techniques would be able to do this.

I took this challenge to heart. Over the following ten years, I practiced yoga and experimented with Tantric meditations from Osho's *Book of the Secrets*, commentaries on the ancient Indian text called *Vigyan Bhairav Tantra*. I began to develop group structures that combined Reichian breathing and body awareness with the more subtle energy meditations described in Osho's book.

The result is a new branch of Pulsation which I call Tantric Pulsation. Here, I emphasize the importance of vital aliveness in the body, side by side with silence, non-doing and a conscious, restful presence. Learning to slow down and relax with a beloved partner deepens inner sensitivity; and a profound melting can happen, dissolving the boundaries between lovers. The two meet in meditation, and the ordinary sex act can be transformed into a spiritual experience.

Individual Session

Joao is forty-three years old, from South America and this is his tenth session with me. He has a ruddy complexion, his arms and legs look strong and well-muscled, his eyes are bright and there is energy in his structure. His chest is an interesting mix: held high, fully charged, suggesting strength, yet at the same time protecting an underlying vulnerability. In Pulsation's typology, we would say Joao is an anger/pain type.

Knowing this, I can expect a lot of energy to move during our session, but I don't yet know how it will play out. We begin with breathing. He is apparently not yet in touch with a feeling, so we can allow the charge to build and grow. With my touch, I direct Joao's attention and breathing into his belly. I encourage him to deepen his breathing – not faster, necessarily, but always a little deeper.

My right hand is checking the tension level in his diaphragm and belly as the breathing deepens. My left hand is checking tension at the back of his neck and then I place both hands on his shoulders and neck to determine their levels of tension.

As we deepen the breathing into the chest, suddenly everything 'slams shut' and a fit of coughing ensues, a kind of choking down of feeling and a gasping for breath. We let the coughing run its course and I notice Joao's neck, throat and chest are flushed and reddish, unable to contain the energy that is rushing up from his diaphragm.

Coughing is often an indication that deeper energy is starting to rise. We resume breathing in the belly and chest, my hands are there, helping to loosen and open the musculature, and before long a wave of feeling comes.

Joao is pounding the mattress with his balled fists and I ask him to let it pour out through his eyes at me. "I hate you!" he screams spontaneously, gasping for breath, and I see that energy is stuck around his mouth, in his throat. I stick out my tongue as an invitation for him to follow my lead and he does so, making the sound "Bllleeaahhh!"

A gigantic roar escapes through his oesophagus. Hatred pours out through his eyes and the rest of his body – arms and legs – join this expression with kicking and pounding. This goes on for quite some minutes, then gradually subsides.

As Joao settles back into himself, his face softens. After a few deep breaths, his mouth, throat and chest open to allow a flood of tears, helplessness and fear, with heart-breaking sobs that roll through and out of his body. No words are necessary. This is a pure expression of unspeakable sorrow.

Eventually, the sobbing softens. Pain and contraction give way to a new inner space. Laughter of relief, of delight, of something beyond words, comes tumbling out of him.

After the session, Joao talked about several important feelings that came up for him – both anger and sadness – particularly in connection with his mother. At the end of the session there was a deep feeling of reconciliation with her, which he could not rationally explain, even to himself.

This was an unusually powerful, clean and straightforward emotional discharge which happens sometimes in the course of

145

ongoing work, when the time is right. It does not necessarily occur in each session or with every exercise.

With experience, one learns how to cooperate consciously with a feeling, to surrender to waves of emotion and ride with them, without preventing, pushing or forcing anything. This energetic discharge, accompanied by a deep letting go, physically and energetically, serves as a step in the process of disentangling old, conditioned patterns of behaviour, thereby restoring natural energy flow and pleasure to the body.

My Life's Work

Osho Pulsation has turned out to be my life's work, as I suspected it would after commencing my training in 1972 with Charles Kelley in the practice of Radix neo-Reichian methods. There is something thrilling about the process, feeling energy moving inside me, giving space for emotions to be felt and expressed. It has given me tremendous joy.

Working with people individually and in groups over many years I see again and again, the healing process that takes place as people open to layer after layer of disowned feelings, releasing chronic tensions of a lifetime. Through the Pulsation process, over time, many are able to perceive a deeper truth, an essential core of strength, a source of trust and joy that resides deep within all of us, undamaged by time and circumstances, always available as a resource.

CHAPTER EIGHT

Body Reading and Body Types

Moumina

Until I was seventeen, I had no real awareness of my body. I hated sports and lived in books. I was going to study English literature at Oxford until I got arrested for performing in a political street theatre. I found that I preferred being arrested to being at school. I moved to a radical community in London and started participating in dance therapy and yoga. It was a completely new world and it was utterly transforming. Previously, all my sensitivity and passion had lived in words, in language and ideas. Now it changed gear and suffused a far richer realm of sensation, feelings and wordless wisdom.

Fascinated by people and the mystery of things, I remember sitting in a pub in London watching bodies and faces. I was learning from dance therapy that the body told a truth I had never known before. I sensed there was a mysterious hidden layer behind people's personalities and I looked everywhere for clues. The soldiers at the bar were laughing together but their bodies spoke to me of a concealed place inside them. I sensed a weight of numbness silencing their emotions and I felt the presence of many things they couldn't express. I wanted to understand more about this. I was convinced there must be a book that explored this, but didn't manage to find it.

I also remember being in a dance class and thinking 'this is the job I want to do.' Through my body I had found a trust in myself. Ever since then the body has been my faithful doorway. The pull of this discovery drew me to India to learn traditional dance forms, which I saw as both mystical and physical, but after a few months I ended up in Pune, at Osho's ashram.

At that time in Pune, the first generation of workshop leaders from pioneering Western growth centres – Esalen in the USA,

Quaesitor and Community in London – had begun to lead groups at the ashram. I participated in as many workshops and meditations as I could, spending from morning to night in either the Buddha Hall or the group rooms.

Then it was decided to train a new generation of workshop leaders and I was chosen to be one of them. I was only twenty and underwent years of the most wonderful training. This included 'Body Reading' which was exactly what I had been looking for, the mysterious art of reading the hidden life of the body. I was so fascinated about what the body could reveal that whenever a body reading was offered I would always jump up and have my body commented on, standing there in my underwear, waiting hopefully to discover something new about myself.

Beyond Theory and Technique

In Pune, at this time everything was a radical experiment. My teacher-therapists were inspired by Osho to explore beyond borrowed knowledge and to trust uncompromisingly in the spontaneous reality of the present moment, the 'here and now'. As a result, most therapists refused to teach any technique. I participated in a fantastic three-month training in massage where we were taught barely two days of actual massage strokes. The emphasis was on knowing yourself and finding the impulse that came from the intuition of the moment, rather than relying on any outer system. I found this challenging and thrilling, even though, at the same time, it left part of me thinking I didn't know enough and was hungry to learn some theory and techniques.

Only later, when I had a therapy supervisor in England, a sannyasin who was an academic psychologist with a PhD, did that hunger dissolve. I assumed she would teach me theory and technique. But when even she said repeatedly that neither theory nor technique were essential to human healing, part of me relaxed into this non-traditional way of working. It was like a cleansing of the need for borrowed knowledge.

Once I had begun to rely on my own inner sense, then I was at last ready to learn more techniques. Although I went on to learn many methods and theories, looking back, I'm eternally grateful I began in this unique way.

This kind of deep-end-first approach lasted the first few years of my training. It was part of a radical willingness to experiment which was going on in every area of life in Pune at that time. Later therapist trainings included more form and method. Nowadays, the essential thing that I carry from those early days is that sometimes, in one of my own workshops, when things may be difficult, the trust never goes away. It is not a trust in my skills and abilities, but in an empty space that Osho has shown me where therapist and client can meet on the level of being.

Gradually, my own style of working began to take shape. I spent many years in training sitting next to therapists who used their psychological insight as an entry to understanding the client. I was impressed they could pick up a conditioning pattern from the words someone spoke and then reflect it back. I used to feel inadequate, because the content of a client's words didn't speak to me in that way. Then I realized it was the client's body that spoke to me. Later, I was trained in Bio-Energetics, which included learning Body Types. Finally, this work gave a frame to my interest in body language and body reading.

When I was twenty-four, I was assisting and co-leading a Bio-Energetics training at Medina, a big therapy and meditation centre in England. I was leading the 'Body Reading' part, because that was what I loved. I vividly remember explaining the body reading for one particular Body Type, when two guys recognized themselves as this type and stood up for a reading. Physically, they were strikingly similar, like twins. Their bodies were like replicas of each other, although one was tall and the other was short.

But something else struck me: one was new to personal growth work, his eyes were dead-looking and far away, his body dissociated, whereas the other had been meditating a while; he was 'inhabiting' his body and his eyes were full of warmth and vitality.

149

I understood something new: bodies take a certain shape as a defence against childhood wounds. When natural impulses have been stopped, you can see the traces of that interruption in the body. This is true for all of us, but we are not doomed to a life sentence, we are not prisoners of our own history. A meditator develops the capacity to follow the impulses that have been frozen and to notice, understand and reintegrate those split-off parts that have been rejected.

When I work with Body Types now, I see that the body, when surrounded by an atmosphere of meditation and acceptance, can begin to unwind, trusting impulses that would once have been rejected. Then it can be seen that these impulses can be a precious resource.

What Are Body Types?

Strong emotions like sadness, joy, anger and terror result in physical movements of the body. If a small child has an intense emotion which he is not allowed to express and release in a natural way – such as crying, laughing or fighting – then the impulse is locked up inside the body and results in a longstanding muscular tension. Children are so plastic and unformed that these tensions actually shape the growing body with permanent effect, just as our experience in the first four years shapes our main ego defences and psychological patterns.

Depending at which time in childhood the strong trauma is experienced, the ego, nervous system and body muscles adopt a certain shape in order to defend against the threat. The results can be seen in five major categories of body shapes, each with its own unconscious defence system. These are the Body Types. Each has a characteristic appearance (sometimes obvious and sometimes not so easy to detect) with accompanying characteristic emotions and life patterns. They generate a whole range of personalities, from the character who is withdrawn, dissociated from the body and not participating in life, to the one who is very outgoing but stuck in endless effort and seeking approval.

The basic blueprint comes from Wilhelm Reich, the pioneering Austrian psychotherapist. He combined his revolutionary discoveries about body energy with the psychological vision of his teacher, Sigmund Freud. He learned how neuroses, created by repression early in life, show in the body. His approach to treatment combined working with body energy and psychology. The five Body Types that Reich's student, Alexander Lowen, formulated. are based on those understandings. Looking at a client's body structure and energy, they identify the particular life situations or traumas experienced in the formative years.

I will mention briefly each Body Type:

• Schizoid. In terms of life history, the Schizoid type is the earliest to be formed. It is based on the feeling of not being welcomed by life or your family, a feeling of being under threat. It doesn't feel safe to enter fully into the physical body. As a result, the person may feel like an outsider, an alien, not able to fully participate in life. The body tends to be thin and contracted. These people have a highly developed sensitivity and visionary qualities which are a great resource when they find a home in their own bodies.

• Oral. The second type to be formed is based on the experience of feeling abandoned during your vulnerable early years. The body is also often thin, but with a slumped quality and childlike look. This person has difficulty recognising their own needs or relying on their own strength. Their inner self-image is of someone weak and helpless and they see life as unfair. They have a capacity to see and understand with great clarity, which is a big resource once they discover their body's ability to take action.

• Psychopath. The third type is to do with distortions around the experience of power. This person has learnt that it's not safe to be vulnerable or in need, and expects to be used or exploited by others. To defend against this they control and seduce others to need them. The body has a larger and more dominant upper half, or, alternatively, seems supple & flowing with tension in the core. They are courageous, generous and perceptive, and these qualities are freed as they begin to know and accept their own vulnerability.

151

- Masochist. The fourth type is when expansive energy and freedom has been inhibited and suppressed. These people have a deep anxiety about exposure and humiliation. Their whole physical structure is built up to bind any expressive impulse that would lead to them being noticed. Guilt and shame stifles their freedom, and their inner sense is that if they express themselves they will hurt someone else. The body tends to be short and thick. They have an inexhaustible creative energy which is released when they learn to trust themselves.

- Rigid. The fifth type has to do with sexuality, love and achievement. This person feels valued only for what they can perform and achieve. They find it very hard to complete something and then rest. They are driven to keep active without any gap. The body is upright and muscled. In relationship, it is difficult for heart and sex to connect. Once they learn to trust in non-doing and letting go, their loving qualities and energetic aliveness are discovered as a great resource.

As you can see, these names are not very flattering. In fact, these labels seem to turn us all into pathological cases, suffering from dire mental diseases. Lowen emphasized that he was not classifying people but only the defensive positions of the body. Nevertheless, many therapists working with these types today tend to use less devastating labels so as not to frighten or offend their clients. Personally, I do both. I use the original names so that people can read what Lowen has said about them and also use less intimidating labels, such as those created by Ron Kurtz:

- Schizoid becomes the 'sensitive/withdrawn' type.

- Oral becomes 'dependent/endearing' or, when there is a compensatory layer, 'self-reliant'.

- Psychopath becomes 'deceptive', tough-generous' and 'charming-manipulative'.

- Masochist becomes 'burdened/enduring'.

- Rigid becomes 'industrious/over-focused' and 'clinging-expressive'.

On the personality level everyone is a combination of several structures and yet is possible to find one, or maybe two, that are most active in us. What I have described so far is not a method but information, a framework of classification to use when working with people. But one piece of the recipe is missing.

If Body Types is a diagnosis of our restrictive defences and self-limiting psychological patterns, then what is the cure? The original therapy was Bio-Energetics, which Lowen developed in partnership with this system of classification. My own approach is a little different. I use Body Types for diagnosis, but I don't use traditional Bio-Energetics as the cure.

The Heart of Everything

As already mentioned, Alexander Lowen was the progenitor of the Body Types, but even though he was a great psychotherapist he was not a meditator. For me, meditation is at the heart of everything, not psychology. So I follow a broad overall pattern which is centred on meditation as the foundation of healing. It goes like this:

I begin by resting into an accepting presence inside me. Then I start feeling for a quality of presence, or 'beingness' in the person with whom I am working. What I am searching for is a specific part of the client's body where 'beingness' is most available. I know I have found it when my own feeling of inner relaxation deepens. This is the resource, the anchor, the foundation for the work we will do.

Next, I look for a body energy that is 'asking' to move or to be seen. It may feel like a quality of aliveness, or movement, which is on the verge of expression by some part of the body. I then respond to this in a supportive way. I may notice a number of emotions or energies, but I leave the ones that don't 'ask' – those that wish to remain hidden, or are not yet available.

I am open to the possibility that, at the right time, the person may experience the denied parts inside them. They may re-live the emotions and body movements that have been rejected. But there is a helpful and an unhelpful way to do this. If someone goes into these places unprepared, they are likely to feel overwhelmed, confused, lost and then contract and be unable to explore further. Re-living is helpful only when the client experiences enough presence and aliveness in the body to handle the situation.

When there is such presence, internally there is a sense that:

(a) I'm okay.

(b) There is a home/viewpoint that creates enough distance to know "This hurt is not all that I am."

(c) It's safe to be in the body.

(d) There is enough trust to feel the painful bits.

When these conditions are met, the pushed-away denied feelings can be allowed to re-inhabit the body. Typically, there will be spontaneous movements and sounds as the person lets go of the denial. They may be loud and cathartic, or it may be a subtle experience – the body's muscles, tissues and nerves can allow impulses without necessarily needing to act them out. Either way, the rejected part is now finding a home for itself in the body once again. The previously trapped energies are out of the grip of the fixed personality and once more become part of the flow of life.

Only now can they evolve and change, because the person is acting spontaneously and is no longer trapped in his/her personality structure. Osho calls this a moment of 'No Mind'. In this state, there is a sense of aliveness and a consciousness that is aware of what is happening, but there is nobody "doing" anything. What I understand Osho to propose is the possibility that all life can be lived in this way. Psychology does not have this vision.

Body Reading

I have evolved a particular way to teach the Body Types. I explain the theory of each type and follow this up with exercises that enable participants to access the memory of key moments in their childhood development. I offer guided body meditations to re-experience the learning that was blocked at each stage:

for example, to trust your own spontaneous way of moving (Masochist), or to let go of effort and be able to receive (Rigid).

Body reading is a key part of the process. Originally, the term 'Body Reading' was used in Rolfing and Postural Integration, studying the structure and shape of the body to check its alignment and bring it into a state of balance.

After volunteering for many Body Readings, all those years ago, my enthusiasm waned. I had heard a number of times where the 'holding' was in my body, or that my face was 'mask-like', and while this was very revealing I didn't know what to do with the information. Even though the reading was a tool for training therapists, I felt it could be also be a more meaningful experience for the model. I felt that there must be more steps to this process.

But what could those steps be? When, as a therapist, I practised doing readings myself, I noticed that a body's energies often begin to shift under my eyes, just from the simple act of being given sensitive attention. Movements or feelings would reveal themselves and come alive as I supported them. I found it was possible to see and connect with incomplete or interrupted events from a clients' past, enabling them to find a fresh, healthy response. I then worked on integrating body reading into a session that allowed room for these new elements. In other words, I wanted the session to be a more useful experience to the model, as well as to any trainees I might be coaching in Body Reading.

In this way Body Reading evolved into a specific process which I do in the context of a training. Its purpose is to help the participants develop their own intuition. At the same time, the recipient has an experiential learning that is much wider than just being given information.

I invite a volunteer. The person stands at the front of the class, wearing shorts and a T-shirt. This is an exposed position for the volunteer, so I spend a considerable time guiding the group in how to look at a person lovingly and non-judgmentally, so the 'client' can feel safe. Mental analysis is intrinsically judgmental and dismissive of a person, whereas observations from the heart, even if confronting, will be felt as nourishing.

In our daily lives, meeting all kinds of people, we develop a certain habit of reading character from face and voice, using these skills in situations such as, for example, "Can I do business with this person? Can I trust him?" But we tend to view the face as the whole person, whereas in reality it is our bodies that reveal our basic attitudes. Their shape and proportion tell the hidden stories by which we unconsciously live our lives.

When you shift from the face to look at the whole body, you see things which are not part of the image a person is presenting to the world, things they unconsciously keep hidden. So, in training we ask: seeing the face as only one part of the body, does the face project one impression while the rest of the body conveys another? Does the face have a concealed expression, different from how this person thinks about himself? For example, sometimes a person thinks of himself as having no problems, whereas his body may reveal a hidden expression of deep sadness.

Aspects of the whole body we may notice in training include symmetry from left to right, whether the top and bottom of the body are equally developed, if the parts of the body fit together, or whether some parts seem to belong to a different person. We may also notice skin colour, the total quantity of energy in the body, the areas that seem energized while others seem depleted. We may ask: is there a sense of implicit movement, or a quality of waiting and enduring? Does this body seem at ease in its surroundings? Is it trying to rise above, or is it being crushed down by its surroundings? Does the body have a free way to move forward, or is it being held back? Do different parts of the body give the impression of going in different directions?

Developing Intuition

The first step in developing intuition is to realize obvious things, which are often examples of universal patterns. For example, the bodies of people who habitually act in a helpless manner are often thin and reed-like. From here, we begin to refine intuition according to people's gifts. Participants learn they have different senses to perceive what the body is saying.

For instance, some people can observe very precise visual details, like the way an ankle is turning. Others receive information through their kinesthetic sense, so what they are perceiving is reflected as a physical sensation in their own bodies. They may pick up emotional qualities like moods or atmospheres. Someone might see a picture that describes a particular energy, or their attention is drawn for no obvious reason to a certain part of the body. As the picture builds, people acquire more insights and understandings, and in this way the body starts to tell its story.

In life, we might look at someone's face to see if they are available or closed. With a little practice, you can also do this with, for example, the legs. Childhood can be described in terms of well-known stages of ego development, but you could instead describe it entirely in terms of the development of the legs, as they grow from soft, pliant limbs to powerful motors of locomotion for dancing and climbing. Everyone is used to judging character from the face, but with practice we can evaluate the same character from the legs.

As an illustration, let's take the Oral Body Type. Very often, someone of this Body Type has started to walk before their muscles are strong enough, or developed enough, to support them. Feeling a lack of support from their mother, they decide to do things on their own and walk too early. As the legs are not strong enough and the arches of the feet are not yet developed, the child needs to lock their knees and strain their inner leg muscles to walk.

This interferes with the development of those inner leg muscles, which have an important function. These are part of the 'core' muscles, which provide our inner sense of physical support and as a result this person will have no underlying sense of self-reliance. The original external situation – lack of support from mother – has been converted into muscle strain and underdevelopment so that, effectively, the Oral type is still carrying around that early sense of lack of love.

157

This can be seen in the physical structure of the legs: the feet will be flat, the knees locked, the legs probably pale and spindly, drawing up and away from the ground rather than coming down to meet the ground with security. As intuition becomes more developed, one may sense the emotional tone of the legs: for example, they may look lonely, or abandoned.

Let's look at some examples of body readings. To understand these, you need to realize it's not a static process of observation. You may have had your body looked at judgmentally, in a medical examination, for example, or you may have had it looked at lovingly, by a lover. Most probably, you have never had it looked at lovingly by a group.

There is a unique dynamic that happens, a feedback loop between the person being observed and the group members. As the person listens to the tentative and partial observations people make, the truth in the body becomes increasingly manifest.

So, as you read these examples, bear in mind it is something alive that has been reduced to a one-dimensional description.

Sample Body Reading: Psychopath

For each Body Reading, I take one Body Type. I don't tell people which type they are, I invite volunteers. During a reading I may see things from the childhood, I may see things from an individual's past lives, I may see a family constellation around the person, I may sense the male and female energies inside him or her. All this, I may use to accompany the body on a journey to reach a healthy landing spot.

Utsav was a curious and intelligent man, very engaged in the group and eager to learn. He stood up as he recognized himself as the Psychopath Body Type.

The group could see that his body was pulled up; in proportion, the shoulders were broader than the lower body, giving a first impression of power, but with underlying insecurity. Although he was standing still, there was no feeling of restfulness. Rather, it seemed his mind and senses were very active behind a semblance

158

of inaction. This gave the impression he was calculating where a threat might come from and that he would move fast and unpredictably to deal with it, to escape from it, or to out-trick it. All this is typical of the Psychopath Body Type.

Utsav readily acknowledged this vigilance as a constant background theme in his life. In fact, he was so busy watching us and evaluating what was going on that people started feeling insecure and were unable to see as clearly as they had with other Body Readings. Again, it is typical of this body type to adopt a checking-out attitude and superior stance. This aims, usually with success, to disable any perception that could sense the underlying insecurity. It also serves to quell any expression from others which could be threatening.

One thing a body may show is a snapshot of a moment in time when something was stopped in childhood. When this comes to the surface we can bring it into conscious awareness. In Utsav's case it was when we reached his face that we saw something he doesn't usually show. It looked like the face of a small child who is watching a scene in front of him and who is desperately trying to find a solution. As this is a childhood scene it is going to be about the family, and in this case I invited Utsav to choose workshop members to represent his mother and father and place them in the room to complete the picture, in a mini-family constellation.

It was a scene of silent conflict. We could see from the mother's body posture, facing Utsav and turned away from her husband, that Utsav was absorbed in her energy-field and his father was excluded. Her words were, "I want to take care of my son," but the words didn't ring true.

Utsav told us his father was useless and neglected his family, but when he said this it sounded hollow, like a second-hand, borrowed opinion – in fact his mother's, which he had taken on as his own. In the constellation, mother and father faced each other and addressed each other, dealing with what was unexpressed between them. As a result, the father took his rightful place in the constellation.

159

As he watched this scene, Utsav experienced a deep relief and his sense of constant vigilance relaxed. He found he was able to feel much more solid support in his own legs, which before had been shaky, and a more healthy balance of male-female energy inside himself.

Interpreting Information

This is a Body Reading I did together with Agni, another body therapist, who was co-leading the training with me. It may be that when you read this, you will wonder where we get the information from. It might look esoteric. All I can say is that, when we are talking to the body, the pictures that come to describe sensations and energies are not the same as the language of the mind. The body's language is different. Also, the body's language varies from person to person, so we get very different symbols from different people.

On the other hand, for centuries, people have been studying the physical, cellular experience you meet when you start enquiring inside. All these different schools of enquiry have symbols that describe states of the body. Some have studied this in great depth and have detailed descriptions. For instance the Chinese use the five elements, wood, fire, earth, metal and water, while the yogis in India have the *chakras*, and the Sufis use the *lataifs*. These descriptions may sound esoteric at first, but once you go into the experience they have a concrete felt meaning. The language we use is a simpler, freelance version of these traditional descriptions.

Our volunteer this time was Jeanette, a dance therapist from Canada. She told us that although she felt strong and confident in herself, she didn't understand why she felt so much mistrust of other people. In this case, the whole group was present, giving her loving attention, but the session was mostly an interaction between the two therapists and Jeanette.

As she stood in front of us, Jeanette told us she was experiencing her left side as flowing – she pictured it as a paradise garden. From that side came her dance skills, her creativity and her sensuality.

It was a positive resource. Through it she experienced satisfaction and happiness. She sensed her hands as having a capacity to form and create material objects. Her left hip had a dancing, flowing, bubbling energy. We noticed, however, that the contact between her left foot and the floor was almost too grounded, hinting at some rigidity and control. Although, according to Jeanette, this side was a positive resource, we were also receiving a sense of strong attachment to these dancing, flowing qualities, maybe to the exclusion of something else.

While the left side was being explored, the right leg seemed to get more and more twisted and stiff. A look of deadness began to appear in Jeanette's chest, her right arm and right eye. She said that on her right side she felt very cold. She didn't like to be made aware of this. She felt it disturbed her flow. She disliked the qualities she found in her right side and wanted to shake them off. We noticed a twist in her pelvis, the right side of her pelvis was tilted up and back, as if she was corkscrewing up and leaving the right side of her body.

We asked her to describe further how she experienced her right side. She had a vivid picture of a brittle, empty room where no-one has ever been. It was suffused with a horrible industrial, artificial, white light. Jeanette wanted to change it, make it nicer. We had an intuition that there was nothing wrong with this white light, which she located in her upper body, but rather that its real home was in the pelvis and it needed to descend there. So we invited her to bring her awareness to her sacrum.

When she began to let this white, empty, dryness settle in her sacrum and genitals something began to visibly relax in her. We accompanied her while she stayed with this alien, brittle quality. It was still difficult to accept and felt like death to her. She wanted to push it out of her body. It made her feel as if she couldn't survive and she kept wanting to get away from it. For a moment, her left hip pushed the other side away, as if it wanted to take over. The desire of her female side for aliveness seemed to be trying to gain the upper hand. But, as we helped her to acknowledge the part

161

of her that felt so threatened, the scary quality began to descend more into her pelvis.

Slowly the right side of her pelvis began to change, to become alive, not like the left side, but softer and more balanced, spreading also into her legs. She discovered gentleness there; pushiness and suspiciousness relaxed. A rebalancing took place in her body. Her pelvis untwisted and there was less quality of effort in the female side. There was a real grounding through both feet. Her right side now participated in movement so there was a fuller flow. There was some jerking in her body as the changes settled in. Her eyes softened and looking out she was amazed to find she didn't feel threatened by people. She could trust, no longer having to protect herself, or be special. It brought simplicity.

Later she told us she had realized for the first time how much her behaviour is governed by fear. She had always seen herself as strong; now she realized how much she was afraid of life and death. Before the Body Reading she had never allowed fear to be in her body and was astounded by the inner safety and trust that she experienced when she did.

Loving Your Body

My work is about loving the body in a very radical way, a way I learned experientially while being with Osho. It is based on a total acceptance of the body, including the whole spectrum of emotions, outgoing and ingoing, that reside there. It respects the body's instinctual authenticity, its capacity to bring you into the moment and also to take you into your unconscious where things have become hidden. Even when the mind gets lost in pain and worry, the body remains spontaneous, impulsive and alive. We don't need to struggle to change ourselves; sometimes we just need to discover the impulses of aliveness already present.

Nowadays, people are desperately trying to make their bodies into attractive commodities by going to the gym and doing yoga. Of course, for some people, doing exercise could be a first step in making contact with their body, in taking care of it, but the attitude to improve and push towards some physical ideal of health and beauty is strong in Western countries. It infects and drives exercise. Bodies are allergic to interference from the mind and at some point resist or rebel. I'm not surprised that many sportspeople end up taking performance-enhancing drugs to drive their bodies further than they naturally want to go.

In my experience, it is only when you can feel your body from the inside that it's possible to love it. I remember one woman in a group who was very overweight. She told us how much she was trying to love and accept her body, looking in the mirror and telling herself she was beautiful. She had the best intentions but it wasn't working. Through working with breath and body awareness she discovered a huge pain inside her and allowed this to be felt. For the first time, she experienced her body as vibrant and light, together with the understanding that all her weight was to cover how intensely vulnerable she felt on the inside.

In the early years in Pune, we had the opportunity to explore all our impulses and bring them to life through our bodies. We learned to know our bodies, with their many unknown territories, from the inside. We would go crazy in Dynamic Meditation, we would merge with a man or a woman in a hug, we would dance with abandon, laugh, cry, beat pillows in rage, clean a room with totality, or rest in silence. Through all this, a trust in the body developed and it became possible to stay present and aware with difficult places inside. Living in that atmosphere of allowance taught us not to cut off our emotions and impulses, but rather to discover a love for the body in its entirety.

I no longer live or work in that kind of wild setting, yet my trust in the body has stayed with me. I no longer feel the need to live out every impulse – it's not the end, the goal. Something more is needed. The fear of what is lurking inside has lost its grip and more trust is available to me now, when I work with people.

163

Spontaneity Plus Awareness

What is needed together with reclaiming the body's spontaneity? Some mystical paths invite you to surrender your body so that it can be moved by the life force... the method named *Latihan* is an example of this. Other methods, like *Vipassana*, emphasise the core quality of meditation, witnessing with detachment any sensations arising in the body as you sit motionless, focusing on the movement of your breathing.

I learnt from Osho that freeing the body can work in partnership with witnessing, and they can even grow out of each other.

Latihan is a good method ... Its function is to bring you into a state where you surrender yourself totally to existence and let your body energy move, not according to your mind but according to the universal spirit. Your bodily energy falls in tune with the universal energy and things start happening in your body: you may start dancing, you may start whirling, your hands may start moving, your legs may start moving ...

And if you add one thing more ... That's why I had to create Dynamic Meditation – it is latihan plus something more, because in latihan you are lost completely. I want you to remain a witness. Don't be a doer. Don't push any action, don't force anything, don't prevent anything ...

You will be surprised that our bodies also collect tension: for example, you wanted to hit someone and you did not hit him ... Your mind wanted to hit the person, your hand was ready to hit the person, but your mind is always in a split. You stopped, for any reason: nonviolence, fear, he is your superior, he is your boss. But what will happen to the tension?

Your hand was ready; the energy cannot go back. There is no system for any energy that has become ready to be expressed to go back to its original source. It will remain in your wrist, it will remain in your fingers, it will remain in your hand. This kind of energy accumulates in different parts of your body – that's why latihan works. In latihan this kind of energy starts moving and you may start hitting an enemy who is not there.

But the witness is absolutely needed so that your body is relieved of all the collecting tensions and you will feel fresh, a beautiful feeling of well-being. ~ Osho[1]

How We Lose Contact

When you feel under threat, your consciousness separates itself from your body. The threat may be in the past, or in the present, you may feel it consciously, or it may operate from your unconscious. All rejected experiences take you out of contact with the body and its capacity to be in the moment – it is your way to survive – and where the trauma has been strong you may be chronically disconnected. But even people who are more physically grounded rarely experience their body from the inside, as they tend to override it with mental programs. Instead of being in the body, they are in their past, in their fantasies, in their dreams and desires. Everywhere, but in the moment.

Those Body Types where the trauma has been earlier and stronger, such as the Schizoid, are more persistently disconnected and often divorced from their physical senses. The type that experienced trauma later, the Rigid, has body connection and will probably enjoy being active, doing sport and exercise, dancing, running. They are able to use the body to achieve things, feel pleasure and have full physical sensations. Yet, although there may be plenty of sensation, their body is being driven by a conditioned program and a whole aspect of its nature is excluded. In this case, experiences such as being receptive and letting go are typically bypassed.

When we do a Body Reading for Rigid types, one thing I always notice is that they are looking straight ahead, their body is primed and ready to 'go there'. It is full of energy, it is capable and it is programmed to reach the goal. Their gaze doesn't move around, or to the sides, or get cast downwards. They are not embarking on a path that might include unknown turns. It is a railway track traveling towards a fixed destination. So for people of this Body

Type to experience receiving and letting go, to trust, to wait in the unknown, is very challenging because it isn't included in their conditioning.

This attitude is very much supported by our present day society, because ambitious, go-ahead people are needed and rewarded. We are expected to get good results, be corporate, be efficient, push ahead, do everything right. The attitude is that the body will serve us, rather than trusting the body to do what it wants, moment by moment.

So if you find yourself lost in your mind, or find you are using your body as a servant, it will be helpful to inquire how an understanding of Body Types will help you reconnect with your body.

Reconnecting Through the Body

Through Body Types and Body Reading we can see which experiences the body has shaped itself to avoid. This is a general truth. We are all going around in fear of certain experiences. Each Body type represents a particular emotional wound. These can be expressed in simple terms:

Schizoid: I am not wanted. There is no safety.

Oral: My needs are not seen and not met. There is not enough for me.

Psychopath: When I am helpless, there is no love. I will be used and betrayed.

Masochist: When/If I act spontaneously I will be punished and isolated.

Rigid: I am loved for what I do not for who I am.

Body Types give you a map that can show you where there is mistrust and holding, where the personality has built a 'No' to protect you from life. It reveals the 'No' and uncovers the 'Yes' that is concealed behind it. For this, meditation is essential. It provides the experience of a 'Yes' that can replace the defensive pattern.

Let's take a common painful experience, for instance rejection, which is fundamental to the Oral Body Type. Let's see how being unconscious of this wound weakens our body. Then let's see how awareness and acceptance enriches us:

First of all, we have the wound of rejection that has stayed incomplete inside us because it wasn't fully felt. So it hovers in our unconscious. This makes us oversensitive to external events because we are constantly scanning for signs of rejection. Our sensitivity is directed away from our own body. We are so highly tuned to anything that could be a rejection that it's like being without a skin. So we are experiencing rejection and at the same time there is a 'No' to it; we don't want to feel it, it is too painful. However our radio station is so highly tuned that we pick it up a lot, certainly more than someone who doesn't have it as their main issue.

The first step is to recognize rejection and feel the body sensations that belong to it. Usually, we are busy with how to stop the discomfort, how to deal with people so that, in the first place, we don't have this painful experience. This takes a lot of energy. Our sensitivity is centred outside us, the antennae are turned outwards. If we begin to feel rejection in the body it probably has some emotions attached to it as well. To experience sensations or feel emotions changes the vibration; it brings the experience back into the body where we can be present with it, with acceptance. From here, we can begin to discover what we actually need in the moment.

If we are caught in a struggle with the denied experience it disconnects us from the body and we are stuck in recycling the old wound. When we are in the moment, here and now, something new is possible. Maybe there is an impulse inside. We may want to touch someone, or lie down on the floor, curled up, hugging a cushion. Maybe we will simply feel full in ourselves – anything might happen.

Working with People

I mostly teach the Body Types as a tool for people who work with people. It is a valuable instrument they can integrate into their own approach. They may have an individual practice as a counsellor or massage therapist. They may work in a social setting, as a social worker, or school teacher, or a business setting, as a coach or consultant.

I once supervised a business consultant, Ross, who had learned Body Types from me. He had been called to an organization where the bosses were having trouble with Hans, the senior manager of a subsidiary. They complained that Hans saw his area as his fiefdom where he could do what he wanted. He was a rogue performer, determined to do things his own way. He ignored instructions given to him and had a history of abusing his authority, such as sacking people on the spot in a dictatorial manner. He would turn against anybody who challenged his authority. Even the bosses were afraid of him.

In appearance, Hans had a solid upper body with broad shoulders, spindly legs, a red face and penetrative eyes. It was hard for Hans to trust people, but he'd felt understood by Ross in a previous session and had requested ongoing coaching with him.

We diagnosed Hans as the Psychopath Body Type. I remembered the words of Barbara Brennan in one of her books: "People who use the psychopathic character defence have probably experienced many lifetimes as warriors, standing up and fighting for a great cause. The cause made them good and the enemy bad ... They are still good at winning. Running a country requires leadership of a different kind. It requires teamwork and cooperation, where everyone is good and a lot of people are right, not just the leader. So people with a psychopathic structure never made it across the boundary from warrior to King or Queen. Psychopathic characters are still warriors trying to win a war that no longer exists. As a result, deep inside they don't trust anyone anymore. Everyone is ultimately their enemy, even their closest associates. They see life as a battleground."

Ross liked this image and felt it could be useful for Hans. He talked to him about the qualities of the warrior and Hans recognized himself. He said his attitude was, "You are either for me or against me. If you cross me you are finished." However he recognized there was a need for change, as he was becoming ill. The attitude that he must control those around him in order to survive no longer served him.

Together, Ross and Hans looked at how he might shift from warrior to king. As the warrior was his default position, Hans felt anxious that, if he dismantled it, nothing would be left. So they explored how, rather than dismantling the warrior, he could come to realize that he was not on a battlefield. He learned to watch his own behaviour so he could recognize when he was in warrior mode and when in king mode. He experimented, shifting his focus to 'catching someone doing something right'. Ross did some simple meditations with him so he could start to get an awareness of his body. They explored ways to feel good, other than winning fights, such as recognizing the value of others in the team, helping them, trusting them.

The fact that Hans trusted Ross enough to have sessions with him was a huge step. He opened to the possibility that there was another way of operating other than fighting to win. This shift of attitude was a huge relief to him and of course to everyone who worked with him.

Although Ross was not in a position to do a deep therapy with Hans, he found Body Types a very useful tool to help Hans gain some distance from his behaviour and get a taste of meditation.

Body Types for the Meditator

This work can be important for a meditator because it gives an indication of which parts of our experience are conditioned and which are free.

Many people have told me that it deeply relaxes them to

understand their Body Type. In the shape of their body, they can see the whole pattern and shape of their life. They see how much of their behaviour is related to their Body Type and can take a step back as they witness those mechanisms at work. They can stop bullying themselves by constantly condemning their negative personality traits. Instead of blaming themselves, when limiting patterns keep repeating in life, they can have compassion. Now they see from where those patterns originate. It makes sense, not just on a purely mental level. Awareness expands and consciousness is strengthened.

The purpose is to free our essence, not to try and cure our conditioned behaviour. We come to the point where we can see the program is not us, rather trying to fix it. Psychology may aim for improvement, but we are working with acceptance, which dissolves the attitude of mistrust and the holding pattern it creates.

In Lowen's work, the therapist attempts to free his client from neuroses. In Radix therapy and Neo-Reichian work, the therapist helps bio-energy flow more freely through the body. We are doing both: becoming aware of the conditioning so we can dis-identify from it while at the same time supporting the free flow of life-energy. With Osho we are not focussed solely on understanding that we are 'not this', but we also experience and celebrate the freeing of body energy that comes when we live in presence.

As in the Enneagram system of identifying personality types, Body Types can indicate how to recover lost parts of our essence. Each of the five types has a 'dark' aspect – the pain and defence which it represents. But it also has a 'bright' aspect, the particular quality – such as trust or creativity – which is a hidden treasure, concealed behind the defence. By letting the 'dark' or traumatized aspect be seen in a loving setting, the bright side can begin to be expressed.

A unique aspect of Osho therapy is that it is impossible to believe that one technique is better than all other techniques. When therapies are not connected to Osho, a message seems to come across that, "This is the best technique and all others are at best ineffective and at worst dangerous." After the training we experienced in Pune, where we were exposed to such a rich variety of methods, it is impossible to believe such exclusive attitudes.

At the same time, each therapist travels deep with the methods they have chosen and is passionately inspired by them. For example, I'm aware that Body Types is just one expression of a vast range of therapy, but it is this particular expression that inspires my creativity. It has given me a frame for all the different skills I've learned, all the different methods to which I've been exposed. That's why I do it.

Guided Meditation: Sensory Awareness

As you sit here, with this book in front of you, take some moments to sense your body, visiting your body without changing anything.

Your breathing can be your companion. There might be some inner movement of breath or energies. Or, there might be a soft outer movement like the rise and fall of the breath.

There could be a bigger movement in a muscle, a hand, a leg, a shifting of position. You can be present with the body no matter what it does.

There is always something to watch, an entry way to meditation.

Allow any small movements that are happening. If your fingers want to move and you allow them, there is more room for watching.

You can forget all efforts to keep a rigid body position and instead accompany this stream of life wherever it wants to go.

As they say in Zen anecdotes, "The Buddha has no fixed postures."

CHAPTER NINE

Twice Born:
Childhood Deconditioning

Premartha and Svarup

Primal, Rock Music and Meditation

Primal Therapy was born at the same time as Rock Bands, in the early Seventies. Both phenomena responded to the same need: the urge of the post war generation to express and release their pent up energy and rebelliousness, curbed in their early childhood by their hard-working and regimented parents.

The youth that populated Rock Concerts was no longer content with following in their small-minded elders' footsteps. Likewise, the people who sought Primal Therapy treatment would no longer function and obey as expected by their parents. They both needed screaming and a lot of emotional release.

But the collective search for a new way of living did not stop with that initial rebellion. After a while, burning bridges with the past became for many youths as repetitive and uncreative as their parents' way of life. At that point, some of them heard the call of spirituality as the best way to search for inner truth and peace.

It was the time of the meeting of East and West. Osho was the first Eastern mystic to introduce new methods that bridged the differences between these two worlds. He understood that to help Westerners achieve true inner silence, methods were needed to erase the voices of the past that were cluttering our busy minds.

For the first time in history, therapy had been given a place in the spiritual field. Osho Primal became a tool used to clean the unconscious mind from the voices of the past and release old tensions in the body before sitting silently in meditation.

Twice Born

Things have changed since the Seventies. Although Rock still occupies a place of honour on the musical Olympus, there are many others sounds that reflect the global spirit of this time.

In the same way, Primal work has changed. Screaming and rebelling are still part of it, but not the only components.

Unexpressed anger is no longer the only obstacle to inner peace. A new and powerful factor has taken centre-stage in our inner struggle: stress.

Stress, the big enemy of the new millennium, requires subtler therapeutic methods. We all get stressed trying to keep up with our fast moving world, and we all end up neglecting our needs and ourselves.

As a consequence, our inner child, who exists inside us as a living emotional reality, again feels wounded and abandoned, and withdraws its energy. We can function, but we cannot really feel. In this state of disconnection from our feelings, meditation cannot go as deep.

To bring back that child into our life, we need time and space to reach it at its frozen core. Pushing will not help.

We first need to contact that child, and find out how we can start nourishing it again. The result is always stunning: once it is acknowledged and embraced, the child in us has a bountiful supply of unused energy and gifts to give back into our adult lives.

Today, Primal as we offer it is for anyone who needs new inspiration and energy. It's for those who want to make peace with the past and move on. It's a rebirth, a door into meditation and inner peace.

This is why we like to call our work Twice Born – Primal-Childhood Deconditioning. This name reflects both the therapy work needed to find out what is conditioned and non-essential in us, and the spaces of meditation where we can individually reconnect with what is natural and essential in us.

It can be done either in a Primal group, or individually through a series of ten Childhood Deconditioning sessions. The group format provides a strong bonding and support system amongst the participants, and the series of sessions offers a more specific insight in one's individual conditioning.

Meeting the Child

In our work we use many techniques involving the body, heart and mind of the participants. But the key to the whole process is one simple technique: learning to consciously shift perspective, being able to experience the same situation from different angles, as a child and as an adult. This is what we will focus on as the golden thread throughout the process.

The first step on the way of the Twice Born process is to contact the child in us through a guided regression journey.

Contacting is more than just remembering how we were as children. It means literally meeting the child as a living emotional reality inside us. It means to see, feel and interact with it.

When we journey as adults back into the past, it's always surprising to discover how the child is always there and ready to meet us, waiting for us adults to acknowledge its existence and take care of it.

Try this simple technique. It will give you a taste of what we are describing:

Sit comfortably with eyes closed, but alert enough to stay present. Have a soft pillow or your favourite teddy bear at hand. Do not be misled by the idea that you have to, 'see' something. Some of us have visual memories, others feel things through the body, and again others simply sense something on a subtle level. Be open for whatever wants to surface.

Remember a time as an adult when you felt caring and loving. Perhaps a time when you were caring for a friend, for a plant, or an animal. Imagine that you can see this time, and the gentle expression of caring and loving it brings, as a picture in front of your eyes at a distance of about three feet.

Allow your forehead to relax, and draw the energy of loving and caring into the place between your eyes. Experience it as an infinite source of loving energy flowing to this place, and from there, flooding through your whole body.

Now visualize or feel the child you, at any age between birth and ten years of age. Focus on its innocence, the sensitivity of its inner world, and also on its pain. Allow your loving energy to flow from the adult-you toward the child-you, reaching all the places inside the child where it got wounded, to bring love and care there. Look at that child through the eyes of compassion, and watch how it responds.

Meeting the child in this way is always moving. It also makes us aware that we are now adults, who can stand up for that child and protect it when needed.

As adults, it's easier to feel our power and readiness to face the unresolved past. This in itself can be a major discovery, a great resource of strength and commitment to one's own life.

For some of us, this meeting is the first difficulty to overcome. There is a part in everyone who would like to forget about the child's helplessness and defeat, its lost gifts and disappointments. We might not see or sense the child clearly because of our own rejection of its pain. It's good to be aware of this tendency: it probably carried us through and allowed us to survive, but it simply won't work in the long run. Part of our energy will remain unused and locked.

Becoming the Child

That's why the next step on the way of this process is to become that child and feel its presence from the insider perspective. It's not as difficult as it seems. In fact, in stressful life situations most of us do it unconsciously on a regular basis. We regress and start reacting like wounded children, out of proportion to the situation that triggered it. And that's how we create misery for ourselves.

Of course, in our Primal process we do it consciously, to create healing. We invite you to take a deep breath and allow your awareness to shift from the adult body into the child's body, becoming the child.

175

Try it just for a moment:

While you continue looking at the child you, take a deep breath and on the outbreath allow your consciousness to float out of your adult body and descend into the child's body. As you do this, shift your position. Take the body posture of the child: maybe you need to stand up, or lay down. Everything around you feels more vivid, larger. The good and the not so good feelings are both amplified.

Now look at the adult you, standing there having journeyed all the way here to reconnect with you ...

Do you recognize this adult as you, or is he/she a stranger?

Would you like to reach out or do you need some distance?

What would you like to say to him/her?

Talk to the adult you. Speak out, loud enough that you can hear yourself talking ...

After a while, take again a deep breath and return to your adult body. If you want, you can hug the soft pillow or teddy bear as if it were the child.

Sometimes the words of the child can really surprise us. We might have imagined that we would find a crushed small being waiting for us, but already on our first meeting we are suddenly confronted with another forgotten facet of that child: it's straightforwardness and truthfulness. Just as it originally would have wanted to speak out to the adults of its past – parents, teachers and religious educators – the child can now look at us adults and show in a very simple way how we are missing out in our lives.

On her first guided meeting with her child, F, a young woman, spent quite some time apologizing to her little girl about her present confusion and her incapacity to make decisions.

She was stunned when she shifted to the little girl and heard herself responding to the adult: "It's time to move on with your life, I've had enough of your unhappiness, you have to follow your heart ... "

This had enormous consequences on F's approach to the work. It was a wake-up call that provoked a new sense of responsibility

176

in her adult self: she recognized how she had adopted the same attitude towards the little girl as her mother had towards her during her childhood.

Like her mother, F was pouring her adult confusion onto the little girl, ignoring the child's needs. Unknowingly, F was deepening her own wound of rejection by behaving in this way.

Once she realized this, F became fully available to the rest of the process. Just through this simple shift of perspective her heart had understood. She took her life into her own hands.

At other times, becoming the child reveals a deeply buried pain that we adults can only perceive as numbness.

A, a man in his mid-thirties, was confused by his girlfriend's love affair with another man. His adult self couldn't understand the reasons for his reaction, because the relationship with his girlfriend was an open one and they were still best friends.

Yet A noticed that, since this episode, he was withdrawing not only from her, but also from his other friends and from life in general. His only outlet was work: his capacity to function remained untouched. For the rest of his time, he would retire to his room and sleep or read.

We guided him to visualize and sense his inner child sitting next to him on his bed, at home, while he read his book. In this situation, as the adult, he felt fine, in good contact with the child. Seemingly, the little boy next to him was peaceful and content.

But once A shifted perspective and became the child, things changed drastically. His facial expression revealed a quiet sorrow – and he could feel this sadness. Suddenly, he realized how the feeling of isolation was familiar to him: he had been a good child and learned that expressing male energy, like his father, would add suffering to his already unhappy mother.

As a child, he learned to contain his outgoing energy. He suddenly realized how much of his life he'd spent trying to control himself. Martial Arts, work, even discipline in the field of meditation – all his usual resources – suddenly looked like isolation cells for the child.

177

The little boy would have wanted to move, explore and be spontaneous and physical, but was now just sitting there, resigned to the lack of contact with humanity at large, ready to go along with what seemed more 'reasonable' and 'mature' behaviour.

The real beauty of this interaction between the adult and the child is that these major insights about one's unconscious behaviour come from inside the client, through direct experience. Our function as therapists is to hold the space, ask questions and maintain a clear distinction between the adult and the child. Because of this, whatever surfaces has an undeniable ring of truth.

The Parents of the Past

The third step along the way is to call forth the other two main protagonists of this inner journey: the parents of the past. As we saw in previous case histories, one or even both of them may show up from our very first meeting with the child, overshadowing our adult image and dominating our connection with the child.

For the child in us, parents are still a living reality, influencing our behaviour on a daily basis. In most cases, they were the only grown-ups who were always around when we were small and held absolute authority over us.

Still now, when we meet people who remind us of them, we unconsciously react to them with the same fear, longing, love and hate that we had for our mother and father when we were small.

These feelings run deep and last long. For the adult, the parents of the past act like secret, hidden control agents, dictating what is good and what is not good from a deeply unconscious place inside us.

They are the foundation of what in therapy is called the Superego, a jumble of injunctions, moral dictates and hypnotic suggestions that 'keep us in place'. Whenever the parental voices of the past fire a message at us from within we shrink, but we also feel strangely comfortable in our restricted area. It's the comfort of having a definition, the need of the child for a map and guidelines. We are simply used to it.

To claim centre stage in our unconscious, parents do not need to be monsters. Especially nowadays, very few parents are intentionally cruel or destructive towards their children. They put limits and give rules to their, 'little ones' mostly out of love and care.

But they are simply not aware how great and long-lasting an influence they have on their sons and daughters. Besides what they actually say, their children pick up and react to a host of signals … the tone of voice, the facial expression … even to things the parents are not fully aware of themselves, such as a mother's unhappiness, a father's sexual frustration.

The child in us feels responsible for its parents' moods and tries its best to appease them. Every time it does this, the little boy or girl in us goes through a mini-shock, loses himself or herself, and starts reacting either passively or aggressively.

Whenever as adults we are burdened by duty, or we retreat too much, or we notice we are criticizing ourselves, most probably there is an inner parental voice behind us, well hidden in our unconscious, pressing down on us or making us feel guilty.

We are so accustomed to thinking of these inner criticisms as our own observations that it takes another shift of perspective to become aware of their real origins. To explore the impact of the voices of the past, try this simple exercise:

Take a notebook and a pen, and make a list of self-criticisms about

- *Your body (I am too fat, too thin, to weak, too strong, etc.)*
- *Your capacity to love (I am selfish, I am a beggar, I am wanting too much, etc.)*
- *Your intelligence (I am slow, I am confused, I am mindy, I am stupid, etc.)*

Take time to write. You will notice that some criticisms will move you more than others.

Now look again at what you wrote, and point out the three strongest criticisms, one per each area you explored (body, love, etc.)

Take a moment time to answer these questions:
From whom did you get this criticism or a similar one?
Whose voice is talking? Keep it simple: mother or father?
If no answer comes, take a moment longer. Ask yourself:
Whom am I covering for?
For whom am I taking the blame?
Is it a male or female voice?

Stand up and repeat that critical sentence out loud a few times, directing it to the child in you. The wording or content of the criticism may have changed with time, but the tone of that inner critical voice is unmistakable; it's either your mother or your father.

Now shift to the child's perspective and hear the parent of the past talking to you in this way. Allow yourself to feel what it does to your body and your heart.

Then visualize and feel the loving adult you are now, somewhere close to you, and ask him or her for support. You can even imagine that you lean back onto his or her larger body.

Shift again to the adult perspective and feel the child in your arms. Talk to the child and tell it that this time you are there, to create healthy boundaries for him or her.

This is a very delicate juncture in our work. As you might have experienced while doing this guided exercise, we are provoking strong feelings towards the parents of the past.

Those strong feelings are already there, inside us, denied and forgotten, because we could not express them when we were small. We were either stopped from speaking out or soon realized that no one would respond. The pain and anger that we swallowed has now become toxic, like a heavy iron ball that hinders our movements.

Emotional release, crying and getting angry, will eventually free up an incredible amount of this blocked energy, and make it available again for life affirmative purposes.

Retrieving Positive Childhood Experiences

If we rush into immediately expressing this emotional load, we risk remaining on its surface. Enmeshed with this load are memories of good moments, hopeful moments, loving moments with the parents of the past – however infrequent they may have been.

Afraid to lose contact with the two people that gave life and nourishment, the child in us holds back and can't fully separate from them. We need to respect this and accept what the child is feeling at any given moment – including love and trust for the parents – without trying to direct the process where we think it should lead. These positive feelings are emotional resources for the child and taking them away would create a new and unnecessary wound.

The phenomenal consequence of this respect for the child's feelings is that the child will trust the adult more and more. It will come to understand that expressing negative emotions doesn't mean denying love for parents.

When the child doesn't need to deny any of its feelings, positive or negative, we as adults will experience a new sense of freedom and expansion in our lives.

Reconnecting with the positive experiences of childhood is as important as processing negative ones.

They are, as we said, emotional resources: they help us unlock the dormant potential in the child.

Recalling her earliest and best childhood memory, F saw herself very young, in the arms of her beloved nanny, in front of a balcony window opening onto a garden full of scented flowers.

Once F shifted perspective and entered the body of the little girl in this situation, she told us how she also could feel the presence in the garden of little elves and gnomes, and other benign presences of light.

"They are my friends ... " she said. Her forehead, often caught in a perplexed frown, started relaxing, and a big smile appeared on her face – the smile of a little girl.

When she came back to her adult body, she maintained the same sparkle around herself. "I can trust my intuition", she told us with firm conviction. She had renounced her intuition long before, when entering the scientific academic world, and had buried this gift together with the rest of her childhood.

This simple guided journey can offer you a direct experience of the release of energy that happens when we remember what is essential in us:

Close your eyes, and allow yourself to recall all the way in which as a child you touched natural spaces of meditation.

Remember moments of wonder in the middle of nature, in which you felt union with the whole.

Or intimate moments at home, when for no specific reason you felt nourished, and full of gratitude.

Or moments of dance, movement, whirling and singing in full abandon ...

Choose the situation that touches you the most, maybe because you feel a deep recognition, or maybe because a sense of longing floods your heart, or for any other reason that is true for you.

Observe what is going on in that situation: where is it taking place? Are there other persons with the child? How is the atmosphere?

Focus on the child you. Notice its facial expression, its movements, or the way it sits still. You might even see an aura surrounding the child.

Take a deep breath and shift perspective. Become the child. Sit or move like that child, allow soft sounds: they can be words or simply gibberish. Allow your senses to open up to the experience and release the happiness, the contentment, the bliss that this moment contains.

Now bring all that released energy back to yourself. Put your hands on your body wherever you feel this energy resonates the most. Allow it to permeate every one of your cells. Breathe it in, expand with it.

Find one or two words to describe the quality that you are

182

experiencing now. It can be silence, or peace, or aliveness, or wildness... Find your own definition. You might even want to whisper, "I am peace ... I am wild ... etc."

Take a deep breath and shift again to the adult perspective. See and feel the child in front of you, acknowledge its gift. Realize how many times you have experienced this quality in your adult life, in meditation, in love or in a creative moment. Understand how this quality motivated you to start seeking for something more than simply doing what is expected from you.

Bow down to the child and receive its gift.

Slowly come back.

If you want, you can take some time writing for yourself how you can bring this quality back even more into your adult life.

Osho Primal: From the Periphery to the Core

The quality that you experienced in the exercise above might reveal something essential about the child in you. The little boy or girl you once were also stands for your simple and true nature on the deepest level, before conditioning enveloped it. This may be the reason why so many spiritual traditions, from Jesus to Buddha, to Osho, talk about becoming a child again.

In this aspect, we differ from the standard therapy offered in the market place. Standard therapy is an incredible help for anyone who needs tools to create a more solid ego-structure and to function in the world in a more mature way. It moves from wounded child to responsible grown up.

The direction of Osho Primal is different: it moves away from the ego-structure, on the periphery, towards the essential in us, the core.

According to Osho, each human being is like an onion: layer upon layer envelops its core, just like layers of rules and roles envelop our original nature.

The child is the closest metaphor that we have to that original nature. We are all born open, unblemished, carrying a potential and a presence that is much vaster than our tiny bodies. Our original task is to simply be ourselves and contribute to existence in the way that is most natural for us.

But from the very beginning we are taught that we are not the way we are supposed to be. Soon enough, we understand that our nature needs to be curbed and we start believing that the roles we adopt are who we really are. We start wearing a social mask. We call this set of fixed responses and reactions to survive and maintain a place in society our 'personality'.

Osho Primal peels layer after layer of childhood conditioning, supporting each person to discard the personality and rediscover our untouched sense of individuality that lies at the core. There, each of us is unique and full of potential, yet deeply connected to other human beings.

Once the experience of this core is touched a seed is planted that will grow and produce its own flowers without struggle or effort. We start living our own life – not someone else's.

In this way, the child becomes more alive in us, and the adult becomes more motivated. We move from nurture to nature, knowing that being oneself generates more happiness and creativity.

Peeling the Onion

Once the connection between adult and child has been established, once the parents of the past have been identified and unmasked from their hiding place in our unconscious, we can start peeling the onion.

We move backwards in time through childhood, from the age of pre-school until the time of conception – the period in which, according to widespread knowledge, the deepest imprinting occurs.

At each stage of development, it is possible to heal the wounds of the child by understanding what happened, and to express through our adult bodies the feelings locked in the child's body, causing armouring and fixed behaviours.

By clearing each specific layer of conditioning, we come to re-experience the natural qualities (such as trust, strength, emotional

184

intelligence and many others) that were lost at that particular point in childhood, integrating them back into our adult life.

The map of emotions, body armours and mental frames created at various stages of childhood is a whole science in itself, too vast a subject to be dealt with in this chapter. For now, it is sufficient to give examples:

G, an attractive woman in her mid-thirties, was a musician. She was introverted and a bit shy, and her attitude seemed to add something extra to her mysterious beauty.

Initially, she came to us because she felt at a loss with men. She could either be 'best friends' with them and remain sexually and romantically dissatisfied, or fall in love with them and become obsessive and jealous.

A whole wave of guilt for her impromptu dramas with men she'd only just met would follow, and she would consequently hide in shame. At some point, she had even renounced playing music, her main expressive outlet, in the hope that men would be less threatened by her talent and seek her out.

It was stunning to hear her talking like a little girl, humiliated and rejected, while looking for all the world like a beautiful and dignified woman.

When invited to contact the little girl inside her, she saw a self-effacing 'bundle' – as she called herself – of a five year-old girl, dressed in hand-me-downs and careless about her appearance. This period in a child's life is known as the time of the Oedipal Triangle.

"How was the relationship with your father in those years?" we asked her.

"He was pushing me to play music for many hours a day and was never quite satisfied ... " she answered.

But her father was also her childhood hero, she told us. His gruff behaviour was more than compensated by the undivided attention he gave her when she played music.

We invited G to take a deep breath and shift to the child's body. She felt numb and indifferent, not connected with her body. We guided her through one of our bodywork exercises designed to release the withheld feelings of a five or six-year-old child. What surfaced in her body was endless shame: shame for disappointing father by being a girl instead of a boy, shame for her own sexual feelings, and even more shame for her passionate heart.

As we guided her to breathe through that layer of resignation back into the original innocence and sensuousness of the little girl, tears were running down her cheeks. Before coming back to her adult body, she whispered a soft and relieved "thank you ... "

She deeply understood that holding her energy back and waiting for men to approach her had the effect of turning them into her father. Her dramas had been her way to release the rage and humiliation that she'd experienced with him.

We advised her to spend the time until the next session exploring joy and pleasure as much as she could, and to connect with women whose style she liked. She came back to the next session radiant: she'd been invited to play in a concert that was important to her heart, and at the same time she had been going out dancing and meeting friends for the whole week: she told us that her little girl, curious and intrigued, had been all the time at her side, enjoying.

This is a significant point to understand: once felt, shame releases the sensuousness that it envelops. When released, each withheld 'negative' emotion leads into its 'positive' counterpart. It seems to be a constant law of our inner world.

The art is to understand in different situations which emotion needs expression. In G's case, going through her shame and rediscovering sensuousness gave her back her sense of self-worth and feeling grounded in everyday life. This, in turn, gave her what she needed in order to enter into the minefield of her unexpressed anger towards father, without becoming self-destructive or feeling guilty.

Everyone Needs a Temper Tantrum
Once in a While

The expression of anger is connected to an earlier stage of development: it's the natural response of an energetic two-year-old child being stopped from moving outwards and testing the world.

For any parent, saying 'no' to such a bomb of energy is not easy. A necessary 'no' can lead to a great temper tantrum: but if the parents can stay present without interfering, the tantrum lasts only for a while, until the pent up energy is released. Once again at peace, the child will move on to another exploration. Unfortunately, not all children are treated like that. They are stopped from expressing their anger and soon learn to compress it and hide it until it becomes toxic.

All of us can feel, even today, how unexpressed anger is held in the tightness of our muscles.

But to release old anger from childhood requires us to dig deeper. To transform it, we need to express it towards the ones who originally provoked it: the parents of the past.

The main paradigm to which we firmly hold is that only when we consciously direct our incomplete anger towards them – expressing it through our bodies – does this anger eventually dissolve.

In our groups and sessions, we dedicate the central part of the process to the expression of the anger of the child through our adult bodies. It's a clean, direct and healthy process. Of course, it's not always easy to access the core of it, but with the right preparation and support it becomes possible. It gives back our sense of direction in life and completes what remains unfinished from the past.

P was a tall and strongly built mountain guide in his forties. He explained to us that he had chosen this work because challenging himself in this way, sometimes under very extreme conditions, was the only way he could feel alive. When he was a very small child, before he even knew he was a little boy, his mother had claimed

187

him for herself. His dad was often away for work and when at home became unpredictable because of his sudden swings of mood.

In his sixth session with us, we supported P into finding his anger towards the absent father of his childhood. It was not easy for him. It was like trying to grasp fog, alternating with thunderstorm.

P went through disappointment, betrayal feelings, helplessness, until he finally broke through into a massive anger. We supported him to express it through the body, encouraging him to feel and release it in the areas that felt more blocked. Amongst other things, he felt in his shoulders the responsibility his father passed on to him to be the man of the family in his absence, and in his heart the wound of betrayal when his father – whenever he was home – pushed him into a corner, taking his mother away from him. We supported him in giving it all back to the father of his past.

P's catharsis was so powerful and clean that it didn't need to last very long. We encouraged him to feel the anger in every part of his body, shout and beat a pillow. In the end, his movements had the fluid and powerful quality of a geyser exploding from underground.

The evening after this session, he had a dream. Here is his report:

I am in a public sauna. I take off all my clothes and hang them on the wall of the dressing room. Instead of going to the sauna, I take a very strong shower. I can sense how much I enjoy the fresh and strong feeling of cleaning myself... It is so joyful that I am smiling.

When I return to my clothes, I see that some items are missing. I can't find my trousers and my underwear... It's ridiculous. My underwear and trousers were well worn, why would someone need them?? I find my watch and other more expensive items, but still no trousers and underwear. I cannot understand why, because these garments don't have any value for anyone else except me...

But then in the middle of it I realize that I do not need them. They are old, and I can live without them.

I collect the rest of my stuff and start walking away.

At this point, I woke up.

I realized that this dream symbolized my farewell with old father's stuff inside me. The worn out trousers and underwear symbolized him as my male model.

Good thing that I understood even during the dream that I did not need this anymore...

Today I experience a healing feeling of emptiness. My mind is calm, just few simple thoughts during a day... It's so healing.

In my previous life, when I felt empty, I felt unsafe and stressed.

It's the first time that I experience void inside and do not worry about anything :)

By expressing his old anger, P released his capacity to move spontaneously. As an adult, he'd already broken free of his mother's excessive holding by climbing the highest mountains around the globe. But now he was also able to retrieve his original spontaneity: just enjoying movement in itself, like a small child, without tension or goals. His catharsis had erased the old imprint of father, the stress of never knowing what to expect and the unfulfilled need for guidance. New possibilities opened up for him in his life.

Like at the end of any detox, after a good release of old anger, just like P describes, we are left feeling empty and light. But, as in any deep cleaning, once the bottom has been reached, new, fresh nourishment needs to come in.

The Delicate Field of Need

With this understanding, we are entering a new developmental stage and the next step of our journey: our first nine months of life.

Love and care are to the soul what food is to the body, especially in the case of small children and babies. They would not survive without an atmosphere of love around them. The love that a baby needs is not personality-based. It's more of an exchange of energy, in which it can feel the oneness it felt in the womb. It's a sharing: what the baby shares, in exchange for the care and love it receives, is a pure state of being, a door into meditation. When you simply hold a small child and close your eyes, you can experience how vast, compared to the tininess of its body, is the presence of this being.

By nature, a baby is trusting and open. Whenever we sit by ourselves and close our eyes, much of the agitation that goes on inside us, at the very moment when we ought to be able to relax, is connected to that baby time. Restlessness indicates a lack of nourishment at the core. It's hard to just be, to trust that we are going to be held in that relaxed state by our beloveds and by existence in a loving way.

If there is not enough emotional bonding and physical presence from mother, or too much mental energy and anxiety surrounding it, the baby cries for a while in an effort to attract attention and receive more of what it needs. Then it stops. That's when we learned in different degrees to retreat, defeated, into a deep place in our hearts and close the doors behind us.

This is the moment when the pathway to trust – as a relaxed state of being – got clogged inside us, and our love became conditional.

At this stage in our work, we enter the delicate field of need. We give time to the emotional expression of the baby's unfulfilled needs, but not too long. Screaming and crying like a baby for too long can easily tear the new delicate tissue that is growing after the big catharsis.

The real transformation of unfulfilled needs is not found in catharsis. It comes through rediscovering our capacity to receive, to invite what is good for us and to be open when life responds, whatever the source of the response is – it can be a person or simply an event.

In order to do that, we need to open the door in our heart that we locked behind us a long time ago.

Behind that door, preserved and almost forgotten, is the imprint of moments, maybe only a few, of true sharing, that did happen with mother and also later with father. It's very individual what surfaces: a moment of shared silence with father, a moment of tenderness with mother. It is always touching, and sometimes surprising what comes.

We guided Z, a bank manager and businesswoman, to return to the time shortly after her birth. Her mother had died few days later from birth complications. The adult Z approached her baby self with some misgivings and a certain brusqueness that she seemed to adopt when she felt over-emotional. She was afraid of not finding any good memories there. But once she shifted into the baby's body, she suddenly felt the enveloping warmth of her mother just after birth.

She looked ecstatic. Amidst the tears, she felt a deep sense of gratefulness. "I belong ... " she whispered softly. For the first time in her adult life, she had a mother.

In the subsequent period of time, Z changed her life circumstances. She followed her dreams and became increasingly female. When we met her again, her gruffness had been replaced by great friendliness.

Allowing past memories of moments of love and merging to coexist with the pain of separation that followed can have an amazing effect on the system. You can try this simple meditation for yourself:

Remember a past experience of separation in your life, at any age, even recently. Choose a situation that still in some way touches you.

You may notice that your heart wants to immediately protect itself. Continue breathing. It's time to complete this event inside yourself, and let your heart relax.

Now take time to describe, loud enough so that you can hear yourself talking, the scenario in front of your inner vision.

How old are you?

Who else is there with you?

What exactly happened?

Focus on your younger self in that situation. Notice how he or she closes and protects his or her heart.

As the loving adult that you are today, connect with him or her, and ask: "What negative decision do you take at this moment about life, love and friendliness?"

Listen to the reply. It might come in words, or through his or her attitude.

Take a deep breath and allow your consciousness to float into your younger self's body, and repeat aloud the decision you made.

Feel where it sits in your heart: you might experience it as a tension, or numbness, or rage in that area.

Keep on breathing and allow it to be there. Your older self, the adult of today, is standing right by you to support you to get through this.

Bring your hands to your heart and gently massage it. Now visualize and feel that you are taking away with your hands the entire psychic debris and tensions that have gathered around that decision inside your heart.

You can move your hands and make soft sounds if you want. With a final sound, throw away what you gathered in your hands: the earth can absorb it and recycle it.

Feel the emptiness that follows. Do not be afraid of it. It will slowly relax, and become just space, receptivity. Receive the love that comes from the adult next to you.

Take a deep breath and allow your consciousness to float back in your adult body. As the adult, take a moment to breathe into your heart and absorb the pain and disconnection that may still linger around your younger self in front of you, and breathe out love and compassion towards him or her.

Now remember all the good moments, the happy moments, the golden moments that happened with the one who was there before the separation took place.

Allow the memories to surface from a very protected and sacred place inside. If tears come, allow them. They are no longer tears of despair. Let the grief for the loss evaporate.

You will notice that after a while the feelings will become softer, more fluid.

It's now time to acknowledge what you received before the separation, and allow yourself to express gratitude for the beauty you shared in those special moments.

Keep it simple; find just one word, like love, or inspiration, or passion to describe the gift received ...

Remember, this gift is also part of your history and inner richness.

Bow down to the person of the past and whisper:

"Thank you for the gift of ... that we shared. I take it and I move my way with it."

If you can, physically turn around, leaving the past behind. Feel the present moment, so full of gifts and nourishment from all kinds of sources, some of them unexpected. Let yourself whisper once more "Thank you ... "

Gratitude nourishes and liberates. Acknowledging the gifs you received makes you free to move your own way, letting go of any grudge.

It also releases those who gave that gift to you, who feel honoured and seen and equally free to move on.

From here on, the remaining part of the Childhood Deconditioning Process is dedicated to positivity: gathering enough spiritual, emotional and physical resources to start living our potential.

A Second Birth

The last step in the process is recalling the period in the womb and the moment of birth. It is not as esoteric as it might seem. In fact, if anyone bothered asking a three-year-old child: "How was it in the belly of your mum?" or "How did you come out?" that child would answer very precisely, even if sometimes through metaphors.

We carry the imprint of the womb in the deepest part of our nervous system and the memory of birth as the first experience of being in a separate body. These imprints are very deep and sometimes traumatic.

In this case, specific techniques and much more time than we would offer at this point are required. Within the field of Osho Therapy, there are other specific and very effective methods that take you back to your original birth and intra-uterine period in order to heal those traumas.

But at this point of our Twice Born Process we take a different turn and offer the participants a new birth.

Our aim is to give each one of them the feeling that he or she can pass through the birth canal, because he or she really wants to be here, in the world, and also the experience that they are being welcomed and held when they come out.

We do a simple and intimate breathing exercise in different stages, guiding the participants in a spacious and loving way through the early stages in the womb, until the last period and then into a new birth. When, at this last stage, the 'babies' come out into life, it is always a celebration; there is much laughter and sweetness in the air.

When things settle in the group room and everyone relaxes into the aftermath of this experience, a great silence descends. It has something sacred and very delicate. In that moment, the last tensions drop. We have reached the core.

Therapy exits the stage and meditation enters. This sacred silence will become a new imprint, a knowing that inside us there is a resting place where we can recharge and relax in between our worldly adventures.

As the sessions or the group are coming to an end, this is also the moment when therapy gives way to integration with daily life, the necessary bridge between all the extraordinary experiences of the process and the world in which we now function.

Before the participants walk out of the group room, back into their own lives, there is one last step to be done: allowing the adult and the child to become one inside them, so that they can re-enter the world aware of both parts and whole.

In the same way, also this chapter ends with a short journey of integration before you move on to the next inner adventure …

As the adult that you are now, walk towards the earlier times in your life, until you reach childhood.

This time, you are going to visit the child, the little girl or boy you, in his or her sacred place. It can be at home, or in nature, or even in an imaginary place where you know the child likes to be in special moments. Look for that place, and when you find it, enter it with the respect.

How does it look?

What is the beauty of it?

What kind of atmosphere is here?

See or feel the child in this place, the way he or she sits, or moves. The child sees you and by now recognizes you instantly: he or she is happy to see you ...

Notice that the child is reaching out with one hand, opening it towards you to show you something. It contains a gift for you from the child. What is it?

Receive it in your own hands and put it in a safe place.

Now it's your turn to give something to the child. It can be an object, a quality, a message ...

Lean closer to the child and with your own words say: "Little ... , this is my gift, I give you the gift of ... so that you ... "

See the child receiving it, and putting it in a safe place.

Then you can notice that the child is moving back to its own world, taking time to rest and play on its own.

Start moving away towards your time, carrying in your heart the knowledge that at any time you can contact that child again ...

CHAPTER TEN

Birth Integration:
Born to be a Buddha

Dwari

For me, the last thirty-five years have been an intense and enriching exploration into the dimension of breathing through body therapy and meditation. It began in 1977 when I came to India and joined the experimental community surrounding Osho, in which the focus of daily life became spiritual growth.

Much has already been said in this book about those days, so I will simply say that therapy became an important element in Osho's community because many of the western seekers coming to Pune were therapists enchanted by the fascinating changes already occurring in the field of Humanistic Psychology.

By the 70s, this form of psychotherapy was no longer focused on healing neuroses and other psychological problems. A new kind of therapy, especially group therapy, developed in which people could explore the limitations of their cultural conditioning and find ways to go beyond it.

Osho encouraged his therapists to create processes for human development and growth in consciousness – often with his personal input – but it was always clear that meditation was his essential vision. Therapy functioned mainly as a bridge to meditation.

Meditation: a Resource

Meditation is an enormous resource as it connects you with your own inner subjective world and the awareness of reality, as it is, in this moment. It strengthens your perception into the felt sense of your body and the changing waves of your emotions, as well as different mental concepts running through your mind.

Through this, you find a new connection to your body and the intuitive intelligence of your 'body-mind-being-system' in the moment, here and now, and you became rooted in reality.

In the meditation methods Osho developed, everyone can find a technique that supports their growth process and deepen the connection with oneself and life. In this way, meditation is an incredible self-empowerment, because you are the one providing the space for yourself to open into more:

- Awareness
- Relaxation and self-regulation
- A non-judgmental attitude to yourself and life

What happens in your personal meditation is independent from any outer influence. It is about you and your connection to yourself. All your energy goes inside – an incredible empowerment for your own strength, into being here and now.

One of the most important statements I heard Osho say was: "I am not interested in your personality, I am interested in how to get the totality of your energy into this moment."

This sentence shifted my understanding about therapy. It is our ego, our personality, our fixed concepts, which come in the way of being in tune with life and the present moment.

Therapy can help us see how unnatural and repressed we have become, how identified with the false personality. Therapy can support the challenging task of dismantling unhealthy false identifications and take obstacles out of the way.

Recognition of the False

The first step is to recognize that our false personality – the way it developed in our early years – was an intelligent instinctive response of our body, mind and being to the challenging, difficult and at times unbearable situation in which we found ourselves when we were very young. We had no choice but to adapt ourselves to outer conditions and expectations demanded of us by our family environment, school and other social situations.

Later on, when we start becoming conscious of ourselves, the deepest feeling we usually identify is a profound sense of not being right the way we are. Facing this basic issue, we have to recognize the extensive survival strategies that we created to protect our vulnerability, as well as the pain of not being supported to grow into a healthy, whole and individual human being.

The second step is to accept who we have become and how our life energy found distorted ways to flow and express itself. With this foundation, we can begin to create a conscious connection to our wholeness; we can begin to expand and to transform out of these defensive patterns that were once helpful and protective, but which are now inhibiting our development.

Restrictive Structures

On the body level, we created a restricted body structure showing armouring and a certain 'holding charge' in the nervous system through:

- Disconnecting.
- Collapsing, withdrawing.
- Moving into a state of high tension

On the level of the mind we develop rigid belief systems:

- About ourselves
- Relationship and love
- Reality and our own capacity to live life

Out of this unhealthy and unnatural situation, behaviour patterns emerge which make it difficult to:

- Be in touch with essential needs.
- Be authentic in showing and expressing feelings and emotions.
- Allow nourishing intimacy.
- Live a fulfilled sexuality.
- Find one's own individual creativity and essential meaning in life.

To accept and became conscious of our individual survival strategies and personality development is an important and necessary step towards transformation. Therapy can help in this process but the real healing happens in meditation.

In therapy, you enter into a mirroring dynamic through relating with a therapist, which is needed for a certain period of time in order to transform.

A therapist who is in touch with his own inner process, who is aware and open to the moment, who is capable of establishing a loving resonance with his client, as well having a skilled therapeutic toolbox in his hands, will be a supportive guide for the client with whom he is working.

Therapy will always be for a limited period of time, focused on rediscovering the client's natural resources, empowering the client to re-establish trust in his or her original life energy and its manifold sensations and expressions.

However, both therapist and client need to bear in mind that inner self-discovery and meeting the challenges of contemporary life is an ongoing process, stretching far beyond therapy.

My Journey into Breathing

Like everybody who found himself in the context of Osho and Osho Therapy, I am in the first place a spiritual seeker. As a seeker, the core question is not 'How can I help others'? The core question is 'Who am I'? And if the seeker is also a therapist, the next question will be 'What is this place inside myself, from where I can offer support and help to other people'?

Early in this quest, my personal path directed me to the awareness of breathing as a guiding thread in my life and my own growth, and also later into specific breath-and-body deconditioning work called 'Osho Diamond Breath' as a therapeutic tool for working with people.

Every state a person experiences physically, mentally or emotionally is reflected in a breathing pattern. Even though most breathing patterns are unconscious, regulated by the autonomous nervous system, the moment one brings awareness to one's breathing it is possible to enter into hidden body memories and open up the possibility for constructive, conscious change.

The first ignition spark for my own search happened when I was around twenty. At the time, I was overwhelmed by my first serious crisis: a relationship break up, accompanied by disorientation and chaotic feelings, a sense of no longer being able to function. In a particularly freaky moment, I somehow became aware of my breathing and without thinking I sat down, focusing on the movement of my breath, in and out, clinging to it as a kind of anchor in the hope that it would somehow make me feel more steady and centred.

It worked. Sitting there, watching my breath, everything inside slowly began to quieten down, relax and shift. My anxious thoughts lost their power and pressure, my emotions began to dissolve. With each breath, the tension in my body noticeably relaxed, as if nothing in this moment was really as great a threat as I'd imagined.

I was surprised, to say the least. I didn't really know what was happening – only that it was somehow calming me. Many years later, I realized that, in this strange and unplanned experience, I had plunged into the essential principles of meditation.

The experience of emotional chaos pushed me to investigate therapy. Aside from this one experience, I had little awareness of my breathing patterns until one therapist, in an individual session, advised "You should do something about your breathing".

I was puzzled by this remark. I had no idea to what he was referring, but I took the hint and tried to find out. What was it about my breathing that was so visible to him and yet invisible to me?

Soon, I discovered that I was in the habit of creating a tense and stressful breathing pattern. For example, whenever I talked with somebody, especially when I was emotionally involved with that person, I forgot to breathe. I took a very short in-breath, which I'd developed unconsciously as a way of suppressing my feelings.

The effect of this automatic breathing behaviour was that my sentences tumbled out rapidly, my voice became high pitched and my body became very tense. This tension was inevitably picked up by the person with whom I was talking, making it hard for him or her to listen to me.

For me, the most remarkable thing about this discovery was that I'd never noticed it before. It had been going on for years and years, as a mechanical habit, without my conscious consent. By becoming conscious of the breathing pattern and the physical response, I was able to look more deeply into the situation responsible for creating this tense expression.

The original cause of this breathing pattern, I discovered, was a childhood experience rooted in fear: "Nobody is listening to me … nobody wants to hear what I am saying … I have to put more effort into my voice … I have speak very fast and say it all at once before I am interrupted or ignored … "

In this single breathing pattern was hidden my whole childhood story. In our family, everybody was talking at the same time, loudly and rapidly, and nobody was really listening. So in relating with other family members there was a continuous sense of frustration and tension.

This realization gave me such a shock – in a positive and healing way – that I began to be very curious about breath and its hidden secrets.

I understood that, if what had happened to me in the past could be so perceptible in the way I was breathing, then I could also do something about it by changing the way I was breathing now, experimenting with different ways of expression and behaviour.

Moving with Breathing

I searched my way through all sorts of breathing methods, such as Middendorfsche Respiratory Therapy, which involved three years of daily training and exploration of my breathing pattern, using movement and sounds. It also gave me a sense of being more 'embodied' in my own physical form. In addition, the training gave me the opportunity to support others in their efforts to develop deeper healthy breathing.

This course was followed by many others: Rebirthing, Bioenergetics, Yoga, Chi Gong, Tai Chi and finally Osho's Breathing Meditations. However, none of this helped me to learn 'correct breathing'. Instead, I arrived at the understanding that 'correct breathing' is, after all, just an idea in one's head – another idea that we think we need to impose on the simple art of breathing naturally.

Breath is much too alive to be locked into a cage of 'correct breathing'. It is constantly changing, tied to the moment, responding to what is happening on a physical, emotional and spiritual level.

This much can be learned from breathing methods: how to open yourself up to your breathing, to experience it consciously; to dissolve old, rigid breathing patterns and go deep inside your own body's history, going back to your natural, original breathing and creating a more healthy contact to being present, here and now, 'in the moment'.

Only when I started experimenting with Osho's active meditations did I realize that movement, expression and awareness go hand in hand. All these active meditations have a phase of charging the body with energy, but also space to release energy in many different ways, followed by a meditative space of silent watching.

Here I found the key for my work. When our energy has a natural flow of expression and release, relaxation follows naturally. We can observe this in the expressiveness of a child. When a child is given freedom to express his natural physical and emotional response to a situation – running, shouting, screaming – it is like a wave of energy going through his little body, which afterwards settles and relaxes ... until the next activity.

This reflects the built-in program of our autonomous nervous system, the sympathetic nervous system (action, movement, expression) and the parasympathetic nervous system (calming down, relaxing). We have an inbuilt balancing system in our body. Naturally supported in its development, it can provide us with an inner regulation and resilience to challenging outer situations.

However, as we grow up, this inner balance is utterly disturbed and the natural flow of energy release and relaxation becomes blocked. This might happen, for example, if the child begins to express anger and the mother or father forces him to be quiet. The balancing flow is interrupted and the energy is inhibited. It can be the same with tears, making too much noise, running around the home ...

These are examples of what happens during the ongoing process of a child's education as a social being. He shifts from natural response to controlling, protective behaviour which is destructive to himself, to others and to environment. We all pay a heavy price for this repressed energy, tension and inner discontent.

Trauma Resolution

In the last twenty-five years, through the development of Neurobiology and Neuropsychology, a deep understanding of the human brain and the complexity of the nervous system has emerged, revealing its significant role in development and growth.

Out of this, a multiplicity of therapeutic approaches have developed methods for dealing with trauma solution, including EMDR (eye movement desensitization and reprocessing) by Francine Shapiro and Somatic Experiencing by Peter Levine. These methods access the new scientific understanding and provide helpful and beautiful tools in order to work effectively with all kinds of trauma issues.

These new findings have influenced the work of Osho Diamond Breath around birth and development trauma, while at the same time confirming experiences in connection with meditation and body/breath therapy.

The Body Remembers

When we consciously follow our breath and allow whatever emerges out of it in the moment, we move into a very individual process of re-owning our life energy. We enter into our body, into old tensions that we hold in different forms, ranging from outer muscle armour to innermost subtle tensions of the nervous system.

We come to our feelings, penetrating through layers of prohibited and suppressed emotions and sensations. We go through many painful contexts of memory from the present into the past, through childhood back to birth and the first breath – even to the time before birth. All this is possible through a deepening consciousness, a containing awareness of the body.

The time in the womb, birth and the first eighteen months after birth are the most important time of our lives. It is the time of our deepest unconscious imprinting and programming. Everything we experience in this time is felt directly through the body. Positive and negative experiences are stored in the developing nervous system as tensions or contractions, remembered in each individual cell of the body – without the possibility of understanding.

Memories from this time can come only through body sensations or inner images as no cognitive mapping existed at the time.

Time in the Womb

In the womb, the child feels at one with the mother. Initially, it floats in the warm amniotic fluid, a salt-containing solution similar to seawater, giving this new being an oceanic sensation of being merged, feeling secure.

Through these nine months, it experiences a symbiotic merging with the mother's organism and all of the child's needs are fulfilled down to the smallest detail. If all goes well during pregnancy, the child feels embedded and well taken care of.

In later years, what remains of this experience is a deep longing for this early sense of merging, for oneness and wholeness – for feeling in harmony with ourselves, the world and others. This is the root of all spiritual seeking.

At the same time, the child increasingly experiences and senses all of the mother's feelings. This occurs directly in the form of vibrations. It feels the situation as relaxing, cosy and melting, or as tense, painful and stressful. It senses the heartbeat, the changes in blood circulation and the intestinal sounds.

When there is stress, this creates extreme rhythms of sound that are almost like techno music. This leads to a fascinating thought: can it be that the younger generation's huge enthusiasm for techno music is just an unconscious attempt to finally resolve the bottled-up prenatal tension of the nervous system? After all, who can endure nine months of a 'techno party' in the womb without being able to let off steam!

Basic Trust or Primal Fear

The unborn child cannot protect itself. The only protection this embryonic organism has is to contract and become tense. This reduces sensitivity and is like a physical reflex, or segment of information stored in the nervous system. If the tension remains unresolved, it later manifests as an indefinable state of anxiety, such as 'I feel threatened' or 'There's no place for me'. It may also manifest in restless, compulsive types of behaviour and breathing disorders: 'I can't breathe!' Or as a rigid attitude towards life: 'Life is just stress for me'.

In this process, the energy field of the uterus can have a variety of auras that are accompanied by the mother's basic mood and attitude towards the unborn child. Every negative climate can later have an effect in the form of psychosomatic symptoms.

Here are a few examples of possible atmospheres in the uterine energy field and their consequences after birth:

● Warm and inviting: the child's body is relaxed and he or she is open to the surrounding environment.

● Ambivalent and over-emotional: the child often suffers from stomach and digestion disorders, or cramps.

- Cold and disturbed: the child seems withdrawn and emotionally toxic. The whole body structure is weak. The child develops slowly and is often ill.

Everything that occurs between the mother and child during this time determines the child's basic attitude towards life. This paves the way for whether we have a healthy sense of trust in our own life force, accepting life and feeling connected with it, or whether a primal fear is lurking within us that blocks every spontaneous impulse and leaves behind a feeling of being cut off and isolated.

Above all, birth is experienced mostly as an extreme trauma.

The mother's womb is the most comfortable situation ... you were just floating in your mother's womb. All your needs were fulfilled.

When the child comes out of the womb, it is the greatest shock of his life. Even death will not be this big a shock, because death will come without warning. Death will come most probably when he is unconscious.

But while he is coming out of the mother's womb, he is conscious. In fact, for the first time he is becoming conscious. His nine months' long sleep, peaceful sleep, is disturbed – and then you cut the thread which joins him with the mother. The moment you cut that thread that joins him with the mother you have created a fearful individual.

This is not the right way, but this is how it has been done up to now.

The child should be taken away from the mother more slowly, more gradually. There should not be that shock – and it can be arranged. A scientific arrangement is possible. ~ Osho[1]

The Natural Birth

It could actually be so simple to give birth to a child in a natural way. A woman becomes pregnant. The child is wanted. The mother creates time in her life for a relaxed pregnancy. She speaks with the little being in her body. The unborn child inside the mother can relax and unfold according to its evolutionary growth. It is cared for, protected, nurtured and is lovingly expected.

In nine months, the embryo experiences six million years of evolution, an incredible achievement – the wonder of life. Even science has not uncovered all the complex and amazing details of this mystery.

The mother prepares for a natural birth. This may happen at home or in a specially equipped hospital, either way without medication. She knows that birth is strenuous and possibly means pain, but she trusts what her body tells her, her body's instinctive knowledge.

Birth stress is necessary and stimulating for the newly-born's organism; in a genial way, it helps it to be able to live in the new, unknown world. It is an intensive, extreme energy experience and the pain that goes with it – if not struggled against – can be lived out almost ecstatically.

Everything in the body of both the mother and the child is designed and set up for this purpose. The body chemistry of mother and child is ruled by a perfect interaction that does not require intervention from anyone as long as nature is allowed to run its course and given the support that it requires.

The mother learns to breathe, to become tense and to relax with the rhythm of labour; at the right moment she can exert all her energy for the contractions.

The needs of the unborn child are considered: no bright light, no loud or nervous voices, no hectic behaviour. Instead, plenty of time, warmth and the possibility of lying close to the mother for a longer time after birth.

Lying on the mother's belly, the newborn child can feel her skin from the outside and re-adjust to the accustomed pulse. The umbilical cord is not cut until the child begins to breathe on its own.

When the baby leaves the body of the mother, immediately a 'love hormone' called oxytocin is released and floods the mother's body, bringing her into a state of ecstatic love towards the child. Her whole body chemistry tunes with the baby and bonds in deep attachment. Feeling this connection, the baby's nervous system can relax and trust.

The First Breath

The first in-breath of air occurs as a natural reflex. Thrust by the pushing contractions of the mother's body, the small baby winds its way out of the birth canal with a spiral motion. Then the enormous pressure eases, making space for the lungs to expand, and the breathing reflex begins with little, careful, pumping breaths of air.

Air on the sensitive mucous membranes is unaccustomed and almost painful. Initially, the two lobes of the lungs are still folded beneath the shoulders ... inhale ... exhale ... inhale ... exhale ... The lungs are pumped up in the chest, breath by breath, through a connected breathing rhythm.

Inhale ... exhale ... inhale ... exhale ... This training of connected breathing will continue for a while as long as the infant's pulsating umbilical cord is still supplied with the mother's oxygen-rich blood.

Directly after the birth, the child requires between twenty minutes and one-and-a half hours to fully develop its lungs and adequately boost its breathing so that it can provide its little organism with oxygen and energy on its own.

Breathing in, breathing out; breathing in, breathing out ... Still being held against its mother's naked body, the baby can now try out its suckling reflex. This reflex is strongest twenty minutes after being born, and only sets in again forty hours later.

When the baby suckles at the nipple, this triggers the milk flow in the breast. At the same time, a hormone is released in the mother's body, telling the uterus "The baby is born, it is breathing, it is alive, it is eating, the little body can sustain itself, so it doesn't need the placenta anymore."

At this point, the placenta begins to separate from the uterine wall and the birth process for the mother is over. Only when all this has been accomplished does the baby's breathing adjust to a new rhythm.

In warmth, the baby can surrender to the natural reflexes of breathing movement, which allows the remaining stress of the birth to dissolve. The spinal column, which was compressed under pressure in the birth canal, dissolves this 'core tension' with light shaking and little waves of motion.

The Umbilical Cord is Cut

Now it's time to sever the umbilical cord. The breathing has unfolded the lungs and set the diaphragm in motion. The wave of breath vibrates down into the belly and reaches the hara, the life centre.

Inhale ... calmness ... exhale ... calmness ... The little human being relaxes into his own belly centre and in this way the soul has fully arrived in its new body. Just as the unborn baby was connected with the mother through the umbilical cord, the child is now connected to his own body through the breath, accompanied by a deep and justified sense of basic trust.

Why 'justified'? Because human beings can absolutely depend on their breath from the very first inhale after birth to the last exhale when dying. Even the smallest movement or emotion is accompanied and supplied by the breath.

The birth has now been completed for the newborn child. A little Buddha is born and life can begin. A good start!

Orientation in Life

If birth would happen like this, there would be no traumatic impact on the nervous system. The biological balance of getting the child ready for the new challenge that lies outside the womb would be supported.

After nine months of merging oneness inside the mother's body, slowly unfolding into a human body of its own, the birth is the first extreme stress experience the baby has to go through.

And everything is ready for this. In birth, all the brain functions get simulated and activated to deal with the enormous stress and changes that follow: light, sound, smell, temperatures, touch, eating ... all the new experiences which need to be processed.

The emotional bonding phase between mother and child immediately after birth, induced by an enormous release of the love hormone oxytocin, is a time for both to relax after the birth tension – for the child to let go of its first extreme stress experience.

This time also enables the mother to be in tune with the baby's energy and its needs in the coming months. The way we respond to stress and challenge in later life very much depends on our early experience, including a healthy bonding and mirroring with the mother in the early weeks of our life. So, this time is meant to give the newborn a safe protected environment in direct contact with the mother's body.

In scientific research it has been discovered a baby can relax as long the mother is within a radius of six meters – the tangible energy field. But direct physical contact with the mother is needed in order to completely relax the baby's body. In this relaxation, the complexity of the nervous system can continue to develop in a natural way.

Lots of physical contact with a newborn will help the infant's brain to develop. Nurturing interactions make the brain produce chemicals and hormones that allow a baby to grow emotionally and physically. For the next one to two years, most of the child's movements will be purely instinctive reflexes in response to the mother's presence.

It is an amazing learning process as the child gains voluntary control over its motor abilities and explores ways to communicate with people and the world around it. A healthy stable contact with the mother will support the brain to create neural networks allowing it to do this, regulating and balancing different sensations, pleasant or unpleasant. These memories stay as unconscious imprints, neurological circuits that create and hold our underlying sense about ourselves and life.

So it is the bonding and attachment with the mother that plays a crucial role in providing an environment of safety and care in which the child can find a resilient orientation to its own body, to the senses and to a stable emotional connection with the outer world.

It will take twelve to eighteen months until the autonomic nervous system is fully developed, giving the baby more mature strategies to respond against stress, threat and danger. It might take a year or longer until the child has a defined sense of time and begins to develop explicit memory, bringing understanding to its experiences.

The biological blueprint of human development contains all that is needed to grow into a healthy sense of self, grounded in the body, trusting one's abilities and open to the challenge of new experiences.

The Second Birth

In my experience, most people have completely lost this child-like connection to the basic trust in their body and their inner centre, unaware they are living with the aftermath and repercussions of an unsolved traumatic birth and what followed later in childhood.

They often feel isolated, at the mercy of the world, lost without knowing why. The 'core imprints' and primal fear of the birth trauma are like an inner barrier that allows no relaxation and no sinking deeply into oneself.

Every intense life experience, such as love, strong sex, separation, death, sudden change and unknown situations may cause fear. This, in turn, triggers a massive defence behaviour that we know so well, but have no idea how to resolve.

In deep meditation, in moments of inner relaxation and 'letting go', this subconscious primal fear also emerges and brings us back to the prison of definable and familiar safety zones.

A 'second birth' becomes necessary, a conscious return to the origins within our body memory, with all the life experience and resources we have developed.

When, in the 'here and now', we can access a resourceful containment in the body, a deep acceptance and understanding of what has happened to us during our pregnancy and birth can be experienced. We also come to know how this process was meant to be by nature, according to our inbuilt biological blueprint.

In all my years of therapeutic work, I am still amazed and touched by people's ability to repair and heal these wounds, growing new qualities in their lives and exploring unknown spiritual dimensions.

Working with Birth Trauma

'Born to be a Buddha' is a birth integration process that has developed out of working, exploring and experimenting with different methods of breathing, bodywork and meditation techniques over more than 30 years. The process is part of the Osho Diamond Breath Training, but is also done as a separate group or individual process.

Birth is a very individual experience and each person has their own story. What will emerge from the process is not predictable, nor can it be pushed. It needs a safe environment, a trusting connection between therapist and client, and the ability to access healthy resources in a client's present life.

At a certain point in the breathing process, while working with a client, traumatic sensations in the form of body memories from birth are likely to present themselves. In the past, in the times when rebirthing was a new method, people often entered into these memories without preparation.

Being overwhelmed, unable to integrate or understand their own feelings, it took a long time to work through the layers of fear and confusion that were surfacing. Times and styles have changed, but I still use 'connected breathing' as one of the main methods in this process. When used in a safe context with different body exercises and preparation, it turns into a conscious exploration of the self-regulating abilities of our body and psyche

Each person can find their own rhythm of breathing, their own pace in body movements, as well as expression of emotions or needs. The active breathing part can go from twenty to sixty minutes, depending on what emerges and how it can be processed and integrated.

Afterwards, there follows a time of relaxation letting the body/mind/being absorb what has opened or been released. Most sessions are accompanied with a therapist, or experienced partner, who knows how to be present and supports the individual in whatever way is needed.

Connected Breathing

Connected breathing is an outstanding method of penetrating the early body memories and to consciously re-live traumatic experiences. Connected breathing means breathing without pause, breathing in and out in an uninterrupted wave or circular movement.

This is not just a breathing technique. It reproduces the breathing pattern of the newborn child. Directly after birth, the child requires between twenty to ninety minutes for the lungs to expand and for breathing to settle. During this time, connected breathing is the child's natural rhythm.

Afterwards, breathing falls into a new rhythm, with a pause at the end of each inhalation and another pause at the end of each exhalation. For a newly born baby, the onset of this new breathing pattern indicates that the initial breath process is complete and it is time to relax, so at this point the baby can remain in a sleeping or relaxed state for the next thirty hours.

In a session, connected breathing often has the effect that the body soon remembers all the traumatic tensions related to birth. One can learn to accept these feelings and consciously flow with them, by letting movements and changes in breathing happen without interfering.

The more you give yourself up to the breathing wave, the more intuitive and natural it becomes. Strong breathing waves get the body to unwind in movement or expression, then dissolve into deeper, more relaxed breathing patterns.

When given space, highly tense emotions such as pain and anger melt away into pleasant sensations. Gradually, a vibrating flow of energy opens up a deep release in the body, in which breathing breaks away from all control and swings back into the centre of the abdomen.

In this deep release, the nervous system's core tension dissolves, the body recuperates and regenerates, and all recently-experienced memory associations become integrated. The life energy flows from the inner core to the periphery and back – the breathing pattern of silence – and the door to life is open again.

Birth: the Core Issue

This Birth Integration session took place in the context of a long process of group and individual work.

Originally, Kerstin came with somatic stress symptoms: difficult sleeping patterns, nervousness, unpredictable sweat attacks, plus stress and anger at not being able to control any of these symptoms.

Her intuitive idea was to go back to the beginning of her life and therefore she wanted to do the birth integration process. She had little information about how her birth had been. When asked, her mother had made a few general remarks, saying everything went fine, then changed the topic of conversation.

Sometimes, Kerstin's sweating attacks happened when there were expectations of certain achievements in her job, or when she had to make a presentation, but also in close emotional situations with friends, or with her love partner.

Kerstin described it as a sudden onset of tension in the body, followed by a feeling of claustrophobia and then extensive visible sweating. The only way to control the sweating was to move out of the situation, which gave her a certain feeling of control and empowerment, but there was no clear sense of what triggered the sweating, or what the original cause may have been.

During these attacks, she had no real sense of fear, just nervousness and a feeling of being closed in. Her response came more in the form of irritation and anger.

From the way she presented her situation, and getting to know more details about her childhood and her life situation, Kerstin's intuition seemed right: behind the symptoms, everything pointed at a possible bonding issue and conflict with her mother.

We had already worked together over a period of several

months and she had participated in some 'breath and trauma' groups as well as a 'birth integration' group process.

There is no specific goal to reach in the 'birth integration process' as every person is at a different place in their exploration and there is always the possibility to learn and discover more about how to regulate life energy.

Birth Session

When she came for the session, Kerstin was excited, having had a dream she felt was very important. This did not surprise me. In my experience, birth experiences often show up for the first time in dreams, with images such as tunnels, being stuck in a car, or falling from a height.

But Kerstin's was especially precise. She found herself in an elevator, not knowing if it was going up or down. At first, she was relaxed and curious about where she was going, but then, as the elevator failed to arrive anywhere, she began to worry and wanted to get out. The moment she wanted to get out, it felt like the walls of the elevator began to close in and there was a strong pressure in her head.

The sessions are what I call an 'open space' to see what happens in the moment and to respond to where energy and movement want to go. With Kerstin, we have developed a pattern of connecting and checking in with each other, followed by a guided meditation or grounding exercise, before going into breathing.

Most often, Kerstin used the sessions to go into a breathing process. She liked breathing as it gave her a sense of let go and empowerment at the same time.

This time, she wanted to begin with a felt-sense guided meditation I'd been doing with her in the previous sessions. She loved the feeling of relaxation plus heightened awareness and liked to remain with closed eyes for some time, which in the beginning had not been possible for her.

Usually, in these guided meditations, I move into a body scan, letting the person sense the different areas of the body: the basic bone structure ... surrounded by muscles ... coming finally to the skin as a clear boundary and definition of the body.

With Kerstin I kept it simple, beginning in the sitting position, inviting her to give space for her legs to feel firmly grounded, for the solidity of her pelvis to carry the weight of her upper body naturally and easily, for a safe feeling of support from the back of her chair.

As we progressed, she seemed absorbed in her inner sensing, and yet there were subtle movements all the time in her feet, hands and neck. In her whole physical presence there was an alert anticipation, which I took to be an expression of the initial excitement with which she came.

I included the excitement of her dream and the physical sense of it in my guidance and within a few moments all movements relaxed. This was an important message for me, showing how essential this dream must be for Kerstin and the need for it to be understood.

When she opened her eyes she described a feeling of space in her upper body and a sense of energy flowing through her legs. I asked her if she was able to sense the safety of my session room as well as the tension building inside her and she nodded.

When I asked her if she needed something, she said she wanted to lie down on the mattress to have the space to let her body move. I encouraged her to allow any movement, but slowly, so she could feel it and connect with it, while staying in contact with me.

Recalling the images of her dream, I asked her if there was a way for her to get out of the elevator, or whether she needed help. In response, Kerstin's body started to move and she raised both hands as fists to her chest. Suddenly, she looked like a stuck baby. With her hands, it seemed like she was trying to pull open the doors of the elevator with enormous effort.

In that moment, the sweating started, the breathing faded and Kerstin's neck and head looked contracted. Feeling safe and in contact with me, she could allow all this without going into shock, panic or cutting off the experience.

216

I offered her to touch her head. She agreed and the moment my hands softly held her neck and forehead, her whole body stretched out in an amazing movement, making the same kind of turning and unwinding motion that babies do as they emerge from the birth canal.

It was a very special moment, yet at the same time it seemed so simple and natural. Her body stretched out on the mattress, shivering a little, breathing and unfolding in all kinds of tiny movements. The breathing went by itself into a connected breath pattern, very easy and flowing.

But then the process was interrupted. Everything stopped and she seemed to be disconnecting from her body. I knew this was a crucial moment. I put my hand on her spine, in the area of the seventh cervical vertebra, as a gentle holding touch – in bodywork, this point is also known as the panic point. My other hand rested lightly on her upper chest, where there was a very shallow breath, as if not daring to flow deeper into the body.

I asked Kerstin to tell me what she was experiencing. She whispered that she clearly could picture herself, high above her body, pulled between an image of her mother lying in a hospital room and a little tiny body in a small bed in a different room. She was totally confused where she belonged.

I asked her to if she could feel my hands. She confirmed that she could and with a gasp her breathing increased. This is the moment where somebody can easily go into an unconscious fear-breathing pattern, but with reassuring touch and encouraging words to maintain contact, one can support the body and the breathing to stay easy and relaxed.

When I connected to her with my touch and voice, again her breathing changed. Now it moved as a soft hesitant wave, breathing into the upper chest. She was in a birth-breathing pattern. Her body released in subtle jerking movements in her upper back and then shivering little waves flowed down the back – this she described as a pleasant sensation.

Her body seemed to relax more deeply into these movements

217

and her breath became stronger and deeper, with gasping sounds on the out-breath. It was beautiful to watch and to feel her naturally reclaiming her body, as if she was that little baby, choosing to inhabit her newborn body.

Her hands went into clear gripping reflexes, just like a baby, snatching my fingers immediately when I offered them to her hand. She smiled and opened her eyes, still breathing naturally. The wave-breathing went on for twenty minutes and energy released in gentle soft movements throughout the whole body.

Afterwards, she went into a profound state of relaxation which she later described as 'finally coming home'.

Reflection

What fascinated Kerstin most in the session was the moment when the sweating started. She felt that if she did not find a way to move she would die, but at the same time she knew she could not do it alone. Even before I touched her, there was an inner impulse – like a cellular information – that it was time for a push and an effort.

The other strong experience happened when she was floating in the air between her mother's body and her own body. There was total disorientation and her whole attraction was to move towards the mother's body, but finally the breathing forced her into her own.

This moment was paired with a deep feeling of desperation and sense of 'lostness'. Only my touch and my voice made it possible for her to stay connected to the body and re-live what she had been through, all those years ago.

I encouraged her to talk with her mother again, approaching her with more precise questions about her birth. This time the information was forthcoming. Her mother admitted that her daughter's birth was far from normal. Kerstin had been stuck in the birth canal for more than 18hours and the mother did not remember how she finally came out. Also, the mother was so exhausted that they took Kerstin away and put her in the hospital's baby room.

Following this session, Kerstin's sweating attacks did not immediately disappear, but she lost her fear of it. This, in turn, made it easier to find resources and tools to deal with the issue in a more constructive manner.

During the time we worked together, Kerstin had chosen to do Devavani Meditation on a regular basis, which includes a fifteen-minute section of making soft sounds of gibberish or nonsense – similar to Osho's No Mind Meditation but much more soft and gentle.

After our session, the quality of this meditation changed and she felt like an alive and happy child, deeply connected with her body, allowing delightful sounds of joy.

CHAPTER ELEVEN

The Roots of Love:
Osho Family Constellation

Svagito

When I came to Osho in 1979 I was a newly-baked psychologist. The first thing I did was throw away all my psychology books and papers. It needed an enlightened Master to make it clear to me that knowledge is not the way to know yourself, nor the main ingredient in working with people. As was once said in a tale about Saraha, the founder of the spiritual tradition of Tantra, the learned has to go to the vital, the false has to go to the real.

In the beginning, I was not in search of any Master, but for something that was missing in my therapy and psychology training. It was meditation. It took me a while to understand that to be with Osho means following your deeper inner truth, not your own mind and not anybody's teaching. After doing other kinds of work in Osho's communes for some years, learning to be more in the present and less in the mind, I started working with therapy once more, but now I was no longer a psychologist and knowledge did not impress me.

I was studying, practising and teaching bodywork, Breath, Pulsation, Energywork and many other therapeutic methods for years and finally, in the late 90s, I discovered Family Constellation. This new approach to therapy – soon to become popular worldwide amongst psychotherapists and health professionals – offered a new way of looking at human beings and seemed to present simple solutions to complex problems.

In my life, I often wanted to get away from my family, was never really interested in my ancestors, or paid much attention to past events in our family. Discovering Family Constellation helped me to understand more profoundly how we are all connected to the past and what it truly means to leave the past behind. I became more conscious of my own arrogance and understood that without a deep love and gratitude towards one's parents self- love remains just an empty word.

Family Constellation offered fascinating new insights about love, respect, freedom, gratitude. But, at the same time, there was a tendency for some people to draw conclusions based on aquired knowledge rather than observation, and use systemic principles as a guide for the right way of living. Family Constellation has the potential to help people come out from their prisons of old beliefs and ideas, but this should not turn into a new conditioning about love and how to behave according to a set of rules.

For me, Osho Family Constellation is a help to self-inquiry, a way to look at yourself and at life from a new perspective without becoming a rigid believer in the principles of this form of systemic therapy. The fullness of life and the many dimensions of an individual cannot be reduced to one path.

These days, I work with many different forms of therapy – some of them described in this book – so it is easy for me to remain unidentified with a single approach. During a Family Constellation session I can easily shift and do something quite different and seemingly unrelated to systemic work, which takes people out of a routine way of looking at life.

Family Constellation is full of surprises – maybe this is why it became so popular. One suddenly finds oneself turned upside down, or better: right side up. Old beliefs about love and relationships turn out to be utterly wrong and we discover unconscious motivations for our behaviours of which we were completely unaware. In fact, we find that we are bonded and connected to a much larger energy that moves us in ways beyond our personal choices, likings and dis-likings.

Ideas about Freedom

Our modern day ideas about freedom of the individual receive a big blow. The movements in this work reveal that we are part of a relational field that not only includes our family, but also our whole culture, nation and ultimately all of life. In this sense, what we observe in a constellation goes far beyond ordinary family dynamics.

We come to therapy with the idea of fixing a problem, gaining a little more insight, adjusting our concepts ... turning a few screws here and there. In a constellation, we suddenly find ourselves turned around completely. Our issues are related to a vast energy field, a complex system, where many people, past and present, are involved, something we never thought about before.

The idea that I am sufficient onto myself that I am a self-made person is just one of the most egoistic attitudes, foolish and false. We are not independent, we are not dependant, we live in a kind of inter-dependence. That is the truth. ~ Osho[1]

Systemic Therapy

First, a short introduction to this work that, since the year 2000, has received so much attention that in almost every country it is well-known in growth and therapy circles.

Systemic therapy is a form of therapy that understands the individual and his problems in the context of a larger group and the relationships within that group – particularly within a family system. In such a relational field, everyone's behaviour, feelings and attitudes have an effect on all the other family members.

Such an approach is neither primarily analytical – like trying to find causes in childhood – nor does it treat symptoms, but focuses on helping a system develop a new way of functioning as a whole, that allows growth. Stagnant behaviour patterns in groups of people are addressed directly, but it is not the therapist who holds the key to change. He is supporting the whole system to change itself.

Family Constellation was originally developed by Bert Hellinger, a German therapist. In the German language, his work is called *Familienstellen*, which has been translated as 'Family Constellation'. Hellinger's approach is unique and differs significantly from other systemic approaches. In his work, people are chosen to represent certain members of a client's family and are placed in an open space without further instructions.

In the original style, the client would place them in relation to each other, so a kind of picture was attained that revealed something about the relationship dynamics between the members of a family. In the latest approach, the representatives are not positioned according to the client's inner picture and are not moved around by a facilitator, but rather are asked to observe their inner impulses and follow them freely.

What becomes manifest is a moving portrait of a certain family to which the client belongs, revealing the degree of intimacy, pain, love, or sense of abandonment that everyone feels in relation to the others. It also exposes deep identifications and entanglements that result from the fact that everyone is bonded to a large system, or collective, that includes many other people from past and present.

Working in this way is not limited to a family. One can place members of any system in a constellation – members of a company, team, or class – and understand something of the relationship dynamics of that particular system.

The Collective Field

A constellation reveals the presence of a collective energy field that has a strong influence on everyone who belongs to it. It makes the effects visible to outside observers, including the client. It also allows people, who have no knowledge about a client and of his family, to step into the field and be moved by it.

For someone watching a constellation session for the first time it is surprising and seemingly miraculous how representatives – who have received no information other than being told whom they represent – start acting in ways that accurately reflect the feelings and behaviour of the family members they represent. This may include, for example, experiencing a physical handicap which the representative knew nothing about.

There is no scientific explanation for this phenomenon other than concluding that there exists an energy field, or knowing field, or 'morphogenetic' field – as various authors call it – into which representatives can tap and allow themselves to be guided. Through these movements, a deep truth about a family system comes to light.

Another unique aspect of this approach is that it shows the strong influence of family members who belonged to former generations, including those who are dead, and also people who are not blood relatives but who bonded with the client's family in some way. This influence of people from other generations has been demonstrated in a science called epigenetics, which studies how experience affects our genes – not only from our own life experiences, but also from those of our mother, grandmother and further back in time.

Epigenetics shows that our experiences and those of our forebears are never gone, even if they have been forgotten. They become a part of us, a molecular residue holding fast to our genetic scaffolding. In other words, you may have inherited not just your grandmother's knobby knees, but also her predisposition toward depression caused by the neglect she suffered as a baby.

This kind of inheritance reveals itself in a constellation. A client may discover a deeper truth about himself, of which he is ordinarily unaware, that shows how the past has a grip on him. In response, he can learn to relax with the past and at the same time discover how to be more connected and in tune with the present.

Another unique aspect of the Family Constellation method is that the client hardly speaks. After representatives for family members have been placed, the client remains an observer for most of the session, although he may be placed in the constellation towards the end – replacing the person who was representing him.

As the client is merely a witness to the process, his mind is less likely to interfere with what the constellation shows. In this way, it is an effective method to by-pass superficial layers of one's mind, where desires, attitudes and beliefs are generated. Instead, it can directly approach the roots of conflict.

The client comes in touch with a deeper part of his mind, beneath his day-to-day level of consciousness. Hellinger calls this deeper layer 'soul', but I prefer to call it 'collective mind'. Either way, this deeper layer is what the representatives perceive and feel within a constellation. So a constellation is actually a mirror of what goes on inside the client on a deeper level, showing how collective and universal forces operate within him.

In Tune with Life

For me, one amazing aspect of working with constellations is to realize that sometimes it is not even necessary to know which family member is being represented. The field still reveals an important dynamic to the client. Even if the client does not consciously understand everything that has happened, the constellation will still have a healing influence on him.

Placing representatives without telling them for whom they stand is different from conventional therapy and even different from the way Family Constellation was done in the beginning, when everything was clearly defined.

In the original style, a constellation moved from an entangled picture to a healing picture, from a problem to a solution. The constellation was guided by a facilitator, who helped everyone find a new and more appropriate position within the system. There were laws to be recognized, rules to be followed and the facilitator had a certain concept about what was right.

Even though this style of work has significance and a healing effect, it appears rather static and controlled. One follows a concept. For me, personally, this is less in tune with how I learned to work with people around Osho, where the emphasis is on energy work and on trusting the moment.

In reality, there is no real distinction between an entangled and a healing picture, as everything is always evolving and entanglement is just part of life. Life is moving towards perfection, but perfection is never reached, since perfection implies an end to growth without the possibility of further development.

In our minds, we have a notion that for every 'problem' there needs to be a 'solution'. But according to Osho problems are only our interpretations of situations, so even the idea of a 'solution' is not really in tune with life.

I have not come across a real problem yet. All problems are bogus. You create them, because without problems you feel empty, nothing to do then, nothing to fight with, nowhere to go.... You create problems, so that you feel life is a great work, growth..... First you create a problem and then you go in search of a solution.
~ Osho[2]

With this in mind, I usually prefer to allow representatives in a constellation to move freely, as they tune into the field. This style of constellation has no beginning and no end. Rather, it is more like taking a clip from a movie of the client's life. I watch a flow of energy, similar to a flowing river, and at the most my job may entail moving some stones, so the water can flow more freely.

Everyone who is present, whether client, therapist or neutral observer, learns something as they watch a constellation unfold. The more objectively and unprejudiced they are able to watch, the more insights will arise. It is like receiving a lesson from life, in which love sometimes flows in strange and unexpected ways.

Session sample: A woman's two uncles – her father's brothers – were shot by a firing squad at the end of a civil war. When, in the constellation, we placed people for the firing squad, the client's representative felt a deep compassion for those who performed the execution. Out of an unconscious identification, she unknowingly took over the emotions and a certain behaviour of the perpetrators. Now the client understood for the first time, why she had such a hidden, unexplainable aggression towards her husband and children and why they experienced her as such a threat.

A Hidden Truth

A constellation brings to light a hidden truth, but there is no 'fixing' or 'solving' a problem in the usual sense. A client understands more deeply why he or she is behaving in certain ways and this in itself may be the solution.

226

This understanding may change things in future, but change is more like a side-effect and not the purpose of the session. It reminds me of one of Osho's comments, in which he said that life will change you, but you cannot change life according to your own inclinations.

Understood in this way, therapy in general and Family Constellation in particular take on a different colour. The primary aim of a session is no more to help a person get what he wants in terms of solving his problem. It is more about falling in tune with life, flowing with life without resistance.

A constellation shows us whether we are in tune with life and, if not, what may be preventing it. We may realize it is time to finally say goodbye to our mother, to stop clinging to her, or we may connect with a deep part in us that wants to remain with her. We may discover that we need to look back at someone in the past and express gratitude which, up to now, we have withheld. Or, we may learn that it is time to stop being so concerned about past events and live more in the present.

In the beginning of a session, no one can know for sure what it means for a client to be in tune with his life. That is why no formula can be applied to any session. The same intervention never works twice in exactly the same manner.

This is evident when working with diseases. Naturally, a client with an illness comes to a session because he wants to heal, he wants to get rid of what is troubling him, but a therapist should not automatically assume he has a right to help a client in this way. Sometimes, a disease has to be accepted and received as part of a client's destiny. In other situations, a disease may have arisen because a client is not in tune with life. He may have excluded someone from his life and the disease is a reminder that there is 'dis-ease' in the family system. In each case, the work of a constellation will be different.

In my view, a good constellation has no goal as such, but will help a client to be more in harmony with his life, letting go of any personal desires that may be in conflict with his destiny.

Our modern conditioning and upbringing gives us a false sense that life is totally in our hands. This reminds me of the American slogan 'yes we can' and how utterly false and misleading it is on a deeper level. In fact, nothing essential in life is ever in our hands. We *cannot* change our life destiny in the sense that we have already been born into a certain family, culture, religion, nation.

A constellation can help a client realize this and become more mature, less childish. For example, a child thinks he is the centre of the universe, an adult knows he is only a small part of the whole. A child wants to be loved by someone else; an adult finds love within himself. A child is willing to sacrifice himself for another, an adult knows about respectful, non-interfering love.

Systemic Laws

By observing the interactions of those who belong to the same system, one can deduct certain systemic laws. These laws guide people's behaviour and way of thinking at an unconscious level. Just as Freud discovered that our actions are guided by our personal unconscious mind, a constellation reveals the collective unconscious and its powerful influence on all members of a family system.

Systemic laws show how the unconscious mind functions. As we grow up, we begin to assimilate values from other people, especially from our parents. We develop a personal conscience and begin to experience feelings of guilt and innocence that tell us when our sense of belonging to our family or social group is strengthened or jeopardised. We feel innocent when we behave according to the values we have been given. We feel guilty when we go against them.

However, there is a deeper conscience unrelated to values acquired from families and social groups. It is universal. It works in all human beings. This collective conscience is made visible in a constellation. We see collective laws operating in families, whether they are from China, Italy or Brazil, whether they are Christian or Hindu or Moslem.

The Law of Belonging

The *law of belonging* is a principle that every member of a system has the same right to be a part of it as any other. This is a simple truth, but we often do not consider it in everyday life. We exclude others in many ways, for example, by judging them, forgetting they exist, ostracizing them, wishing they were not here, or simply by disliking them.

The negative consequences of exclusion are seen in a constellation of a family, where a child of a later generation unknowingly identifies with a former family member who has been pushed out. It can be seen in whole nations, when members of a younger generation adopt behaviour and beliefs from the past, imitating those who were rejected or hated. It can also be seen in companies, where employees identify with those who have been unfairly dismissed.

The deeper spiritual truth of this principle is that, in existence, there are no divisions of better and worse, higher and lower, good or bad. Everyone, even the worst criminals, have their part to play in the drama of life.

A constellation can help us realize the oneness of life and learn to open up to those people, who, for one reason or another, have been excluded, forgotten, judged or disliked. It requires us to give up the childish idea of wanting to be on the side of the 'good' ones. Spiritual growth depends on including what is rejected, judged or ignored – both inside and outside oneself.

The Law of Order

The *law of order* or *systemic hierarchy* is another important principle that, if disregarded, leads to conflict and suffering. In modern families, for example, it is very common that children are either disrespectful to their parents, or dismiss them as out of date, or treat them as children, or as if they are unable to handle their affairs.

This is not necessarily done with bad intentions. In Family Constellation, we see how children often want to save their parents from traumas of the past, which is well-intentioned but misguided because the child is thereby violating the Law of Order, trying to be 'bigger' than his parents. This leads to unnecessary suffering.

For example, a client may be identified with her grandmother, who died early in life, perhaps when her mother was still a small child. As a consequence of this identification, she will tend to relate to her own mother as if she is the real parent and her mother the child. This leads to an unhealthy mother-child bonding, which in future will make it difficult for her to move into relationships and create her own life.

Such identifications become visible in a constellation, perhaps showing a client why she does not want to be in relationship, or to be happy. Remaining in misery gives one a sense of belonging and being loyal. Bonding and loyalty are the main causes for unhappiness and it is not easy to move beyond them. Misery gives us a sense of innocence and goodness, while happiness is accompanied by a sense of guilt – how can I be joyful, if my mother suffered so much? It takes courage to tolerate feelings of guilt, to risk to be an outsider and not accepted by the family or social group.

A Cypriot woman came to a session and reported that she lived outside her country and whenever she returned there, she would be overwhelmed with pain, which could lead to bodily symptoms. It was clear to me that she carried the pains of her people, who were involved in conflicts of the past between Turkish and Greek Cypriots.

She herself came from the Turkish part of the island and when the translator translated 'Greek part' and 'Turkish part' she became annoyed, which indicated her love for all Cypriots.

Rather than guiding her through a whole constellation, I decided to do a small exercise with her, where she practised being an outsider and – as a consequence – would not carry everybody's pain. I invited her to stand in front of representatives for Greek Cypriots and tell them that she was Turkish and loved the Turks. Then I invited her to stand in front of representatives for Turkish Cypriots and tell them she also loved the Greeks.

In each group there were some representatives who loved her for saying this and others who didn't. She accepted that she wasn't liked by some, but was still able to look at all of them with love.

The deeper spiritual truth of this principle is that we all have a unique place in life and a unique destiny that we cannot share with anyone else, not even our own family. In Osho's words: we are all alone here; aloneness is our very nature.

This aloneness or uniqueness, as one could call it, also means that no one can replace us and no one will ever be like us ever again. Existence does not repeat. Systemically speaking, each member of a family system has a specific position and place within the family that belongs only to him.

In the work, I take care that everybody's place and boundaries are respected by all members of the system. Children need to learn to respect their parents' boundaries and come to terms with what they could, or could not, get from them. In other words, children need to accept their parents as they really are, not to remain clinging with an image of how they wanted them to be.

This acceptance includes the essential understanding that what the parents gave was the *only* thing they could give, and this in turn eventually leads to a feeling of gratitude. In fact, all spiritual development is a growth in our ability to feel gratitude.

Family Constellation helps a person to feel a deep 'yes' to life as it is, 'yes' to our parents as they are, and 'yes' to ourselves as we are. Only a person who loves his parents in this way can love himself.

It is important to note that acceptance should not be misunderstood as an attitude of resignation, grudging acquiescence, or saying 'yes' mechanically and habitually. Rather, it needs a quality of rejoicing and gratitude. For this reason, we usually talk about 'receiving' our parents, rather than merely 'accepting' them.

The Law of Balance

The *law of balance* as a systemic principle points to the balancing force in life. On a conscious, inter-personal level, we often have a sense of wanting to give something back, such as after receiving a gift. On a collective level, there is an unconscious drive that wants us to pay for something that our forefathers have done. For example, in constellation work, I sometimes see that children of super-rich families suffer great misfortunes, especially if those riches have been acquired by their forefathers in a ruthless or brutal way, at the cost of others.

Balance shows itself in our sense of justice and wanting fairness in life. Problems arise when we hold on to our personal sense of justice and refuse to move on, when life is not fulfilling our demands, when we do not see the bigger picture.

Collectively, or universally, the balancing principle of life can be observed in the swinging movement from one polarity to the other, as we see in nature: high tide is followed by low tide, summer by winter ... and so on.

Looking at relationships from the perspective of balance, we see two kinds. One is where balance is possible and natural, like the relationship between a man and a woman. The other is of imbalance, which typically happens in the relationship between parents and children.

With the first type, disturbance happens when for example one partner tries to give more than the other. This partner is trying to turn the other into a child and becomes like a parent himself. Such relationships do not usually last long. In the second type, disturbance happens if, for example, children try to give to their parents, or parents try to receive from their children.

The natural state is that parents give and children receive. There is no way for a child to balance what he has received from his parents. Obviously, we are not talking here about small gifts, but about *essential giving*, in the sense of the parents giving life to the child, then nurturing and raising him until he is capable of looking after himself.

The systemic principles outlined above are not really separate, but function in unison with each other. They show the nature of the human mind and its workings on both a personal and a collective level. Moving beyond mind and deeper into meditation may help an individual transcend these laws, since according to mystics like Osho an enlightened consciousness is free from all conditions.

Beyond Systemic Laws, Beyond Family

In Family Constellation we understand our inner functioning, not only on a personal level, but also on a collective level. When we learn to respect what our collective mind is trying to tell us, something starts relaxing in us. I see this happening all the time in constellation work: for example, when an excluded person has been restored to his place in the system, everyone in the room relaxes.

Now the client can be more in touch with his own individuality and follow the calling of his own life, rather than having to carry burdens from the past. This leads to more creativity, freedom, joy and the ability to move into meditation.

Here, one enters another dimension of life, where systemic laws still apply, but without binding the individual. For example, in the normal dynamics between father and son, the son may have a strong feeling that 'I do not want to become like my father', but in spite of this resolve he may eventually discover that he turned out to be rather similar. With the benefit of Family Constellation, the son may genuinely feel love for the father and accept that he shares certain similarities. This, paradoxically, creates the space in which the son has the freedom to develop other qualities that are quite different.

The more one wants to force change upon oneself the more impossible it becomes. What is needed on the path of inner transformation is deep acceptance and love. In Osho's words:

Transcendence comes through experience. You cannot manage it. It is not something that you have to do. You simply pass through many experiences and those experiences make you more and more mature. ~ Osho[3]

In one of his original books, Hellinger states that love has to follow 'order', but this is true only on a certain level of consciousness. At a higher level of awareness, where love is more than a biological drive, love becomes the only law – as so many mystics have pointed out. Instead of adopting Hellinger's view, I would rather say that love has to be conscious.

One of the important systemic principles I've mentioned is that parents essentially give and children essentially receive. This is a truth that applies to the biological dimension of their relationship. Obviously, we all received life from our parents; our physical body comes from them and we have received so many other gifts that there is no way a child can give anything back that comes even close.

But there is another dimension – let's call it spiritual – where children can give to their parents and parents can receive. Here, another law functions: the person with more awareness can give to someone with less awareness and the kind of biological relationship they have is irrelevant.

A child can share his awareness and understanding, which is a different kind of giving. It is not material. It is giving without action, without 'doing'. The child remains the child and the mother remains the mother, but when one is able to stay fully alert and aware then the ordinary, biological aspect of their relationship loses importance.

Here an example from a typical session:

A female client, I will call her Jane, had an issue with her mother. When I placed a representative of her mother and one for herself opposite each other, her mother could not look at her, but kept looking at the floor, which usually indicates that a close relative has died. Asking my client about this, I learned that her mother had lost six children (three pairs of twins) soon after birth.

When we placed representatives of the dead children lying on the floor in front of the mother, the mother became frozen, unable to move or feel anything. Obviously, she could not overcome the pain of her loss. The representative of Jane on the other side was immediately drawn to the children, her siblings, and lay down next to them feeling a kind of relief in doing this.

234

As there was no further movement I interrupted the session and asked my client if she was aware of wanting to die and if she could see the same traumatized expression in her representative's face as in her mother's.

What we see here is an example of the blind and unconditional love of a child towards her mother. We call this love 'blind', because Jane was trying to save her mother from having to feel the pain of the loss of her children, unconsciously saying to her 'I die in your place', without any consideration how her mother would feel about this. She makes herself 'bigger' than her mother, violating the principle of systemic order.

I asked my client, 'How do you think your mother and your siblings would feel, if they would be aware that you want to die as well?' In response, Jane immediately realized they would not like it.

I picked up the constellation again, this time placing the client directly in it. When she looked at her siblings, I asked her to become aware of how calm and peaceful and in tune with their destiny they looked. I also placed a person to represent 'life' behind them.

After a while, Jane also became calm, while tears rolled down her face. She came out from her death-like state and felt love towards her siblings and also towards her mother, who had suffered such a big trauma.

Now for the first time her mother could look at her with a sense of relief.

I asked her to say to her mother: 'Thank you for not giving up and trying again. I will now do something with my life. I stay.'

In this part of the work, one can see how a session progresses from blind to conscious love – how, when we bring awareness to a situation, we come in contact with a higher form of love. The mother gave birth to Jane, but could not be available to her, as she was dealing with her trauma of losing so many children. Jane, as a child, could not understand. She could only feel the grief of her mother and felt like dying herself – maybe wanting to save her mother from the pain.

Now as an adult she can see this would only increase her mother's grief and not relieve her in any way. Seeing the calmness of her siblings, taking their early death as a movement of life, considering what her mother went through, Jane could take a step back from her involvement. She understood that whatever she received from her mother was the best her mother could do, in these difficult circumstances.

Jane changed her perspective from focusing on what she did not get, to seeing what she did receive. In so doing, she not only freed herself, but also her mother. In this way, the parent can benefit from the child's growing awareness. Jane's mother could look at her daughter for the first time and feel relief. Until this happened, it was impossible for the mother to move beyond her trauma and attachment to her lost children.

The parent gives life to the child. On another level, the child can give love and understanding back to a parent and the parent can receive it. But this is a kind of 'giving' that is not a 'doing' and not an effort to save someone from pain.

This kind of scenario happens frequently in a constellation. It shows how traumas get passed on from one generation to the next. The mother's pain becomes the pain of the daughter and – unless this movement is made conscious – she will pass it on to her children.

Still, Jane will need to accept the fact that she lacked her mother's attention and learn how to heal the wound, but it will be easier for her to do so, now she understands the systemic context. So systemic work can be accompanied by somatic trauma work to help a client integrate a challenging life experience, also on the physiological level.

Family Constellation and Trauma Healing

Most events that lead to systemic entanglements are traumatic. The speciality of Family Constellation is that it shows how traumas of past generations and even of a whole country can leave their mark on the individual. While acknowledging the reality of trauma,

Family Constellation offers no specific concept for healing it on a physiological level. This can lead to a neglect of the fact that traumatized clients need to be treated in a way that differs from other clients. Not everyone is able to receive the full impact of a constellation.

The new approach to Family Constellation, where we work more with spontaneous movements of the representatives, usually unfolds in a gradual and subtle way, giving more time for integration. This is closer to the perspective of body-oriented trauma therapy, which considers trauma as an event that affects the body and its nervous system.

It is helpful to understand what actually happens in trauma –ot only psychologically, but also physiologically. It will go beyond the topic of this chapter to explore this subject extensively, but I will mention a few points. Often, traumatized clients are either hyperactive or in a dissociated state. In such cases, before beginning a constellation, it will be helpful to lower a client's level of arousal and help the body to discharge excessive energy that is related to an unresolved trauma. This preliminary process grounds a client in the present moment and makes him more available to observe, absorb and integrate the work.

I have discovered that guiding a client to track his body sensations, moving through cycles of activation and discharge at the beginning of a session – without being too concerned about relating this to family dynamics – can help me discover the most important family member with whom to begin the constellation. The responses of the client's body guides us to what is important.

In this simple example, one can see how working with the physiology supports and prepares the systemic work:

A female client, about forty-years-old, is having a session. She is quite fearful, her body is trembling and she has difficulty speaking with a normal tone of voice. Before inquiring about her issue, I first help her to become more calm. I suggest that she doesn't fight with the trembling feeling, but rather focuses on an area of her body that is less affected and relatively calm. This helps her tolerate the activation more easily and soon she is able to discharge some of the physical tension. I also help her to realize – simply by inviting her to look around -- that she is in a safe and supportive environment.

After grounding and resourcing her in this way, she tells me that a memory is arising of her father suffocating her with a pillow, when she was about six years of age. She remembers that she felt she was going to die. Without going further into this memory, I remind her that she didn't die and, when she relaxes a little, I ask if she remembers where her mother was at the time, and if there was any support available.

She tells me that her mother and other siblings were watching the event and seem to have been paralyzed. She remembers the feeling of letting go and not fighting. I inquire if this response was perhaps what saved her and she agrees. I point out her ability to let go and surrender as a personal resource that saved her life. After this, her energy slowly starts to expand. Previously, her energy had been pulled back from the periphery of her body and held at the core, with her extremities being under-charged and in a state of near-collapse – a typical fear-type physical condition.

Now her body position changes and her arms become more charged with energy. When I invite her to carefully track her body sensations she starts noticing the charge as it enters her arms and hands. As this happens, she makes defensive and protective gestures, especially with her right hand and arm. After following this for a while, she feels more grounded, present and in her strength. I explain to her what happens in the body after such a traumatic event and also the difficulty in developing self-trust that occurs when a parent is unable to be a safe and reliable support for a child.

Now my client is more stable and ready to look at the family dynamics that may have driven her father to become such a threat to her life . It is clear that she will have to solve this issue with her father in order to establish healthy realtionships with men. In her life, she tends to keep men at distance, while at the same time is searching for a father figure.

Letting her face her father in a constellation from the beginning may have been an overwhelming experience for her. Such a confrontation without proper preparation could have led to a strong reaction, or traumatized her further. Now she is more prepared. I ask her if she feels ready to proceed with the constellation and she agrees.

She chooses representatives for her father and for herself, then watches at a safe distance. What shows in the constellation is that her father cannot see his daughter, but took over a murderous impulse from his grandfather, who murdered someone. She, his daughter, identified with the person who was murdered, which led to the re-enactment of this past drama. When this comes to light, both father and daughter are relieved and for the first time can really see each other as who they really are.

Even though a full reconciliation with her father did not happen in this one session, the client for the first time had a sense of being able to relax with her father and was later able to visit him, something that had been difficult for her before. She also felt more at ease about her present life situation, to allow things to grow slowly, without forcing herself into having steady relationships with men.

This leads me to acknowledging how important it is to include bodywork and body-oriented meditations in the work of Family Constellation. We always include Dynamic and Kundalini meditation in all seminars. The body needs to be given the space to integrate insights gained during a session. To become conscious of what our body is carrying in terms of undischarged, stuck energy is even more important for trauma clients. They often suffer from symptoms that need to be addressed physically, not just through understanding the family dynamics.

For example, with clients who have suffered sexual abuse I often do initial work on grounding and discharge before the constellation. Otherwise, it may overwhelm them to see their representative facing the perpetrator and their emotional charge will not allow them to absorb a new insight about the underlying dynamics.

Before and after such a constellation, I give time for sensing the body and feeling how the body is responding to what has been said or seen. Life happens in the body and that is where integration needs to take place. As Osho said: "All growth depends on how one is related to the body."

All trauma work inevitably leads to issues concerning victims and perpetrators and a basic element in the healing of such events is that the perpetrator must be given a place. In order to do this, victims often need to recognize and acknowledge the perpetrator energy inside themselves. In other words, when one is identified with fear, one needs to find anger inside. Conversely, a person who is identified with being angry needs to acknowledge his hidden fear. In this way, inner and outer balance is restored and one experiences wholeness – what was disconnected becomes part of the greater whole again.

In my view, effective therapy addresses all levels – physical, emotional and mental – as they are closely interconnected. For example, a client may understand the importance of honouring his parents, but intellectual comprehension will have little effect unless he is able to open up to the pain that is at the source of his 'no' towards them.

Trauma has the effect of impairing one's ability to say 'yes' to life. A person becomes either disconnected from the flow of life, or develops negative attitudes towards life. At the source of these attitudes is an overwhelming pain, plus the fear of having to face it once again. Only when a person feels safe, grounded in his body and resourced can he allow himself to open up.

Successful therapy completes something of the past, psychologically and physically. It restores a person's capacity to be more in the present and available to move forward in life. Having processed and integrated a painful history effectively, a person develops strength that he would not otherwise possess. Now a true 'yes' to life is possible.

Learning from Family Constellation

Some of the important elements I learned from constellation work:

● Family Constellation is a down-to-earth approach and brings a person in touch with reality within a short time. Deep insights are possible without lengthy analysis. The picture of a constellation talks to our unconscious mind and has a stronger impact than intellectual understanding. Words are less important than movements and action.

● A constellation shows how we are all connected to each other. Often, in life, we behave without this awareness and live in illusion as an isolated 'I'. A constellation reminds us that when we think we are taking a 'free' decision, we are in fact being moved by deeper forces. We do not have the freedom *not* to love our parents, or not to be connected to our ancestors. We may not understand and feel this consciously, but every child loves his parents – it is not his choice. A constellation brings this love to light.

● Through seeing what binds people, we become more open and compassionate. Everyone, who watches a constellation, including myself, can experience how the heart opens to someone after understanding what burdens he has been carrying for his family – something one would have been unable to do in the same way before. Family Constellation helps us to move beyond our judgements in an effortless and natural way.

● Ordinarily, in our relationships, we tend to take the behaviour of others too personally, as if it is related to us – in a positive or negative sense. A constellation helps us move beyond the personal and realize that no one is at fault. The concept of personal guilt loses meaning. We are all entangled in family destiny and unknowingly carrying the feelings of others.

● Often, we think that by knowing the cause of a problem we will be able to control the outcome. Looking at life through a systemic viewpoint, seeing the bigger picture, the problem itself tends to lose importance. Rather, one learns to take life as it is. Ultimately, there is no 'why'. Life is a mystery.

• Observation is the main ingredient in the work, so there is a similarity between Family Constellation and meditation, whose essential quality is awareness, or watchfulness. To allow the energy of the collective soul to reveal itself takes time, patience and a willingness to wait. It does not mean a Family Constellation facilitator does nothing, but a non-doing attitude – with no intention how things should go – is an essential quality. Then the forces of life can manifest and we become witnesses to them.

• Finding to a deep 'yes' to our parents and ancestors, to life as it is, with all past events and tragedies, is similar to the meditative standpoint. Authentic humbleness and gratitude develop naturally.

The Osho Approach to Family Constellation

Recently, in an interview, I was asked what I felt was missing in Osho's teaching that I became interested in Family Constellation. By way of reply, I explained that the opposite was true. First, I felt something was missing in other types of therapy, which is why I became attracted to Family Constellation. Second, I found that something was missing in Family Constellation, which was why the vision of an enlightened mystic was essential.

Meditation eventually leads us to the space of the witnessing consciousness. The witness is not part of any family system. It is a space of pure 'isness'. Love arising from this space is not directed to anyone in particular. It has no roots. It just is.

The work of a Master is not a teaching, it is the destruction of teaching. You do not study how to swim with a Master, you are thrown in the water to find it out. Teaching may be helpful in the beginning, but later it becomes a barrier. I like to use Family Constellation less as a teaching, more as a method that allows us to look at life from a different angle, so new insights become possible.

Teaching has its place when people train in a certain method and wish to become facilitators, but is not the right approach when one wants to learn about oneself. One needs to go through a process of self-inquiry. Osho's emphasis has always been to help people make their own experiences rather than swallowing other people's ideas. Knowledge is handed to us by others. Knowing is our own.

In Osho Family Constellation, we do not replace an old set of rules with a new one. It is not about learning 'the way I was behaving with my parents was wrong and now I will do it right'. It is understanding the implications of my behaviour – what it does to me and others. This understanding in itself leads to change.

Often, after a constellation, people ask me 'And what should I do now?' This is like asking instructions for 'right' living, avoiding the invitation to explore for oneself. When a facilitator falls in the trap of telling people what to do, he destroys an opportunity for intelligence and freedom. Family Constellation should not be seen as a guide book, but as a map that allows you to look at the landscape of life from a new perspective. This encourages one to question old beliefs that have been carried since childhood.

By remaining in a space of inner emptiness without intention or goal, the facilitator creates an atmosphere, where spontaneous awareness can arise.

Any act done in awareness is right and any act done in unawareness is wrong ... The act does not matter; what matters is your consciousness. ~ Osho[4]

So in Osho Family Constellation we do not teach people how they should relate with their families or with love partners. We support them in gaining more awareness. Whether or not a client can respect a parent is less important than whether he is more authentic and conscious in whatever he does. In any case, greater awareness is going to lead to love and compassion for others.

So I prefer to help people see their parents in a new way. In the state of a child, one may see only what one missed from one's mother. With a more mature consciousness, one may be able to understand what one *did* receive from her, in spite of the difficulties and challenges she had to go through.

This is called a change of gestalt, or re-framing. One helps a client reinterpret his experience and the actions of others in a way that allows him to accept them as a resource rather than a deficiency.

The facilitator stands in a different place than his client. By not getting involved in the client's view of the situation, he can help the client change his perspective. This requires an ability to stand alone and respond to each situation in a fresh way, not from a fixed formula. Responding moment to moment and being authentic contributes to establishing a healing field, in which the client can learn to act from consciousness rather than conscience. The more consciousness we gain, the less grip conscience has on us.

All therapy works with the mind and in this way tries to bring harmony and peace. This can be achieved only to a certain degree, because the nature of the mind is to create more problems. The real solution to all problems is to move into a space that is beyond mind.

Often, we are able to enter a state of silence only after sorting out our inner chaos through active meditations and therapy work. This is the point where therapy ends and meditation begins. My greatest satisfaction, at the end of a course or training, is when people become interested in meditation.

Osho Family Constellation sits on the border line between therapy and meditation. Everyone involved, including the client, the representatives and also the facilitator is in a state of alertness, awareness and watching – watching what is unfolding outside and inside. We watch a drama unfold in front of us and at same time observe its effects within. Through this practice, we learn where we are identified, where we cling, and are grateful for any new understanding that arises out of the movements of the constellation.

Ultimately, as understanding grows and meditation deepens, one arrives at the state of the inner 'witness' who is not affected at all.

When nothing is spoken while the movements are unfolding, a constellation can have the quality of a meditation. No comment or analysis is required. The mind stays silent and a quality of presence and love fills the room. Of course, not all constellations are like this, but these are the most touching and profound.

As I mentioned earlier, all of my constellation work is accompanied by meditation. Or, to say it more accurately, meditation is accompanied by constellations. The meeting point of Osho Family Constellation and meditation is when we acknowledge the 'isness' of life and move beyond the idea of improvement. Then spontaneous growth becomes possible.

This, in turn, allows a deep agreement with one's parents, as they are, and also with everything that has happened in the past. Such depth of acceptance may be a life-long learning process rather than the achievement of a single session, but a constellation certainly helps us to move in that direction.

CHAPTER TWELVE

The Learning Love Approach to Growth and Intimacy

Krishnananda and Amana

Most of us long for a deep and lasting love – a love that is vibrant, intimate, safe constantly deepening and growing. Perhaps the issue that causes the most amount of suffering for many of us is missing that kind of love.

What is wrong and how can we change this painful situation?

How can we create and sustain the love we so long for?

This is the issue and these are the questions that most concern us; and the work of the Learning Love Institute is devoted to finding solutions to these questions.

The approach we describe in these pages is based in, and inspired by, the teachings of our spiritual Master, Osho. His unique contribution to inner work and the pursuit of consciousness is an artful mixture of cultivating awareness, aliveness, sensitivity, and the risk to live in love and freedom.

The work is devoted to finding a path towards deep, vibrant, sustained, committed, sexually alive and exclusive intimacy.

Begging for Love

Let's take an example.

Alice is a thirty-five-year-old woman with a long history of troublesome relationships with men. She has always been attracted to men who are not really interested in a committed relationship. When she is with them, she quickly loses herself and becomes a beggar for love and attention, complaining that she is not getting the love and attention she would like. She also says that she is hopelessly jealous and gets depressed whenever the man she is dating even looks at another woman. This only drives the other person away and the man tells her she is too needy and too possessive.

Recently she began a story with a different kind of man, one who really wants to be with her but she finds she is still attracted to her former lover who only wants a casual affair. While making love with her new man, she fantasizes about the other one. She says that she thinks about the other man obsessively but does not want to let go of the new man because she does not want to be alone. When asked what it is for her to imagine to be alone without a man, she says that it is simply too painful. She comes to us wanting a solution to her problem and some advice about how to get her former lover back.

As a child, her father was angry, frequently yelled in the house, and beat her often. Her mother was terrified of her husband and not only did not protect her from her father's rage but also often criticized and yelled at her. She still feels afraid of her father who continues to be a 'rageaholic' and she feels distant from her mother. She admits that she has deep shame and insecurities about herself, especially as a woman, and is full of fear.

The first question that arises for us while listening to Alice's story is, "What is the root of her problem?"

Often, especially when we are in pain, we are looking for a quick solution, a quick fix. This was also what Alice wanted – at first. She wanted some simple advice that would make the pain go away and get back her ex.

But the remedy for Alice's situation is much deeper than finding a practical solution for her problem. The remedy involves deep inner exploration to discover why she is creating this predicament. She is quite typical of a person who is a dependent in relationships and looking for a man to rescue her from her pain, fears and insecurities. She also suffers from low self-esteem and does not feel worthy of love.

There are two basic wounds at the root of her problem: the wound of abandonment and the wound of shame. These wounds *come from experiences in childhood, many of which we may have forgotten, denied, or minimized.*

It is clear that Alice did not have secure, dependable, consistent parental love. She has no inner experience of being loved and valued as a person, or as a woman, from when she was a child, no good role model for functional intimacy, or for a loving male presence.

The lack of these things influences the kind of men to whom she is attracted and the treatment she receives from these men. It has left her with deep wounds of shame and abandonment. But it is not really the wounds that create our problems.

It is what comes as a result of our wounds. It is our false sense of identity, a negative sense of self and of others and of the world in general, an identity of mistrust, deficiency, inadequacy, and terrible loneliness that causes our suffering.

From this false identity, we generate negative and false beliefs, negative and painful feelings of despair, hopelessness, helplessness and destructive automatic behaviours that produce the very results of which we are so afraid. That is what creates our suffering!

Often, we are not aware how profoundly our damaged sense of self influences our life today, especially our relationships. Alice's pattern is just one example of how our wounds and the false identity that comes from these wounds can affect our life today.

Not Safe to be Vulnerable

Here is another example:

Dominick is a fifty-seven-year-old wealthy businessman. Ostensibly, he comes to therapy because of continual conflicts with his girlfriend of three years and would like to find a way for them to be together more harmoniously. He complains that she pressures him for deeper commitment and is often highly reactive and emotional – both of which make him angry and pull away.

He is used to having his own way. He is not accustomed to trusting anyone and he uses his wealth and the considerable force of his personality to get people to do what he wants. He has had three significant relationships in the past including a marriage that produced three children, all of whom are now adults and living on their own.

But he suffered a terrible loss in his family and the pain of that experience caused him to reassess his life, motivating him to seek out therapy.

In his relationships with women as well as with his children, he admits he was never available because he was consumed with his work. Now, he regrets this, especially regarding his children and he feels that his current girlfriend is the first connection that really matters to him. He would like to make it work.

In couple sessions with his girlfriend, they fight. She claims he is selfish, obsessed with being right and in control, and does not embrace her as 'his woman' He argues that all her emotional outbreaks and pressure only make him less willing to give her what she wants.

His greatest difficulty has been to tolerate his vulnerability and to expose it because it was never safe for him to be vulnerable as a child. He grew up with a raging, rigid, unaffectionate and critical mother, and a father who was collapsed, weak and absent. Therefore, whenever he felt frightened, insecure, or out of control, he retreated into his own world.

He has used his considerable intelligence and persistence to excel in school and later to excel and become wealthy as a businessman. He decided very early that it was not safe to be open and vulnerable, that he needed to take care of himself. Intimate relating was not only a low priority; it was not even in his radar. In all his former relationships as well as his current one, as soon as he felt the slightest pressure or expectation, he would run away by losing himself in his work and justify his withdrawal with the belief that all women are 'bitches'.

These are the beliefs that are driving Dominick's behaviour: it is not safe to trust anyone, especially women; he must always be in control; his value and the meaning of his life is based on his success in his work.

The Wounded Child Within

Alice and Dominick have something in common: the wounded child in their psyche, who is filled with a negative false identity and negative beliefs. This is what is running their lives.

The important question, then, is: how can we change this negative sense of self and develop more trust in ourselves, others, and life?

To make this change, we need to understand what we call, 'the wounded child state of consciousness'.

In the child state, we want to avoid discomfort, fear, or pain, in any way possible. The child has no interest or ability to contain, accept, or stay present to any kind of disturbance. It wants harmony, comfort and nourishment.

From this space, in the child state, we will control, manipulate, fight, compromise, rescue, become subservient, or withdraw, whenever we feel threatened, insecure, or unloved.

In the state of wounded child consciousness, it is always the outside circumstances or the other person, or other people, who are at fault and we will try to fight, fix, change, control, or go away, to get rid of the problem.

We will try to avoid any kind of attack, slight, judgment, rejection, failure, or criticism because we don't want to feel the pain and fear these can cause. And if we experience any of them, we will react – quickly, automatically and often unconsciously.

A setback of any kind, a rejection, failure, or lack of attention, can confirm negative beliefs about life, others and, worst of all, about ourselves, all of which have already been present inside of us for a long time.

In the child state, if we encounter a failure, obstacle, or discouragement, we either compulsively and perhaps aggressively push harder, or complain, or we give up and become depressed. The child hates responsibility and may leave messes hoping that someone will magically take care of them.

Or, we may go to the other extreme and become overly responsible, obsessively taking care of things, solving problems and keeping the boat afloat, fully convinced that no one can do it as well as we can.

Furthermore, our child likes to live in fantasies because often reality is too painful and frightening, escaping into spiritual platitudes, rules and ideas.

Recognizing Our Patterns

Do you recognize any of these patterns in yourself? Can you recognize your own child state of consciousness in your relating with others, especially with those closest to you? Underneath these behaviour styles are some strong beliefs that may be determining how we live and how we relate.

For instance:

● "What is the point? I might as well give up."

● "You can't trust anybody. I will never get the love, understanding, or attention I need."

● "I deserve to be loved unconditionally."

● "Other people are responsible for my pain."

● "I need someone to make me happy."

● "It is not safe to be vulnerable because others will take advantage of me."

● "It is important to help people, even if I don't want to."

● "If I stand up for myself the other person will be hurt or take advantage of me."

● "I have to be careful because something bad could happen."

● "I don't deserve love."

● "No one really understands me."

● "I can't make it."

● "Everything is too much."

● "I am too selfish."

● "Life is too hard and difficult."

● "It's all my fault, I am bad and wrong."

These are all aspects of the child state of consciousness. We all get taken over at times by our child state. But are we aware of it and how much do we allow it to run our lives?

The Secret to Finding Love

When we enter a relationship, most of the time, it is not from our mature adult self who has the capacity to see the situation the way it really is. Most often, it is from our wounded child self who doesn't see the other, or ourselves, clearly and fully.

Once we can identity, feel and bring awareness to the child state of consciousness, we have the ability to live and relate from a higher level of consciousness.

The secret to finding love is coming out of our automatic and pervasive child state of consciousness and replacing it with a mature adult state of consciousness.

So, how do we change from living in the child state of consciousness to living in a mature adult state of consciousness?

The first aspect of our healing is recognizing we have been living in our child state of consciousness and then beginning to see how our child thinks, feels, and behaves.

Prior to developing this awareness, we are living like robots. In our work, we use a metaphor to describe this state. We ask people to take a pillow and imagine that this is their wounded child. Then we tell them that, when their wounded child is running their life, it is as if the pillow is on their head.

"Your adult self is not in charge of your life, your child is driving your car."

"Imagine what it is like if your child is driving your car.

"Chances are you will drive into a tree or hit another car, perhaps your girlfriend's car."

Observing and getting to know our wounded child state of consciousness involves noticing three aspects of this consciousness: feelings and body sensations, thoughts, and behaviour.

Normally, in our unconscious state, we do not separate these three aspects of our experience. But if we pay attention, we can begin to observe our child in action.

For instance, Alice already anticipates rejection because she believes this is what she deserves. Inside, she feels profoundly insecure and empty, powerless and unworthy when she is with men. She covers this insecurity with expectations that a man should 'be there' for her, totally present and available. However, her expectations and clinging behaviour drive men away.

We call this, 'abandonment and shame go shopping'.

Dominick is hoping that he will finally be understood, respected and loved unconditionally and he believes this is how a woman should treat him. Inside, he feels profound mistrust. As soon as his partner disappoints him he runs away, fully convinced that he can never trust anyone. He is convinced that the only way to find peace is to be alone and to retreat whenever he feels threatened.

We call this, 'mistrust goes shopping'.

Learning to Feel

However, the awareness of our wounded child's feelings, thoughts and behaviours is just a beginning of our journey. A crucial and essential aspect of the work is to learn to feel what we went through and understand profoundly how and why we are so overtaken today by our wounded child.

It involves stepping into the shoes of a child who was neglected, invaded, unsupported, humiliated, even abused, reliving this experience and feeling the effect it had – and still has on us.

It involves going back in time with the awareness and resources of an adult, re-experiencing all the minor and major disrespects and neglects we had to live through, and seeing the sense of ourselves that we developed as a result.

This stage is not a quick fix.

It takes time and patience.

With skilled guidance, we can begin to feel the depth of the trauma each of us experienced in the different ways that we lost ourselves, developed false ways of being and lost our trust in life.

This process happens in layers of discovery, layers of

remembering, layers of feeling the pain, shaming and terror we experienced – and still experience.

Often, we are hesitant to see and feel our childhood as it really was. We prefer to pretend and hold on to the fantasy that it was all fine. But then we cannot understand where our negative self-image, beliefs and actions come from.

Also, in this deep exploration of our childhood traumas, we are able to feel the pain, shame, fear and even shock that we have been carrying all of our lives and understand how easily small events in our lives can trigger it today.

Let's go back to Alice and Dominick.

As we guided Alice back to her childhood, slowly she was able to feel how painful it was to have to live with her father's rage, and how much terror it instilled in her. She could feel how unprotected she felt with both her parents and how she blamed herself for what was happening. She could not imagine what it would be like to be loved and cared for. But it was healing for her to feel the love and acceptance she felt with us, and from us, and could imagine that we were the parents she never had.

As we helped Dominick to dig into his past with conscious regression, he also could feel where his mistrust started. He could see how he developed a self-sufficient, strongly independent style as a way of surviving – and is still living this way.

He recognized that his little boy inside had no trust that he would be loved, understood, or allowed to be himself. Through a series of breakthroughs, he was able to feel the pain of being raised by such a rigid and cold mother and also his anger toward his father for being absent and not standing up to his mother.

The second step of healing is understanding and feeling how much fear, shock and shame we have inside by allowing ourselves to feel our past as we felt it as a child.

In this stage, we begin to recognize how and why we developed a negative self-image based on insecurity, fear, mistrust and poisonous negative beliefs that run our lives.

And by diving deeply into exploring and feeling the wounds

of childhood, something quite magical happens. They begin to heal and we find ourselves spontaneously making better choices today.

Bringing Awareness into Daily Life

But the journey of recovery is still not over. There is a third aspect to the work. This aspect of the work involves bringing new awareness into our day-to-day lives.

This awareness includes:

● Recognizing in our daily lives when we are in the child state of consciousness.

● Taking new and constant risks that challenge our old way of thinking, feeling and behaving, in spite of our fears.

● Motivating ourselves to raise our level of life energy by moving our bodies on a regular basis in spite of our resistance.

● Opening to intimacy in spite of our mistrust.

● Consciously choosing to move out of our child state of consciousness into a mature adult state of consciousness.

The 'mature adult state of consciousness' is based on what we call, 'core insights'.

● "I recognize that the difficulties I have in my life and in my relationships come from my childhood trauma and I need to commit to work on these wounds in therapy."

● "Taking little risks to become more alive brings more positivity into my life and helps me to get out of my negative mind."

● "I am learning to trust my intuition when evaluating people, and to respect and honour my own needs as well as another's."

● "I am aware that no one is going to rescue me from my fears or pain. Intimacy means that I need to learn to contain my frustration when I am not getting what I want or expect."

● "I am also aware that coming close to someone will challenge me at times to set limits and stand up for myself."

- "I understand that love is based on being responsible with my energy. I need to find ways to regulate my nervous system and stress, make friends with my anger and not throw it on my partner."
- "I am not a victim. Other people and life respond to me according to whether I am living in my child or my mature adult state of consciousness."
- "I recognize that I will receive love if I give it, but I am also committed to being authentic and giving my love in a way that feels right to me."

Commitment to Healing

Alice and Dominick are still in a process of healing and neither is yet in a functional, healthy relationship. But they accept that they need to work on themselves to heal, are committed to making this an ongoing process, and are willing to feel their pain and fear. Furthermore, they have much more awareness of when they are acting out from their child.

Alice recognizes that focusing more on herself helps her not to rely on a man to complete her. She is compromising less with men, is more aware of when she loses herself in trying to please, and is beginning to feel much better about herself as a person and as a woman. She is working out regularly at a gym, more careful about how and what she eats, and more able to risk to express her feelings and set limits.

Dominick recognizes how he has been obsessed with control, how he has – and still does – mistreat women in his relationships and is taking more responsibility for the pain he causes. He sees how automatically he blames and runs away. Now, instead, he risks staying connected and sharing his hurt when he feels abandoned. He, too, is taking better care of his body,

In essence, this third aspect of the work is about awareness and bringing new awareness into our lives. With this new awareness, we can come out of living in a child state of consciousness and embrace a mature adult way of living and loving. Also, by taking regular risks that challenge our negative sense of self and beliefs, we re-program ourselves, gain confidence, and change our feelings toward ourselves, others, and the world.

In these pages, we have attempted to outline the approach we use to help people recover a healthy sense of self and of the world, and build a foundation for a functional relationship with themselves and another person.

We feel that the end point of self-work happens when we are able to find fulfilment in four essential aspects of our lives: our intimacy, creativity, physical health and sense of meaning in life.

To attain this point, it is crucial to find a method that works and confidence in those who are guiding us toward our depth, truth and self-love.

But most importantly, it requires patience, perseverance, commitment and trust in the growth process.

CHAPTER THIRTEEN

Couple Therapy

Vasumati

I came to Osho in 1976 July. At that time I was twenty-five-years-old and had been studying Gestalt Therapy and Bioenergetics in London. One year later, I was asked by Osho to start leading therapy groups in the ashram and this was the start of a rich, life-long journey of learning and experience.

From the beginning, I was aware that therapy with Osho meant more than dealing with the psychological and emotional aspects of human nature. It pointed towards a deeper spiritual truth around the evolution and growth of human consciousness.

When I went to see Osho and asked what approach I should adopt in my new group, he said, "Do nothing. I am leading the group and you are just in the room. So just be present and I will take care of the rest. And remember if it is bad group, it is my group, but if it is a good group, it is also my group."

So that was what I did. I simply practiced being present in each moment without getting identified or invested in the outcome. There were many moments I felt fear, or did not know what to do, except be present to both the not-knowing and the fear, and allow the group to find its own way. Slowly, I learned to relax and see that if we leave things alone they find a natural and profoundly intuitive way of unfolding.

In this way, Osho's guidance pointed to a fundamental aspect of therapy which embraces non-doing. This is not easy to describe, but it is really a space of accessing what I might call the 'true will' rather than the 'false will'. This requires not following my personal agenda, but seeing where the energy of the group as a whole – and through this 'whole' the will of existence itself – wants to go. So, I can say that the 'true will' is in tune with existence and the 'false will' is a manifestation of personal ego.

Working from Presence and Emptiness

My understanding about Osho therapy is that we are vehicles for a greater energy to come through us. Sometimes we called it 'Osho', sometimes 'Existence', sometimes 'the Whole', but it alludes to the fact that we need to be empty. It is our emptiness, not our fullness, that has value and this allows a deeper truth and healing to manifest.

What I have noticed, in this space of 'let go', is that a therapist needs to work more from a state of emptiness and presence, rather than from an ego-driven and narcissistic space.

I fell in love with this work. I became passionate about learning how to get out of the way to make space for Osho's energy to manifest. Sometimes, I could get out of the way and, of course, sometimes not, and I could feel the difference. Sometimes amazing experiences happened, sometimes they didn't, but there was a quality of magic that infused the work.

Osho's presence, his energy field, was – and still is – mystical and transformative. Meditation happens spontaneously, bringing with it moments of 'no mind' and clarity. This, in turn, supports the process of helping participants see through difficult issues that have for years been saboteurs and barriers to a life of fulfilment.

Changes happen quickly, often on an energetic level rather than in a cognitive way. In other words, changes to people in the groups occur in the form of expression, release, transformation – maybe simply as a radiance, a glow in their faces, or a sudden wave of heartfelt love – and only later are we able to figure out what this means on a psychological level. The energy itself has a power and rawness that dissolves stuck patterns.

Tantra: Saying 'Yes' to Life

After leading groups in Pune for some time, I was also asked to lead workshops on Tantra, learning to work with love, intimacy, relating and sexuality. Inevitably, this meant I had to help people get rid of their taboos around sex, their socially-ingrained ideas about relationships, their religiously-indoctrinated attitudes about morality.

This ties in with Osho's view that modern man is so conditioned and repressed that he cannot move into meditation unless this excess baggage is discharged and released. Loving others, I have discovered, is really a secondary issue. The real challenge and the first priority is to love oneself.

At that time, back in the 70s, it was revolutionary to think about self-love in the context of meditation, personal growth and loving others. It was, we realized, all somehow connected. For example, therapy is really the art of looking deeply at yourself and this is possible only by loving yourself – otherwise, all you find is self-judgment and self-condemnation.

This new approach of self-acceptance was radical. And this, for me, is the great teaching of Tantra: acceptance and a total 'yes' to life. Accept things as they are, accept yourself as you are and know that fundamentally, at the core, we are innocent, loving and divine human beings.

So we all dived into therapy with gusto – leaders and participants alike – carrying with us so many old life-negating attitudes and yet learning to embrace life and ourselves with a passionate acceptance and self-love. In this embracing of the reverence for life we discovered our true nature as spiritual beings.

Working with people and exploring the issues around love and relationships, I gradually began to understand that love has nothing to do with attachment, jealousy and possessiveness. These painful experiences may occur as a result of falling in love with someone, but love itself is wild and free – a gift from existence that cannot be tamed.

I also understood that, in order to be intimate with another person in a loving relationship, we need to be able to be alone. In other words, in a relationship we do not need to make prisoners of each other, because we are strong enough to be happy and fulfilled by ourselves.

The Power of a Meditative Community

In the community surrounding Osho, we struggled with the Zen koan of relationship: how to be alone and yet together, how to love and not be attached, how to let go when the time came and not cling to a dying relationship out of fear of being alone.

It was challenging, to say the least, but it was possible because the power of the Buddhafield was so compelling and the atmosphere of love and trust was so strong. There was so much vitality, intimacy and joy surrounding us that we did not need the secure and enduring bond of a steady partner.

It may be hard for others to understand, but in those days, for those of us who'd chosen to become sannyasins and live and work with Osho in Pune, relationships were of less importance than in ordinary society.

We were focused on our meditation, our spiritual growth and the most important manifestation of this, in terms of daily life, was the work we were doing in the ashram. It might be cleaning the floor, cooking meals, working in the office, gardening ... This, it was understood, was our way of working on ourselves.

Of course, sitting silently in Osho's morning discourse, or attending the evening meetings with him, was precious. But the ongoing work of looking at ourselves, seeing the ego, feeling when we were in the flow of collective energy or fighting against it ... all this happened through the work. In this spiritual cooking pot, relationships were enjoyable but not essential.

We had other priorities and I felt grateful for this, because it helped me gain distance and insight into the complex world of love and relating that I may not otherwise have experienced.

Development of Couple Therapy

In order to explain more about relationship therapy and counselling, I need to give a history of couple counselling from the conventional standpoint, seeing how it has evolved in the conventional world and how this was further developed in the Osho context.

This brings us to the subject of the 'therapeutic stance', which is important, especially when working with couples. Every therapist needs to find an inner stance from where she, or he, can work. This means we need to know our core values regarding relationships. This, in turn, determines the style in which we work.

Here, I want to give a short review of some of the cultural influences that shape the way we look at marriage and relationship – I am referring to committed partnerships, not affairs and casual romances.

The first time we started looking at marital or couple issues from a sociological perspective was back in the 1950s. This was a time of traditional marriages and fixed gender roles. Divorce was viewed as a personal failing and brought with it social shame and stigma. Generally speaking, only movie stars got divorced and their sensational escapades filled the gossip columns, avidly devoured by faithful housewives who dared not take the risk themselves.

The 60s and 70s brought about a huge revolution against these traditional values. This was a time of social upheaval, when we saw the beginning of the sexual revolution, the fight against the war in Vietnam, the student revolts on campuses in the USA and Europe. We saw drugs, sex, the pill and Women's Liberation.

The pill had a big impact in the 60s because it gave women power over their own bodies. Now, they no longer needed to worry about getting pregnant. Now, they had the freedom to explore and experiment without risk. Simultaneously, the hippie movement proclaimed 'free love', advocating a more playful, less serious attitude to sex.

This was a huge change in the way relationships were constructed. Young people rebelled against the old cultural conventions. They did not need to marry to have sex. They could cohabit without legal commitment and leave each other without divorce

Now relationships were about personal fulfilment. This was the time of the individual and the 70s were proclaimed 'the me decade'. Not surprisingly the divorce rate soared, with about fifty percent of marriages coming unglued.

Shifting Therapeutic Attitudes

The role of the therapist also shifted. Now, a therapist became less focused on trying to repair a sinking partnership, or papering over the cracks, and more concerned with supporting the wishes of the two individuals involved. If this meant leaving an unhappy situation, so be it. The new ethos was: 'We don't need to suffer together and the world won't end if we decide to break up'.

The 80s and 90s were times of affluence and consumerism. Marriages and relationships tended to follow the business model. The focus became: what can I get out of this, how can I get my needs met, how can we create a win/win situation, how can I gain and not lose.

This saw the beginning of fifty-fifty equality partnerships, with gender-bending implications: women became more independent and assertive, men became more soft and sensitive. The commitment issue was simplified to: we remain together as long as it feels good. Marriage was seen as a context for personal fulfilment stripped of ethical obligations. We looked at marriage as a kind of cost benefit analysis: are the 'pros' outweighing the 'cons'? If the answer is 'yes' then okay, let's continue.

Basic Value System

Therapists doing any kind of work need to know their own basic value system and this is important when counselling couples. For me, this meant I had to know my own personal values, how they may have changed and evolved, and the fundamental teachings I learned from being with Osho.

In couple therapy, especially, such values are crucial. Counselling others, it's really important that you've 'walked your talk': you've been there, you've experienced what these clients are going through, so the values you're sharing with them aren't being pulled out of thin air, or from a best-selling 'how to' manual, or from some holy book.

It's personal wisdom and hard-won experience that gives credibility to therapists in this field, giving authenticity and integrity to the way they work.

For me, there isn't a typical couple session, in which fixed steps are followed. Rather, my approach begins with having no agenda, being present in the moment, being deeply honest with my clients and having the courage to trust myself and follow my heart and energy.

Nevertheless, I do hold to certain values. For one, I am clear that monogamy is the frame for commitment. This means that, if two people want to stay together in a committed relationship, monogamy is necessary.

It is also clear to me that both partners need to work separately on completing themselves through meditation, or some form of spiritual practice. If they try to find total completion through the partner, without looking at themselves, it's not going to work. Then their relationship will be co-dependent and prone to all kinds of false and unsustainable compromises.

Early Trauma Imprint

There are many dynamic developments in couple therapy as it is practiced and taught in the world today. Mindfulness is gaining ground, as is a trauma-based approach called the Psycho-Biology of Love. Many of these new approaches follow the trauma model of understanding how the nervous system and brain determine our emotional responses, especially around attachment wounds developed early in childhood.

We learned how to form bonds in relationship through our first emotional connections – our attachments to mom, dad and other key figures. These theories point to where we suffered developmental trauma, or 'disturbed attachment', or whether we managed to create an optimum state of 'secure attachment'.

Most of us have a history of some form of disturbed attachment that we attempt to heal or repair throughout our lives. Sometimes, we are so traumatized that we are unable to do this, often repeating the same frustrating scenarios we had when we were young. This we call 're-enactment' or 'repetition compulsion'.

The trauma approach is a mindfulness approach that allows us to begin to feel our 'felt sense', or sensations that happen in the body. In this way, the nervous system is able to discharge frozen or incomplete emotional responses, allowing us to slowly return to a healthy state of functioning. As this happens, neural pathways in the brain become rewired in a more healthy way and we learn at a psycho-biological level that we do not need to constantly repeat old traumas.

This process is very similar to meditation, where you gain the sensitivity to be present to what is happening in this moment, here and now, and are able to sensitively track it with awareness, as it unfolds moment-to-moment.

Dependence, Independence and Interdependence

One of the theories prevalent as a therapeutic approach in couple therapy is called the 'Theory of Differentiation'. Differentiation means that each partner in a relationship is able to be whole, complete and free. In this context, freedom is not seen as avoidance or indifference, but being fully integrated in oneself.

This reminds me of Osho's approach to relating, which he calls 'interdependence'. This state is not dependence, which is an unhealthy psychological state, nor is it anti-dependence, which is about avoidance and is really just the other side of the coin from dependence. Both are equally 'undifferentiated'.

One of the biggest gifts I ever got from Osho was to understand this approach of interdependence. In a discourse, where he answered a question of mine, he said:

Vasumati you say, "One of the essential laws of nature seems to be relationship, interdependence". They are not synonymous. Relationship is one thing, interdependence totally another. Relationship is not interdependence, it is a contract between two independent persons. Hence all relationships are false, because basically independence is false. Nobody is independent – and if you are not independent how can you relate? With whom can you relate?

Life is interdependence. Nobody is independent, not for a single moment can you exist alone. You need the whole existence to support you; each moment you are breathing it in and out. It is not relationship, it is utter interdependence. Remember, I am not saying it is dependence, because the idea of dependence again presumes that we are independent. If we are independent then dependence is possible. But both are impossible; it is interdependence.

And the third possibility is of interdependence. That happens very rarely, but whenever it happens a part of paradise falls on the earth. Two persons, neither independent nor dependent but in a tremendous synchronicity, as if breathing for each other, one soul in two bodies – whenever that happens, love has happened. Only call this love. The other two are not really love, they are just arrangements – social, psychological, biological, but arrangements. The third is something spiritual. ~ Osho[1]

Whenever I work with couples, I keep this in mind: relating is neither dependence nor independence, but interdependence. This can also be called 'differentiation' or 'secure attachment'.

A More Human Approach

Traditional therapy, especially those methods that derive from psychoanalytic counselling, believe in the principles of neutrality, abstinence and anonymity. These principles were developed to enhance and protect the therapeutic framework, especially the delicate issue of transference, in which the client projects his, or her, feelings of dependency on the therapist.

In Osho therapy, instead of neutrality, we have been encouraged to be more human and warm in the therapeutic situation. Instead of the cold psychoanalytic approach, Osho has offered something more effective and beautiful. He talked of working from the heart, of working with love, not as an emotion but as a supportive and accepting presence.

In this way, we learned from first-hand experience that love was the most optimal force in the healing of trauma, pain and alienation.

Couple Session

I would like to give an outline of a session, showing how some of the inspiration I have gained from Osho can be put to practical use.

Since Osho has said a great deal about relationship, I want to focus on something that has been of particular importance for me: the idea of 'rising in love' rather than 'falling in love'.

Osho's understanding is that 'falling in love' is something unconscious and biological. We are carried away in the grip of a blind, overpowering force, usually with painful consequences. 'Rising in love', on the other hand, is something spiritual, rooted in meditation and consciousness. It is not in the grip of biology, so it is not based on hormonal instincts. It is something that grows, matures and develops.

In Osho's own words:

Rising in love means a learning, a changing, a maturity. Rising in love ultimately helps you to become grown up. And two grown up persons don't quarrel; they try to understand, they try to solve any problem. Anybody who rises in love never falls from it, because rising is your effort, and the love that is grown through your effort is within your hands. But falling in love is not your effort. ~ Osho[2]

I would like to use this as a frame to describe how I conduct my work. The following session is with a couple I have worked with several times over the years. I will give them fictitious names: Robert and Louise:

Robert and Louise first came to me three years ago because they were fighting and feeling tense towards each other. Both felt hurt and misunderstood by the other.

Robert's narrative about Louise was that he could not trust her because she was 'leaking' her energy with other men and not

267

telling him the truth. Whenever he confronted her, she became withdrawn, defensive and elusive, which in his mind only justified his fears and suspicions about her.

Robert was extremely intelligent and perceptive and had a convincing way of arguing. What was suspect, however, was that he spoke in a highly agitated and emotional manner, so it was clear to me that his logic was not supported by a calm and accurate perception of his partner. He was the more vocal of the two in the session and spent a lot of time talking about Louise as if she were not even in the room.

Robert was an 'expert' on Louise's character. By presenting his analysis of her flaws, he actually depersonalized her to such a degree that he seemed lost in his own trance – out of touch with reality.

When I asked Louise for her version she became sad, feeling defeated that she could not express her truth to Robert and utterly boxed-in by his version of their relationship.

In order to work with this couple, I first had to create enough space for them to come out of the polarization in which they were stuck. To Robert, I needed to point out that his style of describing the situation was self- righteous and attacking.

As I was not personally involved in this relationship drama, I could be loving and yet impersonal, so Robert did not feel judged when I pointed this out. Rather, he slowly allowed the message to sink in and I could see that he was beginning to soften.

When Louise saw this in Robert, she began to feel safer to speak from her heart, explaining how painful it was for her to be consistently mistrusted, no matter what she shared with Robert about her reality.

A technique that can be used for this kind of situation is to create two cushions for each person. One of these cushions represents the individual's 'child' part and the other cushion represents the 'adult' part.

One of the themes I've learned from Osho is how to separate, or dis-identify from the ego. In this case, the ego is the wounded 'inner child' within and it comes with a great deal of intensity, blame, projection, anger and drama.

When this part possesses us, we are totally identified with it, making it difficult – almost impossible – to see or hear the other person with any degree of clarity. Instead, we see them through our projections as the frustrating mother or father. In other words, we do not see them at all.

When both partners are in the 'child' space they are caught in blame and projection, or in blame and defence, and not much insight or growth is possible. However, when we shift from 'child' to 'adult' a change of consciousness is possible.

Inviting both clients to sit on the 'adult' cushion, I asked them to pause for a moment, close their eyes, look inside and see if there was any quality available to them beyond reaction, blame and defence. I invited them to use the present moment, here and now, to go beyond what they were carrying from past inter-actions with each other and find an essential being who was willing to be present.

In this way, I helped each person go deeper into his or her own reality, to go inside and feel what was there.

Sometimes it means feeling fear, pain or emptiness. It also means learning how to be present with these feelings, without immediately making the other person responsible. This requires a non-judgemental attitude and open-minded inquiry.

When the focus of attention shifts from the other back to self, this already represents a quantum shift in the dynamics of the relationship. Immediately, the gestalt and climate changes ... there is more space. When one partner feels the other is occupying an adult role, he or she starts to resonate with this change.

When both of them are in the adult space we can explore the true nature of their distress. We can move from blame to responsibility, from attacking to listening, and from being enemies to being collaborators.

In this session, we have to go from 'child' to 'adult' and back again many times. Sometimes, I invited them both to sit on their 'child' cushions and freely blame, argue and fight, just to experience and understand the futility and lack of creative possibilities involved.

This is the state of being totally identified with the ego as the wounded child, and it is good to see that, in this state, constructive change is not possible. Even when we know, intellectually, we should be behaving in a more adult manner, it is amazing how easily we slip into battle tactics while righteously holding on to whatever grievances we feel.

Ego is a fighter and does not give up easily. But with this method one can coax the ego to allow other dimensions to arise.

One of the stages I took Robert and Louise through was to ask one of them to sit on the 'adult' cushion and listen, without reacting, while the partner shared his or her feelings, hurts and fears.

For example, I asked Robert to listen, without comment, while Louise shared her pain around not being trusted, her feelings of being judged and not seen, and her sorrow about how she was cast as the 'cheater' in the relationship. She was also able to share her anger and frustration that this was not the truth, but something coming from him.

Louise's vulnerability softened Robert. In the past, she had reacted to his accusations by becoming more frozen, distant and mute. Or, if pushed too far, she would defend herself angrily and threaten to end the relationship, which in turn made Robert more enraged and convinced of her guilt.

When it was Robert's turn to sit on the 'child' cushion he became very emotional and really like a child. He talked about how he'd felt abandoned by his mother, who had many affairs. He shared how he could not connect with his mother; how she felt cold and distant from him. As he came in contact with these feelings, Robert began to cry deeply.

He was able to see how he used the defence of his brilliant mind to emotionally protect himself, not only from his girlfriend but from the pain and loneliness inherent in his early relationship with his mother.

As Robert became more vulnerable, Louise began to open her heart towards him, her defensiveness relaxed and she was more present. Slowly, her veil of indifference and coolness towards him also changed and she became more tender and caring.

At this point, I asked them to both be silent, to simply look at each other and feel each other's being; to see the wounded self that has been trying to survive through all the trials and tribulations of life, both as a child and as an adult.

The silence continued for some time and the shifts taking place in the atmosphere of the room felt profound, as both partners understood that their lives could really change and old wounds could really heal. There was a sense of optimism, as if something new was possible.

Now that Louise felt safe, I asked her to go to the 'child' cushion and tell the story of her own upbringing. She recalled that her father was charming but also invasive. He found ways to come close to her that were ambiguous – not just fatherly, but also flirtatious.

The family favoured a liberal approach to child-rearing and were sexually open in their attitudes – not in a direct way, but with innuendo – so as she matured into adolescence she was encouraged to be flirtatious and sexually open.

She was not given a space of safety and did not know anything about appropriate and healthy boundaries with men and boyfriends. As a result, she often felt confused and at times a shocked at the degree of sexuality she was experiencing.

Her flirtatious behaviour had been accepted and supported in her family, so when she encountered Robert's strong reaction to the way she behaved with other men she did not understand.

Sitting on the 'child' cushion, Louise was able to share her confusion and vulnerability with Robert and for the first time he could listen and empathise, rather than immediately going into a frenzy of rage and aggression.

Slowly, both Robert and Louise were able to acknowledge and release their pain and shame from the wounds they'd experienced in their respective childhoods. This cleansing and healing process helped them to be more present, here and now, less governed by past memories.

At the appropriate time, I asked both of them to move to the 'adult' cushion. From this perspective, they could see how they were both lost in childhood dramas and were acting from their respective defences. They could also understand that no one was wrong, that both were simply doing the best they could to create safety for themselves.

Then I invited them to be silent, to be a witness to their own inner workings, and to see with more clarity how their past was destroying the richness of the present. I encouraged each of them to take responsibility for what they were bringing to the relationship: I helped Robert see that his paranoia was really his fear of abandonment. I helped Louise see that her flirtatiousness was a defence against real intimacy.

Obviously, this movement from 'child' to 'adult' does not always happen. But as Robert and Louise were meditators and working towards greater awareness and self-understanding, they were ready for a shift to happen.

The work continued. Robert and Louise followed up with more couple sessions and sometimes individual sessions to deepen these understandings.

In this approach, outlined above, I share one of the basic understandings I received from Osho: that lovers need to learn to cooperate, that they should work together to create consciousness.

This work is an invitation to become friends as well as lovers. When love can also include friendship, a grace arises that carries the fragrance of meditation.

I teach a different kind of love. It does not end in friendship but begins in friendship. It begins in silence, in awareness. It is a love which is your own creation, which is not blind. Such a love can last forever, can go on growing deeper and deeper. Such a love is immensely sensitive. Such a love needs nothing from the other. ~ Osho[3]

CHAPTER FOURTEEN

Diamond Breath:
the Breath of the Buddhas

Devapath

*Ecstasy means to get out – out of all shells and all protections
and all egos and all comforts, all death-like walls. To be ecstatic
means to get out, to be free. ~ Osho*[1]

The Japanese Buddha sits there in ecstasy, showing us with his big
belly that all natural breathing comes from the belly centre. Our
effort in breath therapy is to open the belly centre to allow us to
live in deep trust and inner harmony with the world.

How to reach there, moving towards the opening of the heart
and the belly centre? Osho's vision of therapy and meditation
offers the most beautiful path to connect with "The Breath of the
Buddhas" and that's why I love it.

Writing this chapter, I remember my first deep experience of
breath work. It was in a re-birthing group in Pune in 1980. I went
into connected breathing. To my delight I suddenly found myself
in the womb of my mother. It was an amazing experience to rest
in an incredibly peaceful space surrounded by warm, ocean-like
water. If I understand Osho rightly, our whole spiritual search is
about the longing to experience this beautiful mindless space and
to come home in the cosmic womb.

Osho talks about his psychology as *Parapsychology*, or *The
Psychology of the Buddhas*. This psychology moves from the
known to the unknown and ultimately to the unknowable – from the
body-mind into the mystery of life. Our breath is the most precious
tool on this journey. Nothing else works without it. It is the essence
of life. If we cleanse our body-mind from all its tensions we can
ride on the wave of breath from sex to super-consciousness.

In this chapter, I will present the basic principles of the work called 'Diamond Breath'. I would also like to share the way it has changed me over the past thirty-five years. The way I see Osho using therapy for the preparation of meditation is simply fascinating.

When I arrived in Pune, India, in 1979, after years of searching for the meaning of life, I went through several months of intense group therapy. I fell in love with the direct approach of these groups: leaving no space for the mind, connecting only to my body and helping me to empty myself of the garbage accumulated through social conditioning.

It totally changed my life. I had arrived in the right place. Light and clarity came into my life. Yes, I was also full of fear, but the courage to overcome my fears was the most amazing experience. It made me understand that courage is the most important virtue if we want to follow our longing for a new life – a life where deep natural breathing opens the world of love and meditation.

I heard Osho talking about two kinds of people. One type needs to know what will happen before jumping into an unfamiliar situation and wants to play safe. In terms of spirituality, this type follows Patanjali and his path of Yoga. The other type simply jumps; whatever the cost and however dangerous it might seem to be. This type follows Lao Tzu and his path of Tao. My attraction is for Lao Tzu and this is reflected in my therapeutic work.

I feel a great fascination for Lao Tzu and Chuang Tzu with their sense for paradox:

Easy is right
Begin right and you are easy
Continue easy and you are right
The right way to go easy is to forget the right way
And forget that the going is easy.
~ Chuang Tzu

For me, Osho therapy and meditation feels exactly like this. Breath work is the easiest. It simply bypasses the mind and its tendency to make things complicated.

In my eyes, the most essential quality for a therapist is to create trust by being authentic. Then he can help the individual to overcome fear, including deep, fundamental fears such as fear of madness, fear of sexual orgasm and fear of dying. It's like a mother bird helping her baby bird leave the comfort of the nest and learn to fly alone. Yes, sometimes she needs to kick the baby bird out of the nest, because the baby bird doesn't know yet what it means to fly and to be free.

This is the way I like to use therapy. I help a group or an individual to overcome fear by creating a dynamic therapeutic process. The fire of collective energy burns the prison of personality. You cannot compromise anymore. You long for the real one – the real you – hidden somewhere deep inside. You cleanse yourself from all past conditioning. For the first time, you experience yourself being easy – being in ecstasy.

The first book I read from Osho in 1978 was a Darshan Diary called *Hammer on the Rock,* in which Osho was talking with his disciples on a personal basis and answering their questions. I was fascinated by his full-heartedness, his clarity and directness. It was the last kick to make me visit the 'ashram' in Pune – as it was called at the time.

Now let's come to a description of my therapeutic work. I would like to present this in three parts:

1. Zen in the Art of Group Therapy.

2. The Work of Diamond Breath.

3. An Experience of the Power of Breath.

1. Zen in the Art of Group Therapy

Groups are going to be the future of humanity. Others – psychoanalytical approaches – are really out of date now. The group is going to be the future of the whole of psychoanalysis, psychotherapy. Individual psychotherapy is basically false, because you take the individual as if he exists separately. Group therapies, and later on, communal therapies, will take its place.
~ Osho[2]

This is the way I like to work – to make individual therapy part of the collective process of a group. My focus is on group therapy. It is a much faster way to heal the individual from his or her neurotic past. A group multiplies the energy of each participant. It allows steps I don't see possible in individual therapy, but I'm aware that people who are especially fearful may need to go through a preparation of individual therapy. I myself was never in a long process of individual therapy. Group therapy is my way.

A group is like a healing womb. It's a place where we make ourselves vulnerable, open our deepest wounds and heal in a loving and accepting atmosphere. We experience ourselves reflected in the mirror of many other people and get a more realistic picture of ourselves.

But to heal what? In Pune, in 1988–89, therapy was offered by part of the commune known as the Centre for Transformation. We therapists were sitting together to discuss what therapy is all about. We all had different opinions and finally we decided to ask Osho. The answer was: "Therapy is about sex."

Yes, group therapy gets a sexual vibe when people start opening and enjoying their life energy. It becomes excellent when it has a good foreplay, a play and an after-play.

Here, I would like to mention five topics, which I feel are essential in group therapy:

- The longing for sharing.

- The power of catharsis.

- The journey from personality to individuality.

- Inner transformation by active meditation.

- Sexual healing.

276

The Longing for Sharing

That is the only hope for man – to listen to the heart and to go along with it. Then your life will become a blissful pilgrimage. ~ *Osho*[3]

In this disconnected world we tend to feel alone with our problems. Daily life is preoccupied with survival fears. We compete with each other, feel lonely, miss love, live with a closed heart and cannot trust even ourselves.

Sharing from the heart is a way to understand that we are all haunted by the same issues. We all long for joyful relationships and want to be loved. We search for inner freedom and a deep change for the better in our lives.

That's why we come together. We want to learn to open our hearts and to love ourselves. Deep down we know this is the way to love others, too. We are longing to live with breathing hearts and laughing spirits. We want to overcome the world of separation, the world of the mind.

A participant in a group might share a relationship issue, which, one way or another, is reflected in the experience of every group member. I present this topic to the whole group and show how it affects all our ways of relating. The moment we see that we are not alone with our problems we open ourselves and create a loving atmosphere of togetherness.

Sharing can take so many different expressions: holding hands, looking into each other's eyes, hugging, or just saying: "I love you." In fact, the most beautiful sharing happens when we are silent, deeply relaxed and connected through the gentle rhythm of our breathing.

The Need for Catharsis

My method starts with catharsis. Only when your tensions are released can you jump deep within yourself. ~ *Osho*[4]

Osho's approach to meditation and therapy differs from all traditions. It begins with a cathartic cleansing process to unburden the heart and allow our nervous system to relax. But without meditation catharsis is useless.

In Buddha's time, there was no television, iPad, computer, or iPhone. There was no noise from passing cars and trucks. There was no advertising. The night was dark, not full of artificial light as it is today, so people could sleep more naturally. The air was fresh, not polluted, so people could breathe more joyfully. The mind was based on faith while the modern scientific Western mind is based on doubt.

For all these reasons – and many more besides – our nervous system today is overloaded and therefore in a state of chronic tension. It finds neither time nor space to relax. We try everything from yoga to Tai Chi or Qui Gong to help us cool down, but this seems like a single drop of cold water falling on a burning-hot stove. Our nervous system is basically the same as it was two thousand five hundred years ago, but it gets a thousand times more input. No wonder people get drunk, become violent, or need drugs to escape this madhouse we call our world.

For me, therapy in Pune in 1979 was first of all to cleanse my body-mind and open my heart through catharsis. The next step was learning to love and enjoy myself. The ultimate step was to bring all my energy to this, the present moment, in life. These principles still guide my work: get out of the mind and all analytical therapies – don't give your mind a chance. We already know too much and this knowledge blocks our inner transformation.

When I came back to Pune in 1987 I saw Osho was inviting all kind of therapies, including those focusing more on understanding the mind, throwing his net as wide as possible to attract people. But in the end, just before he died, he closed the circle of Osho therapy by creating his Meditative Therapies, which are certainly beyond intellect and therefore a provocation to all analytical approaches.

Osho's Mystic Rose Meditation is a brilliant meditative therapy process of twenty-one days. It's a reminder that catharsis is the essential cleansing process for the body, mind, heart and spirit. In this way, Osho's vision of therapy gets the final touch: a synthesis of Western encounter therapy and eastern Vipassana meditation.

I heard him mention on several occasions that twenty-one days experience with one meditation technique is needed for a profound change in our being. We use the same model for our Diamond Breath Training. I have done the Mystic Rose many times and it is a great resource for my work with people. A catharsis of laughing and crying liberates the breathing from all its contractions. It's a great preparation for enjoying meditation and celebration.

The Journey from Personality to Individuality

Shallow breathing has become our second nature. Our repressions do not allow us to live our real energy. We feel stuck, trapped in our body-mind structures and unable to express our physical, emotional, sexual or spiritual needs. The amount of unlived energy we carry around with us is amazing. Whoever has participated in group therapy knows what happens if we take even one deep breathe.

The inner journey leads us from a fake personality created by society to what Osho calls individuality, coming home to our original being. This journey passes through four stages:

The first stage is to become aware of the layer of social rules, social behaviour and belief systems – the layer of false personality. Fritz Perls, founder of gestalt therapy, calls it the 'chicken shit layer'. Society is held together by manipulating people in this layer, using fear, greed and guilt. There is no love, only an urgent desire to conform in order to ensure our survival.

We repress our true feelings, our emotions, our childlike aliveness and our innocence. Without knowing it, we sit on a volcano of frustration, negativity and madness. In this context, whoever is a bit more alive and expressive will be judged as being 'crazy'.

The second stage is to release this layer with catharsis. We liberate ourselves from a state of chronic stress that is damaging to our physical health and mental well-being. Not being able to express ourselves is the root cause of depression and suicidal tendencies.

For this layer we need chaotic, dynamic, powerful and conscious breathing techniques. They blow our conditioned structures and allow us to make friends with our physical body. They bring us back to our natural innocent mind and open the door to spirituality. These techniques I call *Power Breathing*.

The next stage is to enter the layer of sexual life energy. Here, we learn to accept the rhythm of pain and pleasure as the basic biological function of life. We realize that we are beautiful sexual beings. We become natural again and see that we need to live this energy, refine it and transform it. We learn to love our body and enter the world of *Tantric Breathing*.

The final stage is to come home to our innermost being. Walking along the divine path of joy and meditation, a day comes when we experience that existence is breathing us. This day we will breathe in Zen.

Inner Transformation through Meditation

Before leaving his body, Osho gave us a beautiful framework for facilitating group therapy as a preparation for meditation. In my work in Pune at that time, as a therapist and director of the Centre for Transformation, I realized how powerful therapy becomes if it is connected to meditation. It works much faster than traditional therapy. It opens doors that traditional therapy could never do.

Our habit is to cling to the old and the familiar, afraid to leave our comfort zone. We don't know what is waiting for us. For example, when I decided to become a disciple of Osho and asked to be initiated as a *sannyasin* – the traditional Indian name for a seeker of truth – I sat in front of my Master and realized I was scared just to look into his eyes. Until that moment, I had never looked into the eyes of an enlightened being. It blew my mind. I knew this was the turning point in my life and I recognized that the groups and meditations I'd done before had given me the strength to say 'yes' to it.

If I want to help people let go of the mind, I need to give something that is deeper than the mind. If I believe that the mind is the only resource in my life, then, obviously, it will be difficult to let go of it. Meditation gives people the experience that their consciousness is not confined within the mind, but is much vaster and basically unlimited.

Having an inner space of growing awareness helps the whole group to move deeper, not getting stuck, or resistant, because in this way we are not so identified with our problems. If we have the choice to suffer or to enjoy ourselves, what will we do? We have suffered so long already. We will choose to enjoy our life and happily let go of the painful past.

Osho's concept of active meditation is unique. It creates the right atmosphere for the inner transformation of modern man. First we bring our male, active energy to a peak and release our tensions, then we relax deeply into the female energy, moving into meditation.

The first meditation is the early morning Dynamic Meditation – a breath-taking journey from therapy to meditation. It's a great model for a therapeutic process: we move from a carbon dioxide and death-oriented chemistry to an oxygen and life-oriented chemistry. Osho says that this method is more psychological than spiritual. It leads ultimately to the spiritual dimension but it starts from psychology.

Dynamic is described in detail elsewhere in this book, but I would just like to say it begins with deep, fast, chaotic breathing, followed by strong catharsis and jumping – a total of thirty minutes vigorous activity – climaxing in an abrupt "Stop!" and then followed by stillness, silence and celebration. As I see it, this allows us to face and overcome our three basic fears: the fear of madness, the fear of sexual orgasm and the fear of dying. The key to dynamic meditation is chaotic breathing.

In one of his early discourses, Osho mentions that all techniques done "vigorously, unsystematically, chaotically", push the meditator's centre of awareness deeper towards his being.

Chaotic breathing pushes the centre down from the head to the heart. Catharsis unburdens the heart from all its repressions and pushes the centre down to the navel centre.

In the late afternoon meditation the group integrates the therapeutic experiences of the day in the *Kundalini Meditation.* About the energy of Kundalini, Osho mentions that breath plays a great role in its awakening.

Kundalini Meditation follows a similar pattern of moving from male energy to female energy: half-an-hour to awaken our life energy and open our breathing by shaking and dancing is followed by stillness and deeply relaxing into our innermost being.

This is Tao. Tao talks about balancing the energies of yin and yang to find inner harmony. This is how Osho's active meditations are working.

The final meditation for the therapist and the group in the evening is the *Osho White Robe Brotherhood,* now known as the *Evening Meeting.* When Osho was alive, he gave a discourse every day. It was an opportunity to fall deeply in tune with him, while listening to his words and imbibing his vision. Shortly before he died, Osho created this unique meditation that we still do today. It begins with a twenty-minute meditation of dancing and relaxing into soft music followed by a video recording of one of Osho's discourses.

In his book, *The Secret of Secrets,* Osho talks about the secret transmission from the master to the disciple in the tradition of Tao, saying that one of the greatest secrets is, that sitting by the Master's side, the disciple starts breathing in the same way the master breathes.

This is the greatest gift for a disciple: to fall in tune with the breath of the master. He can become part of his inner being. This is what happens when I listen to him. This is the moment when I can forget myself and relax into a deeply peaceful energy.

I was always wondering why hypnosis never became a mainstream therapy in Pune. Then I realized that Osho's discourses are themselves a form of hypnosis, or rather de-hypnosis. My therapeutic work is basically a preparation for this moment. I help participants become so relaxed by the end of the day that his words can reach to their innermost being. Breath and body-mind healing I can teach, but for spiritual healing I need to sit in the presence of my master.

For me this is the centre of Osho's work. If I do not offer it in my groups I would feel I was betraying the group and myself. This is the final moment when I leave the world of therapy and enter with my group into the unknowable.

Sexual Healing

Tantra comes in to help humanity, to give sex back to humanity. And when the sex has been given back, then arises Zen. Zen is no attitude. Zen is pure health. ~ *Osho*[5]

Our relationships have many problems because of wrong sexual upbringing. As a result, we are immature even in the first stage of love – physical love, sexual love. In my groups I work on sexual healing with different breathing techniques and exercises.

Western sexuality is dominated by a male mind that is both aggressive and pornographic, which uses sex mainly as a release. I like to present a Tantric approach to sex and to open to the female dimension of life energy, which for ages was either ignored or condemned. Tantric healing is the art to enjoy my body and go with the spontaneous flow of my energy in meeting the other. It allows me to drop all ideas of being a 'real man' or a 'real woman'.

Tantra emerges as a new quality of life when sex and heart connect. Here, we follow the Tantric insight that a man and a woman complete an energy circle. At the level of the sex centre, the man is positively charged with outgoing energy, while the woman is negatively charged and receptive. At the level of the heart and chest, it is the other way around: the woman is positively charged, giving energy out through her heart and breasts, while the man is negatively charged and receptive.

With this understanding, a circle of energy can be created. The woman's energy pours out through her breasts into the man's receiving pole in his chest. The man receives the energy, channels it down through his body to his sex centre and gives it back to the woman through his genitals. She receives the energy through her sex centre, then channels it up through her body to the level of the heart ... and the cycle begins again. To this, we connect the breathing, inhaling when receiving and exhaling when giving, creating a beautiful circle of breath and energy.

Osho talks about three stages of love: sexual love, psychological love and spiritual love. In terms of sexual love, we first of all learn to love ourselves and our own body as small children, then, as we grow from childhood into puberty, we enter the 'rehearsal' stage of 'boy meets girl'.

In my groups, I like to create an atmosphere that recreates this rehearsal phase of sexual development. It's important because this rehearsal is synonymous with foreplay. We dance and play and enjoy our meetings like sportsmen. Nothing is serious yet.

The next stage, from puberty until the early twenties, is about developing a romantic mind and enjoying romantic sexual experiences. This happens naturally when participants lose the fear of their sexual energy. I encourage them to date and write romantic love letters. This is the stage when we learn the art of sexual after-play.

Psychological love happens when we grow beyond our physical and sexual needs and become truly human. In a space of lovingness, friendliness and sharing we open to a deeper dimension of relating. It feels like we are made for each other.

Psychological love is fragile because it is related to our state of mind. For example, one day, we promise our partner that our love will be forever and we really mean it. In that moment, the feeling is true. But then later on, the love may disappear and we feel guilty. This kind of love has become a big challenge to the Western mind and its idea of faithfulness, because the truth is that, from time to time, a new partner comes into our life like a fresh breeze. But if we don't develop beyond the mental age of fourteen we will never be able to get a taste of psychological love

In meditation, we sometimes get a glimpse of psychological love. We feel like merging with our partner and all separation disappears. In this moment, we realize that without meditation no relationship can go very deep. Two minds can meet occasionally, but this is nothing compared to the meeting of two hearts, or the even deeper meeting that connects us being-to-being.

Spiritual love is the state of an enlightened being. The master can transmit this love to his disciples if their hearts are open to receive it. Osho calls it a love affair between the master and the disciple. If I look at Osho, this state of love feels like pure blissfulness and trusting in existence.

2. The Work of Diamond Breath

Breathing is the most mysterious element in man's life. ~ *Osho*[6]

Everything I have described so far relates to the first part of my work, which I have called 'Zen in the Art of Group Therapy'. Now I will talk more specifically about the work of Diamond Breath.

Our breath is a raw diamond covered by the dust of conditioning. If we learn to uncover, polish and play with this diamond it will shine its light into all dimensions of our lives.

There is a growing interest today in the central role that breath plays in our lives and its interaction with the body, mind, heart and spirit. Breath is like the bridge between the body and the soul. We are able to improve the functioning and the efficiency of our heart, lungs, kidneys, intestines, liver, spleen or sexual organs. We are able to balance our emotions. We are able to transform stress and negativity into an energy that we can use for self-healing and personal growth.

In this multi-dimensional way, holistic breath work supports and enhances the quality of our entire life from the physical to the spiritual. Ultimately, the breath is the divine path to experience the joy of ecstasy.

Without doubt, superficial breathing ensures only a superficial experience of ourselves. If we are able to breathe deeply and relax, we take a big step towards preventing many of the physical, psychological and spiritual problems that have become endemic to modern life. Deep, relaxed breathing supports our inner transformation. It sharpens the awareness of who we really are and crystallizes our essential being. Breathing together in love and meditation allows us to heal and grow in our relationships.

I love the view of the Taoist mystics and Chinese medicine that the body is a microcosm of the outer world. Elements like fire, earth, wood, metal and water are reflected in our body and its organs. Chi, the life energy carried by the breath of life, nourishes all our organs.

Diverting from conventional therapy I present a dimension of therapy that moves from analysis towards realising our enormous life energy and spiritual potential. Riding on the wave of deep breathing we can attain the blissful experience of being totally relaxed and fully alert in the 'here and now'.

I have looked into the science, art and mystery of breath from many aspects. It has given me the insight that whatever therapeutic or meditative method we work with, it always affects the way we breathe. A profound understanding of the human breath for healing, wellbeing, sexual fulfilment, loving relationships and the realization of our true being is the key to life.

In other words, knowing the breath we know the secret of life. From native wisdom to spiritual practice the breath is recognized as the fundamental force in existence. In many languages, the word for breathing is synonymous with the word for life itself.

I work with a wide variety of breathing techniques. They allow us to empower ourselves and to heal our childhood wounds. They allow us to explore our sexual energy and to experience bliss and ecstasy. The animal foundation within us has the potential to rise and become a god. Zorba the Greek has the potential to become Gautama the Buddha – Zorba the Buddha.

Dimensions of Breathing

As Osho has said many times, energy moves in waves. Vibrating on different frequencies, their eternal movement stays the same- never ending waves. The one who knows rests in this eternal ocean of waves, passing by and floating towards infinity. The art is to enjoy this existential symphony of music, sound, breath and other waves playing together in never ending space. Osho has also said that their inner secret is eternal silence.

Breath waves connect us to different states of consciousness. A shallow breath wave keeps us controlled by the social mind and imprisoned in repressive conditioning. It keeps us stuck on a very low level of oxygen – a minimum level of life energy.

Tsunami-like chaotic breath waves blow the social mind. They open the door to reconnect with our body. They allow us to dive into the depths of the unconscious mind, cleansing our hearts through a deep catharsis of our whole body chemistry.

Relaxed sensual breath waves allow us to become sensitive beings and enjoy our sexual energy. The deeper, relaxed, and calm oceanic breath waves of a lower frequency help us to find love and inner harmony. When the breath wave nearly disappears we breathe in Zen.

These are the four dimensions of Diamond Breath:

1. Power Breathing
2. Tantric Breathing
3. Oceanic Breathing
4. Breathing in Zen

Power Breathing

Power Breathing is a family of dynamic breathing techniques, such as Trance Energetic Breathing, Chaotic Breathing and several Shamanic Breathing Techniques, which unlock the contractions in our body-mind, shake up the diaphragm and allow the opening of our power centre in the middle of the body.

These techniques also break down our shallow breathing patterns and connect us to our 'inner madhouse' – the unconscious mind. They allow us to release a huge amount of repressed emotions and regain our inner strength. We learn to trust our feelings and to love ourselves as we are.

We support this process with a variety of Dynamic Stress Release (DSR) exercises, which unlock the breath in specific areas of our body. For example, in the back they help us to inhale more deeply and in front to exhale more deeply.

There are many more specific exercises. We can open muscular blockages in the head, chest, diaphragm, belly or pelvis and work with the arms or legs. Joint release techniques open the energy flow throughout the body and special stretching opens the body for deeper breathing. Bio-energetic exercises, elements of primal or encounter therapy, tribal dancing, deep tissue massage and soft touch are other elements that support breath work.

We learn to express ourselves naturally, spontaneously, playfully, innocently and creatively like children. We begin to experience life as an ongoing adventure.

A key technique in my work is Trance Energetic Breathing. It uses a dynamic form of connected breathing, which copies the deep and fast breathing of a jogger. When, for a jogger, breathing through the nose is not sufficient anymore he starts breathing through the mouth to get more energy. Similarly, Trance Energetic Breathing is breathing through the mouth without a break. It is also like the breath of a newborn baby and can lead to the release of the birth trauma.

In a soft way, Trance Energetic Breathing can be used as a hypnosis technique. In a dynamic way, it supports emotional release. Lying down, breathing fast and deep as if you are running creates a paradoxical situation: the mind loses control, the door to the unconscious opens and deep tensions release. Only then do we realize we have carried these heavy tensions all our life.

Near death experiences or long forgotten experiences of physical, mental or sexual abuse may arise. Wounds reaching back to early life, or even to the days of being in the mothers' womb, may be released. The pain of abandonment, or the traumatic experience of living with an alcohol-addicted parent, may surface. The panic of dying in the womb, related to an accident of the mother, or her

288

not wanting the child, or being beaten by her husband ... any of these traumas may come up.

We need these wounds to come to the surface. We need to open these wounds so that they can be healed. Nothing is more poisonous than a closed physical wound, which cannot breathe. Likewise, nothing is more poisonous than a hidden psychological wound, which cannot breathe.

When the storm of catharsis slowly cools down a depth of relaxation happens, which many people have never felt during their entire lives. This can also open the way for an experience of a deep meditative state of being. From total action we move to total relaxation, which is also the secret of active meditation. We close the circle of yin and yang. We are in Tao.

Power breathing hits the diaphragm. This is our biggest breathing muscle, which separates the upper and lower body. It is also called the 'spiritual muscle' and is responsible for seventy-five percent of our breathing. It is special in the sense that here two nervous systems meet: the voluntary nervous system and the autonomous nervous system. These two systems simultaneously express themselves by working with the diaphragm.

With tongue-in-cheek playfulness, bearing in mind the repressive nature of religious upbringing, I call the condition of a contracted diaphragm *Muro Vaticano* – the wall of morality. Powerful breathing breaks this wall and allows the breath to reach down to the sex centre. We reconnect to our sexual energy and enjoy our sexual feelings. When the breath touches the sex centre we have liberated ourselves from all repressive conditioning. We come home, loving ourselves. We are ready to enter the world of Zen, the world of meditation.

The free-floating movement of the diaphragm allows us to liberate the breathing all the way from the upper chest down to the pelvis. We experience the joy of belly breathing. We enjoy the movement of our ribcage and the beat of our heart, which until this moment was badly compressed by so much tension in the diaphragm. We can prevent heart attacks and we can start feeling again.

The movement of the diaphragm is important because it gives a constant healing massage to all our inner organs. It cleans and rejuvenates the organs and allows the whole body to be nourished by a healthy flow of blood that is full of oxygen and life energy. This energy is called *Prana* in India and *Chi* in China.

Here in the middle of the body the ancient Greeks have placed the seat of the soul, with some correctness because it is the centre of our breathing and decides the quality of our life. It is the seat of the solar plexus – the 'sun centre' of our nervous system. When the inner sun of our body is relaxed, it shines and brings warmth to our whole being.

Contrary to Wilhelm Reich and Alexander Lowen, I like to go along with the ancient Greeks and start my breath work in the middle of the body – in the diaphragm segment. From here, I move downwards to the belly and the pelvis segment and then upwards to the chest and the head segment. I see the diaphragm as the central part of the body-mind, where the quality of our breath is created, either being shallow and repressed or open, deep and full of energy.

A great meditation to open the diaphragm is the *Breathing into Life Meditation*. With this method, we imitate the way children keep the diaphragm open and stay emotionally healthy. We play locomotive, bark like a dog, become sensual like a cat, dance and sing like a child, laugh from the belly and cry to release the pain of our heart. Then we are silent and move into the world of inner peace.

A meditation to awaken our power is the *Lion Heart Meditation*. In the world of inner growth we talk about three states of transformation. The first is the camel state: the state of total unawareness. The second is the lion's state: the state of becoming a rebellious spirit. The third is the child state: the state of being innocent and rejoicing in the ocean of love, joy and inner freedom.

This meditation is inspired by a Zen meditation of looking into a mirror and making lion-like faces. First, you breathe deep and slow in order to energize yourself, then you make wild faces and gestures to unlock the frozen energy, roaring like a lion. You dance like a lion and open your lion's heart. Finally you move inside, sit silently, lie down and rest.

It's amazing to see how this little meditation can open the heart. Moving the hands to the middle of the chest and feeling the heart unburdened from all its tensions creates the most beautiful intimate atmosphere.

Tantric Breathing

So, Wilhelm Reich was right, absolutely right, that sex is the problem and all other problems are just by-products of it, branches of it. ~ Osho[7]

Tantric Breathing brings a new dimension of healing, pleasure and well-being to our body and our sex life. Many scientific reports mention the healing force of sexual energy, because fundamentally it is also our life energy. It's the first stage of love and a step towards psychological love.

Power Breathing hits the diaphragm and opens the passage to our sex centre. Tantric Breathing allows us experience ourselves as sexual beings without guilt. We get an understanding of the importance of sex for our physical, mental and emotional health and inner transformation. We learn to enjoy our body and our sensuality.

It is unimaginable how much harm the repression of sex has done to us. Freud and Reich have both made us aware of this fact. At some point, Osho mentions that ninety percent of our mental diseases and sixty percent of our physical diseases would disappear with a healthy sex life.

Tantric Breathing techniques unlock our pelvis from deep contractions resulting from sexual conditioning. We may have experienced these tensions as lower back pain or even more serious problems in the pelvic area. This work helps us to integrate the movement of our pelvis into the harmonious wave of gentle and pleasurable breathing. It awakens our sexual energy and releases many tensions from the spine.

The pelvis moves back with the in-breath and forward with the out-breath. This subtle movement is essential to keep our spine flexible. In the process of mobilising our pelvis and reconnecting to a soft and sensual pelvic movement we find sexual healing. Once our pelvis and spine are flexible again, even the simple act of walking on Mother Earth is a pleasure. We feel how much we are part of this beautiful existence.

This brings us to a shamanic meditation: the *Dragon Breath Meditation*. We connect to Mother Earth by walking like a dragon and bringing our pelvic floor close to the ground. We breathe in the energy from Father Sky and bring it down to Mother Earth. We unlock our fire energy and push our hands forward with strong sounds from the power centre.

Finally we open our arms like the wings of the heart, sending the energy of Mother Earth upwards to Father Sky. We fly towards the open sky. We relax our breathing, sit down, lie down and let go into the mystery of life.

Oceanic Breathing

Tantric Breathing opens our sex centre. We unlock the life energy, which we need for our inner transformation. Now we can grow from sex to love, from sexual love to psychological love. I experience this as a feeling of deep blissful relaxation; a feeling of being one with my partner or being one with existence.

Oceanic Breathing opens us for the ocean of love with beautiful meditations. All these meditations use a gentle and expanding wave of breathing. One meditation moves with the circle of inhalation and exhalation as a way of meditating on love and aloneness.

In the Buddhist tradition, *Atisha's Heart Meditation* uses the power of breath to transform misery into bliss. On the in-breath, we take in the suffering of the whole world and transform it in our heart centre. On the out-breath, we radiate blissfulness and spread it to all the nooks and corners of the world. It's a really wonderful meditation.

Another breath meditation that I use is called *Expanding in Love*. With soft gentle breathing, we expand our love into the space beyond our body, including all living beings around the world in our lovingness. We learn to let go of our boundaries and be in harmony with existence.

A beautiful meditation to create a loving space for partners is the *Breathing in Love Meditation*. Sitting in front of a partner, we bring our hands to the upper chest and breathe from the heart. We look at our partner, as if for the first time, recognizing his or her beauty. With this feeling, we move into soft dancing with each other. Finally, we close our eyes, rest and let the energy work inside of us.

Another heart opening meditation is the *Love and Harmony Meditation*. We sit opposite our partner, cross our arms and hold hands. For ten minutes we sit with open eyes, looking at each other, and then for ten minutes with closed eyes. Then we stand up for ten minutes, swaying to beautiful music, creating an atmosphere of love and harmony.

Breathing in Zen

Facing our madness, cleansing ourselves from the past and regaining our inner strength by Power Breathing is the first step. Connecting to our sexual energy by Tantric Breathing is the second step. Opening our hearts for love energy by Oceanic Breathing is the third step. Now one more step is possible: to breathe in Zen.

Until this point, we can work with therapy and meditation techniques. Breathing in Zen is different: it happens only if we have prepared the garden for the roses of meditation to grow. In Zen tradition, it is called Satori, a moment when mind disappears and blissfulness appears.

This reminds me of the 'energy darshans' with Osho in Pune in the late 70s and early 80s, when groups of tweny to thirty people would meet with Osho in a small auditorium adjacent to his house. At a certain point, the lights were turned off and we raised our hands and started humming. Meanwhile, just in front of us, Osho would be giving energy to two or three guests, surrounded by about a dozen female mediums. The music quickly grew wilder and soon we would all be in ecstasy, absolutely high and totally free.

After a few minutes, the music would suddenly stop and deep silence remained. The world seemed to stand still; one moment felt like eternity. In such moments, the breath of Zen arrives – the breath of ecstasy. Existence is breathing us. We enter the mystery of life.

Imagine being able to bring this feeling of ecstasy into our daily lives – living from moment to moment, without being stuck in the past, or dreaming of the future. This will be the day of our inner liberation.

3. An Experience of the Power of Breath

In this, the third and final section of my chapter, I'd like to describe an experience of the Power of Breath. In general, I'd like to say that the simplest things in therapy often work best. Breathing is the simplest thing in life but because everybody is trapped in the mind few people can appreciate it. On the other hand, many people are scared to move into deep breathing because they risk becoming more alive and less controlled.

I start the group with introducing my work. I present the staff and myself. Then I ask participants if they would like to share why they have come to the group and what are their present issues. Mostly, these issues concern relationships or health problems.

Then I begin the play of the group process. I start with dancing, encouraging participants to meet playfully and joyfully. They open the heart centre by bringing their hands to the chest and breathing gently from the heart. Now I ask them to imagine expanding into an aura of loving energy and to connect by holding hands, hugging or looking into each other's eyes.

I agree with Osho when he says hugging is the best therapy. It's something most of us have missed during our lives; we are afraid of it and it's truly an art we need to learn. Usually, I give a demonstration. Many people don't allow their bodies to fully touch, especially when making contact at the level of the pelvis. Sometimes I make jokes to break the ice, saying "Don't worry, you won't get pregnant just by making body contact!"

As they begin to relax and warm up, trusting the process, I guide them into exercises designed to open the neck and throat. Usually, this begins by provoking fear, but then comes a release of anger. People begin to understand the opportunity being presented: who wants to control and limit expression any longer? Who wants to live life in a fearful atmosphere created long ago by well-intentioned but misguided authorities?

At this point, catharsis can spread through the group like a wild fire and I support this, encouraging participants to keep breathing, keep expressing themselves. Hot anger is the best antidote to fear. A chronic fear contraction is a pre-cancerous state that leads to misery and sickness. We need the hot fire of hate to heat up our system. It cleanses the body-mind like a healing fever.

The opposite to hot hate is cold hate, in which people become mean and hurt others with nasty comments, constant criticism, putting them down, sabotaging others and their own lives. They are afraid of their own hate, which, when released in a safe environment like this one, can open the door to positive life energy.

I enjoy when Osho talks about love and hate. At some point he mentions that, unlike love, our hate is unpolluted because nobody has been teaching us to value it. If somebody hates you, you can trust it. But at the opposite pole, if somebody loves you, then you need to be careful. Love has been polluted by all kind of teachings from people who like to talk about it but have no experience of what love is. Instead, they gave us a plastic substitute in order to prevent us from experiencing the real dimension of love.

I lead the group into dolphin breathing, another strong technique for releasing tension. In shamanism, the dolphin is called the caretaker of the sacred breath. Before he moves into the depth of the ocean he inhales as much air as he can. It allows him to stay under water for a long time. Coming back to the surface after a long dive he releases all his tension with an explosive breath similar to a cork popping from a bottle of champagne.

I then guide the group to lie down and begin Trance Energetic Breathing. This faster breathing opens the door to the unconscious mind and participants start letting go of control even more, moving their bodies and expressing whatever kind of emotion – either negative or positive – that is surfacing at this very moment. It may be anger with a love partner, or some emotion triggered by a primal memory from childhood, or rage resulting from sexual abuse, or a pleasurable feeling of sexuality or sensuality that needs to express itself through dance.

This kind of breathing does not follow any analytical structure. Rather, it brings to the surface whatever needs to be released in our system right now. It is spontaneous, unpredictable and related to our real life circumstances. It's like learning to be a child again and releasing feelings without controlling oneself.

With different kinds of body therapy we help our participants to go deeper into the process, which they create for themselves. For example, we start working with deep tissue massage on the shoulders, or the big chest muscles, to help release contractions from around the heart. We then work on the neck and the spine to release fear, which in Chinese medicine is related to the bladder meridian.

We also work with anger, cleansing the liver by mobilising the arms and legs, kicking away all the people who invaded our space – physically, mentally or sexually. We help to release sadness from the lungs, animosity from the heart and cleanse the gall bladder from feelings of jealousy.

A multitude of pressure points can open the flow of energy all the way through the body from the top of the head to the feet. We touch and massage these pressure points to create an awareness of areas in the body where the energy has been stuck, leading to the release of a multitude of repressed emotional feelings.

This is the moment when we can go a step further in our self-exploration and focus on sexual energy with Tantric Breathing.

The gentle moving of the pelvis related to the rhythm of breathing, the movement of the spine from the pelvis to the neck, opens participants to a feeling of great pleasure.

The next step of our work is to bring our hands back to the heart again. Participants relax into a silent and peaceful space for a long time with soft meditative music. The relaxation after a breath session is simply unique and many people share this experience.

Individual Session within the Group Structure

At the end of the session, Massimo, an Italian man in his mid-forties, raises his hand and shares that he is suffering from depression, paranoia and low life energy – basically feeling suicidal. I ask him about his family background, his relationships and whether he has a happy sex life. In response, Massimo tells us he has had no sex for years and is afraid to come physically close to a woman. He also shares that, from the very beginning of his life, he has felt unwanted. Consequently, he tried to please others in order to be loved but never succeeded.

I ask him how his mother felt when she was pregnant with him and he replies that she did not really want him; he has a strange feeling that something threatening happened during pregnancy but he's not sure what it was. The parents had a bad relationship and the father was beating his wife. Soon after the birth the parents divorced and he went to live with his mother.

I ask him: How did you feel about never being loved, never feeling accepted? Massimo starts crying but his crying is mixed with a deep anger, so I guide him into bio-energetic exercises to mobilise his energy, deepen his breathing and express anger by beating a cushion.

Even I, with long experience of breath work, am surprised at the amount of rage Massimo now releases. His whole life, he was sitting on this rage, using all his energy to stay in control, essentially killing his own energy and that's why he became more and more depressed.

Using breath as a trance technique I guide him back into the

297

womb of his mother. Holding his hand, I invite him to express his feelings of panic and fear, and it is heart-breaking for the whole group to see his pain and desperation releasing in a big catharsis of weeping and tears. Finally, Massimo relaxes into a deeply healing rhythm of soft breathing.

In this gentle space, I ask him if there is any positive feeling inside the womb of his mother and he tells us that, yes, whenever his mother is relaxing there is a beautiful feeling of peacefulness. I suggest for him to take this feeling home with him, after the group has ended, and to make it a resource for his future life. I also tell him this feeling will become stronger if he learns to meditate.

I guide him to bring his hands to the heart and take a moment to just be with himself, free from his parents. Another layer of tears arise, but this time they are without anger. I gently touch his head, helping him relax into his tears, inviting him to find an inner space of loving himself. Massimo's weeping changes to tears of gratefulness, his heart opens and he becomes very silent. He tells me he has never felt such a deep relaxation and love for himself.

The whole group is touched by this experience and many people are crying. I invite them to bring their hands to their hearts and feel this deep longing for love. Then comes the most beautiful moment of the group: just a deep silence – a silence in which we can go into the state of No Mind and we breathe in Zen.

After the session with Massimo, I ask the other participants to share their experiences in groups of three. Now they are in a more open, trusting space and can share with each other in a sincere and authentic way about their inner adventures of breathing. The group session ends with a big, loving hug.

When a group or a participant trusts me we can easily move into the depths of therapy. This is the simple conclusion of my work: love heals and meditation transforms the quality of our lives.

We breathe into a new way of life. We open for *The Way of the Heart.*

CHAPTER FIFTEEN

Sexual Deconditioning and Tantra

Turiya

Sex energy starts at the source of the spine. If a child is taught from the very beginning of his life to be against sex – for example, that sex is sin, and sex has to be destroyed, or at least controlled – and never allowed to go too far or to be spontaneous, and that sexual energy has to be put under many controls, laws, or regulations, then these suppressions become a buffer: the kundabuffer is created. When this happens, the sex energy remains repressed at the source of the spine and does not rise in the spine, preventing full sexual expression. As they say in the East: once the sex energy rises in the spine, you start to become very, very happy. When the sex energy reaches to the seventh chakra – SAHASRAR – you flower into a lotus bloom. Your life then is a deep ecstasy. ~ Osho[1]

I have been working as a therapist and facilitator under Osho's guidance for thirty-five years. When I came to Pune in 1975 with my husband and daughter I was twenty-seven-years-old and within a short time Osho told me I should work with Teertha (Paul Lowe) as co-leader of the renowned Encounter Group.

This was after he'd told me: "Do Vipassana meditation. You don't need anything else, you don't need to do groups."

Vipassana is an ancient meditation technique that requires the meditator to sit in silence with a straight back and watch his breath for forty minutes, then walk in silence for twenty minutes. This cycle is repeated continuously from 5:30 am until 11:00 pm.

This was my first 'Zen hit' and teaching from my Master because it was such a paradox: Vipassana *and* Encounter. The Encounter Group was completely the opposite of a Vipassana retreat. It was being together with twenty people in a small room and daring to be yourself under any circumstances.

Everything was allowed. It was total emotional expression leading to extreme confrontation with yourself and others. Since leading that first Encounter Group, so many years ago, I have been working continuously with groups – beginning in the ashram and then later around the world.

In Pune, after each Encounter Group, the participants and leaders would gather together with Osho at the regular evening meetings (called 'Darshans') and he would ask all of us about the group – how it went, people's personal experiences … and so on. From these Darshans and Osho's teachings I have learned not only how to work with other people and but also how to be with myself.

Another profound experience that has shaped my personal life and work as a therapist was my husband's unexpected death in 1981. That deep loss opened my heart in a painful yet profound way that made it possible for me to learn about real love and compassion.

That experience, along with living with an enlightened Master in a community of very diverse, intelligent and amazing people from all over the world, has taught me so much. Although I cannot name everything I have learned, if I had to condense my understanding and experience into a few sentences, I would say:

- Be still and listen.
- Be a friend to yourself and everybody that needs your help.
- Love and respect yourself and this precious life.
- You are not only your body, your heart and your mind, you are bigger than that. You are an unlimited self in a boxed-up world.

Today, I work with many subjects and use many modalities, each having different themes and often a different way of working. This text is about sexual deconditioning, one of my favourite topics. With this subject, I usually work in groups of about thirty to forty people for seven days. Through a clear session structure and a daily practice of various meditations, participants have a chance to explore and experience the body, mind and heart, heal old wounds and traumas, discover new ways of communicating and being.

Therapy in Service of Meditation

In the past thirty-five years, I have been trained in many psychological and meditative processes. My work as a facilitator has been to build many bridges: between therapy and meditation, between living in the marketplace and living in awareness, moving from the unreal to the real, from death to deathlessness, from the limited mind to an unlimited inner sky.

From my work with thousands of people, I have found that the healing provided by therapy is only lasting if an individual also engages in meditation and learns to be real, authentic and present in his daily life. Unless therapy is grounded in meditative awareness, it can go on forever, as the human mind endlessly produces problems in order to stay in control, to stay in the known, to know where we as individuals are going.

Osho used to say that therapy is a preparation for meditation. And meditation helps to prepare the ground for enlightenment and for waking up.

Basically, my work is to help and support people in a growing-up process, to find a way to mature and realize who they truly are. First of all, this means having the awareness, understanding and insight to recognize the prisons in which they are living. The walls of these prisons are full of ancient stories, traditions, concepts and ideas of our past and our future. By studying the walls, doors and windows of these prisons, they may one day have the courage to break out and live in freedom, in naturalness … in the Now.

Remembrance of Our Magnificence

In a way, I see my work as the remembrance of an ancient sound, a long-forgotten song, or language that reminds us that we are beings of God, or the All-And-Everything, or All-And-Nothing (these are all just words for something limitless that is without name or form).

I don't believe that people are born evil or bad. Instead, I sense that, at the core, we all have a loving consciousness that is full of potential for joy, laughter, beauty, grace and love. Anyone with open eyes and open heart is able to see and experience this, perhaps in a child's smile, in a lover's gift, even in the wag of a dog's tail. It can be experienced in so many ways.

But we often forget or lose this connection to our inherent goodness. When somebody gets angry, hurtful, violent or depressed, I see only someone who is confused, frustrated, in pain and most of all full of self-hatred. A loving individual would never carry out an act of violence. When somebody cherishes and loves himself, he is a joy to be around.

When someone is suffering, therapy and meditation have a big place in uncovering all the old wounds, hurts, beliefs and limiting concepts that keep him from healing and living his life.

A Journey from Ego to Unlimited Self

I see therapy as a process of deep and powerful growth. With the help of another person, or a group, an individual can work through life's crises, challenges and times of transitions. In therapy, the individual is invited – and at other times confronted – to give up old notions and outdated beliefs that might keep him safe and in the known, yet hinder his expansion and growth.

This is an intense process because many people are unwilling to give up these old ideas. In this way, they miss the opportunity to let go of old patterns and welcome a rebirth that helps them make the transition to a greater maturity.

Therapy is a rare opportunity to investigate your beliefs and notions and to develop an always-evolving and maturing attitude towards a forever-changing life. It is a way of remembering that you are a being that is born in essence and innocence, with the opportunity in this life to learn and mature.

Therapy: A School for Life

In school, we learn mathematics, algebra, how to write complicated essays about historical people who are long gone, but we don't learn the most basic subjects of life: How do we love? How do we deal with sexuality? How are we intimate? How do we raise a child? How to be silent? And above all, how do we die?

I see so many young mothers who have no idea what it means to bring up a child. I remember giving birth to my daughter and having no idea what I was getting into. To bring up children with love and awareness is probably one of the most difficult and challenging subjects of our lives. But we aren't in any way prepared. We learn many useless things in school, but not how to connect with our inner being, how to recognize our conditioned mind, how to deal with our feelings and how to love.

I see therapy as an opportunity to awaken certain aspects of the essential self, such as courage, curiosity, love, commitment and honesty, so we can walk our path to our full potential. In my work, I help to orient people towards these qualities in order to walk their lives in authenticity and realness.

My way of working with people has the function of bringing awareness to old patterns of behaviour and thus encouraging healing from old traumas and hurts that hinder us from opening up to life and to love. Most of us come from conditioned families and have consequently learned patterns of behaviour that hinder us from experiencing who we truly are. Instead, we are living borrowed lives that have been pre-ordered, set in fixed patterns of defence and reactivity that don't serve us in being our true selves.

Most of all, my work is to help people to understand their ego and personality structure, to discover how much more they are, to remember that they are truly magnificent and can actually live this here today.

Sexuality: The Source of Creation

Our sexual energy is the most powerful and most profound energy that exists on this planet. Without sexuality, we would not be born or even created. It is the source of creation. A man makes love to a woman, his sperm meets her egg, and out of this meeting a new being is created. For nine months it grows in the belly of the woman and then a miracle: this new being is born.

Through our sexual acts, this creation is happening every second. It is independent of whether we are rich or poor, black or white, creation evolves by itself and pushes its way ahead. So the source of our sexual energy is magical and has an unbelievable power. It is actually something sacred.

Through Tibetan Buddhism, we have found a much deeper understanding of sexuality, related to an inner science through which one can attain enlightenment. The function of sexuality is not only reproduction and the creation of new life, but, as taught in the Eastern traditions, is also a way to enlightenment and realization. Only in the last sixty years have we Westerners discovered a completely new understanding of polarities: the male energy and the female energy as opposites and yet complementary representations of life, sexuality and intimacy.

When I came to Osho in 1975 it was clear to me that he was a Tantric Master who would teach me enlightenment and realization through full acceptance of who I am – not through denial. One of the big Tantric teachings is: "As above, so below". When I heard this sentence for the first time, something in me immediately resonated. It is the truth.

There is no 'lower' in our body. Sexuality is our base energy and needs to be acknowledged and lived so that it can be transformed. As our root energy, if our sexuality is not acknowledged and unlocked, it can never travel to higher levels of consciousness. We are sexual beings and the universe is organized around the opposing polarities of positive and negative, light and dark, day and night, winter and summer, male and female. So, from this perspective, we can say the universe surrounding us is very sexy!

Intimacy and sexuality are doorways to enlightenment. Discovering sex and the alchemy of that potent energy is a vehicle for spiritual transformation.

Repression of Sexuality

Sexuality is one of the most repressed and perverted energies on this planet. Listening to Osho's teachings, I heard him speak over and over again against the repression of sexuality. In my own therapeutic practice, I have seen so many times that repression causes splitting, for instance the puritan versus the prostitute, the saint versus the sinner, the body against the soul.

Repression can never bring freedom. Repression makes you a slave. Repress anything, and that will become your master. So, the so-called celibates in the monasteries – the BRAHMACHARIS – are continuously obsessed with sex and their mind is completely sexual. It has to be so. Or, those that are mad, and are REALLY against the body will start destroying it, succeeding only in becoming a eunuch. ~ Osho[2]

Religion, culture and family interfere drastically with our sexuality. There is an attempt to eradicate sexuality through taboos, bans, and in some traditions even self-flagellation. In some Middle Eastern countries women are stoned for being sexual. Horrors exist such as in New Delhi, India, where a young woman was gang raped on a bus and so severely injured that she died.

In South Africa, a women is raped every four minutes. There is a belief in several cultures that women are at fault for luring men into lust by their seductive beauty and enticing ways. In some African tribes, women are castrated and mutilated so they cannot experience joy while having sex. In some countries, a woman is banned from her family if she has suffered a sexual assault because she is seen as damaged, contaminated and unclean.

Repressed sexual instincts get acted out in the worst perversions or distortions: rape, assault, incest, molestation, abuse, lack of healthy boundaries and invasiveness on a physical, emotional and energy level. You only need to look at what has been happening in the Catholic Church with a whole series of investigations, trials and convictions of Catholic priests – and other members of Roman Catholic orders – for committing sexual crimes against children as young as three years old.

Meanwhile, the Catholic Church has done its best for years to cover up the truth and still supports the practice of celibacy, forcing its priests and monks to obey a series of impossible rules and regulations that make sexuality seem dirty and unclean.

It is always shocking to me to see how many of my clients have been, or continue to be, sexually abused, or abused in other ways. I see it in so many ways, in both women and men. If an individual acts out this abused energy, it becomes very hard to deal with. What he needs to do is free the instinct from repression and reintegrate these perverted splits and misdirected drives into the totality of who we are.

True freedom is based on a healthy respect for sexuality, the self and the other in a sacred context, as opposed to destructive perversion coupled with instinctual drive.

I have heard Osho say that unless the naturalness of sex becomes accepted wholeheartedly nobody can love anybody. The energy of sex is divine energy, godly energy. That is why this energy creates new life. It is the greatest most mysterious force of all. This is why Osho was so insistent that people should drop any antagonism towards sex and acknowledge its sacredness.

One of the major ways of healing is to bring sexuality out into the open. All that is denied, we try to hide. In order to bring awareness to something it has to be brought into the light. As long as one's sexual instinct is kept secret the wounds from repression can never heal and will stay in darkness, continuing to fester and aggravate the wounded. Sometimes it will be covered by guilt and sometimes it will be covered by a deep sense of shame. Neither of these feelings will ever allow true healing.

In the process that I teach, a person can begin to free himself from early conditioning so that a natural sense of sexuality can be restored and used to open new doors. I love the quote from a rare Tibetan teacher who says: "There are three ways to enlightenment – spiritual practice, Tantra and trauma."

Three Energy Centres: Head, Heart, Mind

I work with three centres: basic sexuality, located in the lower belly; the spiritual heart, located in and around the chest; and the mind, located in the head. Each of these centres needs to be open and available in order for one to be present and feel sexually and emotionally alive.

One of the discoveries I have made in working with myself and others is that energy moves upwards, not downwards. Thus, my experience has shown that I need to help a person first to unlock their genital and belly area in order for them to be able to truly experience their heart.

In order to open the sex centre, a person needs to unlock everything that hinders the flow of energy in that part of the body. Being able to feel your genitals and to have an orgasm are all very natural functions of our instinctive body. Once we are in touch with our genitals, one learns that they are an enjoyable part of one's body, capable of pleasure and, at other times, a joyful release.

Loving Yourself

In my work, the first thing I focus on is really loving the whole self, including the genitals and the sexual drive. For many people, the simple act of feeling their genitals is connected with an enormous sense of shame, insecurity and lack of confidence. Part of the work involves participants getting to know themselves and discovering who they are once they give attention to that part of the body.

Wilhelm Reich, a pioneer of body-oriented psychotherapy, used to say that therapy was successful once a person was able to experience a total body orgasm. Of course, this might sound a bit too high a goal, but the idea is that therapy brings a person closer to a natural way of being with his sexuality. It is like becoming intimate with yourself and allowing yourself to take pleasure as a sexual being.

In order to do this, I lead body-oriented exercises, where people stand with eyes closed, allowing their bodies to vibrate. This usually starts with a light trembling that slowly increases until the entire body shakes and in this way slowly becomes alive. Together with the movement, I encourage people to use their voices to make sounds. We are often ashamed of making sounds that expose our sexuality. We are also often afraid of involuntary movements, because these might mean that we are out of control. It is important to allow these movements and allow the sounds to be expressed at the same time.

The Attitude of the Therapist

When we are dealing with such intimate issues as sexuality it is important for the therapist to create a safe place where the client feels completely supported and accepted in whatever issue or feeling he or she will bring up. As this energy has been abused and shut down, all kinds of repressed feelings are likely to surface: old hurts, feelings of humiliation, a sense of failure, feeling rigid and frigid, feeling self-conscious and extremely shy, feeling distrustful. So, especially when working with these issues, it is important that the therapist knows what he or she is doing and is willing to be free of judgements. In my long experience of working with people I've come to understand that one of the most important ingredients in being a therapist is to be free of my own biases, or at least aware of them, so they don't get in the way of a loving and accepting attitude. Especially when you work around sexual issues, this is an absolutely necessary ingredient of the work.

There is so much shame around our sexuality that it is not easy to uncover all the layers of denial, mistrust, deep hurts and wounds. The person coming to you is in some kind of turmoil and needs help, and a big chunk of that help is the feeling that you will never ridicule him, or her, that you will love the person no matter how horrible the story is that he or she reveals or exposes. As a therapist I need to create a safe space so that the client feels valued, heard, and accepted. Otherwise the client will not open up, especially concerning his or her sexuality.

A Signboard: Don't Touch!

As children, sexuality was often a forbidden topic and so much of the enjoyment of the sensuality of the body, which children naturally feel, was condemned or forced to be hidden. Many children are not allowed to touch or play with themselves. From early on, it is as if a signboard was created over our genitals: 'Don't touch!' All this leads to a very charged and unnatural relationship with our genitals.

Part of the healing work is to bring a fresh flow of energy back into the body. It is, in a way, learning to be intimate with yourself before you can actually be intimate with somebody else.

I worked with a young Swedish woman in one of my groups in Denmark. She was very tall, lanky and shy. She was living away from home for first time in her life, but was withdrawn and unhappy. When we started to work on opening up her body, she could not feel anything. Her voice was quiet and her body, in a way, was collapsed. Eventually, she started to open and suddenly remembered that when she was small her father used to drink heavily. When he was drunk he would make condescending remarks about her body, because she was growing up so tall and skinny. She had learned to protect herself by shutting down.

When she remembered this, she broke into uncontrollable sobs, and I could feel her deep pain. Yet for her to open further amid a large group of men and women did not feel safe because anybody could laugh at her, or make some hurtful remark.

To help her, I asked her to imagine having a protector, somebody that would be strong enough to give her full protection. After some hesitation, she chose a man in the group she trusted. Once he stood next to her, holding hand, she slowly started to relax.

I asked her how young she felt when she allowed herself to connect with the little girl inside who'd experienced all that humiliation from her father. After a long while, she finally answered that she was very young. So I let her choose another protector. Sometimes one person is just not enough. When the second person stood in front of her to protect her from the looks of the rest of the group, she finally started to feel safe and could relax.

When the body feels safe, the energy comes back, colour returns to the face, a sense of natural strength is restored and aliveness is embodied and slowly experienced again.

Once my client felt safe, she started to feel more aliveness in her heart, which led to her memory of feeling abandoned by her mother, who was busy working and had no time for her. The realization of that loss found expression in one big sob. Once she allowed the pain to be there, I asked her what was behind the pain when she truly felt into her heart area.

After a moment, she expressed a sense of connectedness to her body that she rarely experienced, a relaxation, or a coming home. At the same time, she also had a sense of being delicate and quite shy.

Feeling safe and protected is the first step in healing, understanding that the body can actually feel different when there is no longer any need to protect oneself. Usually, when people are so disconnected from their bodies, it takes a lot of attention, a totally safe place and a loving and accepting therapist for them to be able to feel again.

I teach you the body: the body is beautiful, divine. Come back to the body. Let the body become alive again, and it will take care; you need not worry about it. The body has a built-in program to keep you healthy, to keep you alive, to keep you vibrant, to keep you young, fresh.

The body has a built-in program: you need not learn anything about it from books and teachings. So when people come to me in the beginning, sometimes they may indulge – but I am not responsible for their indulgence. The priests, the people who have conditioned them, they are responsible. If these people can be here with me for a few days, sooner or later the balance is restored. And with balance comes tranquillity, calmness, a subtle joy and a subtle naturalness. ~ Osho[3]

Learning to Love the Body

In order to be able to feel sexuality and sensuality, a person needs – above all else – to feel and sense his or her body. I have worked with people from many countries, including Croatians, Germans, Jews, Israelis, Swedes and Finns. I have rarely found a person who really loves and appreciates his or her body. Most people have some kind of issue with their body, ranging from minor issues to complete denial that they even have one.

I think the explosion in the number of overweight children worldwide is a result of this disconnection from the body. People can be so judgmental about themselves; one look in the mirror and most people can find something wrong. I am surprised that even the most model-like young women who come to me often make some kind of harsh critique of their bodies. Either the tits are too small or the belly is too big or the legs are too fat.

We live in such a phony, idealized 'Botox' culture, where you see only young, hip, skinny people in the fashion magazines. Many people have lost a natural sense of love for their bodies. But how can you trust and let somebody love you if you hate – or at least not love – yourself? These conflicts result in a disconnection with our bodies and our natural sexuality and sensuality.

Beliefs and Images about the Body

Part of the work of sexual deconditioning is to bring awareness to feelings of self-loathing and to inquire where these feelings come from. Maybe there is a pattern of self-hatred in the family; maybe mom put you down because she was afraid that you were too beautiful and she was envious, or maybe your brother made a remark about your legs that you always remember.

My grandmother, who loved me dearly, always commented on my weight when I saw her. These comments made me feel ashamed and self-conscious. To this day, I start sweating when I stand on scales even though I have an otherwise good connection to my body – loving and accepting it as it is.

311

The first step to deconditioning is to bring awareness to these old patterns. Once a person can see and recognize these patterns, there is a possibility that he or she can create distance and stop identifying with them.

The second step is to allow the body to come alive again. This might be a slow process or it may happen quickly. For some, to be able to feel and sense the body provides an immediate 'coming home' feeling. They are full of energy, juice and zest for life. Their bodies may feel full of expansion and passion.

However, for others, getting to this point may take longer and they may need a lot of encouragement to be able to feel and sense themselves again. They have used dissociation as a way of surviving, meaning they have learned not feel the body at all. Today, so many young people have piercings, tattoos, or have cut themselves in some way ... this, to me, seems like a desperate attempt to feel something.

The final step is to initialize positive experiences where the individual can experience the body as a source of aliveness, sensuousness, and passion.

Sensing Flow in the Body

I do a whole series of exercises that focus on feeling your body again: learning how to touch your arms, your belly, your legs ... as well as learning how to sense your body from the inside.

I have noticed that the more a person actually senses his or her own body, the less judgemental he or she is. To be able to feel and sense your body again from the inside is probably one of the biggest gifts anyone can experience. It allows and helps you to trust your body. It connects you to the ground and opens up the innate intelligence that is inherent in your body. It gives you a sense of freedom and movement as well as the ability to really listen to what your body has to say to you. We pressure our bodies to perform to our idealized standards, but we rarely take the time to listen or pay attention to what the body itself has to say – what it would like to tell us.

Inviting Sensuality

Once you have dared to experience relaxation and are familiar with sensing the body, it is important to invite a sensuousness to flow through your body. This is easier when you close your eyes, because so much judgement comes through the eyes. Once the eyes are closed, you can sense your body from the inside, without even having to think about it. The body can be a great source of aliveness and sensuousness, once you dare to be in it. When I close my eyes and sense my body, I can easily enter a zone of timelessness that seems to have no beginning and no end. Closing my eyes provides a different way of experiencing myself because then I have no choice but to experience myself through my other senses. Meditation is an essential part of this process. Many meditations involve soft movements of the body and these movements help to open the doors to our inner landscape of being.

I worked with a Norwegian man in his fifties. He had been a successful businessman and had divorced his wife about a year earlier. His four children were grown up and did not need him or their mother anymore. Like many Norwegians, he was a runner and kept his body in shape through daily workouts. He looked extremely well-built and healthy, yet when we started working in the group he could not sense his body at all.

As we talked about this, I learned that he felt lonely inside, always feeling like an outsider and a spectator. These feelings were part of an old pattern from his childhood. When he was still surrounded by his family, he was able to cover up these feelings. But now, being alone, these long-denied feelings began to surface. He felt connected to his body when he pushed himself on a morning run or a hard workout in the gym, but he could not really sense himself when he was relaxed.

First, I asked him how he experienced his body. He responded that he could only feel restrictions and a sense of emptiness. I invited him to relax into that, without any expectation, and soon he started to sense his hands. I kept assuring him that he was in a safe place and whatever he experienced was absolutely perfect. I then asked him to sense his legs and see what feelings came up, as his left leg was twitching slightly. Once he became aware of it and allowed that unexpressed sensation, a big surge of energy suddenly arose in his legs.

From this, both legs started shaking and out of this came the impulse to kick. I encouraged him to kick and make sounds. Initially, he held back his voice, but after a while it became more powerful. When I asked him how he felt, he answered "Passionate and full on ... " He kept kicking and releasing energy out of his legs.

When I asked him what would happen next, he experienced a sudden surge of anger, saying it had never been okay for him to be really alive and loud; he'd always had to repress his passion and his fullness. Even his wife told him she didn't like it when he was 'noisy'. She wanted him to behave! Just like his mother.

I learned that his mother was regularly 'fucked' in a loud way by his father, who was always drunk on Saturdays. As a young child, he heard those noises and was terrified. He would hide under his bed and hold his ears until it was over. He also tried to protect his mother by being well-behaved and not making any noises: in other words, not being too alive.

Once he saw and understood all this, I asked him to allow himself to be as noisy as he would like to be and to allow his body to do what it loved to do. His whole body glowed red and started to come alive, full of passionate anger, together with a strong desire to step out of the confinement of the 'good boy' box. As he did so, energy started to flow through his body, which came alive again.

I encouraged him to sense and fully experience the aliveness of the body, then I asked him, "Are you still an outsider?" He looked around and realized he felt connected to everyone in the group. This transformation happened because he felt connected to his own body, which in turn allowed his feelings to open and he could dare to step 'out of the box' and be as alive and juicy as he was meant to be.

From daring to be alive and passionate in our bodies, we can start to explore our sexuality. Ask yourself:

Do I really feel alive in my genitals? Are they a part of my body that I love and appreciate? How do I relate to that basic grounding, passionate energy in my lower belly and in my genitals?

Some people only sense a feeling of a deficiency there, while for others it is pressure. For yet others, it is overcharged and needs to be constantly discharged. In all these different cases my work is the same: to help individuals connect with their bodies and genitals and restore a sense of natural energy flow.

Three Stages of Sexual Development

Osho has said that there are three stages that children go through in their sexual development. The first is an auto-erotic stage, when a young child is in love with himself or herself. In this stage, children love to play with their bodies, enjoy touching their genitals, and naturally enjoy the sensuousness of the body. If parents and society did not interfere with an endless chant of 'don't do that', this would be an enjoyable state of being.

In the second stage, when children grow a little bit older, they become interested in their own sex: boys want to explore with other boys, and girls with other girls. It is a state of curiosity and exploration: "Oh wow, you got a willie too!" or "I wanna see your pussy". If this stage is allowed in a natural way, without parents being immediately alarmed that a girl will become a lesbian or a boy will be gay, children will grow organically into being interested in the opposite sex, the third and final stage. These are the stages of sexual development in children, which, if allowed, are healthy and natural.

Communication of Sexual Needs

The base of our energy is fully alive and grounded. The colour usually associated with the sex centre is a passionate dark red that is full of lust, enthusiasm and zest for life. It is a raw and wild energy that is not yet refined or cultivated. Most people are

315

ashamed of this energy and try to hide it, instead of being open with it. The stage when a person craves a sexual partner and has an enormous sexual appetite can bring up the uncomfortable sensation of wanting or needing. Both are sensations that most people don't like as they make us dependent on others.

I work with many people, encouraging them to express their sexual needs clearly, instead of hiding them, or expressing them in a bizarre or distorted way. Learning to communicate from this place can be very challenging, but can also bring a great relief when it is done.

It is important to bring all the unexpressed emotions and feelings into the light. If we were ashamed of feeling sexual and tried to hide it, these feelings often become distorted because the sex energy is so strong. Many people report how they still feel ashamed of the fact that they masturbated when they were children and teenagers.

But when we start splitting off our sexual desires while pretending to be 'good' these things sit deep in our unconscious and create conflict with our body and minds.

Often, I suggest an exercise where you sit with a partner and share for fifteen minutes each: What would the most sexually fulfilling night with you look like? I make it clear that everything is possible and yet this is just a communication exercise – it doesn't mean that you have to actually follow this up with action.

Maybe at home, it might be good to share this same kind of exposure with your partner. It's important to share all these dreams and needs with another human being. When they remain in hiding, they create a lot of shame and come out in a very unnatural and often destructive, way. Once people start to connect to their bodies in a relaxed way they will naturally open up to their sexuality.

From the Body to the Heart

Once we evoke more aliveness, passion and acceptance in the body these qualities will naturally want to flow into the heart and the area around our chest. This is more than just the physical heart; it is the whole space that is alive in our chest. Once we start connecting with our bodies, this flow can happen very easily.

If we are connected only to our bodies, sexuality can be passionate and almost animal-like, but has no real sensitivity. It is simply fucking or making love without any real connection. Many people prefer this. They are afraid to connect with their feelings because they don't want to get hurt, or too attached, or involved.

But it is only when we connect inside from our genitals to our heart that the sexual act acquires significance and a more gratifying meaning. The raw, animal-like sexual energy gets transformed into loving sexuality that is open to being in a deeper communion with the other person and is willing to give and to receive.

Once a person is connected to his or her body from the inside and learns to love and accept the body as it is, with gentleness and care, he or she naturally longs for the energy to expand and move into the heart centre, because here we experience meaning. Once we can feel our hearts, we can have a sense of worthiness and deep fulfilment.

Heart Connections

Through connecting with the heart we experience love, for which so many people long. It is the longing, above all, to be intimate with yourself and be able to sense your own connection to the heart. Often this connection makes us vulnerable and tender, and once we dare to be present to these experiences we can easily get hurt.

This is one of the reasons why many people build walls around their hearts, even while they are still very young. Many people say "I would rather be alone than feel that pain again." They shy away from life's offerings out of fear of being rejected or hurt.

We often long for intimacy, yet we put so many conditions on it: you should never betray me, or leave me; you should tell me ten times every day how special I am to you; you should keep all your promises under any circumstance; you should support me totally, financially and emotionally. Needless to say, nobody can meet these conditions, even if they try.

I help people to connect with the heart. This means allowing the old ring of protection around their hearts to crack open. To begin this process, I usually introduce a meditation in which I invite people to connect with their hearts. Often, it is a delicate process that needs a lot of love and gentleness. Many of us chose to shut down a long time ago, perhaps through the experience of an early loss, or maybe through not being seen and noticed, or maybe from being humiliated.

A heart meditation is an open invitation to be present again in this area. Once people allow their feelings to surface, they will often cry tears of isolation, as they have been living in that 'separate room' for so long. Even though many of them became accustomed to isolation over time, it still feels lonely and disconnected, not only from the world but from themselves.

I worked with a woman who had been harsh and efficient her entire life. She was around forty years old, very beautiful and successful, working as a doctor in a hospital. She was intelligent, with a high IQ, having studied in top universities in the United States and Australia.

She talked of her longing to be with the 'right' man. She was very demanding in her expectations and not willing to compromise in any way. Her mind was fast, and also very critical. When I asked her who was so critical in her childhood, she laughed and said, smilingly, "Oh, both my parents. No matter what I do, it is never enough for them. No matter what kind of university degrees I bring home, it is never enough for them."

I asked her how that made her feel. She replied that she is always putting herself under pressure and is very self-critical. Digging a bit deeper, I asked her who was her ally, or her guardian angel, when she was little. Eventually, she mentioned her dog, whom she loved deeply, and who died when she was only nine years old.

As she talked about it, she suddenly burst into tears. "I loved that dog so much!" she muttered through her tears. When the dog died, her parents did not spend a moment with her to feel empathy over the loss; life simply went on as if nothing had happened.

They told her not to take the loss so seriously. Their only answer was "you can get another dog." She felt very alone with her deep feelings of loss and pain. At that moment, she made an unconscious decision not to ever open up again, but to be strong, independent and not let anybody see her cry.

In therapy, once she started to open the protection around her heart, she was suddenly more present in her body and faced with all those feelings. She came to realize how lonely she had always felt, how isolated she was as a child and even more so during her study years, when all of her energy had been poured into being intelligent in order to conquer this isolation and loneliness. But, of course, this did not work!

As a result, her energy was up in her head and her heart was extremely protected and frozen. Slowly, she started to open up in the group, allowing herself to feel her pain and loneliness and with it her heart. It brought up a tremendous vulnerability that she had to learn to embrace. It was a process that didn't happen overnight. It took time.

However, when she allowed a friend in the group to see her vulnerability she was amazed at how different it felt. She said, "Suddenly, I can see him as a beautiful man." I reflected it back to her, saying "You see your own beauty in his eyes." She was for a moment seeing the world through the eyes of her heart.

Because of hurts and wounds, we try to protect ourselves. Some of us become hard and cold, others compensate through choosing to do everything by themselves. Some people drown in self-pity. Out of the original wounding comes a whole set of behaviour patterns that offer protection but hinder our ability to live a contented and fulfilling life.

Part of my work is to find the pivotal point when an individual closed off. It can be one event, or it can be many situations, but usually it's an event that was too hard to bear or too difficult to stay fully alive. Once this moment is present, everything can unravel from there. Then the work focuses on looking at patterns of behaviour that were created in order to build a wall of protection – patterns with which the person became strongly identified.

Important Steps in My Work

- Acceptance of what is. This means I invite the person to explore and discover himself or herself, as he or she actually is, instead of trying to be different. It is helpful to learn to accept situations, even if it feels almost impossible to do so. Once a person accepts even the most challenging situation, he or she starts to relax, and once he or she is relaxed there is space for growth and change.

- Creating a sense of inner space. Individuals can sense space. Once a person gets used to space, there is a possibility of looking at the situation from a different perspective, connecting with a new place of understanding and awareness.

- Creating a new perspective.

- Helping the client to find a resource either in their body or in their psyche so the client feels present in body and being.

- Meeting yourself as your best friend means meeting difficult parts of yourself with kindness instead of with rejection.

- Learning to accept and integrate disowned parts of yourself.

- Getting to know and experience yourself in richness and complexity instead of denial and attempts to be somebody else.

- Integrating all these different parts of who we are.

The heart dimension is so rich and so profound that this chapter is not long enough to talk about the incredible depth and transformation that becomes possible once we start to connect with this aspect of our being. It is one of our most powerful centres.

Once we open our hearts and love, the whole world changes: every little blade of grass becomes colourful and significant and every face looks beautiful, no matter what age or what colour. The heart brings innate acceptance and from this arises compassion. Once we connect to our hearts, we become naturally generous and giving, not out of a conditioned sense of duty, but because it flows out of us like a bubbly fountain of water.

Connecting Sexuality with the Heart

When we allow ourselves to sense the connection between our sexuality/belly and our hearts, a harmonious flow of love arises in our bodies and being. Sexuality suddenly has a deeper meaning: it is an experience of gentleness and passion, of both wildness and tenderness. It is a way that the feminine and the male energy can meet and connect with each other.

I find that once I can open to that flow of energy connecting my genitals with my heart, a sensuous feeling of deep satisfaction is created. Once I sense this connection, it is much easier to meet another human being and to merge in a loving and trusting way. From this place it is also much easier to share and respect each other.

For me, one of the most important lessons about exploring sexuality is learning to respect my own boundaries and the boundaries of my partner. In working with sexual issues, I am often surprised how many people have been sexually or emotionally abused. The word "boundaries" was something I'd never heard of until relatively recently – I don't think it had a big place in therapy twenty years ago. It slowly emerged and gained credence in the late 90s when sexual abuse stories were made public.

In my own experience, I relax when I feel safe, and only when I can relax do I connect with my body. What makes me feel safe? The possibility of sensing and listening to myself; that I can say 'yes' and also have the freedom to say 'NO' and be heard and respected in that.

Especially around sexual foreplay and flirting, I have heard many men say, "Oh, when a women says 'no' she actually wants to get laid." In my work with women, I have met many who easily disconnect and dissociate from their bodies while involved in sexual closeness with men. I think it is centuries-old conditioning that women think they have to endure sex and have no right to say 'NO' without being violated or punished.

The truth is: I can only say a wholehearted 'yes' when I also feel I have the right and freedom to say 'NO'.

321

A Healthy Sense of Boundaries

Boundaries are a field of energy that give us the space to be and to sense ourselves. Without boundaries, the only defence we have when we feel unsafe is to dissociate – this often means leaving our bodies and retreating into numbness, denial, daydreams or spacing out.

Boundaries are essential for a healthy sense of being. In order for me to sense myself I need clear boundaries: to be able to express myself, to go slow, to take time and, above all, to express my needs when I am in a relationship. In my experience, sexuality becomes boring or even dead in many relationships because the partners don't know how to respect their own boundaries, or their partner's boundaries, without causing offence and hurting the other.

Most of us endured disrespect of our personal space and choices as children – by parents, teachers and other adults – experiencing that it is 'normal' to be invaded and to be disrespected. Growing up, we get used to this, learning to shut down and simply cope, resulting in a defensive ego structure with deep feelings of shame, helplessness and – at other times – rage and anger.

I worked with a middle-aged English woman who could not feel her body and was mostly focused in her head – that is to say, preoccupied with intellectual concerns and mental activity.

Her issue was a deep fear of speaking in front of large groups. I invited her to describe the fear and paint it on a canvas, then put it up somewhere in the room. Once she had given the fear an image and could see it, she started to breath a bit more and at the same time felt more in touch with her body.

But, as she started to relax, a feeling of anxiety came up. I asked her to sense it in her body and she suddenly remembered that, when she was about five years old, the next-door neighbour's son, who was much older, would come into her room and tell her that if she did not play with him a big red monster that loved to eat small girls would come.

By the time she finished talking about it, her anxiety was alive in her body. I invited her to build a safe place around her – a wall, a tent, or whatever she needed – to keep the monster off. She created an imaginary wall and was able to relax a bit more, again sensing her body. Even for her to be able to do this much was a very new experience for her.

Then I asked her "Who protected you when you were small?" She could not remember anybody. This brought tears to her eyes and she started to gently cry. After this, she could sense her body a lot more and suddenly there was a sensation in her heart space as well.

As she started to connect with her body and heart, she slowly and gently came out of the frozen space. She looked at me and suddenly said "Oh, I'm more here now, how different!" This realization brought more tears. Years of feeling isolated in a family that consumed lots of alcohol and paid little attention to this young girl had made her feel completely unprotected.

As a defence, she went up into her head and became hyper vigilant – it was the best that she could do to survive a very difficult childhood.

I then asked her if there was anybody who could give her support and protection today. She remembered her boyfriend. In her imagination, she brought him into the room and he was allowed to sit with her. With the support of her boyfriend and her wall, she slowly began to come more and more alive. From this place of being in the body, I asked her one more time to have a peek at the monster. As she was stronger, the monster was getting weaker. She was able to stand up and say, "No, I don't want to! Go away!" with force in her voice, instead of collapsing into helplessness.

Working on these kinds of issues in my workshops, I introduce many different exercises to help people have a sense of boundaries, so they can start to relax.

Having boundaries means:

• Slowing down so that you can actually sense what is going on. When you are speedy, you usually cannot feel yourself. It is a defence.

- Take time, no matter how long it takes, and allow yourself to walk step by step.

- Have no goal. Especially around sexuality, we are very driven and goal-oriented. Allow yourself to be present in the moment.

- Be Here and Now.

Once we are allowed to slow down, we become more aware of what is going on inside and outside. This creates safety. Many neurobiological studies show that feeling safe, both emotionally and physically, is an essential ingredient in a healthy and full approach to life.

When the nervous system detects safety, then it is no longer defensive. When we feel safe, magical things can occur. Certain areas of the brain are positively affected, like those feeling pleasure and those that allow us to be expansive, creative and feel enthusiastic about life.

Meditation: An Essential Ingredient

Meditation has an essential part in my work. Unless we learn to slow down and become more conscious of what is going on, I don't think any method or 'how to' can fix our problems.

We need awareness. We need a deep understanding of our intricate and complex psychological inner landscapes and this requires meditation.

Through meditative awareness new neutral pathways are formed in our brains. Simultaneously, new perspectives arise in our minds that allow fresh and innovative ways of being present in our bodies and our hearts. Meditation creates space and presence.

Once we feel more present, we have space to look at our life stories, dramas, challenges, fears and insecurities without being immediately caught up in them. Space creates a clear sense of an unlimited being.

Sex is unconscious, earthly, the lowest form of love. Love is conscious, higher than sex, just midway, a stopping station between the earth and the sky. It is more poetic, but still the poetry is definable, it is contained in the words. The highest form of love is prayer; it is no more expressible, it is not contained any more in any definition. No words are adequate enough to express it. It is inexpressible. And when the highest is felt, you can express it only through tears – or laughter, or dance – very indirectly. And when the highest is felt, it provokes the highest in you: it is felt by the superconscious. ~ Osho[4]

CHAPTER SIXTEEN

Inner Man, Inner Woman

Rafia

I stared at the huge pile of mail in front of me. I was in Athens at Poste Restante and had seen from a ragged list that I had received some mail. It was 1973 and I was hitch-hiking around Europe and North Africa like thousands of other American college students and hippies. I remember reaching into that pile with a muttered groan about the Greek postal system and the seemingly impossible task of retrieving my mail. When my hand came back out holding a small package addressed to me on the first attempt I was stunned and laughing.

It turned out to be a book called *The Secret of the Golden Flower*, an ancient Taoist book about meditation and the balancing of masculine and feminine energies. The book was a translation from Chinese by Richard Wilhelm, a friend of Carl Gustav Jung. It was Jung who had introduced the understanding into Western psychology of a masculine and feminine aspect in everyone's psyche and Wilhelm was exploring how the Chinese had been aware of this for thousands of years. I remember being truly fascinated by this book for some months, but then after a while, I more or less forgot about it until I journeyed to India in 1978.

I had gone to India to visit the ashram of an enlightened mystic, Osho. I didn't comprehend what my inner longing was guiding me towards, and had no real understanding about finding a spiritual Master. But I can see now, in retrospect, I was inexorably drawn to him without any clear concept of why, other than that I felt a pull and a resonance with him that was unlike anything I'd felt before while sampling various gurus, masters, teachers, schools and approaches through attending talks, meditation retreats, satsangs and reading books.

Osho used to give a discourse for an hour or two every morning. To my delight and surprise, the first series I attended was commentaries on *The Secret of the Golden Flower*. I remember feeling a moment of stunned wonder and mysterious synchronicity that first morning listening to him comment on this book.

Energetic Polarity

Over the years he often spoke about relationships and their difficulties, challenges and potential for self-discovery, the masculine and feminine principles, the energetic polarity between sexes and the role of the inner man and inner woman in our inner and outer world. Whenever he touched this subject I would notice a kind of 'extra' alertness as though there was something very important for me personally to understand.

Each individual comes as a single unit, unitary, and then is split. It is just like a ray passing through a prism is split into seven colours. Conception functions like a prism. The one Tao splits into two opposite polarities: man and woman. Remember that no man is man alone, the woman is behind, hidden in him; and so it is with the woman.

If the conscious mind is man, then the unconscious is woman. If the conscious mind is woman, then the unconscious is man. It has to be so. And the desire to meet with the woman or with the man on the outside is not going to fulfill you – unless you know how to meet the inner man and the inner woman.

And that is one of the secret messages of Tao: that you can find your inner woman or your inner man where your conscious and unconscious meet. And once that meeting has happened within you, you are whole. ~ Osho[1]

The Desire for the Other

Some years later, in 1986, Osho was staying in Juhu Beach near Mumbai and was giving discourses in response to questions asked by his disciples. This series of talks eventually became a book called Sermons in Stones. Many of the questions in that series had to do with relationships, the masculine and feminine, as well as 'inner man, inner woman' and I found them very interesting. One night he responded to a question from a woman named Surabhi, who asked: "Osho, The other is a longing within me, because without the other, I can never feel complete, reconciled. Beloved Master, who is the other?" His response impacted me strongly:

Surabhi, your desire for the other, your longing that without the other, you will never be complete, is absolutely true. This is the insight of every human being; that without the other you are not going to have a feeling of wholeness, of completion, of arriving home.

There are very few great discoveries in the world. Tantra can claim the greatest discovery. Tantra's discovery has been standing there for ten thousand years unused, an insight of such great value. The insight is that man and woman are not just one – man just man, woman just woman – no. They are both together: man is half man and half woman, and the same is true about women. And this is the great contribution of Tantra: that unless the man and the woman inside you become one whole, you will remain discontented.

You start looking on the outside, finding a woman or a man who can make a certain organic whole, a unity in your life, so that this constant gap, this something missing, this heavy incompleteness in your being will be removed.

But the basic understanding is right, that somehow man and woman have to merge their energies into one. Just one thing is missing: that miracle can happen only within you, it is not something outside. It is something that as you become silent and peaceful and joyous, as your intelligence becomes more sharp, you will see: the other that you have been searching for is within.[2]

Looking Deeper

After the discourse, I spoke with my girlfriend, Vivek, Osho's personal caretaker. I told her I was very touched by what Osho had said and it made many things clear for me. Later that night, as she was bringing him his evening tea, Vivek mentioned to Osho that I had loved the discourse. She came to me with the message that I should look deeper into the understanding and that it would help me in many ways ... and apparently, with a twinkle in his eye, Osho said it would also help me to not be so reactive to Vivek's ever-changing strong emotional states! Of course, I never forgot that moment and it was then that I got really serious about looking deeper into this subject.

I found myself returning again and again for personal inquiry and meditation on the balance, the polarity and the wholeness of masculine and feminine. I returned to *The Secret of the Golden Flower* discourses and started to practice a meditation Osho suggested for the balancing of the masculine and feminine energy each night before going to sleep. I also started to read more from Jung and Jungian-based approaches and became fascinated by the understanding of what was called Anima (the inner woman) and Animus (the inner man) and how to recognize them in daily life, in relationships and in meditation.

I began to see how these forces were at work in me and how they were affecting my relationships, my feelings, my moods and the expression of myself as a man. I started to be able to recognize a phenomenon called 'projection' – seeing how my fascination with my inner woman was being projected as an illusion on an outer woman – and learned how to consciously withdraw it. A big door of understanding opened for me, which I could test with my inner laboratory on a day-to-day basis. As a result, many issues that had been plaguing me in my relationships became clear and lost their grip on me.

Through a process of meditation, awareness, emotional clearing and deep inquiry, I was able to strengthen and heal my own masculinity which made it more easy for me to integrate my feminine side, and dramatically deepened my connections to, and understanding of, the women around me. It was a wonderful time of revelation, exploration and fun in my life and out of that I developed a real passion to share what I had learned with others.

Falling in Love with Oneself

Liz Greene, a well-known Jungian analyst, writer and astrologer has this to say about projection and falling in love in her book *Relating*:

Animus/anima can only be realized through a relation to a partner of the opposite sex, because only in such a relation do their projections become operative. Relationships which contain any element of falling in love inevitably contain animus/anima projections; and the curious feeling of familiarity one has about the loved one is only too explicable by the fact that one has, in actuality, fallen in love with oneself. This does not necessarily mean that such projections are harmful or negative. On the contrary, they are a necessary catalyst for relationship, just as relationship is a necessary catalyst for self-awareness – the quest for the inner partner is responsible for our embrace of life.

This understanding about projection was particularly challenging for me, as the heady experience of falling love, being in fascination and infatuation, was one of my favourite experiences. Trying to remember to ask myself the critical question: "Do I really know this person?" rather than plunge into romantic entanglement was challenging, because of the intoxicating 'high' of relating to my own projection while at the same time receiving the positive projection of a woman.

However, when I did remember to ask this question – and accept the inevitable answer that I didn't really know her – I noticed that I started to develop relationships that were less super-charged romantically and more based on a mutual seeing and knowing of each other.

Inner Man, Inner Woman Process

Around 1992, I created a group process called *Inner Man, Inner Woman* where I shared many of the lessons I'd learned. A few years later, I started to lead a forty-two-day process with twenty-one women and twenty-one men called the *Tantra Intensive*, which

330

was primarily based on the understandings of *Inner Man, Inner Woman* and its relation to the expression of our sexuality.

In this intensive, we were able to go deeply into inner exploration, seeing and understanding even more clearly the dynamics at play between our conscious identity and our inner 'other' and the way in which this was playing out in our relationships. I am still teaching this work although, as I have matured and experimented, my understanding has deepened and I now refer to the work as *The Essence of Masculine and Feminine* or *The Essential Man and Woman*.

Over the next pages, I will attempt to distil some of the essence of this approach to make it very practical and demonstrate its application through sharing a couple of sessions which deal with typical issues most of us encounter in our inner development and in our relationships.

I have always loved the Indian mythology that says God got bored with being an 'It' and so 'It' decided to divide 'Itself' into two opposites in order to have some fun or *Leela* (in Sanskrit, Leela means sport, pastime or play). So 'It' became God in feminine form and God in masculine form – two halves of one whole that are completely opposite.

In the state of spiritual enlightenment the two halves come together and form a unity that is beyond any duality or separation. However, for the unenlightened, our day-to-day life in which we live, experience, manifest and grow is in the realm of duality. In this realm, energy moves between two opposites and is symbolized by yin and yang, positive and negative, light and dark, feminine and masculine.

In terms of masculine and feminine, the stronger the polarity, the greater the attraction will be, which enhances the potential for relationship growth, conflict, sex and ultimately the spiritual dimension of sacred union.

Rapid Cultural Change

In the last fifty years, we have seen rapid and tremendously powerful cultural changes instigated and accelerated by the women's movement. Women have taken a much stronger position in a world which has been generally devaluing the feminine for many centuries. Although these changes have been good and will hopefully continue to evolve, they have also, in my opinion, created confusion about equality and sameness between the sexes, when in fact the real essences are complete opposites.

At present, we seem to have a situation where many women have become better men than the men. By this I mean they have, for a variety of reasons, developed their masculine sides very well and effectively but sadly, often at the cost of a deep connection to their own femininity. Many women seem to have become faster, smarter, quicker, better than most men, but in that process of developing their masculine side, they have lost contact with the depth of their own femininity.

Over the years, I have met many 'successful' women who really don't have a clue about what they need, feel or value as a woman. After deeper inquiry, these women often find their feminine side stopped developing at a certain age, as though she went into hiding. It is not uncommon when working with a woman with a highly developed masculine side to find that her feminine side, when experienced, is very young, shy, insecure, lacking in confidence and vulnerable to judgments about her feminine feelings and urges.

Men in Western cultures have also grown and evolved during this time and at this point there are many men who live and value the feminine as she exists in themselves and in the world. Men have become more in touch with their feelings, are more sensitive in relationships and in touch with their own softness and intuition, but in this process have lost their sense of direction, clarity, strength and purpose as men.

My investigation has led me to believe that an authentic, embodied presence and vision of the masculine has been missing in this world for a long time. This results in a situation where many men are 'castrated' (the equivalent of feminine devaluation), without a sense of inner support or relaxed confidence as men.

We find men covering this sense of deficiency by behaving very macho, driven by iron-willed determination and performance, or collapsed and withdrawn from the world with an air of moody petulance. In both cases, there is a lack of relaxed confidence as a man and they are usually easily dominated by women with developed masculine sides.

Lack of Authentic Polarity

In the West, large segments of the population are stuck in this lack of authentic polarity and this in turn plays a significant part in the difficulty many people experience to enjoy deep, long-lasting and evolving relationships with the opposite sex.

This distortion has in some ways become politically, socially and even spiritually correct over the last forty years. The outcome is a neutering of the differences intrinsic to natural polarity. This situation may make for great friendships, but in its lack of polarity it also tends to make for bad sex, bad relationships, physical illness, restlessness and unhappiness.

In the Western world, these cultural identity shifts are corrections of imbalances that have been prevalent for a long time and can be seen as part of a process of evolution which is generally positive. However, I believe a next step is needed – and in fact is already happening. A deep synthesis will emerge where men and women live their potential in a relaxed and confident way, grounded in their sexual identity and engaged in fulfilling relationships as a consequence of having integrated their inner man or inner woman.

In order for this to happen, we need to look more specifically at how the distortions manifest and how they can be healed. What I have found in the years of exploring this work is that most of the psychological, energetic and even spiritual problems that arise for men and women have to do with a lack of relaxed confidence in themselves and in their sexual identity.

By relaxed confidence I mean an inner sense of grounded support and acceptance of themselves as the man or woman they are. In order to make a positive integration of the inner polarity (anima or animus), it is important to first resolve issues of being a man or woman and find a way to live that is accepting, relaxed and confident in that sexual and energetic identity.

Once the depth, beauty, receptivity, intuition and flow of the feminine is recognized as intrinsic to being woman and the radiant, clear, solid strength of the masculine is realized and grounded in the man, the integration of the 'inner other' and relationships to outer partners can happen with much greater ease and respect.

To uncover these qualities and integrate them involves deep work on oneself. There are general issues shared by others of the same sex and, of course, there are individual issues and permutations that have to do with the personal history of each person. I will address the general ones and indicate ways to inquire into the more subjective personal ones. To do this, we need to look at how this distortion develops.

Animus Possession

Women who grow up in environments that do not honour, value or celebrate the feminine tend to over-emphasize the masculine part of their psyche. This is an intelligent strategy to survive, to get approval, recognition, respect and safety in a world which has over-valued these masculine qualities. The situation is worsened when someone in the original family was violent or abusive towards the feminine and caused the female to develop her own masculine side to defend herself from the lack of love, violence and abuse.

Through the necessity of protecting themselves and a natural desire for recognition, these women have lost touch with their feminine values, needs and feelings and in this process have abandoned their feminine side, pushing her into the unconscious mind where she waits unappreciated, isolated or forgotten. The operating identity, out of survival and habit, has shifted to the masculine side and functions in ways which are not natural to a woman or to feminine consciousness. This state was named by C. G. Jung as Animus Possession.

A woman who is Animus possessed is usually characterized as being opinionated, judgmental and critical, with a capacity to look at situations and see precisely what is wrong and how everything 'should' be. The word 'should' is central to the view of an animus possessed woman. As Liz Greene puts it:

Often the animus dominated woman holds the conviction that all men are out to dominate her and feels she must prove her superiority to men and never suspects that in reality she is held in domination by the unconscious man inside herself.

One of the most painful aspects of animus possession is that the critical, judgmental side of the inner man is not only turned outwards towards the world, but also inwardly towards the feminine side of the woman herself, thereby causing her to become mistrustful towards her own feminine intuition, impulses, feelings and needs. Impulses of the feminine are judged as signs of weakness and inferiority.

The classic archetypal image of the chivalrous knight protecting the helpless woman in the tower can be seen as an appropriate symbol for this state. Often, at an early age, the masculine side started to dominate and protect the feminine which was not made safe, relaxed and confident about her femininity. It is easy to imagine the masculine as the knight riding around the tower challenging and testing any male that wants access to the feminine. What begins as necessary protection becomes obsessive fighting or testing of all males who approach the woman, becoming so extreme that no man or very few men pass the test and get past the animus, leaving the feminine over-protected and cut off, without the possibility to receive nourishment or love.

Anima Possession

We will look at some examples of how a woman can heal this situation, but first I feel it is appropriate to look at the situation of men and a common state called Anima Possession.

Most men in the Western world have not grown up with guidance, support and understanding for their masculinity. They have not developed a relaxed confidence and ease in their maleness and as a result are endlessly trying to compensate for that loss through pushing themselves, performing, being macho, over-intellectual and over-achieving.

Behind the macho mask, this type of man lives with a chronic feeling of tension, performance-anxiety and disconnection from his own masculine feelings, needs, values and vision. The basic underlying attitude is "I don't have what it takes to do the job", so he tries to compensate through effort and false will. Symbolically, sometimes literally, he has an inner self-image of possessing a small penis. I call such characters 'dickheads'. It is as though, with a feeling of deficiency 'downstairs', the man tries to create a bigger penis 'upstairs' and penetrate the world with his head. This type of man usually has a bad relationship with the feminine, both in himself and in the external world.

Another common manifestation is being stuck as a pleasing little boy, a man who is attuned to the shifts of feeling and energy from any woman. He tries to defend against this fearful state by trying to please the woman, adopting damage-control strategies out of fear. Unable to clearly express his feelings as a man, he will tend to withdraw into moody melancholy or irritable bitchy-ness, blaming others for his weakness and hesitating to make decisions. This is the state that Jung refers to as Anima Possession.

This is called the 'castration wound' as the lack of inner solidity and confidence carries the feeling of having been castrated. I use the words 'loss of relaxed confidence' to indicate castration of healthy masculinity. This is the male counterpart of the devaluation many women have suffered. Liz Greene explains:

Anima possessed man – unconscious of his unpleasant moodiness, compulsiveness, personal vanity and touchiness – will walk around spreading a cloud of poisonous atmosphere; he displays a peculiar pettiness, an indirectness, a weakness in the face of conflict, and a manipulativness that is very slippery and immediately inspires mistrust in women. He often leaves the impression that he is on stage performing a part, rather than relating to individuals.

Healing the Wounds

The goal of the work I do is to help people get a personal assessment of their own state of relaxed confidence, as a woman or a man, to inquire into the history that created this state, to connect with feelings about being castrated or devalued, to begin to find grounding and embodiment of themselves in their own biological sexual identity, to learn to recognize their own 'inner other' and start to integrate the values, feelings and needs of the 'inner other' in a positive and responsible way. When appropriate actions are taken that support these changes, the outcome is almost certainly a happier life, better relationships, better health and deep inner relaxation.

One simple way I have discovered to help people get in touch with the masculine and feminine is by offering guided meditations, using the right side of the body for the masculine and the left side for the feminine. Most people are able to sense their own bodies, so this goes easily and directly to the point.

It is interesting that human beings are, in a sense, cross-wired. The left side of the body is directly connected to the right hemisphere of the brain, which is known to be the side that corresponds to functions we normally call feminine. The right side of the body is connected through the nervous system to the left hemisphere of the brain which generally corresponds to functions called masculine. It is an over-simplification to assign the masculine and feminine to these hemispheres, but for the purpose of this work, using the right and left sides of the body as doorways directly into the masculine or feminine is very effective.

These doorways can be used in group workshops and individual sessions to explore the two sides.

Meditation: Exploring of the Feminine

This meditation is best done in a standing position and can be done with men or women. After doing it two or three times standing, it can be adapted and becomes easy to do in a sitting posture.

Stand in a relaxed posture. Feel your feet on the ground and notice the sense of support you get from your feet and legs. Shift your weight slightly so you are standing a bit more on the left foot, feeling more of your weight through your left foot. As you do this simple exercise, notice what you feel inside. Your left side is like a doorway to your feminine side and you may notice that your way of sensing and feeling yourself has also subtly changed. For example, you may feel more stable, or less grounded, more insecure, or more comfortable ...

Slowly, let your awareness move up your left leg so that the entire left leg is sensed and felt. You may notice that your sense of the feminine is getting deeper as you feel the left leg.

Now bring your awareness to the pelvic area. Sense the left side of the pelvic area including your left buttock.

If the session is with a woman, or if it is a mixed group, I will ask the women to feel their uterus, their womb and to notice how it feels. Is it relaxed and open, or does it have tension, fear?

Let your awareness continue up the body, focusing on the left side of the chest and especially around the heart, which is set just to the left of the mid-line of the body. Take your time to feel this area and breath gently into it, allowing any feelings, sensations or emotions to be felt and if needed, expressed. The heart is deeply connected with our feminine side. Often, if the feminine has been ignored or devalued, hidden or over-protected, you will feel pain in the heart area and some tears may start to flow.

After a while, let your attention rise to the left shoulder, left arm and out to the fingertips. See what happens if you allow your left hand and arm start to move in gentle flowing motions. The essence of the feminine has much to do with effortless flowing energy which is easily expressed and felt by making such movements.

338

As you make these gentle flowing movements, you may also allow your neck to soften, and your head and hips to move in a way that has a feeling of feminine expression.

At this point I may play some feminine sounding music and have the person or group dance or move to the music for one or two songs, just to help this process of embodiment and sensing.

After some time, let the movements slow down and gently feel your inner space. Notice your perception of the world from the feminine perspective.

The meditation ends by having the person, or people, lie down on their backs in a receptive pose, with the hands and legs open, and to simply rest.

At the end of this guided meditation, it is helpful to share your experience with another person who has also done it, or to write about the meditation and make lists of things you felt and noticed.

Meditation: Exploring the Masculine

In some ways, this meditation repeats the process of exploring the feminine, but it has a different flavour.

Stand in a relaxed and easy manner with your eyes closed, sensing your inner world. Feel your feet on the ground and notice that in this way you can easily experience the feeling of being supported by the floor. Notice any relaxation this brings.

Shift your weight slightly, so there is more weight on your right foot. Take time to feel the contact of your right foot with the floor. See if you notice any inner shift of feeling or perception by doing this simple action.

When we focus on the right side of our body, it is as though we open a doorway into the essence of our masculine side, making it easy to feel, sense and know this aspect of our psyche.

Allow yourself to sense, from the floor up, your entire right leg, particularly the right thigh. Feeling the strength in it. Often, there is a feeling that this leg wants to take you forward into life with a sense of purpose and direction.

Allow the sensing to move up your body into the pelvic area. Notice what you feel here. Breathe deeply, down into your lower belly, and notice how this creates more sensitivity in the pelvic area.

Bring your awareness up your right side to just below the rib cage. Breathe into this area. Your liver is located here and although we don't often feel this organ directly, it is on the right side and connected to our masculine essence. The liver is also connected to a sense of strength, vitality and related to the expression of anger. When we suppress our anger it affects our liver in a negative way, making it sluggish and toxic.

What do you notice when you focus here? You may sense aggression, anger or frustration. If so, you may want to stamp your right foot and let out sounds.

This often brings a strong sense of vitality, passion and excitement into the room.

Now bring your awareness up through the right side of your chest, breathing deeply and allowing the chest to expand. Let the energy spread up through your right shoulder and down into your right arm. Let your right hand become a fist and breathe strongly.

Sensing the whole of the right side of your body, let it move as it wishes. The masculine side has a deep longing for freedom. The masculine does not like to be held back.

At this point in the process, I often play strong music – African drums or techno and encourage powerful dancing as an expression of freedom. This can get pretty wild.

Masculine energy is often frustrated from years of holding back and loss of confidence. In its essence, it is neither frustrated nor angry, but has become this way from our social upbringing and conditioning. So, part of the journey into the masculine is to express and release pent-up aggression, frustration or anger.

I often suggest to people that while the feminine contains qualities of prayer, surrender and love, the masculine contains qualities of direction, purpose, clarity and meditation.

At the end of this meditation, I invite people to sit in silence for a while, feeling their back as straight and their inner presence as solid, grounded and dignified.

As with the feminine experience, it is good to end the journey into the masculine by sharing with another participant who has done, or take time to write about any insights, images or feelings that came up.

Session with a Woman on Feminine Issues

There are many ways to work in individual sessions with the masculine and feminine aspects, depending on the issues being explored and the level of inner development of the client. The following is a simple session that allows the masculine and feminine sides to dialogue with each other.

I prefer to do this kind of session sitting on the floor with the use of cushions, but it can be done with chairs. The client has three cushions: one represents a neutral or observer position; one represents the feminine side and one the masculine side.

When the client sits in the neutral position, the cushion on the left represents the feminine, the cushion on the right represents the masculine.

As an example, I will use a session with Isabella, a successful Italian lawyer. In reality, I guided Isabella through three individual sessions, but I am going to condense them into one.

I invite Isabella to sit on the feminine cushion first and, when she is settled, inquire what she notices – how she feels in her body, thoughts and emotions.

Isabella: I feel very small and quite uncomfortable in myself. I feel like I need something but I'm ashamed to even think about it, let alone to say it out loud.

Rafia: Okay, take your time ... keep sensing your body and allow any feelings.

Isabella: I don't feel safe here. I can here many voices in my mind telling me to not do this.

Rafia: Do you have any idea, or sense, of what might make you feel safe and more relaxed?

341

Isabella points immediately to the masculine cushion.

Rafia: Good, it seems you need to spend time on that cushion.

Isabella literally jumps across the space and lands with a sigh of relief on the masculine cushion. She smiles.

Isabella: Now I feel at home. Here is where I want to be. This is safe, familiar and comfortable. This is where I 'live'! (she grins).

I notice she is sitting very straight, relaxed but with a kind of challenging air about her.

Rafia: It seems like you are quite a strong guy. Is that right? Seems like you know what you want, where you're going, that you feel very clear ... right?

Isabella begins to describe her life in detail ... how she never loses a case in court, how she always knows the right thing to do, how much she enjoys winning a case and her skill at instantly seeing flaws in the arguments of other lawyers.

Rafia: How does this guy feel towards the feminine side, sitting on the other cushion, who is feeling insecure and small?

Isabella: Well, she's not good for much and never was. She was always weak and needy. Honestly, there is no space for her in my life. The last thing I need is a crying, miserable woman.

Rafia: I wonder how would it be if we give her time to speak? Would you be willing to listen to her without interfering?

Isabella's male side agrees and even indicates he is interested to know what she has to say. Isabella moves to the feminine cushion and this time is more animated. She sits in a kind of collapsed way but starts to find her voice, expressing her feelings, her needs and what she wants.

Isabella (as the feminine): I am so tired of being judged by him, pretending to be dependent on him. I feel like I have been held in captivity by him and I'm sick of it. I want to have a life. After all, I am the woman here. Being dominated by this guy has got to stop. I need more space and I am sick of his constant judgments!

At this point her voice wavers and she starts to cry, holding one hand on her heart and the other over her womb. The crying, which has started as more of a whine, goes quickly to very deep

*heart-wrenching sobs until at one point she is howling in pain.
She tells me she has painful fibroid cysts in her uterus, that her
relationship with her husband is a disaster, that she hates spending
all her time in courtrooms.*

*She begins to shout at her male side, telling him she needs his
support, not his dominance, endless judgments and criticisms.
When all this emotion has been expressed, she starts to glow
with a healthy radiant look and even cracks up laughing at the
absurdity of it all.*

*At this point I invite her to switch cushions again to see what
the masculine side has to say. As soon as she sits on the masculine
side, it is obvious that something essential has been heard and
understood.*

*Isabella (as the masculine): I really liked it (her strong
emotions). In this moment, I feel attracted to her. I wish she would
be more like this all the time. I want to know more and find a way
to support her.*

*The session went for a few more rounds on each cushion,
developing into an insightful conversation that uncovers old
wounds, memories and starts to be mutually respectful, even a bit
flirtatious. Like a couple that has been stuck in a habitual way of
relating, they are finally having the dust cleared from their eyes
and seeing each other in a new light.*

*Isabella sits on the neutral cushion and comes up with a novel
idea.*

*Isabella: I know what I'm going to do. I don't want to give
up the job of lawyer – I love that – but I seriously need to make
more space for my feminine side. I'm going to buy two watches.
One of them is going to be a power watch, big, dark and chunky.
The other one is going to be very feminine, refined, delicate and
beautiful. I'm going to put two hooks next to the front door of my
house and when I go out to work in the morning I am going to put
on my kick-ass watch and do just that. When I come home, the
first thing I'm going to do is take it off and put on the feminine
watch. Then I'm going to change my clothes into something which*

makes me feel feminine and beautiful – maybe even outrageously so. I'm going to look at how the house is decorated and I'm going to create at least one room with a feminine feeling in terms of the furniture, colours and lighting.

After six months, I was delighted to hear that her relationship with her husband had improved tremendously, that her fibroids had almost disappeared, that she was working much less but enjoying it even more and that she loved feeling feminine and spending time with other women. She still has those two watches.

Session with a Man on Masculine Issues

The following is also a compilation of several sessions but has been distilled to illustrate the essence of the work.

Lars, a Swedish man, came to me broken-hearted from a recent split in a relationship. He also had difficulty finding work that was satisfying and felt depressed about getting his life on any meaningful track. We reviewed his family history and it soon became clear that he had been dominated by his mother and lacked support and meaningful contact with his father.

He was a classic example of an anima possessed man and agreed that the direction for our work would be to strengthen his sense of presence, grounding and direction as a man. He understood that, to achieve this, he needed to get in touch with his deeper feelings and to risk showing these feelings to women, thereby overcoming his fear of women's anger and possible rejection for being honest and direct.

Lars tended to come to a session in a melancholy and withdrawn mood. Between sessions, he spent a lot of time in an isolated inner space, without having the experience of meaningful contact with anyone. He was bitchy and liked to complain, giving expression to hopeless negativity, while at the same time romanticizing his own specialness and deep artistic potential.

We used the structure with three cushions a number of times, but the most powerful work happened when we worked with his masculine side.

Lars: I had a date last weekend and it was going great until I wanted to ask her to come home with me. The moment I started thinking that way, I became completely tense, awkward and felt a strong knot of tension in my solar plexus. I noticed that as soon as this happened she became tired and distracted and there was a palpable resistance coming from her towards me. I lost my ground, my presence, my happiness completely and the whole evening, which had been fun and relaxed went down the drain in a matter of a few moments. This is what always seems to happen. I have been so depressed these last days I just sat at home in front of my computer, wasting time. Feels like the story of my life.

Rafia: As you talk about this, Lars, can you feel the place of tension in your solar plexus, which you talked about last time? Is it still there? Does it become more active when we talk about this incident?

Lars: Yes it's there. When it's there, I feel immobilized in terms of taking any kind of positive action. I can push myself and fake it, but I'm tired of doing that. It seems better to avoid the whole thing and space out.

Rafia: Okay, but now I'm asking you not to space out. Take time to feel into that place and see what happens.

Lars (reluctantly): Okay, but I don't know what good it will do. This is the feeling I'm always trying to get away from. It is destroying my life. This fear that I'm not good enough, smart enough, sexy enough ... If I feel it directly, it becomes even more tense and I feel like the whole lower part of my body is disappearing. At the same time, I notice I'm clenching my jaw, tightening my neck and telling myself I must and will push myself out of this pathetic space.

Rafia: Lars, Can you sense the presence of either of your parents?

Lars: Yes. I feel my mother's coldness and my father's aloofness ... his total lack of being there, or caring about me, or anything other than sitting in his chair and being invisible. I feel furious with them both. But what's the point? I have done that so many times – it doesn't get me anywhere.

Rafia: Stay present in your anxiety without reacting to it, or trying to make it different in any way.

Lars: Okay.

Over the next fifteen to twenty minutes, Lars continued to explore this tension which we decided could be called 'performance anxiety' – a feeling of inadequacy about himself as a man when he is faced with a strong and challenging situation. At one point he started to address his father.

Lars: All I really wanted was for you to show some interest in me, to be there for me in some way. I felt I wasn't good enough to get your attention, then it became a kind of general feeling of not being good enough. Now, when I want to assert myself, whether it's with a woman, or at work, or with other men, I always hesitate, doubt myself and hold back. (He suddenly screamed loudly) This holding back is destroying me!

At this point Lars started to become very emotional, alternating between expressions of frustration and deep sobbing. He stood up and stamped his feet.

Lars (shouting): I can't go on like this. Where were you, dad? Why didn't you support me? Why were you so weak? Why were you so afraid of mom's anger? I need you dad!

I invited him to keep feeling that place where he needed his father. I asked him to feel it as something active in him, in this moment, even though his father was no longer alive and obviously could not do anything. It was the asking that was important; to feel that boyish place inside that always wanted his father's support, love, attention and bonding.

As Lars continued to express himself this way and express his need, his chest started to expand, his eyes began to shine and his body could feel more life and passion.

We continued over a few more sessions to explore Lars' performance anxiety and to allow old feelings of pain about the lack of support from his father. The key was to feel the pain rather than stay locked in the anger, resentment and frustration.

As he metabolized these old feelings it was wonderful to see that his fear of expression with women started to transform. He started to develop an aura of self-love, willing to take the risk of a woman's possible rejection and anger by expressing his feelings, needs, values and vision as a man.

In short, he became attractive and confident, changing his work and his life in many ways that in the past had only been a dream. He became a picture of relaxed confidence as a man. He started to manifest a kind of presence that was loving and respectful towards the feminine.

He realized that when he becomes moody or withdrawn he has to ask himself:

Where did I fail to express myself in the way I wanted to? How did I hold back or let fear dominate me?

He now knows when and where he collapsed and is committed to risk saying the truth and come out of his deadly habit of withdrawal. He wrote to me one day:

Emotional withdrawal is no longer an option.

This series of sessions is classic in the sense of how a man can heal and become rooted in his masculinity. The feeling of 'I can't make it' is a clear indication of being controlled by the castration wound and this makes the man hold back. But holding back is anathema to the masculine presence and creates a downward spiral into depression, moodiness and addictions. When a man works through issues separating him from his masculine presence, his relations with outer women and with his own inner feminine become flowing and respectful.

Destiny Set in Motion

At this point in my life, looking back, I can see my destiny was set in motion when I put my right arm into that pile of letters in Athens, so many years ago, and pulled out *The Secret of the Golden Flower*. Reading that book awoke my impulse to go East and there I found Osho, whose vision embraces both meditation and exploration of love relationships. For me, the key to understanding love relationships can be summed up in the image of my very own 'golden flower' – the discovery of inner male/female polarities.

CHAPTER SEVENTEEN

Male/Female Energywork

Sagarpriya

Recap of Central Themes

Probably you have read the following ideas in this book already, but I repeat them here in a very concise form:

● The quality of presence is the same thing as what an Osho Therapist refers to as 'meditation' or 'meditation space'.

● The absence of presence is the same thing as what an Osho Therapist refers to as 'mind' – desiring, dreaming about a future that is not yet the reality.

● When you make an action which comes from the state of presence, it is a spontaneous, natural response to the situation you are in. It is refreshing and increases the feeling of love in your body.

● When you make an action from desire, it is the opposite of spontaneous. It is calculated to reach a certain goal. It is effortful. It is exhausting.

● You have spent many years in school and later in life learning how to make actions from effort. You plan them by considering various strategies and then deciding which one will be most efficient and effective for reaching the future that the mind is imagining.

● An action from presence cannot be planned. There is no 'how'. It simply happens by itself when you relax. It is a response to the moment which comes as a surprise – often a beautiful and uplifting surprise.

The Art of Waiting

Osho Therapy takes many different forms on the surface, but each therapist is simply waiting to see in their client this 'action from no mind' or 'action from presence'. LaoTzu called it 'Wei Wu Wei' – action from inaction. It has a certain flavor, or taste, or smell. If the therapist has presence in himself, he immediately recognizes when it happens in the client and, in that instant, waiting is over. Of course, the client usually goes out of presence quickly, so the therapist starts patiently waiting again.

When I say that the therapist waits, I don't mean that he or she is doing nothing. The therapist, first of all, stays connected to his own meditative state – otherwise how will he know when the client arrives there? The meditative state is one's natural home. It is impersonal in the sense that it is the same in everybody. No matter what kind of personality you have, you always have the same 'centre' as everybody else. So the therapist makes sure that he (or she) is resting in himself (or herself).

Secondly, the therapist understands that if he can stay rooted in his presence throughout the session, he acts as a catalyst for bringing the other person out of dreams and into presence. So, while it appears on the surface that the therapist is listening to the client, attending to the client, caring for the client, the truth is that he is listening to himself, taking care that his own actions and choices arise from a meditative space, not from desire, because the most supportive thing he can do for someone else is to be present with himself.

When I say that the therapist waits, I don't mean that he is unhappy while he waits and happy when the waiting is over. While he waits, he is creative – that is, letting spontaneous responses roll out one after another, creating a kind of carpet or pathway that surprises even himself. He is happy doing this, and his happiness does not depend on an energetic meeting with the client.

When the client, however, arrives to his center or even stays in his center for some time, the therapist immediately feels the connection. Now the two are connected but the therapist is not more nor less happy than before, just the outer situation has changed from 'aloneness' to 'togetherness'.

Togetherness is a pleasure, but aloneness also has its beauty. The therapist simply sees which of these two is happening and maintains the same vibrant presence in both situations. This means he is not at all dependent on the results of his therapy for his job satisfaction. If he can help someone, good; if not, also good, and it is easy for him to acknowledge that "I can't help you."

Usually, the latter happens when the client doesn't understand the kind of help being offered, which is not about any external condition being fulfilled (for example, the hope that a depression goes away) but rather about the client contacting an internal state of love that he *already has*, a state in which he is already satisfied and is already capable of making a creative response to life.

Working with Energy

My own learning about Osho Therapy evolved in a particular way. I was already a therapist when I first came to Osho. After being a participant in the six groups he recommended to me, I received his instruction to lead a five-day group called 'Urja,' which in Hindi means 'energy'.

It took quite a few Urja groups before it became clear what I was supposed to do there. Just to *be*. Just to watch when something was happening and when it was not. Happenings came like waves, starting small, then increasing to a certain intensity of form, then losing force and fading away finally. In the gap between events there was silence.

I cherished that empty, silent place very much, so I didn't give any direction for what to do in the group – having already exhausted all attempts at managing things in the previous period. I offered no distractions, not even music. At first people slept, then they complained or got angry, and then they started using the same energy creatively. It was so interesting for me to experience in each group that out of doing nothing, such a flowering of joyous creativity would eventually burst forth.

A couple of years after the inception of the Urja group, Osho designed two therapy streams, each containing three groups, to better accommodate the increasing number of people coming to our community in search of themselves. One stream was called 'Awareness and Expression' and the other was called 'Energywork'. My groups were included in the Energywork stream, and at that time Turiya and Rafia were part of the Expression camp.

It wasn't long before I understood something important: one type of person could use the approach I knew, which started out with presence and arrived to action, while another type of person moved naturally in the other direction, from action to presence. This second type of person needed to do breathing, bioenergetics, encounter – all kinds of active things which took one beyond limits – and the experience of being total in action could lead this type to the same silence that I saw between two events.

I say that this discovery was important because it was my first glimpse of male and female. By then, I knew it was the female in me that led groups and my method was feminine, introverted, starting with the inactive presence that you meet in Vipassana meditation. And it dawned on me that other group leaders might primarily use their male aspect in their work: they were more extroverted as a type, and thus more authentic and comfortable in the mode of action and doing.

Male/Female Polarities

Naturally, I did not lead the Urja group forever, but perhaps for the next ten years I remained involved in similar themes: relaxation and energy. Then, there came a change. It happened because my male side woke up. And once I understood that everybody has two sides with completely different gifts and interests, I had to make a structure for my work that included both.

You're going to read a sample of this work very soon. However, before presenting it, I want to mention several points that might give you a better orientation, or reduce the surprise you might feel about what I'm doing.

352

In a session with a client, I know that the person's right leg carries the qualities of the inner male; the left leg is the source for the inner female. If I hold each foot in my hands, sometimes I can define these qualities, if they are developed enough. By the end of checking the feet, it is possible that I have given definition to two characters or personages, one male and one female, but normally this definition is not expressed out loud to the client right away.

I can also feel through the legs how present each character is. The presence is the key. Someone who is present doesn't have to work hard in life. They relax and flow, and the directions and decisions which arise are good for themselves and for others. Sometimes there is no presence in either leg. This does not hinder my work because I also check the chakras and the aura, looking for where I can meet presence. The amount that I find guides the session. The more presence, the more potential for change in a good direction.

Each figure, whether it is the inner male or inner female, is asked to keep all of his/her energy and use it for activities which satisfy himself/herself. They cannot 'share'. One side cannot absorb the other's energy for its own purposes. So there has to be a kind of separation of these two figures in the sense that each one has his or her own home base and they keep all their energy with them on that home base.

Most inner couples (male and female) are not yet functioning properly because one character is dominant and the other is submissive. Sometimes the submission of the weaker character is voluntary: they think they are 'helping' the other part by energetically supporting the other's goals and ambitions.

Sometimes the dominant one, the stronger part, thinks they are 'helping' the weaker one by taking all the responsibility for job, for money, for survival, for decisions regarding the family and so forth. In a healthy relationship, the concept of helping disappears. Each figure is simply present, surrounded by their full energy, and allowing spontaneous response to flow. Then the things they do will be loving, and the whole system starts overflowing with love.

353

Now the case sample, written in the present tense so that you feel you are also there as it unfolds …

Sureela

Sureela is a participant in an Osho Therapist Training which has already been going on for more than a year. She has an unusual background for this training: she is a psychiatrist. Normally, people are coming to this program to learn how to be therapists, but she is here to change her way of being a therapist. When she states the reason why she is taking this demonstration session with me, she says, "I need some guidance, because I don't really enjoy my work fully. I want to take some next steps, or at least one, and I don't know where or how. I feel limited by my role right now."

So I ask her about the job and find out that she is presently working in a clinic that is connected to a hospital. Her patients do not stay overnight, so she has daytime activity in a psychiatric ward.

I already know that she was married before, has children, and is now divorced. I ask her if she has any boyfriend, and she shyly answers that she has a new one, and that she feels "a lot of innocence, joy and peace in this relationship – it's really good for me." I learn that the boyfriend is an architect by profession, but works as a scenographer, making stage sets for a group of entertainers.

Questions finished, I ask her to lie down on a mattress for what I call the 'Energy Check'. I hold the feet, one by one, with my palm under the sole, then place my hand slowly above each of the seven chakras, which are located between the base of the torso and the top of the head.

In the left foot, representing her feminine side, I find the energy diffuse, nebulous, unformed, and the person is not very happy. I don't feel connected to her presence. From my experience, I would guess that this person is not the dominant one in the inner male/ female relationship, nor the one who chose the job situation, but probably she is the one who is asking me for help.

In the right foot, the figure has a very definite form. Here, I see the psychiatrist. He is sitting at a desk, although there is no client in this moment, and directing many people around him. It's a busy place. Everybody except him is in action, and some people (all women) are putting away or pulling out files from the cupboards which line the walls. Everybody is attentive to his instructions. I get the feeling that he likes to have order around him. In spite of all these clear details, there is one big problem: no presence. This figure is absolutely flat and boring; when I seek to find a connection with him through meditation, there isn't one.

Checking the rest of the chakras, I find no presence emanating from them, although the heart and head give me the feeling that some will be coming in the near future. The big surprise is that when I connect with the aura, there is substantial presence, impressively so. To me, this indicates that somebody with a lot of this magical substance is out of the body, and it has to be the female, because the male is very much in the body. Probably only he is occupying the body. No wonder she is nebulous and unformed. Anyway, because of this presence in the aura she will be considered the most loving of the two.

I explain to Sureela that we are going to use the next part of the session to meet these two characters, which means that I will be talking to them, in turn. Then we put them on their own chairs and see who they are. For a while, we will only be observing the situation without any idea of changing it.

Interviews

First I interview the inner female (always the more loving one first). I ask Sureela to cover her right eye with a blindfold, so that the left eye looks at me as 'she' answers questions about job, about qualities which represent her, about her priorities in life. She has a hard time answering the question "Do you work?" because she feels that with her clients she 'enjoys' more than 'works'.

She says, "It just happens. I don't do anything. I have my own small office in another part of town where I see clients and there

I can be a little bit more free. I can just be with the people, for example, when they are facing their anxiety; I'm just there with them." And in this way I learn that Sureela also has a private practice, which wasn't mentioned before, with two or three clients per week.

The female is the one who wants a new work, because she is feeling repressed. When I ask her for two more qualities that represent her besides 'repressed', she says 'intuitive' and 'gentle'. Her priorities in life are:

(1) To be in the daily life in a sparkly way.

(2) Sharing.

(3) Beauty.

Then the blindfold is readjusted so that it covers the left eye. The inner man sees me out of the right eye while 'he' answers my questions. He tells me that he works, but he's very tired of it. He's expected to do a lot of things he doesn't really believe in.

I wonder how he can stay in such a place and he answers, "Because there are possibilities for me to do other things that I do believe in. I've got part of what I like, which is to work together with other people, and I've got the money! (this said with a big burst of energy) I earn the money".

When I ask for three qualities which represent him, he says, "I'm flexible. I'm good at making things happen. I'm quite goal oriented and I always reach the goal." His priorities in life are:

That my children will have good support.

That there are people around me and I have an okay place to live.

To be needed somewhere, to be part in a system somewhere, which is good for the development of humanity.

I immediately give him a feedback about the first two priorities. They both have to do with comfort, living a comfortable life. The first, of course, is for his children, that they should have a comfortable life, and the second is for himself to have a comfortable life, with people around and a nice place to live. I ask him if it's true, that comfort is a top priority for him. He answers, "Yes, I find I can agree to that", and appears to be proud of his ability to create comfort.

And then his last priority is a dependency, needing to be needed by somebody. I ask him if it's true, that he wants to be dependent on somebody needing him. He answers, "I want to be part of a team in some way. I was a soccer player earlier. One of the reasons I chose psychiatry as a specialization was that it was team-working, more than other specializations. So I like team work".

The interview is finished. Sureela closes the right eye and removes the blindfold.

Mutual Descriptions

After some moments of repose, I ask Sureela to sit in the chair that I designate as the one for her female side. This chair is going to represent, for the female, the home base that I spoke about before. Sureela has her eyes closed while I describe the female figure according to what I saw in the leg and according to what she told me. Sureela is supposed to become this female and then describe her according to the present inner experience.

My description, in brief, is that she's innocent, that there are new sprouts of life coming into her, as if it used to be winter and now it's spring – for example, in the heart and in the upper body. But in the depths, she's not happy, even now. She has some beautiful qualities like gentleness and sensitivity, but she's not such a defined person. Perhaps I mean not crystallized – not used to presenting her things and being valued for her contribution. She has a lot of presence in the aura and in her work something happens wordlessly because of this, but she's been unable to give the thing that happens a recognizable shape and form.

Sureela, in her turn, describes the female as "very awake, and always standing a step behind. She is a bit shy, but she has a strength in some way. While she has trust in being where she is, she always wants to take a step forward".

I invite Sureela to move physically to a vacant chair that is directly in front of her, explaining that while the female remains

357

sitting in her chair, the body now moves to a position opposite her and sits in the male's chair. Sureela is to become a man and, looking back at the woman, describe her according to a man's point of view.

His description is quite positive, for example he says that she is fragile but at the same time not breakable. She has soft color, she's sensual, she's beautiful, sensitive, careful. His only complaint is that she is too low profile and lacks courage. Mostly he talks about how she's so comfortable to be with. Apparently she is taking good care of his second priority!

Sureela changes back to the female chair, and looking at the man from a female's point of view, she describes him as "safe; a kind of fatherly caretaker, boring but safe". I think the whole truth isn't coming out yet, so I ask her to tell me one more thing about him. She's reluctant, so I say, "This is my last chance to hear how you see him, so try to be as detailed as possible" And finally she admits, "He succeeds in making a very good comfort zone. However, I can see that at the same time as he protects me, he represses me. Also, he can be boring, because everything is so known".

Adjustments

Now I feel the impulse to get something moving in a new direction. I say to the female, "The way to step out of this repression – if you're courageous enough – is to go out of his comfortable atmosphere and choose your own place to live. We can do it right now! If you are willing, you can take your chair to a place in this room that represents your new location, which is outside the comfortable atmosphere that he is providing for you. And there, it will not be known what's going to happen next, but it's alive! Do you want to try it? "

She moves her chair to various locations, five or six, before finally selecting one.

I ask her (the inner female) to focus now on the idea that she doesn't need the man for what she's going to do next. She has her own house now and she will use her good intuition to decide which action to take – when she gives something to existence, someone will pay her for that. *And I don't believe that it will be in the hospital where the man is working now. Does she think so?*

"No", she answers, "I think it is going to be in the place where I have my room for private patients, a very different sort of clinic. There I have been negotiating already for a job and the first steps were amazingly good. As the discussions continue, I will try to speak more than he (her inner male)".

I'm amazed that she's already done this and nobody told me – almost like it was a secret. I say to her, "Only you! Do all the negotiations yourself! There is no reason for him to be involved, because you are the one making an agreement with the clinic. It's just an old habit to need him, and he likes to be needed. The two of you together are making a bad connection there. What I would like to happen in this session is that he should try to find out who he is, if he's not needed. He doesn't know. So the first thing is that you should not need him! As long as you need him, this repression will continue, because he will give you things, but there is a price!"

The inner woman agrees with that.

Now, at my request, Sureela crosses over to the male chair. I ask the man how he feels, now that "for the first time she took the body out of your sphere of influence. She never asked to use the body before, she just took the spirit somewhere. Now she took the body where she wanted it".

He feels relieved, because he was tired. Confronting the situation that he's not any more needed, he reports, "I'm quite boring. I'm lying on the sofa, or maybe reading, or walking around looking at people".

I say to him, "If you're boring, that means you don't have an inner life. Is that true?"

He answers, "So far I haven't met much of it, yeah. I've been terribly tied up arranging everything. It was tiring". But he says he doesn't know what to do if he stops making so much order in life. "Maybe I just have to be bored with myself for a while until something happens".

I ask him if he likes meditating, and he says, "Yes. It's a very nice journey, but I don't take initiative to do it".

We change back to the female. I ask her, "Does he look different to you, now that you're not in a position of begging him for something?" She says, "He's a good and trusty friend, but now he has taken a step back".

In my own opinion, the male hasn't taken a step back – he has simply revealed what was already the case – but the female has taken a step forward. She continues, "I feel big. He feels smaller, and he seems to be satisfied with that, too. Amazing, his reaction to the new clinic".

I re-emphasize to the female that if she takes the job at the new clinic, she should take it all on herself – everything hers – and let him not work for a while. "And you will come into form, you need form. You will come into crystallization that way. Make the job exactly the way you want it without asking his opinions".

She's just beginning to get it. "So now I can take responsibility for the negotiations! It was really me who said some important things last time and I can say even more." Not only more, but all! She agrees: all.

The Hammer

The session could have stopped here, but – even against the usual principle in my work that the less conscious figure can remain as they are – I find myself going after the man, because he is lazy, still lying on his divan.

So we're on the male side again, and I ask him, "When she does all the negotiations for the new job and then does the job, what happens to you?" He says he wants to share with her, wants to support her.

I snap back at him, "Okay. First of all, she doesn't need your support. And secondly, you don't have anybody inside who can be with her. This is the problem: you're boring. You yourself told me you're boring".

He says, "Then I don't know, I'm quite empty. Maybe I'll take a vacation". I thought to myself, it's another divan.

Change over to the female. I ask her if she chose the new boyfriend. "Yes," she says, "He's one of the first men who has really satisfied so many parts of me".

I say, "The new boyfriend you have does not seem to be similar to this one (the inner man), so I don't think he will end up being the permanent boyfriend (she looks a little disappointed). However, in this moment you need him; you needed something as the female and you have found it. Good! Try saying to the inner man, "I needed something you couldn't provide for me, and that's why I chose the new boyfriend".

She tries this sentence. With a glow on her face, she says it is true, and she even told the inner man that this person would be really good for her. And he is!

Change Over

Question to the inner man: "Did you choose the new boyfriend?" His answer: "No". My comment: "She needed something so she went and got it. She's not so lacking in courage as you led me to believe. Is it okay with you that she has a different boyfriend?"

His answer: "Yes. Because I am quite tired. I had my limits. I think we were bored with each other".

I agree with him. "That's exactly right. So before, even though she hadn't moved out of your house yet, and she was still accepting all the comfort and everything, it was not a good situation – she had already chosen a different man. Now she moved out, she's getting her own job, she's with her new man, and things are much, much better.

So, can you see how crazy it is for you to say, 'I want to share with her, I want to support her' It doesn't fit the situation at all!"

The inner man starts laughing at the absurdity. He says, "I had some sort of separation anxiety".

I respond, "Yeah. Okay. So now, there is a separation. And it's up to you, how much you want to make of your life. You can be her partner, if you want, but it will take some work".

"Umm ... " he muses.

But I continue the pressure: "One can't just say, 'Oh, everything's going to be okay if I just do nothing, if I just lie on the couch, watching television.' You have this section of the training, then the last section, then it's over. Do you see what I mean? Don't let the training pass by without using it!"

He says, "I don't follow now".

"You talked to me about lying on the sofa. You talked to me about taking a vacation. You didn't talk to me about going inside, or exposing yourself to other people".

Now he gets it, "Ah ... okay".

"You didn't talk about love, asking 'Where is the love in me?' or 'Where am I going?' These are the important questions! In the work you're doing now, you are simply pleasing people; whatever they expect, you do. This is a camel behaviour".

"Oh – camel". He is surprised to recognize one of the behaviour patterns he's been learning about, where you get your satisfaction from other people's recognition and you depend on them for your identity. The inner male says, "I will try to grab my innocence inside".

But I know that the words 'try' and 'grab' don't go with innocence. I tell him, "The word 'try' is still in the desire dimension. The real thing is to stay with 'I don't know. I must look! I don't know ... ' like a profound acknowledgement that you're nowhere". And he can agree about this, "Yeah, I am nowhere".

Then I tell him, "Luckily, she has taken you out of your cage. The job at the new clinic is not your job, it's hers. It will be part-time for a little while and that means you'll have the chance to do other things and experiment with what brings you joy. (Brief pause in conversation) I'm a little hard on you just because you go on saying 'Huh? Huh? What? Huh? Hmm?'"

Now the inner man is laughing again. "Yes, be hard," he says, "I trust you".

We change over once again to the female side. I say to her, "I'm glad you're happy over there, with your boyfriend, with your private clients and prospects for a new job, with your negotiation task in front of you. I'm glad you're happy. It's a great step – a great help in the situation".

She is looking radiant and grateful, but she notices that the inner man is quite lost.

"Lost, yes," I comment. "To me the session is about facts: that you're in a good position and he's lost. But it's typical. Don't worry; it's normal".

The inner woman laughs.

"What is not normal," I continue, "Is that this one, the female, has actually taken so many good steps already, with the negotiating, with the new man. Much good movement has happened before you even came to this session".

"Yeah," she says, "And the house is for sale, and I'm moving to a small apartment. I decided it".

Wow! I'm impressed by how much she did behind the scenes. "So everything is perfect right now to shake up this person's life (his life) a little bit. Then he will have to respond. He'll have to figure out, 'Where do I look inside to make a response?' You provoke him! Let everything provoke him – it's good".

We end the session there. I ask Sureela to sit in the neutral chair, the witnessing position, where the session began.

Technicalities

I didn't plan this session, I just took it step by step. But by the end of the energy check of the body, two or three things were clear:

- The female had presence, but it wasn't in the body.

- The male dominated the use of the body, but he had no presence.

- The female needed things to change, the male was not yet initiating a change – he had chosen this job and the ego was benefiting from the present situation. At this moment he was the dominant one in the couple.

So then I did the interviews. I didn't mention it before, but during the interviews, I asked each side separately if she, or he, was a sannyasin. You may wonder what this means. It means, of course, many different things, depending on whom you are talking to, but for the purposes of this explanation it means a commitment to being 'empty' – precisely that space in which the inner male ended the session. A commitment to 'not knowing' in which you acknowledge the helplessness of the mind to bring you anywhere. A commitment to watching the mind desire, but not doing anything about it, waiting for an inspired action from the belly and the heart, not a mental decision of the head.

The master, in this case Osho, is not doing anything at all. He is simply present, and the radiance of that presence supports the natural energy of the 'being' to start moving in the sannyasin's legs, belly, and heart. Anybody who is Osho's sannyasin recognizes the feeling of 'love touching love' and then, of course, soon the two loves can't be divided.

The inner woman told me she was a sannyasin and it was obvious. It was obvious by her priorities (I'll say more in a minute). When I asked the question "Are you a sannyasin?" to the inner man, he waited a while before answering and then said, "Ye-ahhh". Less convincing than the woman's answer but still a 'yes.'

So this was a plus in his favor and it allowed me go after him. If he'd said 'no', he was not sannyasin, not interested in developing his inner being, then the session would have stopped after the woman got support to do her things. The male's closure would have been silently respected.

Priorities that Create Fear

When I do an interview with a character, one of the questions is about priorities in life. The character can choose three and then I look at which category they fit under: love or fear. Some priorities actually create fear in your life, for example, security, comfort, safety, money, and respectability, but there are others.

If you want security and then you relax, security gets less. Life is insecure! So a person who wants security has to become vigilant, tense, rigid, to make sure that security stays at the same level or increases. With every fear priority, the thing you are aiming for decreases when you relax.

By contrast, other priorities increase when you relax. Examples of these are knowing yourself, meditation, creativity, joy, sensitivity, beauty, trust. These lead you to love, because the more you relax, the more you find that your very nature is love.

The female's priorities – sparkling in daily life, sharing, beauty – were love priorities (with 'sharing' being a little questionable, in her case, but normally it is a love priority). The male's priorities were all fear priorities. They were hiding the belief that life won't provide enough comfort for his kids and himself. They were hiding his need for recognition. He can't possibly relax, he will be afraid to let go and, of course, he repeatedly told us throughout the session about how tired he was!

In the mutual descriptions where the figures were on chairs, the female side described the male as 'a fatherly caretaker, boring but safe'. Of course, I knew he must be, but then why had she chosen a boyfriend who was not a fatherly caretaker? The boyfriend was nothing like the inner male, his job was in an artistic area.

When things are working properly, the inner women and inner man want to merge, to fall in love with each other, and nothing will work in life until that happens, but it seemed that this female had given up on her inner partner. Why? She gave us the answer soon, by admitting that she was repressed by him. First we found out that 'repressed' was one of her qualities, but then we found out that she was repressed by him!

Well, when you are repressed, you have to get out of the situation, move to where you can be free and make your own decisions. So that began the next phase of active change. She moved her body out of his comfort zone (one of the most important happenings in the session) and noticed that she was already doing something to create a new job for herself, but she kept expecting to 'share' the negotiating with the inner man.

Now you can see why in this case 'sharing' is a questionable priority! I wouldn't let her share: "Take your choice and do it by yourself!" This hadn't occurred to her before. The conditioning from the man was strong, that 'teamwork' is good. Teamwork is only good when two people are present; it is not good if one is present and the other is a sycophant. Better that the one who is present does it alone, and the one who has no internal authenticity invests his time and energy in self-exploration.

I said to the inner woman early on that 'what I would like to happen in this session is that the inner man should try to find out who he is, if he's not needed'. I hoped that he would arrive to the experience of not being needed and then feel it. But in fact, he arrived to the fact of not being needed but slid away from experiencing it.

He wanted to go to sleep, in a way, and a sofa is a good place to do that. He wanted to distract himself by watching other people, reading books, taking a vacation, or just be bored until something perked him up. Anything except going in! He couldn't initiate a meditation, couldn't recognize that he needed it! He didn't have the thirst to know himself. This is why the inner woman had given up.

Provocation

And now I come to my last point, but with a bit of introduction. If you follow the main principles of Energywork (the female type of Osho Therapy), you support the character that is present, encourage it to be self-confident, strong and happy, and you leave the non-present character alone.

There is no need to touch it, because the relaxation of the awakened part will have a subtle effect on the closed, sleeping part. Soon he (in this case) will look at her (in this case) with half-open eyes, wondering why she is so happy. Then he will close his eyes and go on snoring. Then he will open his eyes again, noticing that she is not disturbed by his absence, that she goes on being happy, and his eyes will stay open longer this time, and the wondering will increase.

366

Slowly, slowly, he enters into the dimension of presence without even noticing that something has happened. If the open part can stay trusting and confident without wavering, the closed part joins it because the relaxation of saying 'yes' to life is more inviting, more easy than saying 'no'.

BUT, as you noticed, I did not leave the male alone. I hassled him. I harassed him. I told him, "Look, the female chose another man because you couldn't give her what she needed". Why did I do that? To tell you the truth, I don't know. It's just that I'm not the same as I used to be, I'm living my male side more than before and I'm as surprised as anybody that I have now joined the Awareness and Expression camp on a part-time basis.

This is exactly the way this type of therapist works with people. I'm reminded of one friend of mine in particular. He provokes. He 'kicks ass'. And so many people love him, and they report to me that they were cruising along with a superficial life and he stopped them in their tracks. They can't thank him enough for that.

So what I want to say is, in Osho Therapy there are times when Energywork is the thing, and there are times when Expression-work is the thing. Life moves back and forth between these two polarities, yin and yang. You cannot know with the mind, you can only know with the heart which direction suits the moment.

I sensed that Sureela's inner male was connected with me somehow, perhaps connected by trust, and I could use a provoking method without damaging him. And perhaps the trust he felt was not especially towards me, but was prompted by his decision to be a sannyasin. All I know is that it felt good to provoke him. Almost like two teenage boys having a scuffle for the sheer joy of it.

Osho used to hammer us sometimes, certainly he hammered me. When you know there's love behind a hammer, you can surrender.

Now I would like to tell you about another session (again in present tense):

Ingeborg

Ingeborg is participating in a different therapist training course than Sureela. She receives a session with the other group members watching. Everybody already knows the main theme she is struggling with: she lives with a man she doesn't want to live with and they both agree to separate, but he doesn't move out of the house – and it's been one year!

When I ask about work, Ingeborg tells me that she has three main activities right now. The first one is working with disabled people and their families when the person is about to die, in the terminal phase. She likes it. She usually meets with the family four times a week and stays with them for half a year. She only works with one family at a time, normally ten to twelve hours on each visit, but sometimes twenty-five hours at a time. Sometimes it's twenty-five hours four times a week! But they also have different caretakers on the other days.

She describes it like this: "In the end, most of them are paralyzed, can't speak, can't even blink their eyes, and I'm doing everything. I'm there in their home, and they die in their home. At the last moment, I'm there with the children, with the mother, with the whole family. I feel I'm very good at holding the space in that moment, connecting, allowing people to let go. They trust me in that process, and they're very calm".

Her second job is working as a counsellor for handicapped people who have a team of nurses in their home. She has to teach them how to be leaders in their own home – the nurse is not a guest but, instead, 'this is a working place now'.

And then Ingeborg is going to school to receive nurse training. In addition to these three job-related activities, she has two children, but one daughter is grown up so she only has to take care of the boy who is now ten.

I start the energy check by holding the left foot. Because we're in a training process, Ingeborg hears this description of her feminine aspect as I tell it to the listeners present.

Female leg: No presence, darkness, and a very unhappy feeling. Slowly I see the picture of a quite substantial woman who is a nurse in a uniform of the past – the nurse's cap of the 1950's and a long dress with thin blue stripes. She seems a rather domineering type to me (different from the Ingeborg I've seen up to now, who is thin, sprightly and very respectful of other people). The face of this woman is serious, the stout legs are a little spread and fixed firmly on the ground. You could almost imagine her arms folded over her chest to take a position about something. But instead I see her active on many fronts, often taking a managerial role. It's not exactly in a hospital, but I can't say where it is that she's active. For sure, this is the dominant one in the pair.

Masculine leg: In this man, there is a search going on. I don't find any presence yet, but he's sniffing for it: "I'm looking for something, where is it?" He's more playful than the other one. He likes to have a good time. He's more sociable. I see him outdoors. Whereas she chooses to be inside a building, this person is preferring to be outside. The figure is not dressed in modern clothes, not jeans for example, but I can't give details. I see him in a small, perhaps middle-sized European town where there is traffic passing on the road which is either horses or wooden carts drawn by bullocks or similar animals. He has many men friends and meets them on the street and makes projects or plans with these people. A friendly person. (pause) But men are friendly in a different way than women: "Hi, how are ya?" with a slap on the back ... that 'tough' kind of friendly when men enjoy each other's company.

While I didn't find any presence in Ingeborg's legs, there is an abundance in the first chakra. This is the chakra of the material world and physical survival. When it has presence, the person has no fear about survival. This is why Ingeborg can work well with dying people, because she is not afraid; she knows that the spirit will survive.

Actually Ingeborg has presence in more chakras, good presence in chakra two (related to job), a little less in the power centre, presence in the heart and in the third eye. So the only places I didn't find any were in the throat and top of the head. On concluding the energy check, I feel that Ingeborg has indeed chosen the right theme for the session, because the pronounced lack of presence in the legs shows that she has a male/female problem.

Interviews

Before I start the interviews, I say to Ingeborg that the female is the dominant one and the male is the most loving – slightly, very slightly, because they are both pretty fixed in their positions. I install the blindfold so that Ingeborg sees me from the right eye only.

When I ask the inner man if he is happy in his life right now, he gets very sad. I ask him to talk about the things that are making him sad, and he says, "I can't speak – I must try ... I can't move. I want to act, but I can't move. (pause) There are walls everywhere. I feel all this space, but there are walls everywhere. I start to feel afraid".

I ask him if he is participating in any of the jobs, and he answers that he made a speech the other day in front of 30 people. He enjoyed it a lot. But other than that, he doesn't contribute to the job. I ask him if he's afraid to disturb her in her job. He says that in general he is afraid of her.

When I ask for three qualities which represent him, he says "vulnerable, joyful, kind". About priorities it's not so easy. I ask him, "Where are you heading in life?" and he answers, "I'm not heading anywhere right now. I'm not even sure I would like to be. I'm not reaching out".

From the conversation that ensues, I learn that in the past he wanted to grow, or 'go further', but he was defeated so many times that he lost faith. Then he set the walls. I encourage him to reconsider what he would do if the walls were taken down. "Otherwise your whole life goes into the building of walls, and then it's over. You say you don't have any priorities, but you are building walls, so there must be a priority – protection or something similar must be a priority".

He agrees. I tell him he can close his eye now, but I have one last thing to say: "I like you". He is touched, but scared at the same time. I say to him, "I can understand. Because if love is a possibility, it means you need to open. Then your whole defense system falls down, and you won't know who you are because those walls have given you your sense of self. But I'm inspired to say to you that I see somebody in there who could be very interesting. I see something good". He answers softly, "Thank you".

I move the blindfold so that Ingeborg's right eye is covered and the female eye – left eye – is open.

I ask her the same thing I asked the man, "Are you happy in your life right now?" She says, "No, I'm not". And the reasons? "I've got too much pressure". And where is it coming from? "From everywhere. And from myself as well. I just keep on moving. I'm like a train – unstoppable. And there are no stations!" Where is the train going? "I haven't the faintest idea. I just keep moving". What feeling would be inside you if you stopped moving? "Emptiness".

We change the subject to the job. She is doing all the jobs. She says that 100 percent of the work comes from her. When I ask her if she thinks the speech the inner male made contributes to the job, she says, "It makes more work!" Clearly she means that the speech was successful and afterwards people asked her to do more things.

Then, out of the blue, she says, "This is really a lonely place. I feel really shut down". I suggest that we use 'shut down' as one of the qualities which represent her, and she should present two more. She says, "Efficient. And I'd like to say powerful, but I think that's an illusion – maybe strong". I agree with her, that it's somewhere between power and strength.

Regarding her priorities in life, the first one is 'order'. The second one is "humanity – to serve people. To help people, to help them die". I'm surprised. "Don't you want to help them live?" She answers, "The people I've been with have been so sick that there was no way out. When I say 'help them die' I mean help them be alive when it's really hard, when you're paralyzed from the neck down, or when you can't speak, to make that a worthy death".

371

"And your third priority?" She is almost embarrassed to say it, so the voice is really low. "Love". I tell her I am quite happy that she said this, and she answers, "Yeah. I say love, but I don't feel it ... so it's hard to ... " "Still," I counter, "I'm glad you included it in your priorities, even if you're far away. Because if you want to get there, you can get there, so it's a very good sign. You might have to give up your second priority for it". She is ready to give up helping people, she says, especially in exchange for a little love instead.

At this point, we remove the blindfold and I arrange two cushions across from each other where soon the male and female will talk to each other. In the meantime, Ingeborg sits on another cushion so that she can be out of both roles for a while. She needs to breathe!

Mutual Descriptions

When she's ready, she sits on the male's cushion with closed eyes and I start describing him. She is supposed to enter into this figure, and 'he' will describe himself in his own words after I finish.

I tell her, "He has a strong body, as if he has done work using his body – probably something outdoors – in the past. He liked being physically strong. And he's been around men who also liked being physically strong, so they had a kind of brotherhood. He's an easy person to be friends with, especially for other men. He has joy sometimes and he's funny, and he's playful. He jokes and he teases people, and laughs. He's a sociable person. I actually think he contributes something to the work when he goes in people's houses and he's joking around and creating good humor, good atmosphere. But he doesn't like to be inside houses, so he gets out as soon as he can.

"He doesn't really know where he's going in life. He acts like he's reached the maximum of what is possible for him, but I don't believe it's true. I think much more internal richness is possible for him, and not even so very difficult".

The inner man adds to the description of himself: "I'm definitely not content. I really love a good laughter. I love color. I'm a bit angry, as well".

Ingeborg changes over to the other cushion and becomes the inner female, who then describes the male from a feminine point of view: "He's pathetic. Weak. Pitiful. I'm just going to say the words that come to me, but they're definitely not nice. 'Disgusting'. Umm. I really don't like him – that's a polite way to say it. My belly is just ... Wwhoosh! I think he's dirty, he's really disgusting, vulgar, stupid".

Now she is asked to describe what happens in her when she is with him. What kind of person does she turn into? "Uptight. Hard. Cold. Much too strict. Judging. Like a mirror, all the things I didn't like are showing up here. Really bad news. I turn into a person that I don't like. I see that these qualities are in myself – the strength, the hardness, the bull – but I would like to open up and be gentle".

I tell the inner woman that she should just be these things and I will help her. "If you start thinking about what you wish you were, I can't help. So be these things. I don't feel any problem that in this moment you are hard or you are judgmental. It's as good a starting point as any".

To Ingeborg I say, "You can open your eyes now and change to the other side".

We are on the male side again and he describes the woman from a man's point of view: "She's not anyone I would like to talk to. Judgmental, stupid actually. She's wasting time. She's much too hard. She's much too stiff. She's not able to move. She's not there. There's no flow".

I ask him to describe himself when he's with her, and he reports that he turns his back to her. He gets a bit flat, like the bubbles of inner champagne go flat. He says, "It's because there's no one to play with. She can't play, because she's stiff. I can't get through".

Adjustments

I say, "If she can't play right now, maybe you had better give the example of how to play". He says, "Now I get really scared. Okay,

okay, I'm willing". (sigh)

I explain that because she's not able to play right now, he will have to play alone. His eyebrows go up in surprise, "I will have to play alone?" "For the moment. But remember what I've been saying to the group: if just one person knows how to be playful, the other one usually catches on after a while. I want to invite you to think of a job that you could do. It should be out of the house, and out of anybody else's house also. It should have nothing to do with helping anybody, it just makes you feel playful. Can you think of any job like that?" First he thinks of an activity: "riding bicycle with my son and some of his friends". Then suddenly he has an idea for a job: "I want to start a small company. I could make that fun. A consulting company for disabled people".

We change over to the other side. I say to the female, "He's going to teach you playfulness by example. He told me he can do this in a consulting firm, where he will work with some disabled people, and he can make it fun. Do you believe he can?"

She answers, "Might". After a tense silence, she says, "I'm angry". Why? "Because you're taking something away from me". I tell her that this is true, she's absolutely right, but the reason I'm doing it is because of her third priority: love. "If what you've got is not making you happy, and I see a way to make you happy, I will take away that thing which is not making you happy". She says, "Okay, I give in". I say, "Beautiful. That's love. Can you feel it? Can you feel some love in your body right now?" "Yeah—bit hard for me to allow myself to feel this", she says.

I make what I think is a simple request, "I'd like to ask you to give him the work in the consulting company on his own. For a while you just ... " but the female moans in agony, "Whooo," while I continue the sentence, " ... watch him do it, and he has it in his hands". She says tightly, "I really don't like that". Why? "Well, can't say I don't like it, I just feel resistant". "Why? I think he'll do a really great job".

Realizing that a deeper part of her wants him to succeed, she slowly relaxes, letting her 'no' change into a 'yes'. I ask her

374

to give her blessing for the new job and working time for those people who need him, and the promise to step out of it and let him take the whole thing. She has a hard time finding the words and her voice is cracking, but she manages to address him with this message. Afterwards she says, "It's really hard, not to recommend or explain or interfere at all".

Change over. To the male, I ask if he likes the idea that it's totally in his hands and he can do the job the way he wants. He's giggling, he's so happy. So finally he has a priority, after all. It is playfulness. What a beautiful priority, to want a life that's playful, and that has jokes in it, and laughter.

"But remember," I say to him, "that your purpose is not to help her 'get it'; your purpose is to give yourself the kind of life you want". "So I have to persist in play", he says. "That's right. And you'll be earning money at the same time and occupying space in the day simultaneously, so it can only be positive from every point of view". "It will be fun", he says, giggling again.

Change over. The female looks at him and finds that he is not so disgusting any more. I say, "Suppose he takes over that job – and he will. He does it very differently than you would, but it's fun and people like it. Could you consider giving him more space for it?" She sniffs, again resistant, "I'd like to say, 'one step at a time'". I respond, "There's a reason I ask you this question. You said you go like a train, and there's so much pressure. Both things would change if he had more time and space".

The female shrugs it off with "I know, I know". "And you could stop. You could stop for a while, and he's carrying things on – even if it's just for a few hours that you stop. He goes and you stop". She's listening. "This will make you softer, because you don't need to keep going, so it can only be positive from every point of view". Again she lets go, "Yes, I could allow him to do more".

Change over. The male reports to me that he no longer feels in a box. I say, "You can do some things that she can't do, up to now. That's why I said to you before, it's really important to have your priorities in life. Let's make a list now ... ".

"Playful is first", he says, cocking his head. "Then, I want to spread happiness. Be happy-go-lucky". He's thinking. "Third is love, acceptance. And including, rather than excluding, other people. (pause) That's me". (he's emotional, sniffing) When I ask him if he likes himself now, he says, "Yes, if you don't count my red nose. Yes. I do like myself".

At this point, we are almost finished and I ask Ingeborg to leave the male cushion and sit to the side, while the rest of the people in the group move closer to us. Now that she has returned to her normal, undivided self, I ask her if there is anything she wants to say before I invite the others to speak. She says, "It was hard".

Not Identified

Certainly, changing is hard. I ask the group to offer their opinions about which changes were hard. Mostly, I agree with their answers, but when one person says that it was hard for the woman to accept the man, I have to clarify something. "Accepting him was the difficulty only on the surface. The real difficulty was, as I told you before, that the dominant figure gets all the energy flowing in their direction, and when somebody pulls a bit of it in another direction, they squawk! Life is supposed to swing between two extremes, but the mind doesn't like that swing. The mind wants one line; it wants to show the world that it has achieved something.

"So all the energy ends up on one side and never changes back. And then a person has to spend twenty-four hours living that polarity: no rest. And then she says, 'I'm on a train and I don't know why, and my train doesn't stop'. It's because everything's going in the same direction twenty-four hours a day. But the minute that there's an invitation to swing the other way, the person says, 'Nooo! That's my *identity*. If I don't have all the twenty-four hours I will feel *empty*'.

"It's normal," (people are laughing) "nothing unusual really. Just think of waves in the ocean. When a wave falls, the rising wave is cancelled out and exists no more. And vice versa, when the wave is rising, the valley – the lovely, curving dip in the water when a wave finishes – is no more to be found. A problem occurs if there is an identification with one aspect: I *am* the rising wave or I *am* the falling wave.

"Ingeborg is identified with the feminine. This is evident in her work also, because she helps people to die. She helps them leave a bodily form that is spent, finished, ready to be discarded. Then the wave is no more, but of course the ocean remains. This is a feminine interest – the disappearance of form, then one can experience a formlessness which is much more vast.

"Now the man comes along with a totally different idea. He wants to help the same people in a different moment, when they have the capacity to live and use the body to create, to enjoy and laugh. While he's doing his thing, the 'falling wave' is no more. There is a short death for the ego of the feminine.

"It's ironic, isn't it, that the female works with helping other people die, but she can't die so easily herself. Meditation helps us in this – not to be identified, not to be something in particular. But in the process of deepening our meditation, this greater death – the death of the ego – is really hard. Love is the only force that can help us do it".

One person from the group says, "I think it was really important that the female part got conscious of how much she wanted love". It certainly was the most important thing in the session, that priority. It made all the difference.

I comment that I really liked the female's ability to say "I feel he's disgusting … he's this … he's that … " and she knew it wasn't beautiful but she was still honest. And she was honest when she said "Love is my priority but I can't love right now". At one point the female said, about her negative qualities, "But I don't want these things, I wish for other beautiful qualities". Ingeborg, remembering that moment, speaks about it. "I wanted to escape; I was a bit ashamed".

I can understand her, but I say to the group, "When you learn meditation, you learn to see all kinds of things you didn't want to be but you are. And then you learn to just be those things and at the same time aware, present, not identified. That's why meditation is so valuable. You don't run away into hoping and pretending, because then things cannot be repaired. We have to assume that where we actually are is a good starting place. And that things can work from here. Just be honest. It can work".

CHAPTER EIGHTEEN

Hypnosis and Hypnotherapy
Premananda and Prabodhi

What is Hypnosis? Many people ask this question because they are attracted to the subject yet at the same time afraid of it. In fact, the state of being in a hypnotic trance is a normal, natural and well-known phenomenon, which occurs in all of us many times a day.

It is the experience of daydreaming or being in a reverie whilst sitting in a favourite place in nature, or experiencing a bonfire at night, or watching a movie, or reading a book, or being absorbed in a task like driving a car, writing an email, or being engaged in a creative act.

In other words, it is a well-known personal experience. Hypnosis has been defined as "a special psychological state with certain physiological attributes, resembling sleep only superficially and marked by a functioning of the individual at a level of awareness other than the ordinary conscious state".

Persons under hypnosis are said to have heightened focus and concentration, with the ability to concentrate intensely on a specific thought, or memory, while blocking out sources of distraction.

Using the technique of Hypnosis for therapeutic reasons is known as Hypnotherapy. Using Hypnosis for entertainment purposes is known as Stage Hypnosis.

The word 'trance' can be said to be an altered state of consciousness from our usual everyday waking state. There are two schools of thought about this. One says that hypnosis is a very special technique that is done to one, or one does to oneself, through self-hypnosis; the other that says the very nature of our everyday lives is extremely hypnotic and that we are in and out of different hypnotic trances all day long. We find this second view to be more useful and appropriate.

The word Hypnosis was created by James Braid, a Scottish doctor, in the 1830s. In Greek it means 'conscious sleep'. The phenomenon of trance and altered states, however, has been around since the beginning of mankind.

So Hypnosis is a very old and basically quite simple art of by passing the conscious mind and communicating directly with the unconscious mind.

Freud: The Two-Mind Model

Freud created the two-mind model, using the metaphor of an iceberg. The smallest part, which is above the water, refers to the conscious mind. The much larger part, which is below the water, refers to the unconscious mind. There are different names for this part of ourselves, like subconscious mind, or other-than-conscious mind. It doesn't matter what you call it as long as the idea of two minds is used.

This model is a useful way of showing the split nature of human experience. The two-mind model is not the whole truth. Other models have many more layers, or levels of mind, like superconscious, universal conscious, archetypal unconscious, etc., etc. But it is a practical way to think about the nature of our experience and a useful way to work with people therapeutically.

We all know the experience of consciously wanting to make changes in our life. We make New Year's Resolutions only to find, after a few weeks, or even days, those resolutions are forgotten. Or, we are unable to sleep and lay awake, tossing and turning, consciously wishing to sleep yet being unable to do so. Or, we suffer from jealousy and try hard to 'not be jealous' and change this painful emotion.

Why can we not make these changes consciously? The reason is, of course, that the unconscious part of our mind has some objection to change, or, there is some unresolved issue lying in our unconscious mind that we are unable to perceive. Permission to change really does seem to lie in our unconscious mind.

Our conscious mind fulfils specific tasks and functions. It is the part of us that makes decisions. It is the part of us that we use to complete various tasks and outcomes. It is also the part of us that Osho frequently talked about as being the 'watcher' of whatever is happening.

It is the part of us that knows where we need to put our attention, or where we choose to shine the torch of attention. So if we need to cross the road, we put our attention on whether there is any oncoming traffic. If we are shopping, we look for what we want to buy. To give an immediate example: if you search the place where you are right now for the colour yellow, you may notice how you do this, dismissing all things coloured blue, green, red and black.

Our unconscious mind is far bigger. As you read these words, are you aware of your heartbeat, the next breath you take, your kidneys filtering your blood, the sensation of this book in your hands and the next thought that you are about to think? You will probably reply, "Yes, I am aware of all these things when you mention them, but I wasn't until you did".

The American Psychologist George Miller in 1953 coined the idea of 'the magical number seven, plus or minus two', which refers to the pieces of information the conscious mind can process at any one moment. It is our unconscious mind that is aware of everything else. Psychologists cannot agree on the exact quantity, but it is thought that we take in thousands of different pieces of information every second through our unconscious mind.

Osho: Hypnosis as Therapy

Throughout his life, Osho was interested in the technique of Hypnosis. He often talked about it and told stories of how he practiced hypnotic techniques on friends when he was a student. He described it as an excellent technique for bridging the gap between therapy and meditation, and also a great way for people to learn how to – as he put it – 'befriend their minds'.

Hypnotherapy was first practiced in Osho's community in Pune in the 1970s by an American therapist, Santosh, who called his work 'Dehypnotherapy'. There was a gap in the mid-80s and then, in 1988, when Hypnotherapy was reintroduced, Osho was very supportive and said he wanted all his therapists to be trained in it. Subsequently, there was a training with seventy people, mostly therapists.

The last meditation Osho introduced, called *Reminding Yourself of the Forgotten Language of Talking to Your Mind and Body*, is based on hypnotic techniques. It involves a process of talking to one's unconscious mind and befriending it, in order to find deeper intentions and motives behind physical ailments.

The form of Hypnotherapy that was introduced in 1988 was the more permissive, non-authoritarian approach developed by the American psychiatrist, Dr Milton Erickson. Erickson became known as the father of modern Hypnosis and made it a respectable and well-known technique.

Two Styles: Authoritarian and Permissive

The difference between authoritarian and permissive Hypnosis is significant. With the authoritarian approach, the hypnotist issues instructions like 'You will relax', or 'I want you to relax now'.

In the permissive approach, the therapist will try to achieve the same result by saying something like "remember a time when you were in a favourite place in nature, a place you enjoy visiting and spending time in, seeing the colours, shapes and views of that place, hearing the sounds, feeling the temperature of the air on your forehead and smelling the air around you".

Naturally, what most people will do is relax, because the hypnotist is evoking a memory in the client where they have already been relaxed.

It is said that the authoritarian approach works well with some people, but certainly not with all. The permissive approach tends to work with many more people.

When you have the experience of Hypnosis, either through self-hypnosis or working with a hypnotherapist, you are learning to befriend yourself and establish an easy flow of two-way communication between both minds.

Many people don't know much about their unconscious minds and tend to be afraid of it. Our unconscious mind has many functions and an important one is to bring about a resolution, or healing, of past traumas and wounds. We all lead busy lives and it seems to be a truism that our unconscious mind records everything that has ever happened to us.

As we are forever moving on with our daily life, we usually don't allow ourselves time to integrate and absorb everything that happens to us. In this way, we treat our unconscious mind as a garbage can, stuffing down everything we can't deal with right now and not giving ourselves time or attention to process it.

But the bodies in the basement begin to stink if left unattended. So it all tends to build up and when we finally pay attention to our unconscious mind it tends to overreact, saying, "Ah, now I have got your attention, let's deal with this … and this … and this … " exposing many old, unresolved issues. It can overwhelm us. Then we get the idea that the unconscious mind is the enemy, which is in fact not true. It just wants to bring about a healing of old wounds.

In addition, people often have a civil war going on inside them. For example, a person might decide that he wants to change his 'bad habit' of staying in bed in the morning and being too lazy to attend an early morning meditation at the ashram where he is staying.

No more of that! He decides that tomorrow morning he will get up at 5:30 am to go to the ashram and participate in Dynamic Meditation. He sets the alarm for that time. The alarm goes off, but, still in a state of sleep, he reaches over and turns off the alarm. Three hours later, he wakes up and immediately feels bad that he missed the meditation – especially since he was so determined to do it.

But his unconscious mind wasn't included in the agreement to do the meditation, so it didn't happen. From these kinds of situations, we can deduce that permission for change lies firmly with the unconscious mind.

Hypnosis is a powerful tool, or technique, to directly address the unconscious mind so that suggestions, ideas and new possibilities can be offered, while objections, fears and limitations can be acknowledged and dealt with creatively.

Subjective Reality

An important understanding about hypnotic work is the realization that everybody lives in his or her own subjective reality, which is profoundly different from that of anybody else. Osho talked about this in *The Hidden Harmony*, discourses on the sayings of Heraclitus, who wrote:

The waking have one world in common.
Sleepers have each a private world on their own.

Osho comments:

That's why, because of so many sleepers, there exist so many worlds. You have your own world. If you are asleep, you live enclosed in your own thoughts, concepts, dreams, desires. Whenever you meet another, two worlds clash.[1]

Only those who are spiritually awakened can speak of experiences in which dreaming is totally absent. However, it makes sense that each of us lives in our own unique world.

Think of the nature of experiencing so-called reality. To see something outside ourselves, a light beam has to arrive at the cells of our retina in our eyes and stimulate an electro-chemical impulse that moves down the optic nerve to create an image in our brain. The same applies to hearing, feeling, smelling and tasting.

This is just the beginning. Having received the impulse, the brain then tries to interpret this new information, using its intelligence to make sense of the new data by placing it in the context of all the billions of impulses and impressions it has already received and stored.

So, in a very real way, we are experiencing life as a result of electro-chemical impulses. We cannot experience whatever is outside us directly. A well-known metaphorical sentence is used to describe this: 'The map is not the territory'. The best humans can do is to create inner maps of whatever we think is there, outside ourselves, in the territory of outer existence.

Responding to Internal Maps

From this, it can be said that people are responding more to their internal maps – what they think is in the territory outside – than whatever is actually out there. Each individual creates his or her own map of the world and this map is neither right nor wrong.

This understanding underpins the Ericksonian approach. It encourages an attitude in the hypnotherapist that one individual map is no more right or wrong than any other. Everybody is unique. There is no single right way. This produces an attitude of deep respect for other people's models of the world and cuts across the self-righteousness of people who think their map is the correct one – even going to war to defend or impose their map as the truth.

In order to function as a society, we sometimes make general agreements on certain points charted on our different maps, but this is a limited arrangement – just enough for us to get along with each other and no more.

We also tend to specialize, developing maps that follow our interests in life. Thus, a medical doctor has a rich map about the physical body, available medicines and what helps healing and what doesn't. A gardener will have a rich map about plants, flowers and how to make a beautiful garden.

If people are responding more to their internal maps than reality itself, then one can say that everyone is in varying degrees of inner preoccupation or hypnotic trance. From this, one can usefully suggest that the nature of everyday life is profoundly hypnotic and that we are all going in and out of different trance states all day long.

Seen from this perspective, the technique of hypnosis becomes a great way to help people widen or enrich their maps so that they can make more appropriate choices, actualizing the changes they wish to make in their lives.

This was Erickson's idea. Osho went much further by suggesting – as mentioned earlier – that Hypnosis can be a bridge to encourage the mind to move more deeply into a state of 'No Mind', or meditation, which is a key characteristic of enlightenment and the fully conscious, awakened state.

Solving Your Own Problems

With this approach, the challenge for the Hypnotherapist is to go beyond the idea that he knows what is best for the client. It is not appropriate in this way of working for the therapist to tell clients what he thinks they should do, or what is good for them, or to give ready-made answers, but rather to support clients in finding their own solutions, their own inner resources and their own healing potential.

Erickson strongly believed that everybody has their own capacity, resourcefulness and ability to solve their own problems, once they discover that the unconscious mind can be activated to do this. A famous sentence he used with many clients was, "You know many things, only you don't know that you know them. When the appropriate situations occur, use your knowings".

According to Sidney Rosen, in his book *Teaching Tales of Milton H. Erickson*, Erickson said this to a certain Dr Pearson who came to him to learn hypnosis. But the message wasn't given to Pearson through normal teaching methods – the doctor had no conscious memory of it being said to him.

Erickson taught his students in a unique way: by putting them into deep trance and teaching them experientially about hypnosis. Many of his students thus learnt how to be effective in the art but had no conscious awareness as to *how* they were so effective. Erickson had taught them unconsciously, so they had very little conscious awareness about how they did what they did.

A few weeks later, Dr Pearson was walking down a street in an American city and as he walked under a scaffold he was hit by a falling brick on the back of his head. So there he was, lying half dead on the street, with the back of his head crushed and half his brains hanging out.

At that moment he heard Erickson's voice saying, "Dr Pearson, you know many things, only you don't know that you know them. When the appropriate situation occurs use your knowings".

He found himself putting his hand at the back of his head to keep brains in, getting up and walking to the nearest phone booth, phoning for emergency help, accurately giving the street address and his location. An ambulance arrived. He was taken to an emergency hospital where he received major surgery to put his head back together again. The doctors said it was a miracle he had survived. He recovered very quickly and was back to normal life in a matter of seven to ten days.

We told this story in a Hypnosis training in Italy many years ago. About four years later, a participant in that training returned to repeat the same course, saying she wanted to deepen her understanding of Hypnosis. Her face, meanwhile, had been badly disfigured and at an appropriate moment we asked her about it.

She said that sometime after the first training she'd been driving along an *autostrada* on a wet and cold night. Her car skidded and hit the metal divider where it allowed a gap between the two carriageways. It was like a knife blade that cut her car in two, nearly cutting her in two as well. She found herself lying on the road, barely conscious, sensing she was about to die.

Suddenly, she heard one of our voices in her head, telling the story of Dr Pearson and Erickson. She realized that she did not want to die and was determined to survive. She told us that she didn't know how she did it, but she was able to stay breathing and cope with the incredible pain until an emergency vehicle arrived and took her to the nearest hospital.

She had a number of major surgeries over the next two years, involving a tremendous amount of pain and discomfort, which she was able to bear because of her determination to live and make something of her life.

This is an example of the power of the unconscious mind. All we need to do is connect with it and ask it to accomplish things in life. However, most people are not aware of the potential power of the unconscious mind.

Another important aspect to hypnotic trance work is the understanding that mind and body are one entity. To think of them as two separate entities is extremely unhelpful. The nature and condition of our bodies profoundly affects our minds, while every thought we have affects every cell of our body.

The Nature of Thoughts

When you learn about the effect of Hypnosis it becomes very important to understand the nature of thoughts – the pictures we make in our brains and the accompanying sound track in the form of inner vocalization, or dialoguing with ourselves. For example, if someone says to you 'do not think of a pink elephant' you will first need to make a picture of the elephant and then somehow try to cancel it out.

People are making these sorts of inner statements all the time. We are all very good at knowing what we do not want in our lives. We often say to others and to ourselves statements like "I don't want to feel sad, depressed and lonely any more". Saying these words, one has to make an inner representation of sadness, depression and loneliness, thereby recreating these states in ourselves. This is a powerful form of what we might call 'negative self-hypnosis'.

Conversely, if we say "I want to feel strong, confident and good with myself", then we need to make an inner representation of these states and in this way help ourselves to create these states in our ongoing experience. It can be said that the biggest problem for most people is not that we don't know what we want, but that we know too well what we don't want.

It is like going to a travel agent in Hamburg. The agent asks "Where would you like to go?" and you reply "Not Hamburg". Or, like getting into a taxi and when the driver asks "Where to?" you say "Not here".

Traditionally, in Hypnosis there is a category of language patterns that people tend to use called Organ Language, which refers to the consequences of this kind of thinking.

For example, someone who complains to himself and others that he cannot 'stomach this job any more' might wonder why he has a stomach ulcer. Another person might say that 'the boss is a real pain in the neck' and then wonder why he suffers from a stiff and painful neck.

The Ability to Self-Regulate

When we learn about Hypnosis and the power of the unconscious mind, we also learn about the body's ability to bring about a state of self-regulation, physically, mentally and neurologically, for balance and bodily health. This includes activation of the autonomic nervous system, which operates below the level of the conscious mind and controls essential bodily functions like heart rate, digestion, respiratory rate, salivation, perspiration, urination and sexual arousal.

One of the desired outcomes for any hypnotic work is to restore balance and self-regulation to the autonomous nervous system and to the functions it controls, because, in our busy society, many people have lost the ability to self-regulate – mainly through lack of rest and relaxation.

It is well known that this system cannot be directly controlled by the conscious mind. Yet it seems that in deep trance, when the therapist has established a rapport with the client's unconscious mind, it will respond and activate on the autonomous level.

Traditionally, Hypnosis has been used for many health issues, both physical and mental, but it's important to understand that it is not Hypnosis or the power of the hypnotist that heals, but the client's own ability to heal themselves. Hypnotic work merely supports and encourages the healing process.

The body and the unconscious mind contain a blueprint for health and healing. It is only because of stress and inner conflict that our connection to this blueprint becomes weakened.

With encouragement, through relaxation, through appropriate suggestions delivered in a way that a person's unconscious mind will accept them, a state of self-regulation, healing and balance can be re-established. Typically migraine, tinnitus and ailments that have no physical cause can be successfully worked with using Hypnosis.

For example, a professor of dermatology at a well-known medical school enrolled in our trainings twice, telling us that ninety-five percent of the skin problems he was asked to examine had no physical cause and could therefore be best treated using Hypnotherapy.

How Hypnosis Affects Clients

Apart from leading many trainings in Hypnosis, we have both given thousands of individual sessions, working with many different issues. Some of the most fruitful have been concerning health. Some have helped clients who possessed a deep level of negative beliefs about themselves, or people who – many years ago and without being aware of it – made self-destructive decisions about themselves and continue to live under their shadow.

Through hypnotic work, these clients have been able to build new foundations in the unconscious mind for a richer, more fulfilled and more creative life. Through suggestions, stories and metaphors, people went through a process of re-educating themselves to the possibilities and potentials of their life, with many more choices opening up for them.

Our understanding of Osho and his penetrating insights into the nature of the human mind, the power of the unconscious, the impact of society on the individual and, perhaps most crucially, the nature of consciousness itself, all serve to inspire us as we work.

Case History: Coping with Cancer

A woman came to us who'd recently had breast cancer. She'd been through chemotherapy and also taken several steps to try and remain cancer free, changing her lifestyle to reduce stress and improving her diet. She asked us for support in this process. We will give her the name Rachel.

Over ten sessions, we worked on a number of issues around the cancer, including the state of her life at the time she'd found the lump in her right breast. Among other things, Rachel recalled having very rigid attitudes and often felt stressed, so we worked specifically on these two issues, with lots of suggestions to her unconscious about healing.

Using what we call 'ideomotor signals' we discovered that her unconscious mind knew how to take care of the cancer cells, and communicated that it would continue to do this so long as the client would support the process by adopting a more relaxed lifestyle.

A number of metaphors were also given during the ten sessions. This woman enjoyed gardening and lived by the Mediterranean. The water at the beach where she loved to go was usually warm and in summer would sometimes become like stagnant bath water. However, every week or so, a storm would occur and a current of water would come to the beach from far out to sea, flushing out the warm water, replacing it with new, cool, cleaner water. This image helped her to ease her rigid attitudes and understand how freshness, change and flow are healing qualities.

In talking about gardens, it was pointed out that a gardener prepares the garden to plant new bushes and flowers and takes away the weeds. Having prepared the garden it is important to then leave it to do its own thing. You don't keep pulling up the newly planted bushes to see how their roots are doing. The gardener does the work and then sits back and lets the garden do its own natural thing. This helped her see how stress leads to unnecessary 'doing', when 'non-doing' is more helpful and nourishing.

It was also pointed out in deep trance that a cancer cell was a poor little cell that had lost its way and didn't know what to do with itself. And that everyone has cancer cells but that our immune system when strong and healthy is very capable to be able to deal with them and that Rachel's immune system had been dealing very successfully with them for many years already.

"So immune system of Rachel, remember you know how to take care of eliminating cancer cells and do it now." If you say this to a person's conscious mind they would immediately ask 'how do I do that'? But saying it to a person in deep trance, bypassing the limited conscious mind, can be very effective. As a hypnotic facilitator, you are always aware to which mind you are talking.

Conscious minds can have understanding and insights and nothing ever really changes. When you have rapport with a person's unconscious mind and you give suggestions either directly or indirectly through stories, metaphors and anecdotes, real change can much more easily happen. The power and truth of this can be seen when you see a client some time later and ask them how they are with the issue that they originally came to you for.

They often say something like 'What issue was that'? and you have to remind them. Clients rarely say afterwards 'thank you for your wonderful work'. However you know that your work was powerful because clients do make changes and they will often later send their friends to work with you.

The Endless List

Rachel's sessions finished and she has remained healthy and cancer-free for sixteen years. Later on, she reported that one aspect of the treatment had been particularly helpful. During one of the sessions, while in deep trance, she had received suggestions from us about learning to relax more and being easier with herself, plus an understanding of how people tend to operate from the idea that one can only relax and enjoy oneself when all the things that 'need to be done' had been completed.

This is a common issue for many people. It is easy to have an endless list of things that 'need to be done' and it becomes a habit to drive oneself relentlessly to accomplish this impossible task.

It is like a weekend, or a holiday, during which one says "I will relax and enjoy myself when I have done the laundry, the washing up, cleaned the apartment, the ironing, written a report and finished reading an important book for my work".

Naturally, there is no holiday at all. Over the weekend, with a lot of effort and stress, you complete some of those tasks but then comes Sunday night and it's all over. Monday morning looms ahead and there is still no time to relax.

Our suggestion to this client was to make a decision to relax and enjoy herself first, regardless of all the things that 'need to be done'. This simple suggestion had radically changed her life for the better. These sessions supported her natural healing abilities and were part of a comprehensive package of changes she made to make her life easier and healthier.

Facticity: Embracing Opposites

Osho was the main influence in the development of the Facticity model, developed by Ragini Michaels, which is a major element of effective Hypnotherapy work. Ragini noticed that Osho and other enlightened beings talk about accepting the 'facticity' of life, including the movement between opposite polarities: how life consists of life and death, light and darkness, love and hate, ugliness and beauty … literally, thousands of opposites.

People tend to get into stress and difficulty when they cling to only one side of a pair of opposites. For example, people make great effort to be as beautiful and intelligent as possible, to always do the right thing and never make mistakes. People focus on life and avoid the idea of death. People seek a lifestyle where no change happens and to live in a 'right way' that will always make them happy.

Much of what Osho talked about was how life includes everything and that when this is understood and accepted, a deep relaxation can occur.

Hypnosis is a particularly effective tool to deliver 'truisms' or universal metaphors to the unconscious mind to allow people to relax with 'what is', thereby resolving a number of problems that people bring to Hypnotherapy.

For instance, many people who are terrified of getting old and dying hold a deep belief they can avoid change. The cosmetic industry is so successful because of this fear. In deep trance, a number of metaphors or truisms can be offered to deal with these fears and invite acceptance of a more holistic and realistic vision:

Trees, as they get older, become more and more majestic with deep roots ... When a tree in a forest falls, or is blown over in a storm, it provides the basis for the growth of new trees ... Within our every-changing bodies, fifteen million blood cells are produced every second and another fifteen million destroyed ... Rivers come from small sources and eventually flow into the sea where the wind will collect that same water and return it to the source as rain ... How even the sun will eventually burn itself out and our planet will die for lack of heat ...

Anatomy of a Session

The first part of any session is 'information gathering': What is the client's problem? Instead of the problem what would they like for themselves? And what resources do they need to help them to get that outcome?

Many different things can happen in a session. The overriding principle is to activate the client's unconscious mind to find resources and solutions so that a satisfactory outcome can be achieved in the client's life.

The Hypnotherapist's task is to use his or her creativity to stimulate the client's own creativity, to support a client's unconscious mind to solve its own problems and find its own solutions.

The therapist might offer suggestions, metaphors, anecdotes or stories that can trigger associations, new ideas, perspectives and possibilities within the client. In this way of working, the Hypnotherapist does not give answers or tell clients what they should do.

Rather, the therapist is carefully calibrating and offering suggestions in an open way, so that if they are not appropriate the client does not need to accept them. This is a different approach from more traditional Hypnosis, which tends to tell people 'to be' and 'to do' certain things.

It is not that the Hypnotherapist has the right answer – in this way of working there is no right answer. There is only the client's potential to find a creative solution to their own issues and to take responsibility for their own lives; to find their own 'ability to respond appropriately'.

This was one of the major messages that Osho gave: to take responsibility for your own life in a profound and meaningful way, developing the ability to respond rather than react.

The Ericksonian way of doing Hypnotherapy helps people connect with a deep part of themselves and makes them aware they are much more than they think they are. It is also helps people befriend themselves on a deep level.

Of course Hypnosis, as a technique, is not a panacea for everything. So much more is involved in a session. When one is working with people, it all comes down to the ability to connect with the human being that is in front of you, to your willingness and capacity to create a stable therapeutic and healing relationship where corrective experiences are possible.

'Yes I Can' – A Relaxation Technique

Here is a technique that we use to help people relax and learn to be more present, more in the 'here and now', especially during a period of quiet meditation, or just sitting doing nothing.

Sitting comfortably, say to yourself three things you can see in this moment.

For example you can say:

"I can see the light coming in through the window".

"I can see the pattern of the carpet on the floor".

"I can see the colours of the wall".

You can follow this with a suggestion to yourself, such as: "And I can begin to relax now".

Then you say three things that you can hear in this moment, remembering to use actual experience.

"I can hear the sound of passing traffic".

"I can hear the sound of music in the room".

"I can hear the sound of my own breathin".

Then you can make a suggestion like "And I can begin to relax even more now and let an inner comfort deepen within".

Then say three things you can feel in the moment.

"I can feel the chair I am sitting on".

"I can feel the temperature of the air on my forehead".

"I can feel the breath I am taking now".

As before, you can follow this with another suggestion, like "I can now relax even deeper and let any worries or concerns drift away".

Then you repeat the whole procedure by saying to yourself two things you see, two things you hear and two things you feel, each followed by suggestions. Finally, you say one thing you see, one thing you hear and one thing you feel.

It is best to begin by familiarizing yourself with the basic technique – seeing, hearing and feeling things – before you start adding suggestions.

The order of the senses was Visual (V), then Auditory (A) and finally Feeling or Kinesthetic (K). You can also do them in a different order, the possibilities being VKA, AVK, AKV, KVA, and KAV. One of these combinations will work best for you. Experiment.

Why does this technique work? Because by reporting ongoing sensory experiences to yourself you are creating what is known as a "Yes set".

I can see the light coming through the window – Yes I can.

I can hear the sound of a passing car – Yes I can.

I can feel the support of the chair I am sitting on –Yes I can.

Having created this mood of 'yes' you can easily add a new suggestion:

I can begin to relax now – Yes I can.

This simple and effective exercise can be very helpful to bring you into the present moment, because you have been pacing your ongoing sensory experience, as it happens, in the present moment. It has the effect of supporting your intention to relax and quieting the mind.

CHAPTER NINETEEN

Art Therapy

Meera

"Now your paintings are beautiful, so you start an Art Group."

This was Osho's message to me as I sat in front of him on November 19, 1979, in *darshan*, our personal evening meetings with the Master. "Start an art group" he said – and that was it. No explanation, no guidance on how to do it. He told me to go back to my seat.

It was a surprise, to say the least, because I hadn't shown any of my paintings to Osho, but in a way I should have expected it. So much experimentation was happening in those days around Osho: all kinds of therapy groups, all kinds of meditation methods, all kinds of music, theatre, handicrafts. It was a rainbow spectrum of human growth and creativity.

My background was that of an artist. I began by studying art as a student in Tokyo, then toured Europe's art museums and finally landed in Toledo, Spain, where I became a founder member of Tolmo, a group of ten international artists. To me, at the time, painting was an all-consuming passion, an end in itself, but then I met Osho and everything changed.

I told my fellow artists, "I'm leaving for Pune and not coming back. There might be a different way to use art … for human growth. Art can serve much more than what we know. I am going to discover that". They were sad, because we had become a close-knit group of friends as well as artists, but what could I do? My heart was strongly pulled to join Osho's work.

So I left my Spanish group and travelled to India, only to be invited by Osho to start another art group! But how to put it together? The answer evolved through the process itself. I soon saw that, when people who have had no education in art start

397

painting together, they bring a new and fresh quality on the paper. In fact, I became aware that knowledge about art can even be a hindrance to discovering one's unique expression.

In Toledo, we'd been very serious about our art. We began at the time when General Franco was ruling Spain as a dictator, so we wanted to use our art to express personal and political freedom indirectly. And we were carrying many intellectual ideas about what modern art should be and how it should influence society.

I was also aware of conventional ideas about art therapy, because during the 60s and 70s people discovered that painting can work directly with the unconscious part of the human mind. One can 'read' the psychological state of a client, or patient, by looking at their paintings and seeing what kind of unconscious forces are being expressed. One can also hope to see a client release stress, neurosis and perhaps even psychosis through this form of expression.

To me, however, art can be used for developing human consciousness, not just for analysing psychological disturbances. For those interested in personal development and human growth, you can use painting as an immediate mirror. What is happening inside you is reflected in your painting, so you look at yourself while you paint.

Osho tells us that everybody is unique. Essentially, we are already that which we think we need to become. So becoming isn't the answer. Rather, becoming is a problem. Being is the answer and we simply need to recapture this forgotten space.

So this is my work: to help people remember the forgotten language of their own being, to realize they are okay as they are and to see what prevents them from singing a song of nature, singing the song they already have inside themselves, making life more rich and meaningful.

Nonverbal Therapy

There are many kinds of therapy, but painting is unique. Picturesque expression is nonverbal and connects directly with the unconscious part of our minds, so the intellectual and rational part cannot interfere. That's why you can be so surprised at what comes out during a painting session – good and bad. In a very short time, this work helps people to understand what is happening in their psyche.

When you stop, look and see what you've done, you have to face it as your own reflection. Then, either you throw it in the garbage so you don't need to acknowledge it, or you look at yourself and accept it.

Most conventional methods of art therapy rely on an analytical approach. But the problem is that the more you analyse yourself, the more you move into the structure of the mind, and the mind has no exit, no way to get you out of the limitations imposed by your own personality.

With the essential, with the immediate, there's a better chance for people to re-experience their original self, hidden deep inside, which is your child-like spirit. This spirit never dies and its most precious quality is innocence. We are trained to forget our innocence, but it is always there, waiting for us to rediscover it.

Saying 'Yes' to the Body

An important aspect of Osho's vision that I use in my workshops is the understanding that the body comes first. The body is the most innocent part of our existence, unlike our busy, chattering minds, which often ignore what the body tries to tell us.

So this is one of the foundation stones: to come back to our body, to say 'yes' to our body, to make more roots in our body. When we do this, we also become more open to the present moment. Bringing awareness to whatever action is happening – drinking, sitting, walking, brushing our teeth – we are brought into a greater awareness of our physical body and in this way directly into contact with the present moment.

I work a lot with body awareness. I come from Japan, where there are many traditions that focus on the feet. For example, Gautam Buddha's Vipassana meditation has a walking stage in which one's awareness is focused on the sensation of the feet touching the ground. In the 'No' dance school, all emphasis is placed on the feet and back. My dance teacher, Kantomoe, who is ninety years old and still performing, used to say to me, "When your back is absolutely present, then you become a dancer – then dance is happening".

Saying 'yes' to the body, means saying 'yes' to ourselves. But we don't say 'yes'. Instead, we hide our nakedness. We have forgotten the grandeur of living naturally, like animals and we have supressed our animal vitality. This vitality is necessary, even essential, on the spiritual path, because energy needs to move if it is to stay alive and vibrant. Whatever we hold back, accumulate and keep bottled up inside us, becomes poisonous.

Saying 'Yes' to Your 'No' Inside

One of the understandings I work with is that paradox is a fundamental law of life and that apparent opposites complement each other. For example, our capacity to say 'yes' is dependent on our ability to say 'no'.

Just think for a moment about when you were a small child and had to obey the authority of your parents, other adult relatives, older brothers or sisters, schoolteachers. You had to say 'yes' even though, on many occasions, you wanted to say 'no'. It was a survival measure.

This 'no' was suppressed because you had no choice, you had no power to resist, but nevertheless the energy of your 'no' didn't vanish into thin air. It was locked inside, buried but not forgotten, and meanwhile you learned to say 'yes' mechanically, out of habit, out of the need to be accepted in society.

The outcome is that your 'yes' is not a real wholehearted YES! It has no energy behind it. It is filled with lingering resentment and half-hearted attitudes. So, if we really want to say 'yes' with our full enthusiasm and energy, which is essential in order to release your creative and artistic impulse, then we must first give ourselves permission to say 'no' with full force.

400

There are many ways of doing this, including the cathartic stage in Osho's Dynamic Meditation, but I have also created special exercises in my painting courses to convey this experience. One of them we will be described in the Primal Painting section of this chapter.

Whatever the method, the aim is the same: to regain our dignity as whole and authentic human beings who, when they say 'yes' really mean it, and the same with 'no'. You may not have thought about it in this way before, but it is a real challenge to be human, because there are so many aspects of our being to explore, reclaim and develop.

Self Portrait

In recent years it has been a common sight in the Osho Meditation Resort to see around fifty people sitting on the marble floor of Buddha Grove with a rather large piece of paper attached to a wooden board, resting on their knees, and a tray of paints nearby, looking into a mirror and painting what they see. It is quite a spectacle and you can see how intensely they are looking; as if these people are determined to find themselves.

Whenever an artist makes a self-portrait it involves more intensity than when making portraits of other people. Painting oneself requires a certain existential drive, energy, or search, as if the artist is deeply asking the question "Who am I ... who am I *really*?"

The face is ninety percent of our identity and yet, when you look at people's faces, they are stiff, almost frozen. Ordinarily, they don't move. They don't change expression. It's as if we have a fixed image of ourselves and don't want to risk going beyond the facade we present to the world around us. This façade has somehow become our trademark.

If you look at children, you notice they are free to move their mouths and muscles of the face in a very alive and expressive way, and this is because they don't cling to an identity like we do.

In my courses, I work a lot with freeing the muscles of the face and one way we do this is to stand opposite a partner and look at each other while doing self-massage on the face muscles, making the face elastic by pulling this way and that. Then I invite them to make faces, as if we have all suddenly become small children who are totally free to make any kind of facial expression. People soon become aware that this is fun and I encourage them by saying things like, "Okay, make your face as angry as you can. Which animal are you in this moment? Are you a tiger, a lion, or a mouse? Show your partner!"

After a while, I ask them to stop and simply gaze softly into each other's eyes, with no effort, which gives people an opportunity to understand something new about themselves – "I'm not just a fixed face with a single expression" – and to also see beauty in the partner's face in front of them.

This is a way to help people loosen up and relax. Then, when they are sitting and settled, I invite them to close their eyes and touch their own faces, to create a deeper understanding of its shape and form. This always reminds me of Helen Keller, the famous blind and deaf American woman who learned to break out of her isolation with the help of her teacher, Anne Sullivan.

Keller travelled the world and in 1955 came to India where she met with Prime Minister Jawarhalal Nehru several times. After Nehru had permitted her to touch his face, Keller said it had "real nobility and a high-domed brow one needs the gift of a poet to describe. It looked like what I had always seen in my mind, a personality that elevates human ideals and goals and shoves the world nearer to true civilization".

This incident inspired me to create a self-portrait group using the same approach. In it, I invite participants to become almost like blind people, developing the same sensitivity and intuition, gathering information through the medium of touch. I tell them: "Close your eyes and start touching, as if you have never touched your face in your life".

I guide them to explore the face through different ways, using fingers, palms, the back of the hand and finally I introduce them to touching like a sculptor working with wet clay, using a strong touch that helps them get a deeper impression of the face – and of themselves.

At this point, I invite them to touch the face with one hand, feeling the shape and form, then grab a sponge with the other hand, dip it into grey paint and give expression to the face's form on the paper with the sponge, as if they are sculpting themselves on paper. We don't use brushes. Touching the paper with a small sponge is the only method.

We have already prepared the colour, which is very specific – a mixture of white, black, navy blue and a little red. The result is a fine tone of grey and this is the only colour we use for self-portrait, which keeps things very focused, raw and stark, so no one can hide their reality behind pretty colours.

Normally, in life, we tend to avoid grey and black. It's a psychological instinct, a fearful feeling that "If I go in there, into darkness, I can't come out again. I will arrive at a dead end". But, by using a hard-surfaced paper, we can bring the needed contrast of light into the portrait.

Beginning with dark grey, we bring in the lighter tones by washing off some of the layers, exposing the paper's underlying whiteness. "You can see where the light illuminates your face – it's obvious, no?" I ask the participants. "So, take a sponge, dip it in water, squeeze it, then stroke it across your portrait where you see the light in the mirror".

This action has a remarkable effect. The white surface of the paper emerges from beneath the grey paint, creating light on the face. The novelty of this method of painting surprises and delights everyone. Light does not have to be imposed. It can be revealed.

Losing Control

Once our participants have 'sculpted' the face, creating a basic shape or outline on the paper, they become more careful and cautious. They want to peek … open their eyes … make sure they don't destroy what they've done. They want to control what happens.

I encourage them to forget about saving what they have created, which can be difficult, because we are so trained in the habit of staying organised in everything we do. But, eventually, they all get the point and soon everyone's paper is completely covered with grey paint.

When I invite them to open their eyes, they get a shock. All form has gone. All has become grey. Then I ask them, "How is it for you, when everything is grey?" And the really interesting thing is that many people say the same thing: "Finally, I can relax. I can let go of my self-image. I don't need to be anybody".

It's symbolic, a reflection of how we live our lives. I want people to become aware how we live in a state of continuous tension because we always want to hang on to something... our bank balance, our love partner, our family ... anything to create a sense of identity. The fear of losing identity is inbuilt in our system and that's why we can't let go, we can't relax.

Looking Softly

The next step is for people to become more conscious of how they look at themselves. I make a distinction between looking aggressively, with energy going out through our eyes towards the viewed object, or looking softly and receptively.

"I want you to be the guest of whatever is being reflected in the mirror". I tell them. "Rather than looking at the person in the mirror, allow the feeling that the person in the mirror is watching you".

This can be a strong experience, because when you allow yourself to be 'seen' in this way you sink deeper into yourself, connecting with more and more impressions and feelings. All your judgements about yourself start to surface ... your wrinkles, you are getting old, your eyes are too big, too small, your lips should be fuller ... People begin to encounter all those wrong beliefs they've been given about what is acceptable, what is unacceptable.

As they go deeper, many participants begin to see the imprint of their parents – their mother, their father – because this face has come from them, through their genes. When this happens, some people really don't want to look into the mirror; they start crying and catharting, saying things like "I thought I was finally free from my father, that's why I changed my name and became a sannyasin, but when I look in the mirror I only see him!"

Self-portrait means you can't get away from your parents, you have to face them, because there is every possibility that either the mother or the father will be seen in the mirror, looking at you through your own features. When this happens, I guide participants into a gestalt dialogue, using two cushions, one for the parent and one for themselves. In this way, they can experience being the parent, open a channel of communication and resolve any conflict that may still be lingering. For example, one may start to understand "I thought my father was making my life hell, but now I can also see it from his perspective".

I also use Family Constellation, guiding participants to choose representatives for the mother, the father, and in this way exposing the energy dynamics of the original family situation. This type of therapy is described elsewhere in this book, so I will simply say it brings a much deeper understanding of one's parents, their destiny, their emotions and the love with which they brought their children into the world.

One exercise is particularly strong, in which I guide the participants to enter into the mother's body, becoming the mother. This is helpful to understand the mother's life and her emotions. Everybody carries a strong imprint of the mother, although normally we experience this only from the child's perspective.

When these exercises are combined with the ongoing process of looking into the mirror and painting, participants gradually experience a state of acceptance, not only of their parents but also of themselves and how they look.

Slow Construction

As you can see, self-portrait has many dimensions, using many exercises that are not directly concerned with painting, but after each exploration that takes us away from the paper, we always come back to it again, enriched by new insights and new experiences. In this way, the portrait slowly acquires depth, unique expression, containing glimpses of who we are beneath the surface. But of course, our tendency is to be in a hurry to establish form, structure and detail. For example, it's a strong temptation to put in the eyes very quickly. It is a common tendency in almost everyone.

I warn them, saying, "Take your time, no hurry, don't put the eyeballs yet!" Because once you put in the eyeballs, you become paralyzed. You can't move. The proportion may be wrong, they may be too close together, too far apart, they may be too far up the head – a very common mistake, because not many people realize their eyes are actually half-way between the chin and the crown of the head.

So I invite people to really take their time, like a constructor at a building site, beginning with the foundation, which is, as I mentioned before, to embrace the face they see in the mirror through the medium of touch.

It's not uncommon for me to say, "Take off your eyes. It is not time yet for us to do that. Now touch your face again, with eyes closed, yes, that upper part of your head from the crown down to the eyes … feel how big it is … ".

This is how we create the self-portrait. A time comes when we are able to say 'yes' to our inner being reflected in the mirror, to the Buddha inside. Beyond the imprints of our father and mother, beyond all the judgements, we see our original being, looking out at us from the mirror.

That's the point when I say, "Look into your eyes. See how much they shine. Don't waste this opportunity. Receive this energy. Receive yourself through the mirror".

Now participants begin to understand. This isn't just a class in creating a portrait of themselves. This is a long, deep look inside.

This is an encounter with themselves at soul level. It is an act of creating oneself.

Darkness and Light

Darkness is scary. When it surrounds us, we get panicky. We want to change things fast. We want to get out of it and move towards the light. Therefore, one of my important tasks is helping people become comfortable with darkness and make them feel that "darkness is my home".

In Pune, I take them down into the Resort's underground therapy chambers where it is possible to create an atmosphere of total darkness. For most people, this is a very unusual experience. Rarely, if ever, do we choose to put ourselves in a total blackout.

I've written about this extensively in my book, ReAwakening of Art, but it's worth going over again because it's an essential process in personal transformation.

Each participant stands close to the room's padded walls. When the lights go off, I invite them to face the wall and to struggle against darkness, pushing hard against the wall while remembering impossible situations from their lives – situations where they felt trapped.

It's symbolic, but very effective. In this atmosphere of darkness, it's easy for people to connect with an overwhelming feeling of hopelessness: the struggle to achieve what we think will make us happy, the fight to get rid of what we think makes us unhappy; this inner conflict has been going on a long, long time in everyone's life.

There is another, level, too. Darkness is associated with death. This all-pervading space of blackness, of nothingness, has a feeling of finality. It looks like the end of everything, the end of our story. Darkness is death. There seems to be no way out, with no bottom to it, no further step to take in any direction. In terms of colour, too, we have reached the end -- darker than black doesn't exist. I encourage people to continue pushing against the wall for at least 15 minutes in order to create the opportunity for a dramatic change in gestalt.

As they stop struggling and relax into the arms of darkness, I read a quote from Osho, in which he explains that darkness is the absence of light. In a way, it goes deeper than light, because light comes and goes; light has a transient quality. Even our sun will burn out one day, grow dim and then go dark. Osho points out that darkness is an eternal quality of existence, a universal principle, neither negative nor positive. And it is always there. From this darkness we come. To this darkness we return.

I don't encourage an emotional reaction to these experiences, because the connection to darkness goes deeper in silence, but sometimes it happens on its own. For example, on one occasion, in this part of this exercise, a young Italian woman started weeping. When I asked her what was happening, she replied, "I've never used black in my life. I've been studying art for twelve years and never used black because somehow it's too intense. Now I see how much I've been avoiding this colour, because it reminds me of death".

All of these attitudes are reflected in painting. When I see that people haven't even taken the lid off the black pot, I know they are avoiding hidden qualities in themselves. So the next step is to sit with a plain sheet of paper and begin to paint on it, using only black.

While they are absorbed in this work, after a few minutes, I suddenly turn off the lights. "Keep your eyes open and continue to use your brush on the paper", I tell them.

There is something magical about painting blindly – really blindly. I can guarantee that nobody in this group has done such a thing before. Your eyes are open, your hand is moving, painting is happening... yet all you can see is darkness, absolute darkness. In such a situation, you are helpless and also innocent, because none of your normal control mechanisms can function.

I guide them to paint, first with their eyes open and then later with eyes closed, so that gradually there is a merging of inner darkness and outer darkness. In this way, slowly, they are becoming friends with darkness. And even though they can't see what they are painting, they start to sense that painting is a process happening inside themselves.

After a while, I light a small candle, softly illuminating the room. Now, I give out pots of white paint, because the next step is also significant. First, we moved away from light into darkness. Now we are moving back from darkness to light.

In this way, we play with black and white, gaining flexibility to move in both directions: from darkness to light, from light to darkness. Gradually, we are moving into a state of balance, in which opposites are allowed and embraced.

This is my understanding: if people are motivated to explore their psychology, becoming aware of how they are suppressing their energy, emotions and fears, they will naturally begin to include darkness in their paintings.

After this experience balance becomes easy. If the painting seems too dark, light can be added; if it's too light, darkness can be added. And what you learn through painting, you can apply in your daily life, too.

Partner Painting Portrait

One of the strongest experiences I had in my life was being a model for a sculptor. He was working with clay, creating sculptures of my face and I was modelling for about three hours a day. I didn't know anything about meditation at the time – I was only a twenty-year-old student – but while modelling I had a very powerful experience that life consists of something more than just the physical body.

There was an inner light shining through me and out of myself through my eyes and even through my skin. The artist was looking at me all the time and it seemed that this inner light of mine responded to the attention he was giving me.

It may not be the same for everyone, but I have found in my workshops that the experience of being a model for an artist is a beneficial one for most people. You really become aware of your inner qualities when other people are looking at you and painting, or modelling. So I bring this into my courses in a structure called 'partner painting'.

Partner painting is a good preparation for the intensity of creating a self-portrait. I invite participants to choose a partner, then sit in front of each other with eyes closed. I ask one to be the active partner while the other is passive. I guide the active partner to come closer to the passive one and gently touch this person's face, exploring its structure, curves and detail. The passive partner simply receives. After a few minutes, they stop, switch roles and repeat the exercise.

Then we place two pieces of paper next to each other between the two partners and one becomes the painter, while the other becomes the model. The most important element in this exercise is to maintain eye contact, so both people have their eyes open. What is happening on the paper is not the priority, but the feeling that is being created between an artist and a model.

For this portrait, we use watercolour or ink, which gives the painting a transparent quality and I know, from the beginning, it is going to be kind of chaotic, because – with the emphasis on eye contact – not a great deal of attention is being paid to the form of the painting itself.

After fifteen minutes, I ask them to change roles and now it is the turn of the other partner to be the painter. In this way, we change over every fifteen minutes until the paintings are more or less complete. Then it is time for the two partners to share their experiences: how it was to be the model, how it was to be the painter, and so on.

Primal Painting

Primal Painting is the backbone of my teaching. Childhood issues are touched in almost all my workshops and trainings, but in Primal Painting we make it the main focus, taking a long, deep look at attitudes and feelings that we've kept locked inside ourselves since we were very young.

Everybody carries beliefs about themselves that were formed

410

during those primal years, including all kinds of notions about one's own creative abilities. Unfortunately, these beliefs are usually negative. Even therapists who have worked on childhood issues in other ways often say things to me like, "Painting? It's not for me. I have two left hands!" Meaning, of course, they have no talent.

Yet when I look at small children, under the age of three, they never question their creative abilities. If the materials are given – crayons, paints, charcoal – they just use them, following their curiosity and natural sense of playful adventure.

For example, I used to take care of my sister's child when she was two years old. One day, as an experiment, I gave her several big pots of colours, big brushes and many papers, without any instruction. I didn't say, "Now paint a house," or "Now paint a tree". I just left her alone to do whatever she wished. She stayed there for hours, continuously inventing new ways to paint on different papers.

That's when I understood it's not right for adults to say things like "I have no talent". It's pure nonsense. Of course, not everyone can be a Picasso or a Van Gogh, but everyone can access their natural sources of creative energy. It's our birth-right. It's a gift from the generosity of existence.

One of my first tasks is to guide people back in time to one of those childhood moments when creativity was blocked. To do this, I invite them to sit in front of a blank sheet of white paper and pay attention to memories and feelings triggered by this simple act.

"Maybe you wanted to impress somebody – your teacher, your mother – and you couldn't manage it," I suggest. "Maybe you painted a picture and one of your parents expressed disappointment. Maybe somebody told you 'Don't paint this way... that's not right!' Maybe you were pushed or pressured too much.

"One way or another, you got the message to be somebody else than you are, and in order to be loved, to be accepted, you trimmed and adjusted your creative energy to match the expectations of others. Slowly, these restrictive patterns became an ingrained habit in all aspects of life. Whatever the activity – relating, working, dancing, talking – the same negative attitudes were repeated".

It's my aim to uncover those memories where shock occurred, because this is one of the keys to undoing the damage. Once you start remembering, once you consciously re-live a traumatic experience with the wisdom and compassion of an adult, healing starts to happen. The blocked creativity begins to flow again.

A playful attitude can be very helpful in healing trauma. Having evoked unpleasant memories by asking participants to sit in front of a blank piece of paper, I then encourage them to find as many different ways to play with the paper as possible.

Like Children on the Beach

In general, even though the atmosphere in the room is playful, people want to make some sense of what they are creating – as if somebody is watching and judging what they are doing. So I encourage them to remember when they were small children on the sea beach, spending hours building a sand castle, then treading on it and destroying it with carefree happiness. These two opposite impulses of creativity and destruction were naturally present in us when we were children.

Encouraged by my words, the room soon becomes a circus: people are flying paper kites and aeroplanes, poking their heads through holes, making animals, tearing papers and throwing pieces at each other … everyone goes crazy and bits of paper are flying everywhere. It's a great way to release energy that has been trapped in negative attitudes.

Then I tell them to put all the paper in the middle of the room – a small mountain arises – and stand in a circle around it. It is a great moment. Looking at this pile of paper, we can dismiss it as rubbish, but through innocent eyes it can also be seen as a beautiful sculpture, full of unknown forms and contrasts of light and dark.

Exchanging Paintings

Another exercise we use in Primal Painting is to create a painting, then find a partner, exchange paintings and continue to paint – on the other person's painting. This simple act can create strong feelings. Of course, when somebody interferes with 'my painting' or 'my precious creation' we don't like it. We feel indignant, invaded, overpowered. We want to protect our own territory, our possessions. So this is an effective exercise to show us our attachments, our blind spots, our patterns.

After painting on the other's artwork, the next step is to give expression to the triggered feelings, beginning with the statement "I don't like what you did to my painting … " and then going into detail, connecting with one's feelings and expressing them.

This is an opportunity to say 'no' very clearly and directly, which, as I explained earlier, isn't something most people generally like to do. During our upbringing, we learned to compromise, to hide what we are really feeling and this developed into a chronic condition, a habit.

With this kind of suppression, pressure keeps building up inside, year after year, so that when release finally happens it is likely to be an explosion. In such a situation, there won't be much communication – just two people reacting against each other. So we create a safe space to allow and express a clear 'no'.

When this has been fully expressed, we switch to the opposite expression. Now I encourage participants to say "I like what you did to my painting" and explore with an open mind how the painting has been improved by this contribution from another person. Whenever you say 'no' to another person with sincerity and authenticity, something magical starts happening: it creates a space in which a genuine 'yes' can follow.

This sudden switch in perspective can give rise to profound insights. We see that what we have been rejecting is really an unlived part of our own creative potential. We see that we have been repressing our spontaneity, our willingness to take risks, our curiosity to explore new styles. We have been playing safe, because that's what we learned as children.

Now we are being pushed out of our comfort zone in a search of our authentic creative energy. This becomes apparent when people come to the end of the exercise and begin to work on their own paintings once more. This is when they experience a new freedom to go beyond their old ideas about 'my creativity'.

These are all ways of helping to focus people on their psychology and have a deeper understanding of what they have been hiding and suppressing, as well as giving them a vision of just how big and unlimited their creative potential can be.

Group dynamics are tremendously helpful in this process. For example, I invite people to notice what opinions they have of each other's work, because it's inevitable that when you criticise another person's work you are making a projection and denying something in yourself. We are all mirrors to each other, reflecting infinite possibilities.

Sharing is given a big role in the group process because it brings us closer to our real feelings, challenging us to be continuously aware of what is happening inside. So many people, so many different nationalities, so many perspectives, all gathered in a single workshop … naturally, in a short time, our problems are being exposed and mirrored by others. In this way, we learn sincerity and honesty.

Giving Birth

I help people to be a midwife to their own painting. In other words, I bring them into a psychological space where they are willing to let a painting give birth to itself – where they are not 'the doer' but just helping it along. When they don't apply ideas about where the brush strokes should go, when they're not in their heads, painting becomes simple, maybe even easier than dance or music.

Painting is instinctive; it is one of mankind's earliest achievements. Before any sophisticated language existed painting was part of our lives – ancient cave paintings are testimony to this fact – and this reflects a truth which remains with us today: pictures go deeper than words. They make a stronger impression.

But words can block the paintings that want to express themselves through us. As I've said before, criticism inhibits creativity, judgements limit our vision, so I've developed many ways to bypass them. For example, one is to invite the participants to stand up, move around, and stand in front of a painting they don't like. I put on music and ask, "If this painting makes you dance, what kind of dance will it be? Receive this painting in a soft way and let your body respond to what your heart is feeling ..."

Some people feel an earthy quality, so their bodies make slow movements that reach down towards the ground. Others feel light and airy, so they are almost on tiptoe, reaching upwards as they move to the music. So you become the translator of the painting, expressing its impact on you. It's a telegraphic message without words, so people become more connected to their own sense of beauty through a painting, which, at first glance, was not pleasing to their eyes.

"Imagine bringing your own painting here and merging it with the beautiful aspect of this painting. What kind of painting will it become?"

Something incredibly important can happen in moments like this. As the participants stand before this painting, imagining their own painting merging with it, they are painting with their hearts. Nothing is happening on the outside, but inside the painting is happening, in their private inner space.

This can be an important healing experience, because many of our psychological wounds are created and sustained through separation or alienation – the feeling of being an island with no bridge to the rest of humanity, or to nature.

This simple exercise helps people become part of this beautiful existence, because through it you can keep on painting, anytime, anywhere, without paints, paper and brushes. After all, who cares about material painting? What is really important is your own energy and your way of looking at life. You can participate in the creativity of nature. You are creating, each moment, without doing anything.

An Osho Therapist

In my work, I not only facilitate workshops; I also teach participants how to work with other people by using art and therapy together. So it's important, here, to say something about the attitude and approach of an Osho Art Therapist.

We feel good when a certain person is around, sensing that, as a result, our own inner state becomes more silent, more relaxed, more at peace. Something in us is touched through this person's presence and we feel an inner expansion, lightness, warmth, or sense of well-being that is beyond the usual feeling of friendliness, beyond the level of personality.

Many people know this experience from going to a doctor with an ailment. If the doctor is good, just his presence starts to make you feel better; it has its own healing effect. The same goes for a therapist. His job, or her job, is to 'hold the space' for the participants, so they feel safe and supported in their exploration of their own psyche. Slowly, in a workshop, people build confidence that it is okay to relax their defences and open up to each other.

One of the best ways to create this collective atmosphere of trust is to work with participants individually, in front of the whole group. It touches the hearts of everyone when an individual really starts looking into his or her inner darkness, which consists of all those things like energy blocks, or psychological issues, which up until this moment in life have prevented a free flow of energy and creativity.

Then other people get the feeling: it is a pity to hide, to hold back, because through hiding you can't work on yourself. One by one, they take support from each other and gain courage to share their own issues, looking at patterns that may have been stopping their spontaneity and aliveness, whether it is with a lover, a family, or at work, with a boss … and so on.

416

The only way to reach to another human being's heart is to be a real human being yourself. To be real, you need to look into yourself and for this meditation is essential. A watching space, an ability to see one's own character is needed and out of this watching love arises naturally. Love is a by-product of meditation. So the therapist's job is not so much to give advice, but to help people catch the fire of watchfulness – this is the key for working with people.

This is the purpose of my work. I want to give a hand, helping people open up to everything, both inside and outside, because life can be so rich, so beautiful, and can offer so much opportunity to grow.

CHAPTER TWENTY

Gurdjieff Sacred Movements

Amiyo

Once, I heard Osho say that when he will die, he will dissolve into his sannyasins, and this is how I experience it. When I transmit the Gurdjieff Movements, I feel that Osho is being expressed through them: the inner stillness, the quality of presence, the love that radiates towards my students, the deep respect and gratitude I have for Gurdjieff and his body of movements.

I have spent my whole life searching for deeper experiences of myself through different techniques of dance. I saw the Gurdjieff dances for the first time in 1989 in a movie called *Meetings with Remarkable Men*. At the time, I was living in India, in Osho's commune in Pune. Osho handed me a video of this movie, saying "There is nothing remarkable about this movie except the last ten minutes" – referring to the part where the dances are being performed.

This fragment of the movie, made in 1979 by Peter Brooke and Madame de Salzmann, and based on the book of the same title written by Gurdjieff, was the first ever public display of Gurdjieff Movements. Osho told me to find the keys hidden behind the movements. Little did I know that I was engaging in what would become a major part of my outer and inner life.

At first sight, the vision of these movements electrified my skin. I could hardly breathe! In my many years of different dance practices, I had never seen anything like it. I spent three days and nights continuously watching the strange movements, concisely edited in the movie, trying to decipher the choreographies. In those days, we had only very basic videotape, so slowing down the movie was not possible.

It was not easy, as I did not know anything about the Gurdjieffian logic and mathematics behind the choreographies. In fact, Gurdjieff himself was not so forthcoming about his methods, nor from where they came. Born in 1872 in Armenia to a Greek father and Armenian mother, he absorbed spiritual teachings from many different cultures, including ancient temple dances.

In the early part of the 20th, Gurdjieff became a mystic in his own right, stating that the vast majority of people live in a state of hypnotic 'waking sleep' and asserting that it is possible to transcend and awaken to a higher state of consciousness.

Clearly, the dances in this film were part of Gurdjieff's effort to help others 'wake up'. But how? The film was carefully cut so as not to unveil the secrets that had been kept hidden for so long. But supported by my Master's trust I suddenly had a shout of 'Eureka!' as all became clear.

Osho sent me wholeheartedly into the discovery of the secrets hidden behind the outer form of the Gurdjieff Movements and, to this day, the journey continues. Three months later, when Osho left his body, I felt that this offer was a beautiful farewell gift from him.

Although the dances were beautiful and charismatic, it was not their aesthetics that were mesmerizing, but something behind the visible movement, an inner state that was reflected through a particular quality of presence in the eyes of the dancers. I was witnessing a dance 'technique' which involved not just the body but the whole of the 'being'.

A dance was not created; rather dancers were created through it. They seemed to be animated by forces that belonged to the movements themselves, by a new quality or substance. Was this the 'dancing soul' Osho had talked to me about?

The Meeting of Meditation and Dance

Behind the dance there was an absolute, unmoving state of consciousness and also a unique pulsation within the group as an organic unity. I sensed that each outer movement was just the tip of the iceberg. Inner forms lay within, like a living path and a path for life. Maybe, I would finally have an opportunity to embody my long years search for a meeting between meditation and dance.

This search had taken me in 1978 to Pune and Osho. Prior to that, in France, I had reached what seemed to be the pinnacle of my life as part of a modern dance company, where I had a lot of freedom to be creative, with no financial worry, as the company was paying me a decent salary.

But I remained dissatisfied. Dancing facing a mirror, dancing to impress the public, constantly pushing the body to its limits in order to stay abreast of the latest trends, always on the lookout for something new, better, unique and original, seemed so superficial. Intuitively, I knew that dance was more than this ... that a spiritual dimension existed, but wherever I turned the answer would not come.

Until a friend told me about a place in India, where many of the meditations included both movement and stillness. This brought me to Osho. After being in Pune for few months, I was trying to decide whether to return to my company, to share what I was experiencing, or to stay in the commune, when Osho asked me to start a dance group. Speaking to me in *darshan*, the time of intimate talks between a Master and his disciples, Osho told me:

So you can continue here and you can start teaching here. And dance is not really a thing to be learned. It is not an art; rather, it is a meditation. To think in terms of art is to miss the whole point. You can learn it technically and you can become a technical dancer, but you will miss the reality of it. It will be just the body – the soul will be missing.

The soul comes through being meditative. The dance is not the real thing, but a dancing soul! Then the body moves of its own accord. You can make the body move but the soul will not move. The centre never follows the circumference but the circumference always follows the centre.

Now it is time to go ahead on your own. So, dance, help people to dance, and develop your own style, develop your own ways, develop your own technique. One has to be innovative. People try to be imitative. Learning from somebody else is good in the beginning. A little bit of information is helpful, it prepares your body, but one should not be too much attached to it. [1]

All and Everything

During this period, Osho asked all the group leaders working in his commune to be trained in bioenergy and bodywork. I vividly recall how much I hated going down into the soundproof basement chambers every evening, screaming, beating pillows and suffocating in the humid closeness of sweating bodies. But to this day I'm grateful it happened, as it gave me a deep, inner experience of energy movement, unlocking the body, and showed me the intimate connection between emotions, breathing and movement.

Many different therapies were being offered in Pune and I had the opportunity to experience them, which helped me understand that my dancing path was not the only way to awakening; that many beautiful roads were leading to the same goal. Osho's vast vision did, indeed, include 'all and everything' – the name Gurdjieff gave to his three-volume trilogy on mysticism.

Sitting and listening to Osho, day after day, I learned to include and respect views that were different than mine, to avoid the dangerous pitfall of fanaticism and narrow vision, which I'd come across so many times during my earlier adventures into the spiritual world.

I loved hearing him speak on Taoism, Yoga, Tantra, Buddhism, Zen ... and so often on Gurdjieff. It was clear that Osho had an abiding affection for the Armenian mystic – mostly, I suspect, because they both shared a love for being rebellious, disturbing people and making trouble.

During these years, hearing Osho speak daily on physical, emotional and mental awareness, on the true meaning of discipline, on the importance of stillness and silence, on meditation ... I slowly absorbed these qualities in my daily life.

Being born French, I grew up on cheese, jealousy and emotional dramas. By nature, I loved movement, intensity and action.

Sitting silently in meditation was foreign to my usual behaviour. However, by and by, I learned to understand that true movement comes from stillness, that an agitated and restless person cannot create anything of value.

All these years prepared the ground for me to be able to welcome, respect and honour the extraordinary quality of Gurdjieff Movements. Again and again, I find myself in an inner state of awe, seeing the genius and richness of Gurdjieff, who so masterfully reproduced such a body of movements – perhaps two hundred and fifty in all – so different, so simple, so complex, so 'prayerful' or warrior-like, all leading us to the experience of being 'in the moment' in a state of wakefulness.

These dances are a fragment of a larger teaching that can be felt directly and clearly through the experience of practicing the movements: calmness, alertness and focus being some of the qualities acquired; agitation being one of the main obstacles to receiving the benefits of the process.

So, after living and teaching for eleven years close to Osho, I must have been prepared for what lay ahead of me, when Osho decided it was time to start practicing the movements in his commune. Three days after I'd decoded the movements on the film, Osho told me to start teaching them.

Transmitting the Movements

I had the feeling Osho was pushing me into the swimming pool before I could even swim. But I trusted and loved him, so, in spite of my fear, I happily dived, body and soul, into what would become a totally new discipline for my body, mind and heart.

A little while later, help came from the outside world and I met my teachers. These were former students of John G. Bennett, the British mathematician, scientist and mystic, who'd been a close disciple of Gurdjieff and who'd founded a spiritual school in the UK based on Gurdjieff's methods, including the sacred movements. Bennett died in 1974.

At first, the work of learning the dances involved a great deal of coordination, rhythm and inhabiting the body in a new way, through these unheard of positions, transitions, sequences: feet doing one rhythm, right arm another, left arm another; or strangely asymmetric sequences, with one part of the body doing something round and soft, the other part doing something staccato.

But I discovered that the process offers much more. It also acts at the level of energy channels, unlocking emotional knots, discarding old belief systems. Sometimes, I felt inner restructuring at the level of the brain, as if untrodden paths were suddenly being transformed into open circuits, new bridges were being opened between the two hemispheres.

The right hemisphere of the brain learns through pictures, intuition, merging and love. The left hemisphere learns through precise patterns, exact perception, observation of details. So this sense of the two hemispheres coming together was a meeting of science, art and religion, or as Osho puts it: mathematics, music and meditation.

When the music and the movements stopped, I watched a new quality of energy running powerfully inside the body, and the joy that this realization brought swelled up in my heart. I had never experienced this in my whole dancing career.

I started to be emotionally involved, yet detached through watching. I started to investigate all the different fragrances of the movements: the peaceful inner space of the dances Gurdjieff refers to as 'prayers', the longing and nostalgia awakened by others, the heart-tearing feeling of knowing that 'I' is much more than what I am living; the inner fire, passion and determination triggered by dervish dances, and also the humour contained in some pieces.

Teaching others was a great way to go deeper into the movements myself. I started to embody in my flesh the language of the different positions and transitions from one to another. It is not just reaching to the position that matters. It is the way 'there', this continuous uninterrupted message given by the movement in the positions and in the transitions – sometimes a small change in the spatial position of the fingers and the meaning changes drastically. And the underlying feeling, coming to me again and again that someone is 'home', watching, realizing that BEING stands in front of DOING.

The movements show me there is no in-between state. Either I am present, with the three centres – physical, emotional and intellectual – supporting each other, or I am not present.

From Abstraction to Experience

Hearing Osho speak so clearly about awareness and going beyond the mind prepared me to receive the movements. And now, practicing the movements helps me to viscerally experience the awareness and No Mind that Osho talked about so often. The movements are a vehicle to create consciousness. As life is movement, it is a basic, existential method.

Before Gurdjieff and Osho entered my life, the state of meditation was for me a pure abstraction, an interesting idea but far away and foreign, because like most people in the West I was identified with an active personality. Aware of modern man's compulsion to be always active, Gurdjieff, as well as Osho, introduced the movements as a way to enter into meditation.

Now, entering into the movements is for me like putting on silk gloves: entering in a space of quietude, smoothness … finally coming home. Even in the midst of the most active dervish dance, there exists a centre where all is stillness. In this peaceful, still spot, is my real existence.

Each movement starts in stillness, beginning with an inner preparation and then moving outward into expression. Only the one who has understood stillness, which is the source, can understand the movement. Only the one who has understood silence can understand the word. This is why most people are speaking, speaking, speaking … without understanding what they are saying, and without understanding what is contained in the word, because they do not understand silence, which is the source of all words.

It is the same thing with movement. For most people, movements are an escape from themselves, from their own stillness, from their own silence. They enter the movement as an escape. This is why some people like to practice Gurdjieff movements, rather than to sit silently, because in the movements they still can escape from themselves. But one day, if they continue, they discover stillness within the movement.

Through the movements, I can feel this state, the more subtle vibrations emanating from it, when the mind stops. Yet, in this 'no mind' state, I am not a just mindless zombie. Thinking stops, but 'seeing' and 'awareness' continue. I see myself as I am, I see what is around me, so clearly, I receive the music and its quality, I am aware of the inner and outer world. I am aware that I am here ... I am.

Searching for Balance

Movements belong to the hygiene of inner life, as an inner discipline and a door to freedom. Through them, we see our life, our oscillation between the external world and the inner world. Through them, we are searching for a balance where we can have 'one eye out' and 'one eye in', not being taken and overwhelmed by outside events or people, and not withdrawing into the deepest recesses of ourselves, unable to communicate and to act.

Learning the dances, one of the first realizations is that our scope of attention is very small, a few seconds and then the mechanical train of our thoughts takes us away. This is reflected immediately by a 'mistake' in the outer form, or we lose the true grace inherent to the movements. This continuous temptation to be distracted mirrors the daily life of most people, who are manipulated by emotions such as joy, love or pain, according to the strings that are pulled by the wheel of life.

But by and by, with a quality of attention becoming more sustained and subtle – merely a question of practice and intention – another vision unveils, a new sensation of the body, not in its different fragments, but as a whole, vibrating, living being.

And the taste of these two states is so different. One is the foggy taste of sleep, doubt, anxiety; the other one is the taste of freedom, spaciousness, harmony and silence.

425

In our daily life, most of the time, our attention is scattered: "I still have five e-mails to answer before going out ... brushing my teeth with one hand ... cleaning the sink with the other ... must remember to call my mother ... listening to the news on the radio ... trying to put on my shoes ... check my mobile for messages ... " This goes on all day long. Then we wonder why we are so tired at night.

In this multi-tasking society, to remember Gurdjieff's statement seems more appropriate than ever: "When you do a thing, do it with the whole self. One thing at a time."

Sincerity not Seriousness

Just imagine you are entering a group room and watch this scene: a few people are sitting with their eyes closed, resting quietly inside. Others are lying on the floor, relaxing the body-mind. A few are working as a little group on a sequence of the movements, helping each other and comparing notes. At this very moment, there is an atmosphere in the room of collected attention, friendship, inner discipline and relaxation, silence, care, effort and non-effort. I feel utterly at home ...

To work by ourselves can be very arduous. For me, a group is the beginning of everything, a group of people seeking to live in a more conscious way, and, most importantly, sincere but not serious. Humour can do miracles on this path. Both Osho and Gurdjieff were very humorous mystics. Osho helped me not to become too serious on this strongly disciplined path of teaching the movements:

A sincere person is totally different. He is true, but not serious. He is seeking, but not as a goal. He is seeking it just like a child seeks things: if he finds, it is okay: if he doesn't find, it is okay also. A child is running after a dog, and just in the middle he finds a butterfly; he changes. He starts running after the butterfly; and then, by the side, there comes a flower – and he has forgotten the butterfly and the flower takes his total attention. He is not serious, but very sincere.

When you can pay your total attention to something, it is sincerity. And when you are paying your attention only as a means, you are cunning. You really want to reach the goal, and this is only a means. You are exploiting; you are exploiting the path to reach the goal. For the child, the path is the goal. And for the religious person also, the path is the goal. Wherever I am, it is the goal. Whatsoever I am, it is the goal. ~ Osho[2]

In this relaxed, yet sincere attitude, the group grows in awareness and love, away from stiffness, competition, comparison, judgments. Osho is a constant reminder of the importance of compassion and non-judgmental awareness in the work. Yes, the path has rigour, it asks for efforts at first, but Osho taught me that the basis remains love, a friendly attitude that includes moments of easy flow as well as moments of difficulties.

Soon, the students become my friends, my family. We share the same love, the same passion, the same search, and this creates bonds that go far beyond time and space. Usually, the process develops over a few years, not just one seminar, so it gives us the opportunity and the time to develop a deep intimacy, a communion of presences, not based on personality, or verbal exchanges, but on a common search and the closeness that a silent awareness brings.

If you meditate alone it will be more difficult to enter into it, but if you meditate with a group it is very easy, because the whole group works as a unit. After two or three days your individuality is no more; you become part of a greater consciousness. And very subtle waves are being felt, very subtle waves start moving, and the group consciousness evolves. So when you dance, you are not really dancing, but the group consciousness is dancing; you are just a part of it. The rhythm is not only within you, the rhythm is also without you. The rhythm is all around you. ~ Osho[3]

The Warrior and The Lover

It is said that Gurdjieff's path is based on will, so there is a danger: if we are not alert, the practice of the movements can bring more rigidity to someone who already has this tendency, and it can attract people who are thirsty for power.

Trying to focus the mind in a new and unfamiliar way, it is possible for a student to create friction; to fight with his own mind and in this way create a certain feeling of being powerful. Conquering the outer form of a movement, a feeling may arise of strength and victory over inertia, clumsiness and lack of coordination. With this, the ego rejoices. One feels a sense of invincibility: "Ah! I made it!" In this way, power reinforces the ego and prevents the most important experience: the deeper feeling of mystical revelation that the movements can give.

As Osho puts it:

Concentration will make you a man of will. Meditation will make you an emptiness.[4]

Gurdjieff's path has often been presented as masculine and wilful, a path of effort ... effort ... and more effort. In my understanding, effort is needed, of course, but we have to emphasize the right balance between effort and relaxation. I find myself adopting a more feminine approach, inspired by Osho's vision and also by Madame de Salzmann, one of Gurdjieff's closest disciples.

Before his death in 1949, Gurdjieff gave responsibility for transmitting his teaching to one of his main disciples, Madame de Salzmann, an accomplished musician and dance teacher who had worked with him for thirty years. In particular, he gave her the work of transmitting the movements, which she did with extraordinary intelligence and love.

Madame de Salzmann added a more feminine touch. She emphasized receptivity, letting go and an acceptance of what is. She also introduced silent sittings and meditation in the practice, which were unheard of with Gurdjieff. In fact, she seems to be the bridge between Gurdjieff and Osho, whose books she was reading, by the way, during the last years of her life. She died in 1990, the same year as Osho, at the age of one hundred and one.

During the practice of the movements, when the body is utterly relaxed, when the heart is at peace and the mind still, a point comes of letting go, of surrendering to a higher force, which is the force of the group, of the music, of the movement itself. This moment of transition between effort and non-effort is subtle and individual: there can be too much effort, or not enough; on one hand, inertia, on the other, a certain form of violence.

While Osho was alive, I was invited to be one of his 'mediums' during energy transmissions to disciples who sat in front of him during evening *darshan*. These were precious moments of totally letting go into ecstasy, abandon, as he was touching my third eye, and it felt like the ocean was taking possession of me, while everyone around me was humming and swaying, accompanied by wild music.

As mediums, we allowed ourselves to become one with this powerful wave of energy and yet, at the same time, we had to be able to come back to this earthly plane, with our feet on the ground, as soon as the music stopped.

Through Osho, I learned what would be repeated during the practice of the movements: the beauty of allowing the inner movement to take possession of me, surfing on a collective wave of music and grace, a living embodiment of the archetype that each movement represents. For example, in a dervish movement, my whole being burns with an intense and dynamic awakening. In a prayer, a fragile yet vibrant link is established to an inner space of peace and union.

My life with Osho, within the practice of Gurdjieff's 'Fourth Way', has shown me how important it is to live the dimensions of love and will together, in one sensitive harmony.

As I mentioned earlier, the movements bring us in touch with the existence of an inner force, with the power of our will, with our potential, which could lead to a dangerous misunderstanding: a certain domination of ourselves and others.

But this is not real power. The real power is not to dominate others, or even ourselves. Our power lies in the incredible aliveness of our vital force, an inner flame that wishes to affirm itself in its totality and helps us accomplish our higher destiny.

Real power gives us multi-dimensional sensitivity and the strength to surrender to a higher dimension.

In deep gratitude, I bow down to this universal wisdom so beautifully transmitted to us by Osho and Gurdjieff.

CHAPTER TWENTY-ONE

Satori: Awareness Intensive

Ganga

Satori is a powerful and intense method of inquiry into oneself. In Japanese, the word *satori* means glimpse of enlightenment. This process aims at establishing a solid connection with the source of life in us – our Being. We all have glimpses of it, but they mostly happen accidentally, for example when watching a beautiful sunset, holding the hand of a beloved, or swimming in the ocean.

To come out of this accidentalness we need to discover how we can arrive at the same space consciously. For this, we use a set of questions as a device to move through the layers of our thoughts and feelings into a state of no-mind and Being.

To distinguish these questions we call them koans, because a koan doesn't have an intellectual answer in the way that ordinary questions do. A koan needs to be experienced directly. Thinking about a particular question is not enough. One has to embody it, moment to moment. One becomes the living answer in each moment – new, fresh and alive.

These koans are called life koans because as long as one is alive they can be experienced directly. However, there are no final answers as a completion to one's quest. Rather, one needs to sense, feel, explore into *how it is now* – over and over again.

The awareness needed to pursue this ongoing self-inquiry has given the process its name: Awareness Intensive.

Who Am I?

The most famous and well-known life koan is "Who am I?" which grew out of ancient Indian spiritual traditions. It was popularized and attracted global attention in the mid- through the teachings of an enlightened mystic living in South India called Ramana Maharshi.

The actual structure of the process, originally called Enlightenment Intensive, was created by American therapist and spiritual seeker Charles Berner in 1968. In a stroke of genius he put together three elements:

The question "Who am I?" which, as I say, came from India.

The Western method of co-counselling, developed by American psychotherapist Carl Rogers.

The discipline of working on a koan in the Zen Sesshin tradition facing the wall in silence.

Berner's intention was to evoke in his clients the 'sense of self' – as he called it – without having to face a wall in meditation for endless years. His observation was that people who acquired this sense of self made faster progress in a therapeutic situation than those who didn't. Looking for a solution, he came up with the Enlightenment Intensive structure.

When it arrived in Pune, the process was renamed Intensive Enlightenment by Osho and was one of the first groups to be introduced. From 1976 onwards, hundreds of people arriving at the Shree Rajneesh Ashram (as the Osho Meditation Resort was then called) took part in the Intensive Enlightenment process on Osho´s recommendation.

Ashram facilities were very limited but the number of participants in the group kept expanding. The biggest one took place with two hundred and fourteen people who had access to only six showers. Yes, you might say, we were dedicated to the search!

In the late 90s, Osho replaced "Who am I?" with the question "Who is in?" and there is a story about how this happened, which I will relate shortly.

Other Life Koans

Other life koans that we have used over the years include: "What is love?" "What is another?" "What am I?" "What is trust?" "What is freedom?" "What is life?" "What is surrender?" "What am I like if completely alone?" "What is relaxation?" "What is consciousness?"

Any of these koans represents a key to unlock the door of one's Being and all are inherent in the master key "Who am I?"

Why use so many koans? Because, in our experience of working with all kinds of people, different forms of social conditioning create different types of personality which tend to be lopsided in their development.

As a result, people tend to be in touch with some aspects of themselves and not with others. By creating a range of questions, we invite participants to approach the core from different directions, some of which will prove fruitful while others less so. But the goal of all koans is one and the same: to have a direct experience of Being.

The Being is that always-present, healthy, free, whole, luminous, loving and mysterious core and source in us, out of which we emerged through the door of birth and into which we will disappear through the door of death; the direct experience of that will come in due time ...

The Structure

In Pune, the Intensive Enlightenment process was structured to last three days. The Satori process was developed as an extension of Intensive Enlightenment, lasting five days, a week, ten days, or even longer. Both Intensive Enlightenment and Satori come under the umbrella title Awareness Intensive.

The purpose of the Satori process is to reconnect with our core, with what we are born with – that which we can never lose but might have forgotten.

For this to happen, we need to let go of what is not ours – what we are *not* born with – but took on board during our education, conditioning and socialisation process of growing up, i.e. beliefs, habits, ideals, self-image ... to name a few. In a single word: personality.

Looked at from this angle, it is a paradoxical work to search for what I already have inside me (Being) and discard what never was mine (personality).

433

Now that we know what tool we are using and what we are looking for, we can proceed to a description of how to use it.

The main work happens in Dyads, meaning two people face each other and communicate in a structured way. One will listen and be passive, while the other will inquire and be active. As the process starts, the passive one will say: "Tell me who is in" (or whatever the partner's koan is). Then he will listen with his full attention (including head, heart & being) but without any reaction or comment, simply being attentive, being present, taking in what is being expressed.

After five minutes, the roles are reversed and the partner who was listening will now be asked by the one who was speaking, "Tell me who is in." She will take the koan inside, intending to have a direct experience of herself and her koan in this moment. She will open to the experience and whatever comes to her consciousness – as she is holding the koan – she will communicate to her partner.

She will repeat the sequence for five minutes until she hears the gong, when, again, the roles will change. This goes back and forth for forty minutes, after which people will be asked to find a new partner and begin the process again.

These Dyads are spread out over the day, from early morning till late evening.

Other elements of the process include daily active meditations: Dynamic Meditation and Kundalini Meditation. Another, is the time set aside each day for work meditation – cleaning, cooking, gardening and other simple tasks – with the intention to bridge the spiritual with the mundane, to bring meditative presence into daily activities.

And of course there are meals, walks, naps and occasionally another of Osho's active meditations, such as Mandala, Chakra Breathing, No Dimensions, Nataraj. During the whole day everybody is in silence (apart from the Dyad work).

The main difference between the original format of Berner's Enlightenment Intensive and the subsequent development of Osho's Intensive Enlightenment is that Dynamic Meditation and Kundalini Meditation have been added to the process, providing opportunities to experience oneself directly through active meditations that involve the body as well as the mind. Also, less emphasis was paid to diet.

Emptying the Mind

The technique is simple and very effective. By and by, all is said. What one did in the past (the story, the memories), what one wants or should do in future (hopes, ideals, expectations), what one is and is not (identifications), what one believes or does not believe. When these usual ways of describing and defining ourselves have been covered, the thinking mind with all its statements *about* oneself tends to be exhausted.

Now the journey into *directly* experiencing oneself can begin. Now it gets interesting because ... how to do that? Going blank, realizing *I don't know* and feeling empty inside are all challenges that need to be faced. This is the end of our comfort zone. Once this hurdle is managed, the journey becomes very alive and wondrous, at times psychedelic, full of insights, enjoying the senses.

But this, too, is not the end of the journey. It goes on and on until all separation disappears between what is experienced and the experiencer herself. Subject and object become one. One radiates in oneness, one is oneself, one is at home.

Shift to "Who Is In?"

As the years went by, a significant change took place in the 90s as a reflection of the process becoming less goal-oriented. Gradually, we came to understand that to focus on having an 'enlightenment experience' didn't seem so helpful as it created an immense tension for the spiritual ego to somehow 'get it'.

On the other hand, if the focus was on being present with 'what is', in the moment, accepting 'who and what I am right now', a participant will quite naturally end up in a direct experience of himself or herself. In this way, it was easier to come to the core and root of Being and experience a gap between the personality and 'the real me'.

The deeper one settles into Being, the more one's personality recedes. It's like the leaves of a tree. Any leaf can guide me to the roots of the tree if I follow it backwards, retracing how it grew: from leaf to branch to stem to roots. Likewise, I can use any sensation, feeling, emotion or thought – any event – to come back to the core by asking "Who is experiencing this?"

Then I will not get lost in events. They will not lure me away from myself. Instead, they turn into an opportunity, a stepping stone on the way back home to the real me, to that part of myself that never changes and which is always there. It cannot be escaped, whether we recognize it or not.

Another historical nugget happened in 1989, during a series of discourses given by Osho called *Yahoo! The Mystic Rose*. In one of these discourses, Osho hammered "Who am I?" as the most stupid question ever asked. This was very surprising to many listeners, since on other occasions Osho had made it clear he was very fond of "Who am I?"

Anyway, next day I sent him a question, asking if I should look for another job, since I was working in a process where we did nothing else but ask this 'stupid question' all day long. His answer came back: the new question is "Who is in?"

A new ball game altogether.

Osho's Personal Guidance

I leave it to everybody to discover for themselves what the differences are when working with this new koan. And I will add two personal titbits:

In 1976, I went to darshan and spoke with Osho. 'Darshan' is the traditional Indian name for personal meetings between a mystic and his disciples, and for many years Osho was available to us in this way, every evening.

I told him that I was feeling split inside during the meditations. He answered, "It will be good for you to do Intensive Enlightenment, because it bridges the left side and right side of the brain."

Well, there I was! Osho was guiding me back into the same

process in which I had taken part the year before as a total greenhorn to meditation – and which had totally changed my life. So that's how the love affair started, which is still unfolding after thirty-eight years.

The other situation also happened in darshan, a little later. I asked Osho if I should stay in a relationship or get out of it. He took out his Zen stick and said: "Such minor things as who you are together with, you can decide yourself." This left me dumbfounded, because all my attention had been focused on this love affair. Osho left me wondering what could possibly be more important than a relationship with a man.

I mention this to illustrate how Osho's guidance influenced my understanding of the process and moulded the way I work with people.

He set pointers but left it to me to figure out what is involved, be it paying attention to building bridges between the two sides of the brain, or looking for what is important in life.

Interviewing Participants

After introducing people to the Awareness Intensive method and letting them know how the days ahead will be structured, the main medium for working with people individually is the interview. It's a one-to-one meeting, conducted during the process, in which I find out how a person is getting on with the koan.

I focus on four points:

• Is the person taking the koan inside, or is he looking outside and comparing his own 'performance' with the way others use the koan?

• Is he intending to have a direct experience of himself and his koan? Here, I'm looking at the intensity of a person's motivation: does he really want to find out? If not, why not? Usually, the reason has its roots in deep personal wounds, such as of lack of self-worth and a resigned, hopeless attitude to life.

• Is he open to what comes to his consciousness spontaneously, as he is holding the koan, or does he have a pre-planned agenda of what he thinks he should be experiencing?

- Is he communicating what he finds authentically, or is he selecting and editing?

In the first interview, my attention is mostly on the mode of inquiry – very little on the content of what is being said.

In the second interview, I focus on how the horizontal and vertical dimensions are represented. By 'horizontal' I mean the dimension of time, matter, events, like sensations in the body, feelings, emotions, thoughts; in short, that which comes and goes, plus whatever we took on board during our life's journey – memories, stories – and also whatever is currently happening in the outside world.

By 'vertical' I mean the dimension of the eternal, the soul, spirit, godliness, being ... howsoever you like to call it. In short, that which doesn't change, that core of consciousness with which we are born.

In any given moment both the vertical and horizontal dimensions are present in us. However, due to the nature of mind, we tend to be more aware of the horizontal dimension because something is usually happening there. The mind is restless, constantly in motion, seeking novelty, entertainment – it's a real junky for change and sensation.

Meanwhile the vertical dimension is peacefully resting in the background all along, a pool of energy and *isness*, a storehouse of the potential, of resources, of the un-manifested. One can easily forget it because nothing ever happens there. It just is. It's the *I am* before I move into action.

After a day of working with koans, most people are quite skilled in expressing what they feel, but if I suddenly say "Stop!" while they are speaking, they look puzzled or even annoyed. Usually, I make this intervention after they say "I am ... " and before they specify what the content of their experience is, like "I am bored, angry, happy, my foot is itching ... "

I ask them to slow down, to experience this *I am, I exist,* without the usual content that follows. For many, this is a turning point. They consciously experience their existence for the first time. The foundation stone is laid. The anchor is cast. They are no longer oblivious of their existence, nor do they take it for granted anymore. It's like being born for the first time. Puffs of love and gratefulness fill the air.

So, in this interview, the subject of the experience – the experiencer – is emphasised and brought into the foreground. This often triggers a self-empowering experience in the participant which finds its expression in statements like: *This is me, I am me, I am, I am here*. End of playing mouse – beginning of living like a queen or king.

Accepting without Judging

In a further interview, I might check on how a person deals with her experiences. At this stage, we are dealing with the conceptional overlay, that which is not part of the facticity of the moment, but which is piled on top of it. Here, we are getting into attitudes and interpretation of the facts.

For example, is this person appreciating or judging whatever is arising in the moment? Does she say 'yes' to the experience or reject it? Is she hooked on ideals and busy touring fantasyland and the future? Does she have the courage to welcome and embrace herself, just as she is right now, without trying to change and improve herself? Can she let go of ideals, comparison and beliefs – just for this moment? Can she stop adding more suffering to herself and allow herself to just be?

In this context, contracts with other people – parents, teachers and spouses – often come to the surface and these need to be addressed before the individual can stand up for herself and enjoy being who she is without feeling guilty.

For example, it may emerge in an interview that a participant is feeling angry and this she judges as bad. Perhaps, as a child, she learned never to be angry – her parents condemned her for it, or she wanted to please her mother or father by being a 'good girl'.

So now it becomes difficult for her to get into the experience of anger – just for what it is.

Or perhaps she doesn't dare to experience her divineness, because she has been taught it is a sacrilege to declare oneself god-like in nature. But if this is happening, what to do? She needs to feel this and give herself permission to express it. I will help her face her spiritual attitudes and religious beliefs so that she can allow and enjoy the experience.

Again, the focus is solely on how the person deals with her experiences, not on what she is experiencing. As far as experiencing is concerned, whatever is, is. There is no right or wrong.

Another method of support in an interview is to help a participant anchor his or her experiencing in the body. For example, a participant might tell me "I am bored". In response, I ask "How do you know this? How do you recognize it?"

Usually, there is a moment of bewilderment and then new understanding arises: "Oh yes ... My breathing is shallow ... my eyes feel tired ... I slump over in my chair ... "

It's a bit like using reverse gear to go back to our experiences as kids. As children, we are what we feel, we have an experience in the body, but we don't have a name for it – we are not yet intellectually articulate. But soon we learn to give it a name. For example, mother says "Don't be shy!" That's how we learn to label our feelings, realizing "Aha! This uncomfortable sensation that I'm feeling is called shyness".

As grown-ups, we need to reconnect with the physical experience of feeling in the body. If we want to live our energy, then we cannot simply make an intellectual report of what is being felt – it might be safer than really allowing a feeling, but is not much of a life.

Signs of Truth

Yet another topic in the interview is reading the signs of truth. How do I recognize if truth is spoken, either when listening to somebody else, or when hearing myself speak?

This can be a complex issue, because we tend to describe our experience of truth according to our so-called 'learning styles', which have been categorized as Visual, Auditory or Kinaesthetic. These categories were developed in the 1970s as part of a new approach to communication and personal growth known as NLP – neuro-linguistic programming – pioneered by psychotherapists Richard Bandler and John Grinder.

The system asserts the following:

● Visual learners have a preference for *seeing* what they're being taught – by reading written words, for example – and they also tend to think in pictures.

● Auditory people learn best through *listening* – attending lectures, joining discussions, listening to CDs and tapes.

● Kinaesthetic people prefer to learn via *experience* – by moving, touching and doing (for example, conducting science projects).

Depending on what perception type my participants may happen to be – visual, auditory, or kinaesthetic – they will describe their experience of truth accordingly. Since many of them are unaware how to detect and communicate it, I help them become aware of it.

For example, truth may be like a clear visual image for some, or something that rings true and 'sounds right' to others, or a feeling that gives 'goose bumps' on the skin, while others just have an inner knowing.

It's good for people to know how they experience truth, because the deeper they move inside themselves, the more they move into aloneness. On this inner journey, it's helpful to have some landmarks, because there is nobody to ask and it's easy to get lost.

Participants may also need assistance concerning the 'answers' given. It can happen that an inquirer does not recognize he's had a direct experience of himself. It can also happen that someone declares "I've had a direct experience" when this is not the case.

Addressing the group as a whole occurs when issuing instructions, clarifying the technique, or pointing out the stages one tends to go through during the process. In this context, I want to mention a beautiful book by Osho containing all the steps of the inner search called – very appropriately – *The Search*. In this book, the classic story of the Ten Bulls of Zen provides the basis for Osho's discourses. The story is told in three different forms: as pictures, as poetry, as commentary.

General Reflections on the Process

Awareness Intensive is a meditation process, not therapy. Nevertheless, it is very therapeutic. It is all about accepting and relaxing into *who I am* – not about growth, improvement, or becoming anything other than I am already. Once the seed of acceptance is planted, love, trust, awareness, compassion, sense of humour and joy are the flowers of this immanent transformation.

The brain has two sides and both are equally activated in the process.

In step one, when taking the koan inside, the right side comes into play through the act of receiving.

In step two, when intending to have a direct experience, the left side is active and masculine qualities like focus, motivation, setting the frame of mind for the task are in demand.

In step three, when opening up to whatever is present in the moment, the right side brain is called for and feminine qualities are involved, like being receptive and surrendering to what comes. The material coming up is full of pictures and metaphors, often chaotic, bits and pieces, incoherent and discursive.

In step four, when communicating what has been found, the left side with its concepts and logic is challenged to bring this 'mishmash material' into a concise understandable expression without losing all the nuances, poetry and flavours of the inner.

Even in the position of being the listening partner, both sides are present. Giving the instruction "Tell me who is in?" is a left side job, being receptive and listening is a right side job.

This continuous and equal stimulation of both sides of the brain bears fruit in easier access to intuition and inner resources. There is less fear to go in and face oneself and the unknown. Verbal expression becomes clearer, more precise and colourful with many shades – not just black and white.

I see the integration of polarities and opposites, the welcoming and embracing of whatever is there, as an integral part of Osho's teaching, whether it is left-right, male-female, good-bad, holy-mundane, material-consciousness, moral-immoral, effort-relaxation. I see the effects of this understanding reflected in the attitudes of participants as they go through the changes demanded by the Awareness Intensive process. Their horizon becomes wider.

Since all is allowed and nothing needs to be condemned or excluded, since everything has its place, a relaxation starts to happen. One is less judgemental and more loving and friendly towards oneself and others. A life affirmative attitude arises and in its wake participants can enjoy a sense of humour and playful creativity.

Years ago, I saw a funny animation film depicting a great striptease. When the woman was naked I expected the movie to end, but no, she kept on going ... taking off her hair, her eyes, ears, nose and tongue ... ending up as a dancing skeleton. Very seductive!

Well, the Awareness Intensive takes striptease one step further: even the skeleton, the final straw, has to go. Nothing, or no-thing, is left and only consciousness remains.

Perhaps the experience of this ultimate state of utter nudity is best expressed by the famous *Heart Sutra* of Mahayana Buddhism:

Gate gate paragate parasamgate bodhi swaha.

Gone, gone, gone forever, never to return. What ecstasy! Alleluia!

Poetry often replaces prose when mystics attempt to describe this state. There is a poem by Jalaluddin Rumi, the celebrated Sufi mystic, translated and published by Coleman Barks, which is dear to my heart because it sheds light on the Awareness Intensive's essential koan:

Who Says Words with My Mouth

All day I think about it, then at night I say it.
Where did I come from, and what am I supposed to be doing?
I have no idea.
My soul is from elsewhere, I'm sure of that,
and I intend to end up there.
This drunkenness began in some other tavern.
When I get back around to that place,
I'll be completely sober. Meanwhile
I'm like a bird from another continent, sitting in this aviary.
The day is coming when I fly off,
But who is it now in my ear who hears my voice?
Who says words with my mouth?
Who looks out with my eyes? What is the soul?
I cannot stop asking.
If I could have one sip of an answer,
I could break out of this prison for drunks.
I didn't come here on my own accord,
And I can't leave that way.
Whoever brought me here will have to take me back home.
This poetry, I never know what I'm going to say.
I don't plan it.
When I'm outside the saying of it,
I get very quiet and rarely speak at all.

Frequently Asked Questions

Who can take part?

Anybody who wants to find out who is in.

The youngest person taking part in an Awareness Intensive facilitated by me was sixteen, the oldest eighty-four.

A certain amount of life experience is helpful (frustration is a great trigger for the motivation to look in) and some physical fitness is needed (tight schedule, lots of sitting).

The process provides a space for self-inquiry. It does not

444

provide therapeutic guidance. It totally respects the individual process and the themes, speed, pace and mode of inquiry of each participant, without interfering with the content presented. This also means each one has to find his or her own way through the maze by trial and error.

That is the beauty of the Awareness Intensive. It holds the space for everybody, in trust that each can do it. We all suffered much from being told to 'do it this way' or 'do it that way', and from 'this is right' and 'this is wrong'. I recall, as a child, my beastly brother once looked at me with wide eyes and said: "Uh, you are chewing the wrong way round", which slowed down the intake of my breakfast considerably.

The Awareness Intensive is not suitable for people who are in the middle of a severe emotional crisis or nervous breakdown. They need a more guided or even medical support than provided in the Awareness Intensive.

Are there any requirements?

Yes, wanting to know: "Who is in?" Apart from that, everybody has what it takes. It's like a bud that knows how to open and a seed that knows how to sprout. Everybody is perfectly equipped by existence with all the necessary tools: a body with its senses, a heart to feel, a head to think, consciousness for witnessing, and a being resting in oneness.

Is there a right way to work in the Awareness Intensive?

There are as many ways as there are people. Some take a bungee jump straight to the core without paying attention to what they meet on the way. Others collect many insights on the way and carefully clean up the house as they move in. There is no right way to do it; there is only *your* way to do it. It is a journey into your uniqueness.

Can I repeat the process?

Definitely, since it is a meditation process, there is no end to it. But if you expect to have the same experience as last time you ask for trouble. You cannot repeat any experience, nor can you continue where you stopped last time. It is always fresh and new and it is most helpful to stay in the beginner's frame of mind of not knowing. Hence the Zen saying: "Not knowing is the most intimate … "

Can I do it with my partner?

Yes, though sometimes it is better to have the space all to yourself. With a partner we usually have contracts, which can get in the way of moving into the unknown and opening new facets of yourself.

Couples or very close friends are asked not to work together for the first two days until both are settled in the technique. Then they can face each other. The simple fact that each has equal time to communicate, to listen and to be listened to, can be very transformative for a relationship. This is especially true if both are speaking in an *"I–me"* language that focuses on, for example, "I feel hurt," or "I feel sad," thereby exposing vulnerability, rather than slipping into the *'you'* language of blame and interpretation, such as "You are always … " and so on.

Do I choose my koan?

Everybody starts with the koan "Who is in?" or "Who am I?"

Usually, the next koan will emerge from an individual's responses. The way he expresses and communicates his experience of "Who is in?" will provide me with an indication of what other koans will be helpful and then these aspects of his essence can be explored deeply … and so it continues.

But, as I said before, the master key "Who is in?/"Who am I?" can open all doors of the inner world. There is no graduation from lesser koans to more significant ones.

What do I get out of it?

Most of all, I learn to make the famous one-hundred-and-eighty-degree turn from the outer to the inner. It makes all the difference, because through discovering my own core I also experience my essential connection to the Whole. I no longer live a life of separation and isolation. I no longer believe I am like a single leaf on a tree – continuously in danger of be blown away and dying a lonely death. Rather, I am living as the tree itself, with its infinite potential to produce millions of leaves as the seasons come and go, deeply rooted in life. I will notice the effects of this by having more trust in life, by having more distance from the personality and the procession of ego problems. I learn not to bite the finger pointing at the moon, but turn to see where it is pointing.

The moon represents a few things. It represents the feminine, the soft, the poetic, and one has to move towards the feminine, towards the soft, towards the poetic.

To live outside oneself, logic is enough, arithmetic is enough. To live outside oneself one needs to be hard, violent, aggressive, one needs to be competitive, cruel, cunning; but to go inside just the opposite is needed. Logic is a barrier there, and hardness of being won't allow you to go in. One has to become soft, one has to melt; one has to disappear as a rock and become a flower. Only the flowers become enlightened, only the flowers come to know what life is all about. The rocks only struggle but they never arrive, and the flower has already arrived. ~ Osho[1]

Another metaphor for what happens in the Awareness Intensive is presented in the symbol of the double-edged sword of awareness: one side points to the object of the experience (changing), one side points to the subject of the experience (not changing). Mind oscillates between the two sides and tends to be oblivious of the middle.

In the direct experience of oneself, one sits – so to say – in the middle, aware of both sides at the same time, one sword with two edges.

In this state, there is no process, there is no separation, only oneness.

Always be attentive to that which never comes and never goes, just like the sky. Change the gestalt: don't be focused on the visitors, remain rooted in the host; the visitors will come and go.

Of course, there are bad visitors and good visitors, but you need not be worried about them. A good host treats all guests in the same way, without making distinctions. A good host is simple a good host: a bad thought comes and he treats the bad thought in the same way as he treats a good thought. It is not his concern whether a thought is good or bad ...

Gurdjieff used to say that only one thing is needed: not to be identified with that which comes and goes. The morning comes, the noon comes, the evening comes, and they go; the night comes and again the morning. You abide: not as you, because that too is a thought – as pure consciousness; not your name, because that too is a thought; not your form, because that too is a thought; not your body, because one day you will realize that too is a thought. Just pure consciousness, with no name, no form; just the purity, just the formlessness and namelessness, just the very phenomenon of being aware – only that abides. ~ Osho[2]

A further outcome of the process is: I will be more self-oriented and less other-oriented. A participant expressed this very beautifully: "I found a reference point inside which I'd never had before; a place of home, of knowing that even in the middle of emotional turmoil there is something else. A gratefulness that, after so many years I know now what the Himalayan Peaks are that the mystics speak about. The light went on and never really went off again – something I was waiting for after years working in therapy and with the personality. This meditation retreat gave the feeling that IT IS POSSIBLE."

The implication is that the point of reference is now inside myself, not in the other. I am orientating myself on my own experiences and values. In consequence, I need to take response-ability for my actions, including the mistakes I make. In other words, I claim my own authority and withdraw it from others. But, be aware! This attitude also means the end of blaming others and playing the victim's game of 'poor me.' It also opens the door to a great deal more breathing space, freedom, spontaneity, fun and love for myself and others.

Epilogue

Each chapter of this book is written by a different therapist and, as the reader may have noticed, their views sometimes differ. Each contributor emphasizes a slightly different aspect of Osho Therapy.

These differences illustrate a significant point: Osho Therapy is not a system with a definite set of rules. It is less concerned with concepts and structure, more focused on accessing a state of being. Therefore, the emphasis is not on what technique or method is being used, but on the way in which it is applied.

Osho Therapy is a subtle phenomenon, more like a flavour than a dogma. While journeying through a kaleidoscope of many methods of therapy, this book is aimed at giving the reader a taste of this flavour.

Often, our need to study, learn and improve ourselves arises from an attitude in which we do not honour our own innermost qualities – who we are already, rather than who we might wish to become.

In Osho Therapy, we are reminded of our own inner beauty and what is really essential in life. Then the need for self-improvement, achievement and social recognition starts fading in significance. In other words, this kind of therapy leads to a meditative lifestyle.

In all aspects of Osho Therapy, meditation plays a central role. Dynamic Meditation and Kundalini Meditation are an integral part of most therapy courses. All Osho therapists agree on the central role of meditation in their work and the importance of love as a healing force.

In this regard, there is no essential difference between a therapist and his clients. A therapist is an expert in a certain field, but when it comes to the fundamental challenge of moving beyond the mind, expertise and knowledge are of no help. At this important threshold, therapist and client alike must be willing to leave knowledge behind.

To be a therapist is one of the most difficult things in the world, because you have to know to help, and on the other hand, you have to forget all that you know to help. You have to know much to help, and you have to forget all of it to help. A therapist has to do a very contradictory thing, and only then does therapy happen. ~ *Osho*

Svagito

About the Authors

Anando (1)

One of the women in the ASHA Foundation's list of 240 'influential, inspiring women from all walks of life and from around the world who are outstanding in their fields'. Formerly a lawyer and business manager, Anando worked closely with Osho for many years, as personal secretary and one of his caretakers. She has over 30 years' experience of practicing and working with his meditations and transformative techniques. Her book *YES – A Practical Guide to Loving your Life* is available in many languages. Her guided meditation CDs are produced by New Earth Records.

www.Lifetrainings.com

Anubuddha (2)

Since the mid-70s, Anubuddha has been an innovator and pioneer in bridging Meditation, Yoga, Touch-based healing arts, and Love. Under Osho's guidance, he helped create and teach Osho Rebalancing, Osho Neo-Yoga, Osho CranioSacral Balancing and Osho Hara Awareness, as well as being appointed the Founding Director of Osho International Academy of Healing Arts. He was also Osho's personal touch-based 'doctor' and gave him over 150 sessions in a wide variety of methods. In 1994, he and Anasha created and began teaching 'ARUN Conscious Touch' worldwide. ARUN is lovingly dedicated to the ongoing evolution of creative Human Touch.

www.arunconscioustouch.com

Prem Shunyo (3)

Originating from London, Shunyo travelled to India in the 70s and her training in awareness began while living close to Osho for 14 years, as part of his household. She has been practicing Osho's meditation techniques for over 35 years. Shunyo now shares her experience, facilitating meditation courses and groups for women as she travels to many countries. She also conducts trainings for people who would like to teach meditation to others. Music, dance and celebration are an important part of Shunyo's work, and this coupled with her intuitive heartfelt way of working, allows participants to touch deep levels of peace and silence. Her book *Diamond Days with Osho* has been translated in eight languages.

www.meditantra.com

Leela (Lydia Itzler) (4)

Came in contact with Osho in 1973 and explored Dynamic Meditation in London. She travelled to Pune and from 1979 worked in the commune's Press Office for two-and-a-half years, dealing with journalists from all over the world. Later, Leela taught massage and energy healing and also co-ordinated the commune's Therapy and Meditation Department. In 1988, she was requested by Osho to design, develop and facilitate three meditative therapies: The Mystic Rose Meditation, Born Again and No-Mind. She has offered these processes around the world for the past 25 years and continues to do so. These three meditations are known as Osho's Meditative Therapies of which Leela is the Director.

www.mysticrosemeditation.com

Tarika Glubin MA (5)

Has a Master's degree in Psychology and has spent the better part of the last 40 years helping people to enhance their quality of life. Tarika calls herself an Osho Therapist because the primary inspiration for her work comes from this enlightened mystic. She combines meditation techniques with various therapeutic modalities. Her greatest joy is watching people learn to love themselves. In her search for deeper understanding, she created the Transessence Technique (a tool for essential living) which she shares with individuals and groups throughout the world.

www.free4being.com

Pratibha (Gianna de Stoppani) (6)

Began experiential research into shamanism in Latin America. The power and secrets of the human voice and sounds started to be revealed to her during these transformative experiences. Returning to Europe, she continued to explore sound, voice and language. At that time, she started her involvement in humanistic psychology and her connection with the teachings of Sufism and Taoism. Finally, the urgency to find a living spiritual mystic, whose vision and techniques were geared to the complexities of modern man, led her to Osho in 1976. She has integrated her discoveries and experiences with Osho's vision to create her own unique transformational approach called VOICING®.

www.voicing-institute.com

Aneesha Dillon (7)

Trained in neo-Reichian education with Charles Kelley at the Radix Institute in California from 1972-74. Her long association with Osho and his work (since 1976) has brought about a unique synthesis of Eastern and Western techniques of human growth and inner exploration called 'Osho Pulsation', a merging of the breathing and bodywork of Wilhelm Reich with meditation. Over many years, she developed Tantric Pulsation energy work which is rooted in the body's natural capacity for pleasure and joy, and the spirit's longing for silence and meditation. Aneesha lives in Northern California and leads groups and trainings worldwide. Her book, *Tantric Pulsation* is available in several languages, including English, Russian, Italian Spanish, and Portuguese.

www.oshopulsation.com

Moumina Jeffs (8)

Trained in Laban technique dance therapy in London. She went to India in 1977 where she studied Indian dance at Kalakshetra Fine Arts College in Chennai. From there, she went to live in Osho's commune in Pune. She is trained in Pulsation, Primal, Tantra, Star

455

Sapphire Energywork, Family Constellation and Non-Violent Communication. Formerly a director of the Centre for Transformation in the Osho International Meditation Resort, she now works all over the world, and in the past 32 years has run workshops and trainings in South America, India, Japan and Europe.

www.body-psychology.com

Svarup and Premartha (Manuela Disegni and Wilhelmus de Koning) (9)

Are lovers, friends and partners. They have been working together since 1986. Out of their combined experience they have created a large variety of groups, courses and trainings. The focus of their work lies in the areas of childhood and sexual deconditioning. Both are trained facilitators in the Essence work. Together they developed the Twice Born Childhood Deconditioning process, an in-depth individual journey of ten sessions into childhood, going backwards from the time of pre-school until conception. Trainings in this method are offered at Osho centres in Europe and America. Their book, *TWICE BORN – Healing the Past Creating a New Future*, has been published in English, Italian, German, Turkish and Czech.

www.primaltantra.com

Dwari Deutsch (10)

Has been working with people for over 30 years. After studying in Cologne and Berlin, she worked for five years as a teacher. Through teaching, she became interested in somatic developmental psychology and family systems. She trained for three years in Breath Therapy with Professor Ilse Middendorf in Berlin. Further training followed in Rebirthing, Counselling, Primal Therapy, Tantra work, Family Constellation and Somatic Experiencing. Meeting Osho in 1977 shifted her focus toward meditation. She is a co-director and trainer in the Osho Breath Energy Training and teaches Family Constellation in different international therapy institutes. Her work with people focuses on inner transformation and holistic healing.

www.dwari-lifeskills.net

Svagito Liebermeister (11)

Holds a degree in psychology from Munich University and has been working with people since 1981. His training programmes specialize in Family Constellation, Neo-Reichian breath work, Counselling, Male-Female Energy work and Trauma Healing (SE). For many years, he coordinated the Osho Therapist Training at Osho International Meditation Resort in Pune. Every year, he travels extensively through Europe, Asia and South America, offering courses and trainings in over 15 different countries. Svagito is the author of two books: *The Roots of Love. A Guide to Family Constellation* and *The Zen Way of Counseling- a meditative approach to working with people*, which both have been translated into nine languages.

www.family-constellation.net

Krishnananda and Amana Trobe (12)

Have been leading seminars together since 1995. They are the founders and directors of The Learning Love Institute whose work deals with helping people to learn how to love themselves and others. Krishnananda is a psychiatrist, educated at Harvard University and the University of California. Amana is a therapist, trained in Cranio-Sacral Balancing, Counselling, Inner Child Work and Non-violent Communication. Together, they have written six books: *Face to Face with Fear*, *Stepping Out of Fear*, *From Fantasy Trust to Real Trust*, *When Sex Becomes Intimate*, and their latest, *The Learning Love Handbook, Book 1 Opening to Vulnerability* and *Book 2 Healing Shame and Shock*. Their books are translated into twelve languages.

www.learningloveinstitute.com

Vasumati (13)

Has been a sannyasin since July 1976 and holds a degree in Psychology and Anthropology from the University of Cape Town, South Africa. She has led many workshops in the Osho commune in Pune and has also been a therapist and trainer worldwide. She specializes in working with relationship issues, helping people to transform their partnerships from co-dependency to conscious relating. She has done extensive training in the USA and has studied many of the cutting edge approaches available in therapy today. Her passion is the interface between therapy and meditation, through which love can be transformed into a spiritual dimension.

www.vasumati.info

Devapath MD (Jochen Peters) (14)

Earned his medical degree in 1978 in Germany, has been an Osho therapist for the past 33 years and is the director of the International Breath Energy School. He was the co-founder of various European growth centres and the director of the Centre for Transformation in the Osho Multiversity in Pune, a position he held for five years. For several years, he created and coordinated the four-month long Osho Therapist Training and educated therapists in Counselling, Primal and Breath therapy. With Osho Diamond Breath he created a multidimensional therapy including 'The Power of Breath', 'Love, Tantra and Zen' and 'Aquaprana Healing'. He has published a book called *The Power of Breath*.

www.devapath.com

Turiya Hanover (15)

An internationally known therapist who has been leading self-development workshops and trainings worldwide since 1973. She is trained in Humanistic Psychology, Gestalt therapy, Somatic Experiencing™, Enneagram & Diamond Logos. In 1975, she became an Osho sannyasin and began her work as a therapist in Pune, leading a multitude of groups. She was responsible for creating an array of new self-development processes during that time. Turiya uses the alchemy of spiritual therapy and meditation in her work, giving room for the unique transformation of each individual's journey. Today, she continues to lead workshops and trainings worldwide and is one of the founders & creators of the Path of Love. She also co-leads a new certified therapist training called 'Working with People'.

www.divinemeetings.com

Rafia Morgan (16)

Born in San Francisco and attended UC Berkeley during the late 60s and early 70s. He was a committed social and political activist until it became clear to him that the transformation he was seeking needed to happen within himself. This started an inner search which in 1978 led him to Osho. After that, he spent many years living in Osho's communities. He had the privilege to travel the world with Osho for nearly a year. Over the last 35 years he has developed many spiritually-based therapy groups and meditations and to this day continues to travel the world leading groups and training people in the work he has created. When not traveling, he resides in London.

www.rafia.info

Sagarpriya DeLong (17)

Started her career at the Esalen Institute in California, where she directed the massage program and subsequently invented the bodywork technique 'Psychic Massage'. She has written two books about this method: Psychic Massage and The Master's Touch: Psychic Massage; the second one was inspired by Osho's influence. Sagarpriya is well-known for another original invention, 'Star Sapphire Energywork'. This verbal therapy method delineates the inner male and female 'characters' inside the body and improves the way they relate to one another. Her recent book about inner man and woman, Le due sponde dell'amore, was published in Italian in 2009. Sagarpriya lives in Italy, where she continues to teach and to direct the association Conscious Living.

www.consciousliving.it

Premananda and Prabodhi
(Roger Vaisey and Greta Mildenberg) (18)

Have worked with hypnosis for the past 30 years. Both are certified members of the European Association of Psychotherapy, NLP master trainers and Hypnotherapy trainers with the American Board of Hypnotherapy since 1996. Prabodhi was born in Columbia and brought up in Germany, where she trained as a lawyer. She is also a Pulsation teacher. Her passion has been to go beyond the artificial expression of body and mind, focusing on supporting people to live from their core, strengthening the unity of thinking, feeling and acting. Premananda was born in the UK. His vision through working with hypnosis is to help people to awaken to their own creative possibilities and to access resources they were not consciously aware they have.

www.isnlp.de

Meera Hashimoto (19)

Born in Ishikawa, Japan, she studied in Musashino Art University and then travelled all over Europe, visiting all the famous art museums. She settled in Toledo, Spain, where she studied and painted for seven years, becoming a founding member of the art group known as TOLMO. In 1974, she became an Osho disciple and a few years later was invited by him to start an art group at his commune in Pune. Meera has held many painting exhibitions all over the world. She studied and integrated other therapeutic methods in her courses, including Star Sapphire energy work, Family Constellation and Dance therapy. Her Osho Art Therapist Training is held at Osho International in Pune, Osho Miasto in Italy and Amalurra in Spain.

www.meera.de

Amiyo Devienne (20)

Learned to become a dance teacher, choreographer and dance therapist in France and became a sannyasin in 1978. Soon afterwards, Osho asked her to start leading a dance-creativity group in his Pune commune and this continued at his community in Oregon, USA. In 1989, having returned to Pune, she started teaching Gurdjieff Movements with her partner Chetan, an accomplished musician, violinist and opera singer. For the past 20 years, they have been travelling worldwide to give courses in Gurdjieff Movements, plus instructor trainings, as well as public demonstrations.

www.gurdjieff-dances.com

Ganga (21)

Born in Germany, Ganga graduated from the University of Heidelberg and trained as a Clinical Psychologist. In the early 70s, she undertook her first long meditation retreat at a Buddhist monastery in Thailand and in 1975 went to India and became a disciple of Osho. She is the founder and director of the Academy of Awareness and Creative Expression. She leads trainings in Awareness Intensives, including 'Who Is In?' and 'Satori', in countries all over the world. Her other skills include various bodywork methods, life coaching, intuitive Chinese Calligraphy and gardening.

www.awareness-academy.com

For further information on Osho, Osho meditations and Osho meditation centers:

www.osho.com

References of Quotations

Introduction

1 Osho: Light on the Path, Ch16
2 Osho: Come Follow Me, Vol.4 Ch 14

Chapter 2

1 Osho: Om Shanti Shanti Shanti, Ch 27
2 Osho: Hammer on the Rock
3 Osho: I Am That, Ch 1
4 Osho: From Unconsciousness to Consciousness, Ch 30

Chapter 3

1 Osho: The Secret of Secrets, Vol 1 Ch 12
2 Osho: The Art of Ecstasy, Ch 3
3 Osho: Jharat Dasahu Dis Moti, Ch 14 (translated from Hindi)
4 Osho: The Transmission of the Lamp, Ch 46
5 Osho: The Dhammapada, Vol 5 Ch 5
6 Osho: Vigyan Bhairav Tantra, Vol 1 Ch 39
7 Osho: Vigyan Bhairav Tantra, Vol 2 Ch 11
8 Osho: Vigyan Bhairav Tantra, Vol 2 Ch 21

Chapter 4

1 Osho: Ya-Hoo! The Mystic Rose, Ch 30
2 Osho: Ya-Hoo! The Mystic Rose, Ch 21
3 Osho: The Art of Dying, Ch 10

Chapter 5

1 Osho: The True Sage, Ch 4.

Chapter 6

1 Osho: Gita Darshan, Ch 6

Chapter 8

1 Osho: The Path of the Mystic, Ch 3

Chapter 10

1 Osho: From Unconsciousness to Consciousness, Ch 25

Chapter 11

1 Osho: Take it easy, Vol 2 Ch 2
2 Osho: The Tantra Experince, Ch 2
3 Osho: The Beloved, Vol 1 Ch 4
4 Osho: The Dhammapada: The Way of the Buddha, Vol 5 Ch 6

Chapter 13

1 Osho: The Book of Wisdom, Ch 12
2 Osho: Sermons in Stones, Vol 2 Ch 12
3 Osho: From Death to Deathlessness, Ch 36

Chapter 14

1 Osho: Dang Dand Doko Dang, Ch 8
2 Osho: Blessed are the Ignorant, Ch 16
3 Osho: Satyam Shivam Sunderam, Ch 18
4 Osho: The Eternal Quest, Ch 3
5 Osho: The Diamond Sutra, Ch 2
6 Osho: In Search of the Miraculous, Vol 1 Ch 6
7 Osho: Meditation, the Art of Ecstasy, Ch 3

Chapter 15

1 Osho: The Divine Melody, Ch 10
2 Osho: The Divine Melody, Ch 3
3 Osho: The Secret of Secrets, Vol 2 Ch 15
4 Osho: Philosophia Perennis, Vol 1 Ch 2

Chapter 16

Chapter 18

Chapter 20

Chapter 21

Epilogue

Back Cover